AP®* Calculus
AB/BC
Preparing for the Advanced Placement® Examinations

Maxine Lifshitz (Ret.)

Mathematics Department Chairperson
Friends Academy
Locust Valley, New York

with

Martha Green (Ret.)

Mathematics Teacher
Baldwin High School
Baldwin New York

D1530335

AMSCO SCHOOL PUBLICATIONS, INC.,

a division of Perfection Learning®

Reviewers

Anthony DeLuca
Math Teacher
Saint Cloud High School
Saint Cloud, FL

Dr. Chuck Garner, Ph.D.
Mathematics Department Chair
Rockdale Magnet School for Science and Technology
Conyers, GA

Diane M. Mayer, M.S.
Math Teacher
Oak Harbor High School
Oak Harbor, WA

Tim Walsh, M.Ed.
Mathematics Department Chair
Exeter Township Senior High School
Reading, PA

MaryLou B. Wood, M.S.
Math Teacher
Holly Hill Academy
Holly Hill, SC

Mary Eschels, M. Ed.
Math Department Chair
Ballard High School
Louisville, KY

Dr. Christopher Goodrich, Ph.D.
Instructor of Mathematics
Creighton Preparatory School
Omaha, NE

Holli Prior, M.S.
Math Teacher
Prosser High School
Prosser, WA

Peter Wisniewski, M.S.
Math Department Chair
Villa Joseph Marie High School
Holland, PA

Cover design: Mike Aspengren
Typeset by Lapiz Digital Services

© 2017 by Amsco School Publications, Inc., a division of Perfection Learning®

Please visit our websites at:
www.amscopub.com and *www.perfectionlearning.com*

When ordering this book, please specify:
Hardcover: ISBN 978-1-63419-958-2 or **1532901**
eBook: ISBN 978-1-53110-106-0 or **15329D**

1 2 3 4 5 6 EBM 21 20 19 18 17 16

Printed in the United States of America

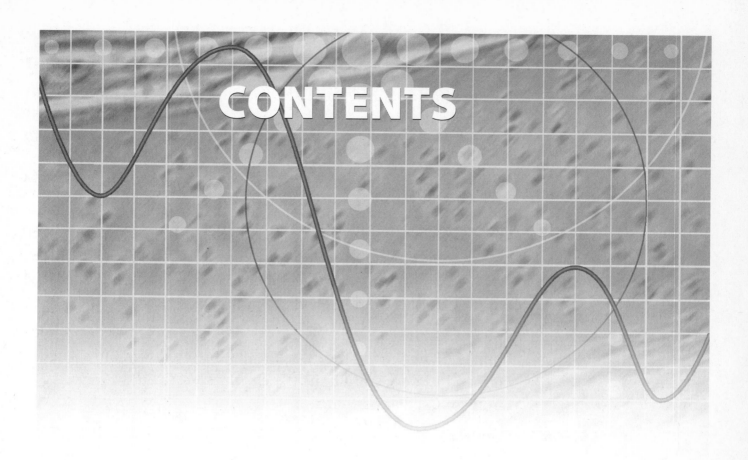

CONTENTS

INTRODUCTION

This book will provide you a thorough review as you prepare for the AP Calculus Exam on either the AB or BC level. As of May 2017, the College Board is changing both the AB and BC courses and exams to reflect a more comprehensive and cohesive curriculum. In response, we have changed the structure of our book, which will help you as you prepare to take this important exam.

As you move through this book, you will see that we have divided the content into five Main Idea units:

- Prerequisite Ideas
- Limits
- Derivatives
- Integrals and the Fundamental Theorem of Calculus
- Series (BC Exam Only)

Each Main Idea unit is divided into Lessons to provide a focused review. These Lessons contain concise explanations of the concepts, definitions of important terms (in **boldface**), and necessary formulas. The Lessons also feature Model Problems with a variety of multiple-choice and free-response questions, mirroring questions that have appeared on previous AP Calculus examinations. Each lesson ends with a set of multiple-choice and free-response AP Calculus Exam-Type Questions, which provide additional practice with all tested objectives. Finally, this review book also contains a Diagnostic Exam, Summary Assessments, and Model Exams.

How to Use This Book
Your teacher will provide you with specific instructions on the use of this book in your classroom. In general, this is not intended to be a textbook, but rather it is an organized review of concepts already studied and a source of practice problems. Ideally, this review book will be used as a companion to a classroom textbook, supplementing each concept with concise explanations and problems.

The AP Calculus AB and BC Examinations
The College Board has designed these tests to assess your understanding of the concepts of calculus, your ability to apply these concepts, and your proficiency in making connections among multiple representations of

mathematics. The revised AP Calculus Exam continues to contain both multiple-choice and free-response questions, and, as in the past, there are sections of the exam on which you are not allowed to use your graphing calculator. To do well on this test, it is important that you have a strong foundation in algebra, geometry, trigonometry, and elementary functions. You must also practice problems daily to develop a thorough understanding of the concepts presented in this review text.

The two AP Calculus Examinations are organized in the same manner. Both consist of Section I and Section II, each of which has two parts. The two sections of the exam contribute equally to determining your examination grade.

Section I: Multiple Choice

- Each question will have four answer options.
- For Part A, you will have 60 minutes to complete 30 questions.
  - No graphing calculator allowed.
- For Part B, you will 45 minutes to complete 15 questions.
  - Graphing calculator allowed.
- Bubble in your answers on a bubble sheet.

Section II: Free Response

- This section requires that you solve a more complex problem using an extended chain of reasoning.
- For Part A, you are allowed 30 minutes to complete 2 problems
  - Graphing calculator allowed.
- For Part B, you have 60 minutes to answer four questions.
  - No graphing calculator allowed.
- For this section you will write your answers in an answer booklet.
  - If you finish Section II, Part B with time remaining, you are allowed to return to the problems in Section II, Part A, but without the use of your graphing calculator.

We provide a summary of this information:

Section I—Multiple Choice Questions				
	Number of Questions	Time Allowed	Graphing Calculator Allowed?	Answer Format
Part A	30	60 minutes	No	Bubble Sheet
Part B	15	45 minutes	Yes	Bubble Sheet
Section II—Free Response Questions				
Part A	2	30 minutes	Yes	Booklet
Part B	4	60 minutes	No	Booklet

Graphing Calculator Information

The AP Calculus Examinations are written with the assumption that you have access to a graphing calculator with the following built-in capabilities:

1. Plot the graph of a function within an arbitrary viewing window.
2. Find the zeros of functions.
3. Numerically calculate the derivative of a function.
4. Numerically calculate the value of a definite integral.

Note that the test writers take care to ensure that exam questions requiring the use of a calculator do not favor students whose graphing calculators have more extensive built-in functionality. You can find a list of graphing calculators approved for use on the AP Calculus exam at https://apstudent.collegeboard.org/apcourse/ap-calculus-ab/calculator-policy.

Throughout this review text we provide calculator notes for the TI-83/84/84+/89. Where keystrokes differ substantially, we provide instructions for the TI-*n*spire. Note that the TI-*n*spire OS is frequently updated. Go to www.education.ti.com to download the most current OS.

You will not be required to clear the memory of your calculator prior to the exam.

Finally, when writing solutions to the free-response exam questions, you must use standard mathematical notation and NOT calculator syntax. For example, you must write

$$\int_1^3 2x^2 \, dx = \frac{2x^3}{3}\Big]_1^3 = 17.333$$

and NOT

$$\text{fnInt}(2x^2, x, 1, 3) = 17.333.$$

You should note that all answers are expected to be accurate to three decimal places.

Examination Scoring   The multiple-choice questions in Section I are machine scored. High school and college teachers selected by the College Board grade the free-response questions in Section II. These teachers, called "readers," are trained to use a grading rubric, which ensures the grading is as consistent as possible. Remember that your raw score on each Section contributes equally to your final score. After machine scoring and reading, your raw score is tallied and converted into a numbered grade from 1 to 5. A score of 3 or better is generally acceptable for either advanced course placement or a semester or years' worth of credit at a participating college. As the amount of credit awarded by colleges for AP test scores varies from institution to institution, you must consult with your individual college choice for more information.

Test-Taking Tips
- Follow the directions given for each question on the examination.

- Read each question carefully and consider your answer thoughtfully. Long explanations are not required for the free-response questions. Readers are looking for a concise and clear response based on an appropriate theorem or technique.

- Include all of the necessary information in your response, such as units of measure.

- Be mindful of the list of the four capabilities required of the graphing calculator you will use on the exam (see p. x). Answers to free-response questions will not receive full credit without supporting work.

- Become proficient with the graphing calculator you will use on the exam AND learn the mathematics needed to respond to the questions. It is important to know when to use your calculator and when to rely on your brain. An overdependence on technology will not only hinder your development of calculus concepts, but it will also waste valuable time on the test!

- Thoroughly practice both multiple-choice and free-response questions. This review text contains both types of questions in every lesson to help you become proficient.
- Remember that the readers scoring your exams are not your calculus teacher who is familiar with your knowledge and work style. You must write complete answers using correct mathematical notation to show what you know.

Final Thoughts The AP Calculus AB and BC exams are a challenging exercise for even the most hard-working student, and they require extensive preparation. It is important to practice problems daily and endeavor to truly understand what is presented. We know that throughout your AP Calculus course there will be times that you are frustrated or lost in the material or notation. Do not give up. Instead, ask questions of your teachers and peers to help you understand the concepts. Continue working through challenging problems and using this review book as a source of concise explanations and additional practice. It is important that you understand all of the problems in this book as they were developed from past examinations and it is likely they will again appear on the exam. Good Luck!

CALCULUS AB/BC

SECTION I, Part A

Time – 60 minutes

Number of problems – 30

A graphing calculator is not permitted for these problems.

1. $\lim\limits_{x\to 0} \dfrac{\frac{1}{2+x} - \frac{1}{2}}{x} =$

(A) $-\dfrac{1}{4}$

(B) 0

(C) $\dfrac{1}{4}$

(D) $\dfrac{1}{2}$

For Questions 2–4, consider

$$f(x) = \begin{cases} \left|x^3 - 4x\right|, & x < 1 \\ x^2 - 2x - 2, & x \geq 1 \end{cases}.$$

2. $\lim\limits_{x\to 1^-} f(x) =$

(A) -3

(B) 1

(C) 3

(D) Does not exist

3. $\lim\limits_{x\to 1^+} f(x) =$

(A) -3

(B) 1

(C) 3

(D) Does not exist

4. $\lim\limits_{x\to 1} f(x) =$

(A) -3

(B) 1

(C) 3

(D) Does not exist

5. The average rate of change of $f(x) = 1 + \sin x$ over the interval $\left[0, \frac{\pi}{2}\right]$ is

(A) $\dfrac{\pi}{2}$.

(B) $\dfrac{2}{\pi}$.

(C) $\dfrac{1}{2}$.

(D) $\dfrac{1}{\pi}$.

6. If $y = 3 - 7x^3 + 3x^7$, then $\dfrac{dy}{dx} =$

(A) $7x^2 + 3x^7$.

(B) $-7x^2 + 3x^7$.

(C) $21x^2 + 21x^6$.

(D) $-21x^2 + 21x^6$.

7. If $y = \dfrac{2x + 1}{2x - 1}$, then $\dfrac{dy}{dx} =$

(A) 1.

(B) $-\dfrac{4}{2x - 1}$.

(C) $\dfrac{1}{2x - 1}$.

(D) $-\dfrac{4}{(2x - 1)^2}$.

8. If $r = \tan^2(3 - \theta^2)$, then $\dfrac{dr}{d\theta} =$

(A) $\sec^2(3 - \theta^2)$.

(B) $-4\theta \sec^2(3 - \theta^2)$.

(C) $-4\theta \tan(3 - \theta^2)\sec^2(3 - \theta^2)$.

(D) $4\theta \tan(3 - \theta^2)\sec^2(3 - \theta^2)$.

9. For what value(s) of m is
$$f(x) = \begin{cases} \sin 2x, & x \le 0 \\ mx, & x > 0 \end{cases} \text{ continuous at } x = 0?$$

   (A) All real numbers
   (B) $m = 2$
   (C) $m > 0$
   (D) $m \le 0$

10. Find the second derivative of $\sqrt{(x^2 + 1)}$.

   (A) $(x^2 + 1)^{-1/2}$
   (B) $(x^2 + 1)^{-3/2}$
   (C) $x(x^2 + 1)^{-1/2}$
   (D) $2x(x^2 + 1)^{-3/2}$

11. Write the equation of the line tangent to $y = \sqrt{x^2 - 2x}$ at $x = 3$.

   (A) $y = \frac{2}{\sqrt{3}}x - \sqrt{3}$
   (B) $y = \frac{2}{\sqrt{3}}x + \sqrt{3}$
   (C) $y = \sqrt{3x} - \sqrt{3}$
   (D) $y = \sqrt{3x} + \sqrt{3}$

12. Write the equation of the line tangent to $x = 2 \sin t$, $y = 2 \cos t$, at $t = \frac{3}{4}\pi$.

   (A) $y = x + 2\sqrt{2}$
   (B) $y = x - 2\sqrt{2}$
   (C) $y = 2x - 2\sqrt{2}$
   (D) $y = 2\sqrt{2x} - 2$

13. Which one of the following functions could lead to $f''(x) = x^{1/3}$?

   I. $f(x) = \frac{9}{28}x^{7/3} + 9$
   II. $f'(x) = \frac{9}{28}x^{7/3} - 2$
   III. $f'(x) = \frac{3}{4}x^{4/3} + 6$
   IV. $f(x) = \frac{3}{4}x^{4/3} - 4$

   (A) I only
   (B) III only
   (C) II and IV only
   (D) I and III only

For Questions 14–17, $f(x) = \dfrac{1}{\sqrt[4]{1 - x^2}}$.

14. Over which interval is $f(x)$ concave up?

   (A) $[0, 1)$
   (B) $(-1, 0]$
   (C) $(-1, 1)$
   (D) None

15. Over which interval is $f(x)$ concave down?

   (A) $[0, 1)$
   (B) $(-1, 0]$
   (C) $(-1, 1)$
   (D) None

16. Over which interval is $f(x)$ increasing?

   (A) $[0, 1)$
   (B) $(-1, 0]$
   (C) $(-1, 1)$
   (D) None

17. Over which interval is $f(x)$ decreasing?

   (A) $[0, 1)$
   (B) $(-1, 0]$
   (C) $(-1, 1)$
   (D) None

For Questions 18–20, $\displaystyle\int_1^3 g(x)\,dx = -2$,

$\displaystyle\int_3^7 g(x)\,dx = 5$, $\displaystyle\int_6^7 g(x)\,dx = 3$.

18. $\displaystyle\int_1^7 g(x)\,dx =$

   (A) 2
   (B) 3
   (C) 5
   (D) 6

19. $\displaystyle\int_{3}^{6} g(x)\,dx =$

(A) 2

(B) 3

(C) 5

(D) 6

20. $\displaystyle\int_{1}^{6} g(x)\,dx =$

(A) 2

(B) 3

(C) 5

(D) 0

21. Find the area between the x-axis and the graph of $y = \sin x$ over the interval $[0, \pi]$.

(A) 0

(B) 1

(C) 2

(D) π

22. Evaluate $\displaystyle\int_{-1}^{1} (3x^2 - 4x + 7)\,dx$.

(A) -16

(B) -4

(C) 4

(D) 16

23. $\displaystyle\frac{d}{dx}\int_{2}^{x} \sqrt{2 + \cos^3 t}\,dt =$

(A) $\sqrt{2 + \cos^3 x} - \sqrt{2 + \cos^3 2}$

(B) $\sqrt{2 + \cos^3 x}$

(C) $\dfrac{3\cos^2 x \sin x}{2\sqrt{2 + \cos^3 x}}$

(D) $\dfrac{3\cos^2 x}{2\sqrt{2 + \cos^3 x}}$

24. Evaluate $\displaystyle\int_{0}^{2} \sqrt{4 - x^2}\,dx$ by interpreting it as area and using a geometric formula.

(A) π

(B) 2π

(C) 3π

(D) 4π

25. Find the indefinite integral $\displaystyle\int\left(x^2 - \frac{1}{x^2}\right)dx$.

(A) $\dfrac{x^3}{3} - \dfrac{1}{x} + c$

(B) $\dfrac{x^3}{3} + \dfrac{1}{x} + c$

(C) $x - \dfrac{1}{x^3} + c$

(D) $x^3 - \dfrac{1}{x} + c$

26. Which slope field best fits $\dfrac{dy}{dx} = x - y$?

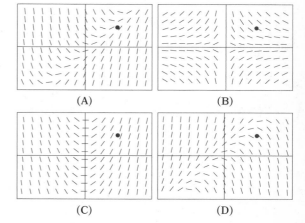

(A)   (B)

(C)   (D)

(A) Graph A

(B) Graph B

(C) Graph C

(D) Graph D

BC 27. Use integration by parts to find $\displaystyle\int 3x^2 e^{2x}\,dx$.

(A) $x^3 e^{2x} - \dfrac{3}{2}x^2 e^{2x} + \dfrac{3}{2}x e^{2x} + \dfrac{3}{4}e^{2x} + c$

(B) $\dfrac{3}{2}x^2 e^{2x} - \dfrac{3}{2}x e^{2x} + \dfrac{3}{4}e^{2x} + c$

(C) $\dfrac{3}{2}x e^{2x} + \dfrac{3}{4}e^{2x} + c$

(D) $\dfrac{3}{2}x e^{2x} + c$

28. Solve the initial value problem $\frac{dy}{dx} = y + 2$ when $y(0) = 2$.

(A) $y = e^x - 2$

(B) $y = e^x + 1$

(C) $y = 4e^x - 2$

(D) $y = 2e^x + 1$

BC **29.** Use partial fractions to find $\int \frac{x - 12}{x^2 - 4x} dx$.

(A) $\frac{|x|^3}{(x - 4)^2} + c$

(B) $\ln \frac{|x|}{(x - 4)^2} + c$

(C) $\ln \frac{x - 12}{(x - 4)^2} + c$

(D) $\ln \frac{|x|^3}{(x - 4)^2} + c$

30. Find the volume of the solid generated by revolving the region bound by $y = x^2$, $y = 0$, and $x = 2$ about the x-axis.

(A) $\frac{8\pi}{5}$ cubic units

(B) $\frac{16\pi}{5}$ cubic units

(C) $\frac{32\pi}{5}$ cubic units

(D) $\frac{64\pi}{5}$ cubic units

CALCULUS AB/BC

SECTION I, Part B
Time – 45 minutes
Number of problems – 15

A graphing calculator is required for these problems.

1. $\lim\limits_{x\to\infty}\dfrac{3x^2+7}{4x^2+5}=$

   (A) 0

   (B) $\dfrac{3}{4}$

   (C) $\dfrac{7}{5}$

   (D) ∞

2. The equation of the line tangent to $y=\dfrac{x^3+1}{2x}$ at $x=1$ is

   (A) $y=\dfrac{1}{2}x+1$.

   (B) $y=x$.

   (C) $y=\dfrac{1}{2}x+\dfrac{1}{2}$.

   (D) $y=2x-1$.

3. For $y=\dfrac{4}{\cos x}$, find $\dfrac{dy}{dx}$.

   (A) $\dfrac{4}{\sin x}$

   (B) $-\dfrac{4}{\cos^2 x}$

   (C) $4\sec x\tan x$

   (D) $4\sec^2 x$

4. The equation of the line tangent to $x+\sqrt{xy}=6$ at $(4,1)$ is

   (A) $y=-\dfrac{5}{4}x+6$.

   (B) $y=-\dfrac{4}{5}x+6$.

   (C) $y=-\dfrac{4}{5}x$.

   (D) $y=-\dfrac{5}{4}x$.

5. A person who is exactly 6 feet tall walks at a rate of 5 feet per second toward a streetlight that is 16 feet above the ground. At what rate is the length of the person's shadow changing when that person is 10 feet from the base of the streetlight?

   (A) -5 ft/s

   (B) -3 ft/s

   (C) 3 ft/s

   (D) 5 ft/s

6. Find the average value of $y=\sec^2 x$ over the interval $\left[0,\dfrac{\pi}{4}\right]$.

   (A) $\dfrac{\pi}{2}$

   (B) $\dfrac{2}{\pi}$

   (C) $\dfrac{\pi}{4}$

   (D) $\dfrac{4}{\pi}$

7. The expression $\dfrac{1}{20}\left(\sqrt{\dfrac{1}{20}}+\sqrt{\dfrac{2}{20}}+\sqrt{\dfrac{3}{20}}+\cdots+\sqrt{\dfrac{20}{20}}\right)$ is a Riemann sum approximation for

   (A) $\displaystyle\int_0^1\sqrt{\dfrac{x}{20}}\,dx.$

   (B) $\displaystyle\int_0^1\sqrt{x}\,dx.$

   (C) $\dfrac{1}{20}\displaystyle\int_0^1\sqrt{\dfrac{x}{20}}\,dx.$

   (D) $\dfrac{1}{20}\displaystyle\int_0^1\sqrt{x}\,dx.$

8. Find a Trapezoid Rule approximation for $\int_0^\pi \sin x \, dx$ when $n=10$. Round your answer to four decimal places.

(A) 0.9980

(B) 1.9835

(C) 2.0082

(D) 3.2402

9. $\int_0^{\frac{\pi}{2}} x^2 \sin 2x \, dx =$

(A) -4.935

(B) -2.467

(C) 0.734

(D) 1.142

10. Solve the initial value problem $\dfrac{dy}{dx} = \dfrac{y}{x}$, $y = 2$, when $x = 2$.

(A) $y = x$

(B) $y = x + 2$

(C) $y = -x$

(D) $y = -x - 2$

11. A bank account that is earning continuously compounded interest doubles in value in 7.0 years. At the same interest rate, how long would it take the value of the account to triple?

(A) 4.4 years

(B) 9.8 years

(C) 11.1 years

(D) 21.0 years

12. Find all points of inflection for $y = x^{\frac{1}{3}}(x - 4)$.

(A) $(0,0)$

(B) $\left(-2, 6\sqrt[3]{2}\right)$

(C) $(0,0)$ and $\left(-2, 6\sqrt[3]{2}\right)$

(D) There are no points of inflection.

13. Find the interval(s) over which $y = 4x^3 + 21x^2 + 36x - 20$ is concave up.

(A) $\left(-\infty, -\dfrac{7}{4}\right)$

(B) $\left(-\dfrac{7}{4}, \infty\right)$

(C) $\left(-\dfrac{7}{4}, \dfrac{7}{4}\right)$

(D) $\left(\dfrac{7}{4}, \infty\right)$

14. Use the first derivative test to determine all local maxima of $y = x\sqrt{8 - x^2}$.

(A) $\left(-\sqrt{8}, 0\right)$

(B) $(2, 4)$

(C) $\left(-\sqrt{8}, 0\right)$ and $(2, 4)$

(D) No local maxima

BC 15. Use partial fractions to solve the initial value problem $\dfrac{dp}{dt} = 0.006P(200 - P)$ when $P = 8$ and $t = 0$.

(A) $P = \dfrac{200}{1 + 8e^{-1.2t}}$

(B) $P = \dfrac{200}{1 + 8e^{-0.6t}}$

(C) $P = \dfrac{200}{1 + 24e^{-0.6t}}$

(D) $P = \dfrac{200}{1 + 24e^{-1.2t}}$

CALCULUS AB/BC

SECTION II, Part A
Time – 30 minutes
Number of problems – 2

A graphing calculator is required for these problems.

1. On Earth, if you shoot a paper clip straight up into the air with a rubber band, at an initial velocity of 64 feet per second, the height of the paperclip above your hand t seconds after firing will be $s(t) = 64t - 16t^2$.

   (a) Find the equations for the velocity and acceleration of the paper clip as functions of time, t.

   (b) How long does it take the paper clip to reach its maximum height?

   (c) What is the paperclip's maximum height?

   (d) On the moon, the same force will send the paper clip to a height of $s(t) = 64t - 2.6t^2$ after t seconds. How long will it take the paper clip to reach its maximum height on the moon and how high will it go?

2. Water is flowing at the rate of 50 m³/minute from a reservoir that is shaped like a cone with its vertex down. The base radius is 45 meters and its height is 6 meters $\left(V_{cone} = \frac{1}{3}\pi r^2 h\right)$.

   (a) At what rate is the water level falling when the water is 5 m deep?

   (b) At what rate is the radius of the water's surface changing when the water is 5 m deep?

CALCULUS AB/BC

SECTION II, Part B
Time – 60 minutes
Number of problems – 4

A graphing calculator is not permitted for these problems.

1. Suppose that functions f and g and their first derivatives have the following values at $x = -1$ and $x = 0$.

x	$f(x)$	$g(x)$	$f'(x)$	$g'(x)$
-1	0	-1	2	1
0	-1	-3	-2	4

Find the first derivative of the following combinations at the given value of x.

(a) $3f(x) - g(x)$ at $x = -1$

(b) $f^2(x)g^3(x)$ at $x = 0$

(c) $g(f(x))$ at $x = -1$

(d) $\dfrac{f(x)}{g(x) + 2}$ at $x = 0$

2. A charter's buses each hold 60 people. The fare charged, p, in dollars, is related to the x number of people who buy a ticket by the formula $p = \left(3 - \dfrac{x}{40}\right)^2$.

(a) Write a formula for the total revenue per trip that is received by the bus company.

(b) What number of people per trip will make the marginal revenue equal to zero? What is the corresponding fare?

(c) Do you think the bus company's fare policy is good for its business? Justify your answer.

3. Find the average value of

(a) $y = \sqrt{x}$ over the interval $[0, 4]$.

(b) $y = a\sqrt{x}$ over the interval $[0, a]$.

4. Consider $\int 2 \sin x \cos x \, dx$.

(a) Evaluate the integral using the substitution $u = \sin x$.

(b) Evaluate the integral using the substitution $u = \cos x$.

(c) Show that the answers to parts a and b are equivalent.

CORRELATION CHART

Use the given charts to mark the questions you missed. Then work through the suggested lesson(s) to improve your understanding of the concepts.

Section I, Part A (No Calculator Allowed)

Missed?	Question Number	Review the information in Lesson (Main Idea #. Lesson #)...
	1	1.2
	2	1.3
	3	1.3
	4	1.2, 1.3
	5	2.1
	6	2.2
	7	2.2
	8	2.2, 2.3
	9	2.5
	10	2.6
	11	2.5
	12	2.5
	13	2.6
	14	2.6
	15	2.6
	16	2.6
	17	2.6
	18	3.4
	19	3.4
	20	3.4
	21	3.3
	22	3.2, 3.3
	23	3.3
	24	3.4
	25	3.1
	26	2.9
	27	3.1 (BC Exam Only)
	28	3.9
	29	3.1 (BC Exam Only)
	30	3.7

Section I, Part B (Calculator Required)

Missed?	Question Number	Review the information in Lesson (Main Idea #. Lesson #)...
	1	1.2
	2	2.5
	3	2.2, 2.3
	4	2.5
	5	2.7
	6	3.6
	7	3.2
	8	3.2
	9	3.3
	10	3.9
	11	3.6
	12	2.6
	13	2.6
	14	2.4
	15	3.1, 3.9

Section II, Part A (Calculator Required)

Missed?	Question Number	Review the information in Lesson (Main Idea #. Lesson #)...
	1(a)	2.7
	1(b)	
	1(c)	
	1(d)	
	2(a)	2.7
	2(b)	

Section II, Part B (No Calculator Allowed)

Missed?	Question Number	Review the information in Lesson (Main Idea #. Lesson #)...
	1(a)	2.2, 2.3
	1(b)	
	1(c)	
	1(d)	
	2(a)	2.7
	2(b)	
	2(c)	
	3(a)	2.1
	3(b)	
	4(a)	3.1
	4(b)	
	4(c)	

PREREQUISITE IDEAS

Lesson 1: Functions

Calculus is the study of how things change. We use functions to describe or model the quantities that are changing. Functions may represent areas, volumes, distances, or other quantities. Functions may also represent the rates at which quantities are changing. This unit provides an overview of basic function information. You may want to return to it as your study more complicated concepts that are built on this foundation.

A function is a relationship between two or more variables. It is often expressed as a rule that relates the variables. AP Calculus deals with functions of a single variable, usually expressed as $y = f(x)$. By definition, a **function** is a set of ordered pairs $\{(x, y)\}$ such that for each x-value there is one and only one y-value.

On a graph, the vertical line test determines whether a graph represents a function. The **vertical line test** states that if any vertical line intersects the graph more than once, then the graph is not a function.

Analyzing the properties of a function and then applying the techniques of calculus allows us to solve many types of problems. For instance, given the perimeter of a rectangle, we can find the dimensions of the rectangle that has the maximum area. Given information on the initial height and velocity of an object, we can determine how fast the object is moving when it hits the ground. In these examples, the area of the rectangle and the velocity of the object are represented by functions.

The Vertical Line Test

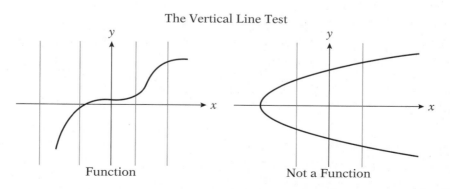

Function   Not a Function

Polynomials
A **polynomial** is a sum of terms of the form ax^n, where n is a nonnegative integer. The largest value of n is the **degree** of the polynomial, and the coefficient of the term of the highest power of x is called the **leading coefficient.** Polynomials include linear, quadratic, and cubic functions. For example, $4x^3 + 8x^2$ is a polynomial. Its degree is 3 and the leading coefficient is 4. This polynomial can also be expressed in factored form as $4x^2(x + 2)$. The zeros of the polynomial are found by solving the equation $4x^2(x + 2) = 0$. The zeros are $x = 0$ (a double root) and $x = -2$.

The graph of the polynomial $f(x) = 4x^3 + 8x^2$ shows that there are two turning points, or places where the graph changes direction. We can also determine the number of turning points by noting the degree of the equation. The maximum number of turning points is equal to $n - 1$, where n is the equation's degree.

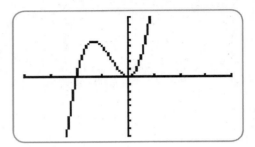

Calculator Note

A graphing calculator can be used to find that the coordinates of the turning points of the polynomial $4x^3 + 8x^2$ are $(-1.333, 4.741)$ and $(0, 0)$.

Using the TI-83/84

Enter the function into Y= and press ZOOM 4. Then press WINDOW and change Ymax to 7. Press GRAPH.

To find the coordinates of the turning point in the second quadrant, press 2nd CALC 4. To enter the Left Bound, scroll to the immediate left of the turning point and press ENTER.

Now scroll to the immediate right of the turning point and press ENTER. Press ENTER and round the coordinates to $x = -1.333$ and $y = 4.741$.

The second turning point appears to be located at the origin. With the polynomial still in Y=, press 2nd CALC 3. Scroll to set the Left Bound and the Right Bound of the turning point. To enter Guess, scroll as close as possible to the turning point. Press ENTER. The calculator confirms that $(0, 0)$ is the turning point.

Using the TI-*nspire*

There are several ways to access the graphing capabilities of the **TI-*nspire*.** From the home screen, you can go to the Scratchpad, then select B Graph, or use the graph icon on the bottom row.

To find the coordinates of the turning points, enter $y = 4x^3 + 8x^2$ in *f1(x)*. Make sure you have a standard window. You can check this by accessing MENU then **Window/Zoom** and then select **Zoom-Standard.** To find the coordinates of the turning points, press MENU, **analyze graph, maximum,** and then press ENTER. When prompted for the lower bound, use the track pad to move the vertical line to a value that is clearly to the left of the maximum, such as

–2, and press ENTER. At the upper bound prompt, use the track pad to input a value to the right of the maximum, like 0, and press ENTER again. The screen will display the maximum value located at (–1.333, 4.741). To confirm that the minimum is the origin, repeat the steps outlined above using the minimum function, found under MENU, **Analyze Graph, Minimum**.

End Behavior

Two factors, the degree of the polynomial and the sign of the leading coefficient, determine the end behavior of the polynomial. The **end behavior** of a polynomial is a description of how the right and left sides of the graph behave.

Degree
- Polynomials of even degree have ends pointing in the same direction.
- Polynomials of odd degree have ends pointing in opposite directions.

Sign of the Leading Coefficient, a
- The end behavior of polynomials of even degree is similar to $f(x) = ax^2$.

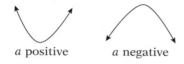

a positive a negative

- The end behavior of polynomials of odd degree is similar to $f(x) = ax^3$.

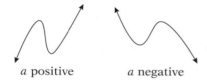

a positive a negative

Algebraic Functions

Algebraic functions that appear frequently in calculus are square roots and cube roots of a polynomial. For example, $\sqrt{(x - 3)}$ has the domain $\{x \geq 3\}$ and range $\{y \geq 0\}$. Its graph is shown below.

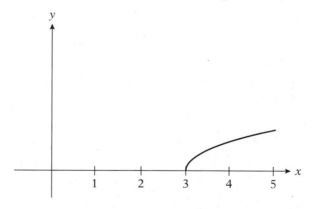

Rational Functions   A **rational function** is the ratio of two polynomials. Unlike polynomials, the domain of a rational function may not be the set of all real numbers. When the polynomial in the denominator is zero for some values of x, these values are excluded from the domain. In addition, rational functions may have vertical and horizontal asymptotes. An **asymptote** is a line that the graph of a function approaches very closely.

> **To find the vertical asymptotes of a rational function:**
> - Set the denominator equal to zero and solve for x.
> - Find the values of x that make the denominator equal to zero, but do not make the numerator equal to zero. The equations of the vertical asymptotes are these values of x.

If a value of x makes both the numerator and the denominator equal to zero, then there is a break or a hole in the function at that x-value. When using a graphing calculator, this hole may or may not be visible, depending on the [WINDOW] in which the graph of the rational function is viewed.

> **To find the horizontal asymptotes of a rational function:**
> - When the degree of the numerator is less than the degree of the denominator, the function has the line $y = 0$ as a horizontal asymptote.
> - When the degree of the numerator is equal to the degree of the denominator, then the equation of the horizontal asymptote is:
>
> $y =$ the ratio of the coefficients of the highest degree terms
>
> - When the degree of the numerator is greater than the degree of the denominator, the rational function has no horizontal asymptote.

MODEL PROBLEMS

1. Find the equation of the vertical asymptote of $y = \dfrac{2x + 4}{x - 1}$.

Solution

$x - 1 = 0$ Set the denominator equal to 0 to solve for x. The equation $x = 1$ is the function's vertical asymptote.

$x = 1$

2. What is the equation of the horizontal asymptote of $y = \dfrac{2x + 4}{x - 1}$?

Solution

Note that the expression in the numerator has the same degree as the expression in the denominator. When this occurs, we divide the coefficients of the leading terms to determine our answer. Thus, $\dfrac{2}{1} = 2$ and the equation is $y = 2$.

Below we show the graph of the equation $y = \dfrac{2x + 4}{x - 1}$ with the asymptotes depicted as dashed lines.

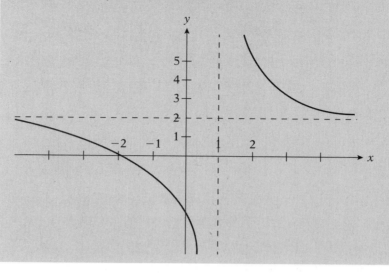

Trigonometric Functions

One of the basic topics in precalculus is learning the properties of, and graphing the sine, cosine, and tangent functions, as well as finding the amplitude, frequency, and period of these graphs.

Generally, a sine or cosine curve of the form $y = a \sin bx$ or $y = a \cos bx$ has amplitude $|a|$, frequency $|b|$, and period $\dfrac{2\pi}{|b|}$.

For example, in the function $y = 2 \sin x$, the amplitude is 2, the frequency is 1, and the period is 2π. Its graph is shown below.

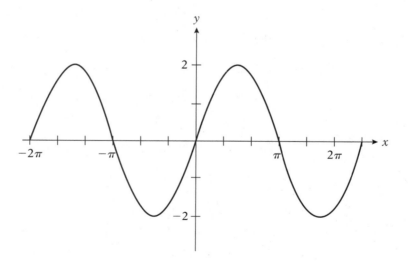

As another example, the graph of $y = -\dfrac{1}{2} \cos 4x$ has amplitude $\dfrac{1}{2}$, frequency 4, and period $\dfrac{2\pi}{4}$, which simplifies to $\dfrac{\pi}{2}$. The negative sign causes the graph to reflect over the x-axis. The graph is shown on the next page.

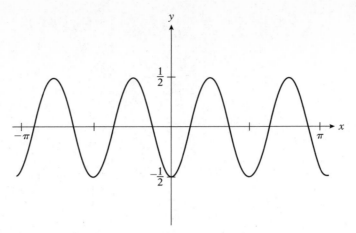

Tangent curves do not have amplitude. A tangent curve of the form $y = a \tan bx$ has frequency $|b|$ and period $\frac{\pi}{|b|}$. The graph of $y = \tan 2x$ has frequency 2 and period $\frac{\pi}{2}$. Its graph is shown below.

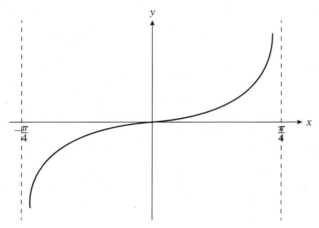

In addition to graphing trigonometric functions, it is also important to be able to solve trigonometric equations. Solve the equation $2\sin x - 1 = 0$ for values of x between 0 and 2π, in the following way.

First solve for x.

$$2\sin x - 1 = 0$$
$$2\sin x = 1$$
$$\sin x = \frac{1}{2}$$

When $\sin x = \frac{1}{2}$, the equation $2\sin x - 1 = 0$ is true. There are, however, infinitely many values of x that make $\sin x = \frac{1}{2}$ true. It is necessary to find the values of x in the domain given, between 0 and 2π. Since $\sin x$ is positive, x is an angle in quadrant I or II. The solution in the first quadrant is $x = \frac{\pi}{6}$. This value is used as a reference angle to find the solution in the second quadrant, which is $\pi - \frac{\pi}{6}$, or $\frac{5\pi}{6}$.

To solve trigonometric equations, it is necessary to know the values of sine, cosine, and tangent functions for the boundary angles 0, $\frac{\pi}{2}$, π, and $\frac{3\pi}{2}$, and the standard angles $\frac{\pi}{6}$, $\frac{\pi}{4}$, and $\frac{\pi}{3}$, as well as which functions are positive or negative in each quadrant. The values in the table on the following page are often used in solving trigonometric equations.

Degrees	0°	30°	45°	60°	90°	180°	270°	360°
Radians	0	$\frac{\pi}{6}$	$\frac{\pi}{4}$	$\frac{\pi}{3}$	$\frac{\pi}{2}$	π	$\frac{3\pi}{2}$	2π
Sine	0	$\frac{1}{2}$	$\frac{\sqrt{2}}{2}$	$\frac{\sqrt{3}}{2}$	1	0	–1	0
Cosine	1	$\frac{\sqrt{3}}{2}$	$\frac{\sqrt{2}}{2}$	$\frac{1}{2}$	0	–1	0	1
Tangent	0	$\frac{\sqrt{3}}{3}$	1	$\sqrt{3}$	undefined	0	undefined	0

Each of the standard angles is a reference angle for another angle in quadrants II, III, and IV. The following wheels illustrate the standard angles and the angles in the remaining quadrants in radian measure.

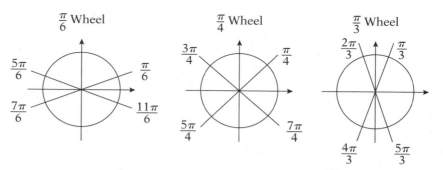

MODEL PROBLEMS

1. Solve for x: $2 \sin^2 x - 1 = 0$ for values of x between $-\pi$ and π.

Solution

Solving for sin x first, we have $\sin x = \pm \frac{\sqrt{2}}{2}$. The solution to $\sin x = \frac{\sqrt{2}}{2}$, $x = \frac{\pi}{4}$, provides the reference angle for the remaining solutions. There are four solutions, one in each quadrant. The solutions are: $x = \frac{\pi}{4}$, $x = \frac{3\pi}{4}$, $x = -\frac{\pi}{4}$, $x = -\frac{3\pi}{4}$.

Trigonometric Identities   The following trigonometric identities are necessary in calculus, particularly in AP Calculus BC:

Pythagorean Identities

$$\sin^2 x + \cos^2 x = 1$$
$$\tan^2 x + 1 = \sec^2 x$$
$$\cot^2 x + 1 = \csc^2 x$$

Reciprocal Identities

$$\csc x = \frac{1}{\sin x}$$
$$\sec x = \frac{1}{\cos x}$$
$$\cot x = \frac{1}{\tan x}$$

Quotient Identities

$$\tan x = \frac{\sin x}{\cos x}$$
$$\cot x = \frac{\cos x}{\sin x}$$

Double-Angle Formulas for Sine and Cosine

$$\sin 2x = 2 \sin x \cos x$$
$$\cos 2x = \cos^2 x - \sin^2 x$$
$$= 2 \cos^2 x - 1$$
$$= 1 - 2 \sin^2 x$$

Inverse Trigonometric Functions

The **inverse of a function**, f^{-1}, is itself a function only if there is a one-to-one correspondence between the domain and the range. Interchanging the x- and y-values of a trigonometric function results in a relation that is not a function. For each new x-value, there will be many values of y. To obtain inverses of the trigonometric functions that are themselves definable as functions, the domains of the trigonometric functions must be restricted as follows:

- $\sin x$ is restricted to $-\frac{\pi}{2} \le x \le \frac{\pi}{2}$ to obtain arcsin x.
- $\cos x$ is restricted to $0 \le x \le \pi$ to obtain arccos x.
- $\tan x$ is restricted to $-\frac{\pi}{2} < x < \frac{\pi}{2}$ to obtain arctan x.

Arcsin x and arctan x are the inverse trigonometric functions that usually appear on the AP Calculus exams. The graphs of arcsin x and arctan x are shown below.

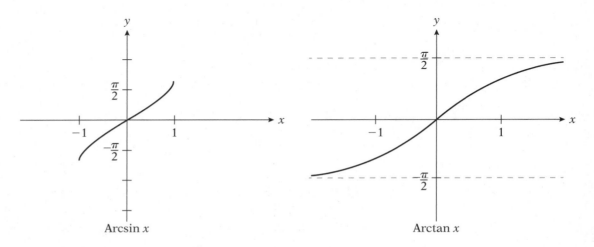

Arcsin x Arctan x

For example, arcsin $\frac{1}{2}$ is the angle (in radians) whose sine is equal to $\frac{1}{2}$, and we know this angle is $\frac{\pi}{6}$. Therefore arcsin $\frac{1}{2} = \frac{\pi}{6}$. Since it is a function, arcsin $\frac{1}{2}$ has only one answer, which must be in the range of arcsin x.

Similarly, arcsin $\left(-\frac{1}{2}\right)$ is the angle whose sine is equal to $-\frac{1}{2}$, and we know this angle is $-\frac{\pi}{6}$. Therefore arcsin $\left(-\frac{1}{2}\right) = -\frac{\pi}{6}$. Since it is a function, arcsin $\left(-\frac{1}{2}\right)$ has only one answer, which must be in the range of arcsin x.

Arccos $\frac{1}{2}$ is the angle whose cosine equals $\frac{1}{2}$, and we know this angle is $\frac{\pi}{3}$.

Arccos $\left(-\frac{1}{2}\right)$ is the angle whose cosine equals $-\frac{1}{2}$. Since the range of arccos is from 0 to π, the only solution to arccos $\left(-\frac{1}{2}\right)$ is $\frac{2\pi}{3}$.

Exponential and Logarithmic Functions

Exponential functions are functions of the form $y = b^x$, where b is a positive number, $b \neq 1$. The domain of $y = b^x$ is the set of all real numbers, and the range is $\{y > 0\}$.

Properties of Exponents

$b^0 = 1$

$b^1 = b$

$b^x \cdot b^y = b^{x+y}$

$\dfrac{b^x}{b^y} = b^{x-y}$

$b^{-x} = \dfrac{1}{b^x}$

$(b^x)^y = b^{xy}$

The inverse of the exponential function $y = b^x$ is the logarithmic function $y = \log_b x$. Therefore, the domain of $y = \log_b x$ is $\{x > 0\}$ and the range is the set of all real numbers.

Properties of the Logarithmic Function

$\log_b 1 = 0$

$\log_b b = 1$

$\log_b x + \log_b y = \log_b(xy)$

$\log_b x - \log_b y = \log_b\left(\dfrac{x}{y}\right)$

$\log_b x^y = y \log_b x$

The graphs of $y = b^x$ and $y = \log_b x$ are reflections of each other across the line $y = x$. The graphs of $y = b^x$ and $y = \log_b x$ are shown in the figure below.

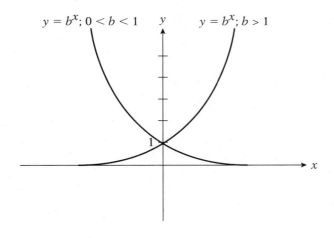

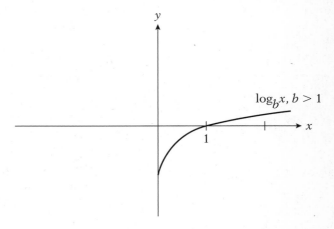

In the special case, where $b = e$, the graphs appear as follows:

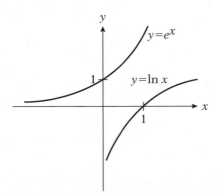

Piecewise-Defined Functions

Piecewise functions (also called **split functions**) are functions defined by more than one rule in each part of their domain. The pieces of the function may be connected or not. These functions may be graphed on a graphing calculator, but you should practice graphing them by hand until you become proficient at it. Two examples follow:

$$f(x) = \begin{cases} x + 2, & \text{for } x < 1 \\ 2 - x, & \text{for } x \geq 1 \end{cases} \qquad g(x) = \begin{cases} x^2, & \text{for } x < 0 \\ 2x, & \text{for } 0 \leq x \leq 1 \\ x + 1, & \text{for } x > 1 \end{cases}$$

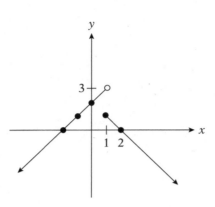

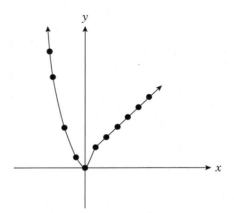

Calculator Note

The graphing calculator is a useful tool for examining functions and investigating their properties. At times, there will be exercises in this book to be done *without* a graphing calculator. Exercises done without a graphing calculator emphasize basic knowledge of details of a function. Since about half of the AP Calculus exam is done without any calculator, it is essential that you gain experience by doing exercises without a calculator.

The graphing calculator can be used to graph functions, help determine their domains and ranges, and find points of intersection of graphs. In this book, there will be exercises in which a graphing calculator is necessary to explore a concept or practice a technique. You should be aware that calculators might provide misleading or even incorrect information. It is vital that students of calculus understand the processes of calculus and be aware of the pitfalls of believing everything they see in the calculator window.

A student in an AP Calculus course should be skilled at using the graphing calculator to perform the four procedures allowed on the AP Calculus exam:

1. Get a complete graph of a function using the WINDOW key. (A complete graph is a graph that shows all the essential parts of the function.)
2. Find the zeros of a function.
3. Find a derivative numerically.
4. Find an integral numerically.

It is also useful to be able to find points of intersection of two graphs, and the maximum and minimum values of a function using the 2nd CALC menu on the TI-83/84 series (or the F5 Math menu on the TI-89).

On the **TI-nspire,** the MENU button is used to access available functions in the graph window.

1. **Actions** are generally used when creating programs or activities.
2. **View** hides or displays axes, and gridlines, and more.
3. **Graph Type** opens a menu that allows you to change the graph type.
4. **Window/Zoom** enables you to change the parameters of the viewing window.
5. **Trace** permits you to trace one or more graphs on your screen.
6. **Analyze Graph** is where you can find the commands to locate points of intersection, minimum values, maximum values, and zeroes.

MODEL PROBLEMS

1. Use a graphing calculator to sketch the graph of each of the following functions. Below each graph, state the window size used. State the domain and range for each.

   (a) $y = e^x + 1$

   (b) $y = \ln |x|$

   (c) $y = \sin^{-1} x$

   (d) $y = \begin{cases} x^2, x > 1 \\ 2x, x \le 1 \end{cases}$

   Solution

   (a) Domain = {all real numbers}, range = {$y > 1$}

   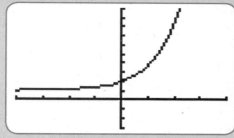

   $x[-4, 4], \quad y[-3, 10]$

   (b) Domain = {$x \ne 0$}, range = {all real numbers}

   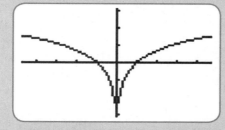

   $x[-4.7, 4.7], \quad y[-3.1, 3.1]$

(c) Domain $= [-1, 1]$, range $= \left[-\frac{\pi}{2}, \frac{\pi}{2}\right]$

$x\,[-\pi, \pi]$, $\quad y\,[-1.5, 1.5]$

(d) Domain $=$ {all real numbers}, range $=$ {all real numbers}

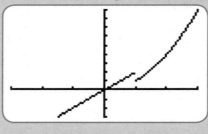

$x\,[-3, 3]$, $\quad y\,[-3, 9]$

Exercises

Multiple Choice Questions
No calculator is allowed for these questions.

1. The zeros of the polynomial function
   $f(x) = x^4 - 3x^3$ are

   (A) 0 and 3
   (B) 0 only
   (C) 3 only
   (D) 3 and 4

2. Arctan $\sqrt{3}$ is equal to

   (A) 1
   (B) $\frac{\pi}{4}$
   (C) $\frac{\pi}{6}$
   (D) $\frac{\pi}{3}$

3. Find the number of solutions of the equation
   $\cos^2 x - 1 = 0$ for values of x in the interval
   $[0, 2\pi]$.

   (A) 0
   (B) 1
   (C) 2
   (D) 3

4. Solve for x: $e^{2x} = 9$.

   (A) ln 9
   (B) ln 4.5
   (C) ln 3
   (D) ±4.5

5. Find the range of the piecewise function defined by $f(x) = \begin{cases} (x-1)^2, & x < 1 \\ 2x - 3, & x > 1 \end{cases}$.

(A) {all real numbers}

(B) $\{y > -1\}$

(C) $\{y \geq -1\}$

(D) $\{y \neq 1\}$

6. Find the equation of the horizontal asymptote of $y = \dfrac{5x}{x-1}$.

(A) $y = 0$

(B) $x = 1$

(C) $x = 5$

(D) $y = 5$

7. Find the equation of the vertical asymptote of $y = \dfrac{5x}{x-1}$.

(A) $y = 1$

(B) $y = 0$

(C) $x = 1$

(D) $x = 5$

8. Given $f(x) = 2x - 3$, find $f(x + h)$.

(A) $2x + 2h - 3$

(B) $2x + h - 3$

(C) $x + h$

(D) $x + h - 3$

9. If $f(x) = (2x - 1)(x^2 + 1)(x - 5)^2$, then $f(x)$ has how many real roots?

(A) 0

(B) 1

(C) 2

(D) 3

10. Solve for x: $\log_9 x^2 = 9$.

(A) 1

(B) 3^3

(C) 3^9

(D) $\pm 3^9$

11. $2 \ln e^{5x} =$

(A) $10x$

(B) $5x^2$

(C) $25x^2$

(D) e^{10x}

12. The values of x that are solutions to the equation $\cos^2 x = \sin 2x$ in the interval $[0, \pi]$ are:

(A) $\arctan \frac{1}{2}$ only.

(B) $\arctan \frac{1}{2}$ and π.

(C) $\arctan \frac{1}{2}$ and 0.

(D) $\arctan \frac{1}{2}$ and $\frac{\pi}{2}$.

13. The graph of $f(x) = \dfrac{x^2 - 1}{x - 1}$ has

(A) a hole at $x = 1$.

(B) a hole at $x = -1$.

(C) a vertical asymptote at $x = 1$.

(D) a vertical asymptote at $x = -1$.

14. If $\ln x^2 = 6$, then $x =$

(A) $\pm e^6$

(B) $9^{\sqrt{6}}$

(C) $e^{\sqrt{6}}$

(D) $\pm e^3$

Free Response Questions

A graphing calculator is required for some questions.

1. Find the domain and range and sketch the graph of $y = e^{\ln x}$.

2. The rational function $y = \dfrac{ax}{bx + c}$ has a vertical asymptote at $x = 2$ and a horizontal asymptote at $y = 3$.

(a) Find a and c in terms of b, and express y in simplest form.

(b) Graph the function, showing the vertical and horizontal asymptotes.

3. Write a piecewise function that has domain = {all real numbers} and range = $\{y \neq 2\}$.

4. Solve the trigonometric equation $4 \sin^2 x - \cos x = 1$ for values of x in the interval $(0, \pi)$.

5. For each of the following functions, graph $f(x)$, $|f(x)|$, and $f(|x|)$. Using these graphs, write a statement about the relationship between the graphs of $f(x)$, $|f(x)|$, and $f(|x|)$.

(a) $f(x) = \cos x$

(b) $f(x) = \sin x$

(c) $f(x) = x^2 - 2x$

6. (a) Write a fourth-degree polynomial that has roots 3 and $1 - i$. (There is more than one correct solution.)

(b) Write a rational function that has a vertical asymptote at $x = 1$, a horizontal asymptote at $y = 2$, and a hole at $x = -1$.

Lesson 2: Lines

Recall the following formulas related to linear equations, which you have learned in previous math classes:

The Formula for the Slope of a Line

$$\text{slope } m = \frac{\Delta y}{\Delta x} = \frac{y_2 - y_1}{x_2 - x_1}$$

Three Forms for the Equation of a Line

slope-intercept form	$y = mx + b$
point-slope form	$y - y_1 = m(x - x_1)$
standard form	$ax + by = c$

When the y-intercept is known, use the slope-intercept form. In most cases, however, the y-intercept is unknown, and the point-slope form should be used.

The Equations of Vertical and Horizontal Lines

horizontal line	$y = b$ (a constant)
vertical line	$x = a$ (a constant)

The Relationship Between Parallel and Perpendicular Lines

• If two lines are parallel, their slopes are equal.

• If two lines are perpendicular, their slopes are negative reciprocals.

MODEL PROBLEMS

1. Use the slope-intercept form to write the equation of a line with slope 5 that passes through the point (0, 7).

Solution

Since the slope is 5, and the line intercepts the y-axis at (0, 7), the equation of the line is $y = 5x + 7$.

2. Write the equation of a line that is parallel to the line with equation $4x + 3y = 9$ and that passes through the point (0, 7).

Solution

Method 1   To find the slope of the line with equation $4x + 3y = 9$, rewrite the equation as $y = -\frac{4}{3}x + 3$. The slope is $-\frac{4}{3}$ and since the line passing through the point (0, 7) means that the y-intercept is 7, the line parallel to the given line has the equation $y = -\frac{4}{3}x + 7$.

Method 2   A line parallel to the line with equation $4x + 3y = 9$ has the same slope and has an equation of the form $4x + 3y = k$, where k is a constant. Substituting the values of x and y in (0, 7) into the equation $4x + 3y = k$, we find the value of k is 21. Therefore, the equation of the line, in standard form, is $4x + 3y = 21$.

3. Write the equation of a line perpendicular to the line with equation $2x - y = 8$ that passes through the point (4, 5).

Solution

Method 1   The line with equation $2x - y = 8$ can be rewritten as $y = 2x - 8$. Since its slope is 2, the slope of any line perpendicular to it is $-\frac{1}{2}$. Using the point-slope form for the equation of a line, we find that the perpendicular line that passes through (4, 5) has the equation

$$y - 5 = -\frac{1}{2}(x - 4).$$

Note: On the AP exam, the equation of a line may be left in this form and the student will receive full credit.

Method 2   The slopes of perpendicular lines are negative reciprocals. A line perpendicular to the line with equation $2x - y = 8$ can be obtained by exchanging the coefficients of x and y, which results in the equation $x + 2y = k$, where k is a constant. Substituting the values of x and y into $x + 2y = k$, we find the value of k is 14. Therefore, the equation of the line perpendicular to the given line is $x + 2y = 14$.

4. Write the equation of a line parallel to the x-axis and passing through the point (–1, 4).

Solution

A line parallel to the x-axis is a horizontal line. Since it passes through (–1, 4), its equation is $y = 4$.

Exercises

Multiple Choice Questions
No calculator is allowed for these questions.

1. Write the equation of the line parallel to the graph of $4x + 3y = 8$ that passes through the point (2, –1).

   (A) $4x + 3y = 5$

   (B) $3x - 4y = 10$

   (C) $4x - 3y = 7$

   (D) $3x + 4y = 2$

2. Write the equation of the line perpendicular to the graph of $2x - 5y = 0$ that passes through the point (–2, 3).

   (A) $2x - 5y = 11$

   (B) $2x + 5y = 11$

   (C) $5x + 2y = -4$

   (D) $5x + 2y = -16$

3. Which is the equation of a line with slope -3 that passes through the point $(-1, -5)$?

(A) $y - 5 = -3(x - 1)$

(B) $y - 5 = -3(x + 1)$

(C) $y + 5 = -3(x - 1)$

(D) $y + 5 = -3(x + 1)$

4. If the point with coordinates $(3, k)$ is on the line $2x - 5y = 8$, find the value of k.

(A) $-\dfrac{14}{5}$

(B) $-\dfrac{3}{5}$

(C) $-\dfrac{2}{5}$

(D) $\dfrac{2}{5}$

5. The equation of the line joining the points $(-1, 2)$ and $(5, 6)$ is

(A) $2x - 3y = 8$

(B) $2x - 3y + 8 = 0$

(C) $2x + 3y = 8$

(D) $2x + 3y + 8 = 0$

6. Which of the following are the equation of a line?

I. $y = 2x - 5$

II. $y = x^2 - 5$

III. $2y - 3x = 0$

(A) I only

(B) III only

(C) I and III

(D) II and III

Free Response Questions

No calculator is allowed for these questions.

1. Given points $A(2, 4)$, $B(0, 0)$, and $C(4, 0)$,

(a) write the equation of line l, the perpendicular bisector of segment BC.

(b) is point A on line l?

(c) write the equation of line m, the perpendicular bisector of segment AC.

(d) is point B on line m?

2. Given points $A(2, 4)$, $B(0, 0)$, and $C(5, 1)$,

(a) find the equation of the line through A and parallel to line BC.

(b) find the coordinates of point D so that $ABCD$ is a parallelogram.

Lesson 3: Function Properties

The **domain** of a function is the set of its x-coordinates. The x-coordinate is called the independent variable. Often the easiest way to find the domain of a function is to locate the values of x for which the function is not defined. In a rational function, for example, the function is not defined at those values of x for which the denominator is equal to zero. The domain of a function is the set of x-values excluding those for which the function is not defined. In the case of polynomials, the domain is always the set of all real numbers. This is one of the reasons that polynomials are the functions we study first.

The **range** of a function is the set of its y-coordinates. The y-coordinate is called the dependent variable. The range of a function depends on the values in the domain.

Finding the range of a simple function such as a line or parabola is a straightforward process. An arbitrary function may have maximum and minimum values that are difficult to locate. In some cases, therefore, finding the range may require using the methods of calculus.

Function Notation The value of a function $f(x)$ at $x = 2$ is denoted $f(2)$. If the function is $f(x) = 4x + 1$, for example, then $f(2) = 4(2) + 1 = 9$.

Similarly, $f(a) = 4a + 1$, and $f(x - 1) = 4(x - 1) + 1 = 4x - 3$.

Symmetry of a Function and Asymptotes If a function $f(x)$ is **even,** its graph is symmetric with respect to the y-axis. An equivalent algebraic statement is that $f(-x) = f(x)$.

If a function $g(x)$ is **odd,** its graph is symmetric with respect to the origin. An equivalent algebraic statement is that $g(-x) = -g(x)$.

If 0 is in the domain of an odd function $g(x)$, then $g(-0) = -g(0)$, or $g(0) = -g(0)$. Therefore, $g(0) = 0$. That is, if 0 is in the domain of an odd function, then its graph must pass through the origin.

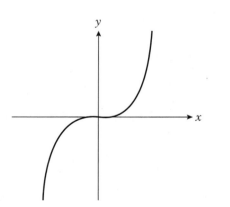

An Odd Function
Symmetric with Respect to the Origin

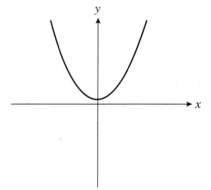

An Even Function
Symmetric with Respect to the y-Axis

If there are values of x for which a function is undefined, then the function may have a **vertical asymptote** at these x-values. Many rational functions have vertical asymptotes.

If a function is not a rational function, it may still have vertical or horizontal asymptotes. Vertical asymptotes are located by finding the values of x for which the function is undefined. Finding horizontal asymptotes may involve evaluating the limit of the function. We discuss limits in Main Idea 1.

Multiple Representations of a Function

The AP Calculus courses emphasize the importance of being able to represent a function in multiple ways. You should be able to represent functions graphically, numerically, algebraically, and verbally. You should also be able to convert flexibly from one representation to another. Much of the power of calculus derives from being able to approach problems from different perspectives. Students who are skilled at representing functions in multiple ways are able to approach problem-solving situations from a variety of perspectives and can choose from a number of techniques and methods when working toward a solution.

For example, looking at the graph of $f(x) = \dfrac{x}{x^2 + 1}$ shown on below, we might suspect that the function is odd, since it appears to be symmetric with respect to the origin.

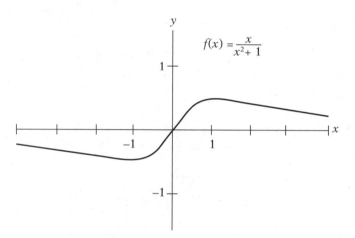

Investigating further, we evaluate the function for several values of x. Thus,

$$f(2) = \frac{2}{5}, f(-2) = -\frac{2}{5}, f(0) = 0, f(1) = \frac{1}{2}, f(-1) = -\frac{1}{2}.$$

The emerging pattern further indicates the function is odd. We prove it algebraically:

$$f(-x) = \frac{-x}{(-x)^2 + 1} = -f(x).$$

We conclude that $f(x) = \dfrac{x}{x^2 + 1}$ is an odd function because $f(-x) = -f(x)$, which is the definition of an odd function.

MODEL PROBLEMS

1. Find the domain and range of the function $y = \sqrt{x - 8}$.

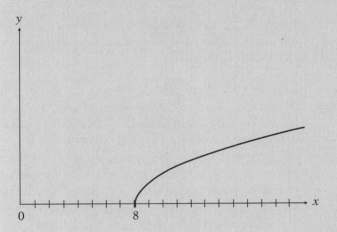

Solution

The quantity under the radical must be greater than or equal to zero; therefore, the domain is $\{x \geq 8\}$. Since the y-values are greater than or equal to zero, the range of the function is $\{y \geq 0\}$.

2. Find the domain and range of each function.

(a) $y = e^x - x$

(b) $y = |x| + x$

(c) $y = (x + 1)^2$

(d) $y = \dfrac{\sin 2x}{x}$

Solution

(a) Domain = {all reals}, range = $\{y \geq 1\}$

(b) Domain = {all reals}, range = $\{y \geq 0\}$

(c) Domain = {all reals}, range = $\{y \geq -1\}$

(d) Domain = $\{x \neq 0\}$, range = $\{-0.434 \leq y \leq 2\}$

3. Is the function $y = \dfrac{e^{x^2}}{x}$ even, odd, or neither? Explain your answer both graphically and algebraically.

Solution

GRAPHICALLY Graph the function on the calculator to see if it is symmetric to either the y-axis or the origin.

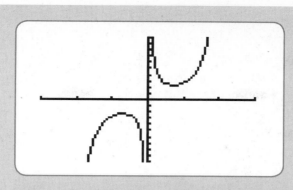

The function appears to be symmetric with respect to the origin, so we suspect it is odd.

ALGEBRAICALLY Choose several x-values to see if either $f(-x) = f(x)$, or $f(-x) = -f(x)$.

$$f(-x) = \frac{e^{(-x)^2}}{-x} = \frac{e^{x^2}}{-x} = -\frac{e^{x^2}}{x},$$

which is $-f(x)$. Therefore, $f(x)$ is odd.

Calculator Note

To see if a function is even or odd using your calculator, enter the function in Y_1. Then enter $Y_1 (-x)$ Into Y_2. Now graph Y_1 and Y_2.

If the function is even, then Y_1 and Y_2 are the same function, and only one function will appear on the graph.

If the function is odd, then Y_1 and Y_2 are opposites, and two opposite functions will appear on the graph.

On the **TI-*nspire***, enter one function into $f1(x)$, then enter $f1(-x)$ into $f2(x)$. If the function is even, $f1(x)$ and $f2(x)$ are the same function and only one function will appear on the graph. If the function is odd, then two functions will appear.

Zeros   The zeros of a function $f(x)$ are the x-values such that $f(x) = 0$. Sometimes we can find the zeros by factoring or by approximating them on a calculator. In the case of complex roots, we need to use algebraic methods.

MODEL PROBLEMS

1. Find the equations of the vertical asymptote(s) of $y = \frac{x + 2}{x^2 - 1}$.

Solution

The vertical asymptotes are found by solving $x^2 - 1 = 0$.

The solutions are $x = 1$ and $x = -1$. Since neither of these values makes the numerator zero, both $x = 1$ and $x = -1$ are equations of vertical asymptotes.

2. Find the asymptotes of $f(x) = \frac{x-1}{x^2-1}$.

Solution

Since $f(x)$ is a rational function and the degree of the numerator is less than the degree of the denominator, $f(x)$ has a horizontal asymptote at $y = 0$.

To find the vertical asymptotes, set the denominator equal to zero and solve for x. There are two solutions, $x = 1$ and $x = -1$. Since $x = 1$ also makes the numerator zero, $f(1)$ is not undefined (it is called indeterminate). Thus, there is a hole at $x = 1$ and no vertical asymptote. The function has only one vertical asymptote at $x = -1$.

3. For the functions that follow, find

(a) the zeros.

(b) the end behavior.

- $f(x) = (x - 2)^2(x + 3)$
- $f(x) = (x - 2)^2(x + 3)^2$

Solution

For $f(x) = (x - 2)^2(x + 3)$,

(a) the zeros are $x = 2$ and $x = -3$.

(b) since $f(x)$ is a third-degree polynomial and the leading coefficient is positive, the graph of $f(x)$ goes up to the right and down to the left.

For $f(x) = (x - 2)^2(x + 3)^2$,

(a) the zeros are $x = 2$ and $x = -3$.

(b) since $f(x)$ is a fourth-degree polynomial and the leading coefficient is positive, the graph of $f(x)$ rises on both the left and right sides.

4. (a) If $(1, 2)$ is a point on the graph of an *even* function, what other point is also on the graph?

(b) If $(1, 2)$ is a point on the graph of an *odd* function, what other point is also on the graph?

Solution

(a) By the definition of an even function $f(x) = f(-x)$. Since $(1, 2)$ is a point on the graph of an even function, the point $(-1, 2)$ is also on the graph.

(b) By the definition of an odd function, $f(x) = -f(x)$. Since $(1, 2)$ is on the graph of an odd function, the point $(-1, -2)$ is also on the graph.

Exercises

Multiple Choice Questions

A graphing calculator is required for some questions.

1. If $f(x) = x^2 - x + 1$, then $f(x+1) =$

(A) $x^2 - x + 2$

(B) $x^2 + x + 1$

(C) $x^2 + x + 3$

(D) 1

2. Find the domain of $f(x) = \sqrt{x^3 - x^2}$.

(A) $\{x \geq 1\}$

(B) $\{x \geq 1, x = 0\}$

(C) $\{x \leq 1\}$

(D) $\{|x| \geq 1\}$

3. Which of the following is an even function with a domain of all real numbers?

(A) $\ln x^2$

(B) $e^{x^2} - x$

(C) $e^{x^2} - x^2$

(D) $e^{x^3} + 1$

4. Find the domain of $f(x) = \ln(\tan x)$ on the interval $[-\pi, \pi]$.

(A) all x in $(-\pi, \pi)$

(B) all x in $(0, \pi)$

(C) all x in $\left(0, \dfrac{\pi}{2}\right)$

(D) all x in $\left(-\pi, -\dfrac{\pi}{2}\right)$ and $\left(0, \dfrac{\pi}{2}\right)$

5. $f(x) = \dfrac{(x-1)^2}{x^2 - 1}$ has

(A) holes at $x = -1$ and $x = 1$.

(B) vertical asymptotes at $x = 1$ and $x = -1$.

(C) a horizontal asymptote at $y = -1$.

(D) a hole at $x = 1$ and a vertical asymptote at $x = -1$.

6. $f(x)$ is an odd function and the graph of f contains the point $(6, 5)$. Which of the following points is also on the graph of f?

(A) $(-6, 5)$

(B) $(6, -5)$

(C) $(-6, -5)$

(D) $(-5, -6)$

7. If $f(x) = \sqrt{x-2}$, then $\dfrac{f(x+h) - f(x)}{h} =$

(A) $\dfrac{\sqrt{x-2} + \sqrt{h-2}}{h}$

(B) $\dfrac{\sqrt{xh-2} + \sqrt{x-2}}{h}$

(C) $\dfrac{\sqrt{x-2+h} - \sqrt{x-2}}{h}$

(D) $\dfrac{\sqrt{x+h} - \sqrt{2}}{h}$

8. If $f(x) = \dfrac{1}{x+2}$, then $\dfrac{f(x+h) - f(x)}{h} =$

(A) $\dfrac{h+4}{h(x+2)(x+h+2)}$

(B) $\dfrac{-1}{(x+2)(x+h+2)}$

(C) $\dfrac{-1}{(x+h)(x+h-2)}$

(D) $\dfrac{1}{h(x+2)(x+h+2)}$

9. Which of the following functions are odd?

I. $y = \ln(x^3)$

II. $y = |x^3|$

III. $y = e^{x^3}$

(A) None

(B) II only

(C) I and II

(D) II and III

10. Which of the following functions are even?

    I. $y = \ln |x|$

    II. $y = |\ln x|$

    III. $y = \left|\frac{1}{x}\right|$

(A) None

(B) II only

(C) I and II

(D) II and III

Free-Response Questions

A graphing calculator is required for some questions.

1. Find all the zeros (real and complex) of
$f(x) = x^3 + 2x - 3$.

2. (a) Enter into the calculator [Y=]: $Y_1 = x^3 - x$, $Y_2 = Y_1(-x)$. Sketch Y_1 and Y_2 and describe the relationship between them. What property of the function in Y_1 is the basis for this relationship?

    (b) Enter in [Y=]: $Y_1 = x^2 + 1$, $Y_2 = Y_1(-x)$. Sketch Y_1 and Y_2 and describe the relationship between them. What property of the function in Y_1 is the basis for this relationship?

3. Sketch $f(x) = \dfrac{x - 1}{x^2 - 3x + 2}$, and state the vertical asymptote(s), horizontal asymptote(s), and holes, if any.

4. Find the zeros and describe the end behavior of $f(x) = 2x(x - 1)(x + 1)$. Is $f(x)$ odd, even, or neither? Explain.

Lesson 4: Inverses

If a function is **one-to-one,** then the function has an inverse. The inverse of the function $f(x)$ is denoted $f^{-1}(x)$, and is read as "the inverse of f." Do not confuse $f^{-1}(x)$ with $\frac{1}{f(x)}$.

We can use the **horizontal line test** to determine if a function is one-to-one from its graph.

> **Horizontal Line Test**
> If a horizontal line intersects the graph of a function no more than once, then that function is one-to-one.

If a function is not one-to-one, it may be possible to restrict its domain in order to make it one-to-one. $y = \sin x$, as we stated previously.

The graph of the inverse of a function is the reflection of the graph of the function (on its restricted domain) across the line $y = x$.

The equation of the inverse of a function can be found by exchanging x and y in the equation of the function, and then solving for y. The domain of the inverse is the range of the function, and the range of the inverse is the domain of the function.

Calculator Note

The TI-83/84 and TI-89 calculators have a built-in draw inverse feature.

Using the TI-83/84
Enter the function into Y=.
  Press 2nd DRAW 8 to get DrawInv on the Home screen.
  Press VARS Y-VARS 1 ENTER.
  The calculator will display the graph of the inverse of the function.

Using the TI-89
Press GRAPH WINDOW F6 3: DrawInv, then enter the function (for example, Y_1 or Y_2) and press ENTER.

Using the TI-nspire

Enter the function in $f1(x)$. Then press MENU, **Actions, Text** and type in $x = f1(y)$. Using the hand, grab the text and drag it to the x-axis. The inverse function will appear.

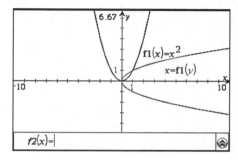

MODEL PROBLEM

1. For the functions $f(x)$ and $g(x)$ where $f(x) = x^3 - 4$ and $g(x) = \ln(x) + 2$,

(a) state the domain and range of the function.

(b) find the equation of the inverse of the function.

(c) state the domain and range of the inverse.

(d) graph the function and its inverse on the same set of axes.

Solution

For $f(x) = x^3 - 4$,

(a) the domain is the set of all real numbers. The range is the set of all real numbers.

(b) the equation of the inverse is $y = (x + 4)^{1/3}$.

(c) the domain and range of the inverse is the set of real numbers.

(d)

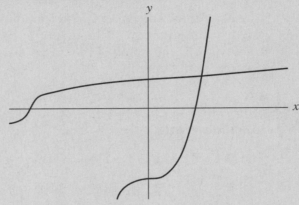

For $g(x) = \ln(x) + 2$,

(a) the domain of $g(x)$ is $\{x > 0\}$. The range is the set of real numbers.

(b) the equation of the inverse is $g^{-1}(x) = e^{x-2}$.

(c) the domain of the inverse of $g(x)$ is the set of real numbers. The range of the inverse of $g(x)$ is $\{y > 0\}$.

(d)

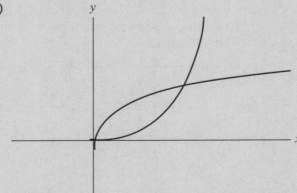

Exercises

Multiple-Choice Questions
No calculator is allowed for these questions.

1. Which of the following graphs show(s) a function that has an inverse?

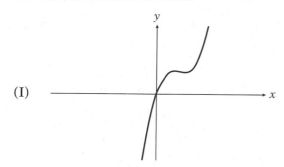

(I)

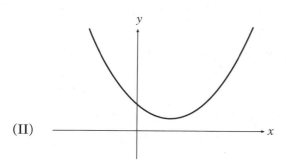

(II)

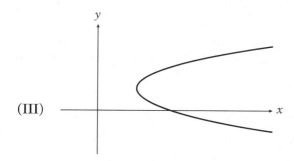

(III)

    (A) None
    (B) I only
    (C) II only
    (D) I and II

2. Find the inverse of the equation $y = 2x^3 + 1$.

    (A) $y^{-1} = \dfrac{2}{x^3} + 1$

    (B) $y^{-1} = -2x^3 + 1$

    (C) $y^{-1} = \sqrt[3]{\dfrac{x-1}{2}}$

    (D) $y^{-1} = \dfrac{\sqrt[3]{x-1}}{2}$

3. The graphs of a function and its inverse are reflections of each other across

    (A) the x-axis.
    (B) the y-axis.
    (C) the origin.
    (D) $y = x$.

4. The composition of a function f and its inverse is equal to

    (A) -1
    (B) 0
    (C) 1
    (D) x

Free-Response Questions

A graphing calculator is required for some questions.

1. (a) Sketch the graph of $y = -e^{-x}$. State its domain and range.

    (b) On the calculator, enter [2nd] DRAW 8: DrawInv Y_1, and sketch the inverse you see on your screen onto your graph from part (a). the inverse onto your graph.

    (c) Solve algebraically for the inverse of $y = -e^{-x}$.

    (d) Enter the equation of the inverse in Y_2. Graph it and examine the symmetry to check that it is in fact the equation of the inverse.

2. (a) Find the domain and range of the function $y = \sqrt{x-2} + 1$, and sketch the graph.

    (b) Find the domain and range of the of the inverse of y, and solve algebraically for the equation of the inverse.

3. Sketch the inverse of the function shown here.

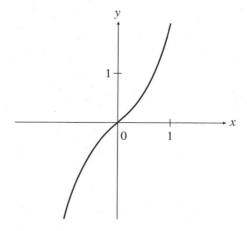

Lesson 5: Translations and Reflections

When the graph of a function is moved to the left or right, or up or down, or is reflected across the x-axis or the y-axis, the graph maintains many of its properties. When the graph of a function is shifted or flipped, the rule for the function changes, though the graph remains essentially the same.

Rules for Translating and Reflecting Functions

- If a function $f(x)$ is translated to the right c units, its new equation is $f(x - c)$.
- If a function $f(x)$ is translated to the left c units, its new equation is $f(x + c)$.
- If a function $f(x)$ is translated down c units, its new equation is $f(x) - c$.
- If a function $f(x)$ is translated up c units, its new equation is $f(x) + c$.
- If a function $f(x)$ is reflected across the x-axis, its new equation is $-f(x)$.
- If a function $f(x)$ is reflected across the y-axis, its new equation is $f(-x)$.

For example, if the graph of $y = x^2$ is moved 5 units to the right, the new rule is $y = (x - 5)^2$.

If the graph is moved down 3 units, the new rule is $y = x^2 - 3$.

If the graph is reflected across the x-axis, the new rule is $y = -x^2$.

When the graph of a parabola is shifted or reflected, the graph remains a parabola with properties similar to those of the original graph.

If the graph of $y = \ln x$ is shifted to the left 2 units, the new rule will be $y = \ln(x + 2)$.

Practice in graphing both by hand and using a graphing calculator makes it easier to recognize that a group of functions can be understood as one function that has been shifted and/or reflected.

MODEL PROBLEM

1. Describe the translation and/or reflection that changes

   (a) x^2 to $(x + 3)^2$

   (b) $|x|$ to $-|x - k|$, $(k > 0)$

   (c) 2^x to 2^{-x}

   (d) $\cos x$ to $-\cos x$

Solution

   (a) The graph is moved 3 units to the left.

   (b) The graph is moved k units to the right and reflected across the x-axis.

   (c) The graph is reflected across the y-axis.

   (d) The graph is reflected across the x-axis.

Exercises

No calculator is allowed for these questions.

1. The following functions have been shifted as described. Circle the equation that matches each description, then sketch its graph.

   (a) $y = \ln x$ shifted right 2 units.

   $y = \ln(x + 2)$ $\qquad$ $y = \ln(x - 2)$

   $y = \ln x + 2$ $\qquad$ $y = \ln x - 2$

   (b) $y = 2^x$ shifted down 1 unit.

   $y = 2^x - 1$ $\qquad$ $y = 2^{x-1}$

   $y = 2^{x+1}$ $\qquad$ $y = 2^x + 1$

   (c) $y = |x|$ shifted left 3 units.

   $y = |x + 3|$ $\qquad$ $y = |x - 3|$

   $y = |x| + 3$ $\qquad$ $y = |x| - 3$

   (d) $y = x^2$ shifted up 2 units and right 4 units.

   $y = (x - 2)^2 - 4$ $\qquad$ $y = (x - 2)^2 + 4$

   $y = (x^2 + 4) + 2$ $\qquad$ $y = (x - 4)^2 + 2$

   (e) $y = \sin x$ reflected across the x-axis.

   $y = \sin(-x)$ $\qquad$ $y = \sin(x - 1)$

   $y = -\sin x$ $\qquad$ $y = -\sin(-x)$

2. Write the domain for each of the following functions. Then sketch the graph.

   (a) $y = \ln x^2$

   (b) $y = |x + 2|$

   (c) $y = -\ln(x - 1)$

Multiple Choice Questions

A graphing calculator is required for some of these questions.

1. The graph of $y = x^2$ first reflected across the x-axis and then shifted down one unit is

   (A) $y = 1 - x^2$

   (B) $y = 1 + x^2$

   (C) $y = 1 - x^{-2}$

   (D) $y = -1 - x^2$

2. The graph of $y = x^2$ first shifted down one unit and then reflected in the x-axis is

   (A) $y = x^2 - 1$.

   (B) $y = 1 - x^2$.

   (C) $y = 1 + x^2$.

   (D) $y = 1 - x^{-2}$.

3. The inverse of the function $y = x^2$ with domain = $\{x \leq 0\}$ has equation.

   (A) $y = x^2$.

   (B) $y = \sqrt{x}$.

   (C) $y = \pm\sqrt{x}$.

   (D) $y = -\sqrt{x}$.

Free-Response Questions

A graphing calculator is required for some questions.

1. Sketch the graph of $y = \frac{1}{x}$, and then use it to sketch the graphs of the following functions without a calculator. Check your results by graphing each equation in the calculator.

   (a) $y = \dfrac{1}{x - 1}$

   (b) $y = \dfrac{1}{x} - 1$

   (c) $y = \dfrac{1}{x + 2} + 2$

   (d) the inverse of $y = \dfrac{1}{x}$

2. Describe the translations and/or reflections that transform $y = x^{2/3}$ into the following:

   (a) $y = x^{2/3} + 2$

   (b) $y = -x^{2/3} - 3$

   (c) $y = (-x)^{2/3}$

   (d) $y = (x - 1)^{2/3} + 1$

Lesson 6: Parametric Equations

Functions in calculus are usually of a single variable. There are also functions defined by a set of parametric equations, where x and y are both dependent variables expressed in terms of an independent variable t, called the **parameter.** Parametric functions appear in the following form:

$$\begin{cases} x = f(t) \\ y = g(t). \end{cases}$$

Parametric equations allow us to graph a wider variety of functions and graph curves, called relations instead of functions. Unlike x and y, the parameter t does not appear as an axis in the coordinate plane. It is a third variable, often representing time, used only to define the values of x and y.

Calculator Note

To work with parametric equations on the graphing calculator, the MODE must be set to Par (for parametric). Expressions for both x and y may then be entered in Y=.

Press WINDOW to enter values that will define the viewing window. In addition to Tmin and Tmax, there is also a Tstep, which controls the number of points that are plotted. The bigger Tstep is, the fewer points are plotted and the less accurate the graph. The smaller Tstep is, the more points are plotted and the more accurate the graph. It also takes the calculator longer to produce a graph with a smaller Tstep.

Once the functions are entered, you can press GRAPH, and then TRACE, to display the values of x, y, and t.

To change to parametric mode on the **TI-nspire,** press MENU, then select **Graph Type, Parametric.** Minimum and maximum window values for x and y may be altered by the accessing **Window/Zoom** and then **Window Settings.**

MODEL PROBLEMS

1. Use your calculator to graph the given parametric function. State its domain and range.

    $$\begin{cases} x = t^2 \\ y = t + 2 \end{cases}$$

    Graph the function in the WINDOW: Tmin = 0, Tmax = 3, and Tstep = 0.1, Xmin = 0, Xmax =10, Ymin = −3, Ymax = 9.

Solution

Press $\boxed{Y=}$, and enter $x_{1T} = t^2$ and $y_{1T} = t + 2$. Define the window and then press $\boxed{\text{GRAPH}}$.

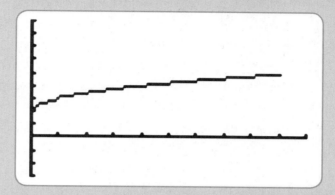

Use $\boxed{\text{TRACE}}$ to find that the domain for t is $[0, 3]$, the domain for x is $[0, 9]$, and the range for y is $[0, 5]$.

2. Using the parametric function from Model Problem 1, go to $\boxed{\text{WINDOW}}$ and change Tmin $= -3$, and then press $\boxed{\text{GRAPH}}$. Find the domain and range of the graph.

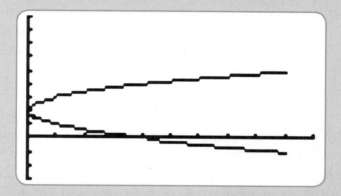

Solution

Notice that the graph is not that of a function. It is now a relation. The domain of t is $[-3, 3]$. The domain of x is $[0, 9]$. The range of y is $[-1, 5]$.

By eliminating the parameter t, the set of parametric equations given in Model Problem 1 on page 44, $x = t^2$ and $y = t + 2$, can be transformed into a single equation in terms of x and y. Solve for t in $y = t + 2$, $t = y - 2$, and substitute t into the equation for x, $x = t^2$. Thus, $x = (y - 2)^2$. This is the equation of a parabola, but there is still a restriction on the values of x and y, depending on the values of t that are used, say t between 0 and 3 or t between -3 and 3. It is extremely important to remember that when eliminating the parameter, the values of x and y are still limited by the values of t specified in the problem.

MODEL PROBLEM

1. Using your calculator, graph the parametric function in the window given.

$$\begin{cases} x = te^{-t^2} \\ y = t + 2 \end{cases}$$

Graph the function in the following WINDOW: Tmin = −2, Tmax = 2, Xmin = −2, Xmax = 2, Ymin = −1, Ymax = 5.

(a) Sketch the graph and indicate the direction of increasing t.
(b) Estimate the domain and range of the graph.

Solution

(a) With the calculator in parametric mode, enter the following into Y=:
$x_{1T} = te^{-t^2}$, $y_{1T} = t + 2$. Set the WINDOW and press ENTER.

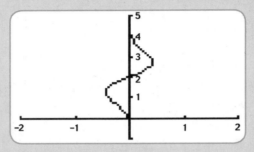

(b) The domain is approximately [−0.429, 0.429], and the range is [0, 4].

Exercises

Multiple Choice Questions
No calculator is allowed for these questions.

1. For the pair of parametric equations $x(t) = 2\cos t$ and $y(t) = \sin t$, eliminating the parameter gives which equation in the variables x and y?

(A) $x^2 + y^2 = 4$
(B) $x^2 - y^2 = 4$
(C) $x^2 + 4y^2 = 4$
(D) $4x^2 + y^2 = 4$

2. For the pair of parametric equations $x(t) = t^2 + t$ and $y(t) = t$, eliminating the parameter gives which equation in the variables x and y?

(A) $y^2 = x + y$
(B) $y^2 = x - y$
(C) $x^2 + x = y$
(D) $y^2 = x^2 + y$

3. Which of the following is a part of the graph given by the system of parametric equations $x(t) = t^2 + 2t$ and $y(t) = t$?

(A)

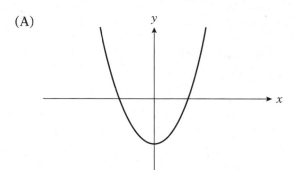

(B)

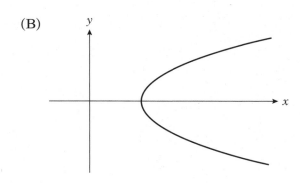

(C)

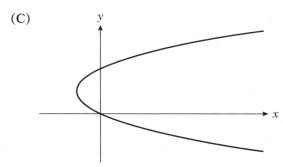

(D)

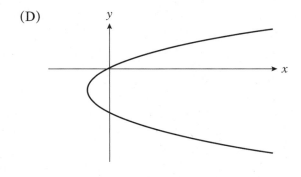

4. The parametric equations $x(t) = 2t + 1$ and $y(t) = t - 1$, for t in the interval $[0, 4]$, represent the equation of

(A) a line.

(B) a ray.

(C) a line segment.

(d) a circle.

Free Response Questions

A graphing calculator is required.

1. Using the given parametric equations, sketch the curve and indicate the direction of increasing t.

$x(t) = 2\cos t$ and $y(t) = \sin t$,

for t in the interval $[0, \pi]$.

2. Sketch the graph of the parametric equations, indicating the direction of increasing t, and use the graph to identify the curve.

$x(t) = t^2 + 1$ and $y(t) = t - 1$,

for t in the inverval $[-3, 3]$.

Prerequisite Ideas
Summary Assessment

Multiple Choice Questions

1. Find the slope of the line with equation
   $2x + 3y = 5$.

   (A) $-\frac{3}{2}$

   (B) $-\frac{2}{3}$

   (C) $\frac{2}{3}$

   (D) $\frac{3}{2}$

2. Find the equation of the line parallel to the line with equation $x - 2y = 6$ and passing through the point $(2, -3)$.

   (A) $x - 2y = 11$
   (B) $x - 2y = 8$
   (C) $2x + y = 7$
   (D) $2x + y = 1$

3. Find the equation of the line perpendicular to the line with equation $3x + 4y = 7$ and passing through $(0, -1)$.

   (A) $4x - 3y = 7$
   (B) $4x - 3y = 3$
   (C) $3x + 4y = -4$
   (D) $3x - 4y = 4$

4. How many vertical and horizontal asymptotes are there to the graph of $y = \dfrac{x^2}{x^2 - 1}$?

   (A) 2 vertical and 1 horizontal
   (B) 1 vertical and 1 horizontal
   (C) 1 vertical and no horizontal
   (D) 2 vertical and no horizontal

5. The graph of $y = e^{-x} + 1$ has a horizontal asymptote with equation

   (A) $x = 0$.
   (B) $y = 0$.
   (C) $x = 1$.
   (D) $y = 1$.

6. The graph of $y = \ln(x + 2)$ has a vertical asymptote with equation

   (A) $x = -2$.
   (B) $y = -2$.
   (C) $x = 0$.
   (D) $y = 0$.

7. The domain of $y = e^{-2x} + 1$ is

   (A) $\{x > 0\}$.
   (B) $\{x \neq 0\}$.
   (C) $\{x < 0\}$.
   (D) $\{\text{all real numbers}\}$.

8. The range of $y = \ln(x + 2)$ is

   (A) $\{x > 2\}$.
   (B) $\{x > 0\}$.
   (C) $\{x \neq 0\}$.
   (D) $\{x > -2\}$.

9. The end behavior of the graph of $f(x) = x^4 + 3x^3 - 6x$ can be described as

   (A) both ends up.
   (B) left up, right down.
   (C) left down, right up.
   (D) both ends down.

10. The end behavior of the graph of $f(x) = -3x^3 + x^2$ can be described as

    (A) both ends up.
    (B) left up, right down.
    (C) left down, right up.
    (D) both ends down.

11. Find the value(s) of $\arccos(1)$.

    (A) 0
    (B) π
    (C) 0 or π
    (D) $\frac{\pi}{2}$

12. Solve the equation $\ln x^2 = 5$.

(A) $x = \pm e^{5/2}$

(B) $x = e^{5/2}$

(C) $x = \pm e^{\sqrt{5}}$

(D) $x = e^{\sqrt{5}}$

13. The function $y = \log_2(x - 4)$ has an x-intercept at $x =$

(A) 1.

(B) 2.

(C) 4.

(D) 5.

14. The function $y = \ln x + 2$ has a y-intercept at $y =$

(A) 0.

(B) 1.

(C) 2.

(D) e.

15. Solve the equation $e^{2x} - e^x = 2$.

(A) 2 only

(B) -1 or 2

(C) $\ln 2$

(D) e^{-1} or e^2

16. The graph of an even function has

(A) no symmetry.

(B) symmetry with respect to the x-axis.

(C) symmetry with respect to the line $y = x$.

(D) symmetry with respect to the y-axis.

17. If the point with coordinates $(2, 1)$ is on the graph of a function, then which of the following is on the graph of its inverse?

(A) $(2, -1)$

(B) $(-2, -1)$

(C) $(-2, 1)$

(D) $(1, 2)$

18. The inverse of $y = 2\sqrt{x}$ is

(A) $y = \frac{1}{4}x^2, x \leq 0$.

(B) $y = \frac{1}{4}x^2, x \geq 0$.

(C) $y = \frac{1}{4}x^2$.

(D) $y = -2\sqrt{x}$.

19. The real zero(s) of $f(x) = x^3 + 2x^2 + 9x + 18$ are

(A) -2 only.

(B) $-3, -2$.

(C) $\pm 3, -2$.

(D) $\pm 3, \pm 2$.

20. If $f(x) = x^2 - 2x$, then $f(2 + h) =$

(A) $h^2 + 8h + 3$.

(B) $h^2 + 2h + 3$.

(C) $h^2 + 2h + 3$.

(D) $h^2 + 2h$.

21. The domain of $f(x) = \dfrac{x - 3}{\sqrt{x - 2}}$ is

(A) $x \geq 2$.

(B) $x > 2$.

(C) $x > 3$.

(D) $x > 2$ and $x \neq 3$.

22. The range of $y = 2|x - 2| - 2$ in the interval $[0, 5]$ is

(A) $\{0 \leq y \leq 5\}$.

(B) $\{2 \leq y \leq 5\}$.

(C) $\{-2 \leq y \leq 5\}$.

(D) $\{-2 \leq y \leq 4\}$.

23. Which of the following has an inverse?

(A) $x = y^2$

(B) $y = |x|$

(C) $y = \ln x$

(D) $y = \sqrt{4 - x^2}$

24. Which of the following functions are even?

I. $3y = x^4 + x$

II. $y = |x - 2|$

III. $y = e^{x^2} - 1$

(A) I only

(B) II only

(C) III only

(D) II and III

25. For which of the following functions does $f(a) + f(b) = f(a + b)$?

(A) $y = 2x + 3$

(B) $y = 2x$

(C) $y = x^2$

(D) $y = \sqrt{x}$

Free Response Questions

1. (a) Sketch the graph of each function below by hand.

$$f(x) = x^4 - x^3$$
$$g(x) = \ln x$$
$$h(x) = x - 1$$

(b) Graph the 3 functions in the calculator and use $\boxed{\text{ZOOM}}$ Box centered at $(0, 1)$.

(c) Write a sentence that describes the relationship between $f(x)$, $g(x)$, and $h(x)$ for the values of x near $(1, 0)$.

(d) Find the range of $f(x)$.

2. (a) Graph $f(x) = x^3 - x$.

(b) Does $f(x)$ have an inverse? Explain your answer and find the inverse if it exists.

(c) Graph $g(x) = x^3 - 1$.

(d) Does $g(x)$ have an inverse? Explain your answer and find the inverse if it exists.

3. Copy the table below and fill in the domain, range, roots, symmetry, and asymptotes (if any) of each of the following functions. Then sketch the graph of each function without using a calculator

Function	Domain	Range	Roots	Symmetry	Asymptotes
(a) $y = x^2$					
(b) $y = \ln x$					
(c) $y = 2^x$					
(d) $y = \sin x$					
(e) $y = |x|$					

4. (a) Sketch the graph of $f(x) = (x - 2)^2 (x - 4)^3 (x - 6)$.

(b) Find the degree of function and the roots, and describe the behavior of the graph near each of roots.

5. (a) Give an example of an odd function which has $x = 0$ in the domain and which passes through the origin.

(b) Use the definition of an odd function to prove that the conditions in part (a) are true for all odd functions.

Main Idea 1
Limits

Lesson 1: Limit Definition and Basics

- Definition of a Limit
- Numerical and Graphical Estimation of Limits
- Using Limits to Describe Asymptotic and Unbounded Behavior of Functions

Explain: Definition of a Limit

A limit of a function $f(x)$ is a real number, R, that the function approaches as x moves arbitrarily close to a number, c. We denote this by

$$\lim_{x \to c} f(x) = R$$

To determine the value of the limit R, we take values of x that are closer to c, both from its left- and right-hand side, which we substitute into the function and observe the behavior of the value of the function. If, in both cases, the function tends to a specific number, we say the limit exists and is equal to the value R. Otherwise, the limit does not exist. In addition, if the value of $f(x)$ tends to be increasingly larger or smaller without bound, we say the limit does not exist.

MODEL PROBLEM

1. Find the limit of the function $f(x) = 4x$ as x approaches 2.

(A) 4

(B) 2

(C) 16

(D) 8

Solution

We choose values of x on both the left- and right-hand side of 2. Suppose that $x = 1.99$. Then, $f(1.99) = 7.96$. If $x = 1.9999$, $f(1.9999) = 7.9996$. These values appear to be heading toward the real number 8. Is this true on the right-hand side of 2? If $x = 2.01$, then $f(2.01) = 8.04$, and if $x = 2.0001$, $f(2.0001) = 8.0004$. The values $7.96, 7.9996$ approach 8 from the left-hand side while 8.04 and 8.0004 approach 8 from its right-hand side. Therefore, the limit exists and is equal to 8. Using the limit notation, we have $\lim_{x \to 2} 4x = 8$ and choice (A) is correct.

FR **2.** The limit of a function $f(x) = 3x - 1$ as x approaches -2 is a number t. What is the value of t?

Solution

This question is worded differently than in Model Problem #1, but it is asking us for the same information. We consider values of x that approach -2. From the left-hand side, if $x = -2.01$, $f(-2.01) = -7.03$ and if $x = -2.0001$, $f(-2.0001) = -7.0003$. It appears that $t = -7$. To finish this problem, show that the values on the right of -2 also approach $t = -7$ so that $\lim_{x \to -2} 3x - 1 = -7$.

Explain: Numerical and Graphical Estimation of Limits

We can estimate the limit of a function by numerical substitution as well as by graphical methods. In the previous section, we briefly reviewed how to use numerical substitution to estimate limits. In this section, we proceed to the use of a table of values and examination of the graph to estimate the limits of functions.

Let's consider the limits of two functions, $f(x) = \frac{\sin x}{x}$ and $g(x) = \frac{1 - \cos x}{x}$, each as x approaches 0. For $\lim_{x \to 0} \frac{\sin x}{x}$, we determine the values of the function $f(x) = \frac{\sin x}{x}$ when the x values are less than 0 and also greater than 0, but not actually at 0, using the TABLE function on our graphing calculators as shown.

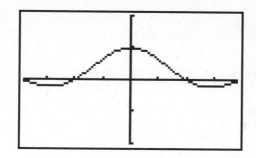 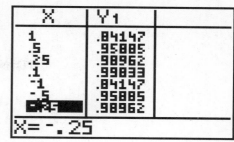

We see from the table that as x tends to zero, the values of the function move closer and closer to 1. Therefore, we estimate the limit of the function to be 1 and $\lim\limits_{x \to 0} \frac{\sin x}{x} = 1$. Generally, $\lim\limits_{\theta \to 0} \frac{\sin \theta}{\theta} = 1$ where θ is any function that approaches 0 as θ approaches zero.

We now evaluate the limit of the function $g(x) = \frac{1 - \cos x}{x}$ as x approaches 0. We graph the function using our calculators and examine the table.

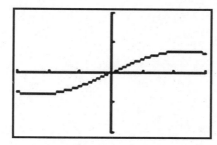 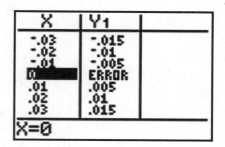

It certainly appears that the function's limit as x approaches 0 is 0, but can we prove it? We will use trigonometric substitution to try to find an expression that is equivalent to $g(x) = \frac{1 - \cos x}{x}$.

$\lim\limits_{x \to 0} \frac{1 - \cos x}{x} = \lim\limits_{x \to 0} \frac{(1 - \cos x)(1 + \cos x)}{x(1 + \cos x)}$	We multiply both the numerator and the denominator by the conjugate of the numerator $(1 + \cos x)$.
$\lim\limits_{x \to 0} \frac{(1 - \cos x)(1 + \cos x)}{x(1 + \cos x)} = \lim\limits_{x \to 0} \frac{1 - \cos^2 x}{x(1 + \cos x)}$	Use the quadratic identity $(a + b)(a - b) = a^2 - b^2$.
$\lim\limits_{x \to 0} \frac{1 - \cos^2 x}{x(1 + \cos x)} = \lim\limits_{x \to 0} \frac{\sin^2 x}{x(1 + \cos x)}$ $= \lim\limits_{x \to 0} \frac{\sin x}{x} \cdot \frac{\sin x}{(1 + \cos x)}$	Recall that $\sin^2 x + \cos^2 x = 1$ and that $\sin^2 x = 1 - \cos^2 x$.
$\lim\limits_{x \to 0} \frac{\sin x}{x} \cdot \frac{\sin x}{(1 + \cos x)} =$ $\lim\limits_{x \to 0} \frac{\sin x}{x} \lim\limits_{x \to 0} \frac{\sin x}{(1 + \cos x)}$	We apply a limit law. This law is explained in Lesson 2, page xx.
$\lim\limits_{x \to 0} \frac{\sin x}{x} \lim\limits_{x \to 0} \frac{\sin x}{(1 + \cos x)} =$ $1 \cdot \frac{0}{1 + \cos 0} = 1 \cdot 0 = 0$	Use the result we found, $\lim\limits_{\theta \to 0} \frac{\sin \theta}{\theta} = 1$, and the fact that $\sin 0 = 0$.
We have shown that $\lim\limits_{x \to 0} \frac{1 - \cos x}{x} = 0$.	

These two special limits of trigonometric functions can help us determine the limits of other trigonometric functions, as we will show in Lesson 2.

MODEL PROBLEMS

1. Using a table, evaluate $\lim\limits_{x \to 0} e^{2x}$.

(A) 1

(B) 0

(C) e

(D) -1

Solution

We choose values of x arbitrarily close to 0 then substitute these values into the function and determine the corresponding output values.

x	$f(x)$
-0.5	0.36788
-0.05	0.90483
-0.0025	0.99501
0.0001	1.0002
0.05	1.0101
0.1	1.2214

From the table above, we see that when x approaches zero from both the left- and right-hand sides, the value of the function tends to 1. Therefore $\lim\limits_{x \to 0} e^{2x} = 1$ and choice (A) is correct.

FR **2.** Using a table, evaluate $\lim\limits_{x \to 0} \dfrac{\sin 4x}{x}$.

Solution

Follow the procedure outlined in Model Problem #1 and the information given in the text regarding special trigonometric limits to solve this problem (see page 62). If you use your calculator, be sure it is in radian mode. Explain your work.

Explain: Using Limits to Describe Asymptotic and Unbounded Behavior of Functions

Asymptotic Behavior Recall from your previous math courses that an asymptote is a line that a function approaches. Asymptotes can be vertical, horizontal, or slant (sometimes called oblique) and are common with rational functions. Since functions approach asymptotes, they provide a limiting description of the function at that point.

If a rational function has a vertical asymptote at $x = a$, then the function $f(x)$ is undefined at $x = a$, but can approach ∞ or $-\infty$ as the value of x approaches a from the right or the left.

In symbols, we write

$$\lim_{x \to a} f(x) = \infty \text{ or } \lim_{x \to a} f(x) = -\infty$$

If a function has a horizontal asymptote, $y = b$, where b is a real number, then $\lim_{x \to \pm\infty} f(x) = b$.

A function has a slant asymptote at $h(x) = mx + c$ if $f(x)$ approaches a linear function $h(x) = mx + c$ as x approaches $\pm\infty$. In symbols, we write

$$\lim_{x \to \pm\infty} f(x) = h(x) = mx + c$$

We picture each type of asymptote below.

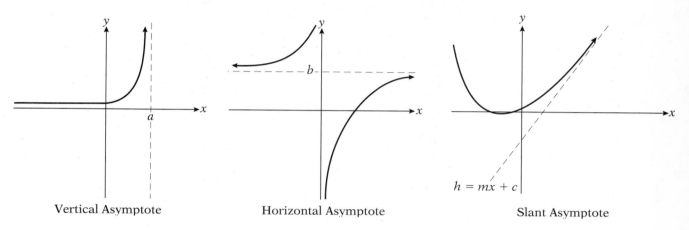

Vertical Asymptote   Horizontal Asymptote   Slant Asymptote

The table below shows a summary of limits.

LIMITS		
Notation	**Meaning**	**Asymptotes**
$\lim\limits_{x \to a^-} f(x) = \infty$	$f(x)$ approaches ∞ as x approaches a from the left.	vertical asymptote at $x = a$
$\lim\limits_{x \to a^+} f(x) = -\infty$	$f(x)$ approaches $-\infty$ as x approaches a from the right.	vertical asymptote at $x = a$
$\lim\limits_{x \to \infty} f(x) = b$	$f(x)$ approaches b as x approaches ∞.	horizontal asymptote at $y = b$
$\lim\limits_{x \to -\infty} f(x) = b$	$f(x)$ approaches b as x approaches $-\infty$.	horizontal asymptote at $y = b$
$\lim\limits_{x \to \infty} \big(f(x) - h(x)\big) = 0$; $h(x) = mx + c$	$f(x)$ approaches $h(x) = mx + c$ as x approaches ∞.	slant asymptote at $h(x) = mx + c$
$\lim\limits_{x \to -\infty} \big(f(x) - h(x)\big) = 0$; $h(x) = mx + c$	$f(x)$ approaches $h(x) = mx + c$ as x approaches $-\infty$.	slant asymptote at $h(x) = mx + c$

MODEL PROBLEMS

FR 1. Find the vertical asymptote of the function $f(x) = \frac{2}{6x - 3}$. What can we say about the limit of $f(x)$ at that point?

Solution

To find the equation of the vertical asymptote, we set the denominator of the function equal to 0 and solve for the variable. In this case, $6x - 3 = 0$, $6x = 3$, and $x = \frac{3}{6} = \frac{1}{2}$. Hence, there is a vertical asymptote is $x = \frac{1}{2}$. At the point $x = \frac{1}{2}$, we know that $\lim_{x \to \frac{1}{2}^-} f(x) = -\infty$ and that $\lim_{x \to \frac{1}{2}^+} f(x) = \infty$.

FR 2. Find the horizontal asymptote of the function $f(x) = \frac{5x}{8x^2 - 3}$. What is $\lim_{x \to \infty} f(x)$?

Solution

The degree of the function in the numerator is 1 while the degree of the function in the denominator is 2. Since the degree of the numerator is less than that of the denominator, there is a horizontal asymptote at $y = 0$. Use the chart on page 55 to determine the limit.

FR 3. Find the slant asymptote of the function $f(x) = \frac{6x^2 + 4x - 1}{3x - 1}$. Show that $\lim_{x \to \infty} (f(x) - h(x)) = 0$.

Solution

Recall that you can use polynomial long division or synthetic division to find the equation of the slant asymptote and then use that equation as $h(x)$ to show the limit above is true.

Unbounded Behavior We can describe the end behavior of functions in terms of limits. When a function increases or decreases without bound as x approaches positive or negative infinity, we describe this in terms of limits. Thus, if $f(x)$ approaches ∞ as $x \to \infty$, then $\lim_{x \to \infty} f(x) = \infty$. For example, the quadratic curve below has $\lim_{x \to \infty} f(x) = +\infty$ and $\lim_{x \to -\infty} f(x) = +\infty$.

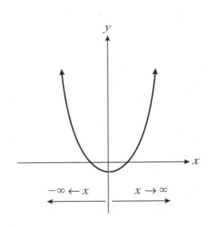

MODEL PROBLEMS

1. Identify the end behavior of the function $f(x) = \sqrt{4x^2-1}$.

(A) 0

(C) ∞

(B) $-\infty$ and ∞

(D) $-\infty$

Solution

There are several strategies we can use to solve this problem. We will examine very large positive values and very large negative values of x using the calculator's TABLE function.

X	Y1
130000	260000
140000	280000
150000	300000
160000	320000
170000	340000
180000	360000
190000	380000

X=160000

X	Y1
-1E5	200000
-90000	180000
-80000	160000
-70000	140000
-60000	120000
-50000	100000
-40000	80000

X=-70000

We can see that for very large values and for very large negaive values of x, $f(x)$ increases without bound. The correct answer is (C).

FR 2. Identify all the asymptotes of the graph shown below. What is the end behavior of $f(x)$ as x moves toward ∞?

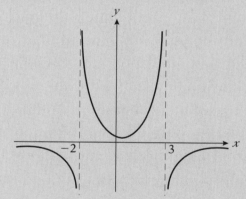

Solution

From the graph above, we clearly see two vertical asymptotes. Is there a third asymptotes or more? Are any of the asymptotes related to the end behavior of $f(x)$ as the function moves toward positive infinity?

3. Find the value of $\lim\limits_{x \to \mp} \dfrac{2x}{x + 2}$.

(A) 0

(C) 1

(B) $\dfrac{1}{2}$

(D) 2

Solution

How can we use our knowledge of asymptotes and the end behavior of this function to determine the value of the requested limit?

AP Calculus Exam-Type Questions

Multiple Choice Questions
A graphing calculator is required for some questions.

1. Find the limit of $f(x) = 6x$ as x approaches 3.

   (A) 3
   (B) 9
   (C) 2
   (D) 18

2. Evaluate $\lim\limits_{x \to 0}(1 - 2x)$.

   (A) -1
   (B) -3
   (C) 1
   (D) 3

3. Use tables to evaluate $\lim\limits_{x \to 3}(1 + 3x - 5x^2)$.

   (A) 55
   (B) -35
   (C) 37
   (D) -5

4. Use tables to evaluate $\lim\limits_{x \to -2}(7 - 8x - 2x^2)$.

   (A) -17
   (B) 15
   (C) 31
   (D) -1

5. Determine the limit, using tables, of the function $f(x) = \dfrac{\cos x \sin x - \sin x}{x}$ as x approaches 0.

   (A) 0
   (B) 1
   (C) -1
   (D) ∞

6. Find the equation of the vertical asymptote of the function $f(x) = \dfrac{1}{x - 2}$.

   (A) $y = 2$
   (B) $x = -2$
   (C) $y = 0$
   (D) $x = 2$

7. Determine the horizontal asymptote of the function $f(x) = \dfrac{5}{2x - 6}$.

   (A) $x = 0$
   (B) $y = 3$
   (C) $x = 3$
   (D) $y = 0$

8. Determine the equation of the horizontal or slant asymptote of the function
   $$f(x) = \frac{4x^2 + 2x - 3}{x - 2}.$$

   (A) $y = 4x + 2$
   (B) $y = 2$
   (C) $y = 9$
   (D) $y = 4x + 10$

9. Find the equation of the vertical asymptote of $f(x) = \dfrac{6x}{2x - 8}$.

   (A) $x = 4$
   (B) $x = 0$
   (C) $y = 4$
   (D) $y = 5$

10. Find the equation of the horizontal asymptote of the function $f(x) = \dfrac{3x^2 + 1}{9x^2 - 6}$.

    (A) $x = 3$
    (B) $y = \dfrac{1}{3}$
    (C) $x = \dfrac{1}{3}$
    (D) $y = 3$

11. Evaluate $\lim\limits_{x \to \infty} \dfrac{4x - 3}{2x - 5}$.

    (A) 2.5
    (B) $\dfrac{1}{2}$
    (C) 2
    (D) ∞

12. Find the equation of the vertical asymptote of $f(x) = \csc x$, where $0 \leqslant x \leqslant \frac{\pi}{2}$.

 (A) $y = \frac{\pi}{2}$

 (B) $x = 0$

 (C) $x = \frac{\pi}{4}$

 (D) $y = \frac{\pi}{3}$

13. Find the value of m such that $\lim\limits_{x \to m^-} \frac{6x + 2}{x - 3} = -\infty$.

 (A) 6

 (B) $\frac{1}{3}$

 (C) 3

 (D) $-\frac{1}{3}$

14. Determine the equation of the slant asymptote of the function $f(x) = \frac{x^2 - x + 4}{2x + 1}$.

 (A) $y = \frac{1}{2}x + \frac{19}{8}$

 (B) $y = \frac{1}{2}x - \frac{3}{4}$

 (C) $y = \frac{1}{2}x + \frac{1}{2}$

 (D) $y = \frac{1}{2}x - \frac{19}{8}$

15. Find the equation of the vertical asymptote of $f(x) = \tan x$, where $0 \leqslant x \leqslant \pi$.

 (A) $x = \frac{\pi}{2}$

 (B) $y = \pi$

 (C) $y = 0$

 (D) $x = \pi$ and $x = 0$

16. Find the equation of the vertical asymptote of $f(x) = \frac{1}{(x - 2)^2}$.

 (A) $x = 2$

 (B) $x = 1$

 (C) $x = 4$

 (D) $x = 0$

17. Find the equation of the horizontal asymptote of $f(x) = \frac{2x^2 + 3}{(x - 1)^2}$.

 (A) $y = 0$

 (B) $x = 2$

 (C) $y = 2$

 (D) $x = 0$

18. Find the equation of the vertical asymptote(s) of $f(x) = \frac{(x - 2)^2}{x^2 - 4}$.

 (A) $x = 4$

 (B) $x = 2$ and $x = -2$

 (C) $x = 2$

 (D) $x = -2$

Free Response Questions
A graphing calculator is required for some questions.

1. Find the equation of the vertical asymptote of $f(x) = \cot x$, $0 \leqslant x \leqslant \frac{\pi}{2}$.

2. Determine the vertical asymptote(s) of $\frac{3x + 2}{12x^2 + 16x + 5}$.

3. Evaluate $\lim\limits_{x \to 2.5}(2x^3 - 5x + 1)$.

4. Evaluate $\lim\limits_{x \to 3.9}(2 - 3x^2)$.

5. Find the value of t given that $\lim\limits_{x \to t} \frac{x - 1}{x^2 - 1} = \infty$.

6. Determine the horizontal asymptote of $f(x) = \frac{19x + 20}{(38x - 10)^2}$.

7. Evaluate $\lim\limits_{x \to \infty} \frac{3x^2 + 1}{3x^2 - 1}$.

8. How many asymptotes does the function $f(x) = \frac{x + 3}{x^2 - 9}$ have? List all of their equations.

9. Can a rational function have both horizontal and slant asymptotes? Explain.

Lesson 2: Calculating Limits

- Limit Laws
- Limits as x Approaches a Finite Number, c
- Trigonometric Limits and the Squeeze Theorem
- Limits at Infinity and Beyond

Explain: Limit Laws

In the last lesson, we estimated limits using different techniques. In this lesson we move to actually calculating limits. In general, we can find the limit of an expression by taking the limit of each individual term within the expression and then combining the results using appropriate mathematical operations. Limit laws help us do this.

Suppose that c is a constant and we have two functions, $f(x)$ and $g(x)$ whose limits $\lim_{x \to a} f(x)$ and $\lim_{x \to a} g(x)$ exist. Then,

---

1. $\lim_{x \to a} [f(x) + g(x)] = \lim_{x \to a} f(x) + \lim_{x \to a} g(x)$

2. $\lim_{x \to a} [f(x) - g(x)] = \lim_{x \to a} f(x) - \lim_{x \to a} g(x)$

3. $\lim_{x \to a} [c \cdot f(x)] = c \lim_{x \to a} f(x)$

4. $\lim_{x \to a} [f(x)g(x)] = \lim_{x \to a} f(x) \cdot \lim_{x \to a} g(x)$

5. $\lim_{x \to a} \dfrac{f(x)}{g(x)} = \dfrac{\lim_{x \to a} f(x)}{\lim_{x \to a} g(x)}$ if $\lim_{x \to a} g(x) \neq 0$

6. $\lim_{x \to a} [f(x)]^n = \left[\lim_{x \to a} f(x) \right]^n$

7. $\lim_{x \to a} c = c$

8. $\lim_{x \to a} x = a$

9. $\lim_{x \to a} x^n = a^n$

10. $\lim_{x \to a} \sqrt[n]{x} = \sqrt[n]{a}$

11. $\lim_{x \to a} \sqrt[n]{f(x)} = \sqrt[n]{\lim_{x \to a} f(x)}$

These are known as the limit laws.

MODEL PROBLEM

FR 1. Evaluate $\lim_{x \to 4} (2x^2 - 3x - 4)$ and justify each step.

Solution

We take the limit of each term.

$\lim_{x \to 4}(2x^2 - 3x - 4) = \lim_{x \to 4}(2x^2) - \lim_{x \to 4}(3x) - \lim_{x \to 4}(4)$ By Law 2

$= 2\lim_{x \to 4}(x^2) - 3\lim_{x \to 4}(x) - \lim_{x \to 4}(4)$ By Law 3

$= 2(4^2) - 3(4) - 4$ By Laws 7, 8, and 9

$= 16$

The answer is 16.

Explain: Limits as *x* Approaches a Finite Number, *c*

To evaluate a limit algebraically as x approaches a finite number c, substitute c into the expression.

1. If the result is a finite number, that number is the value of the limit.

2. If the result is of the form $\frac{0}{0}$, we have an **indeterminate** form. In this case, one of the following techniques may be useful in evaluating the limit:

- Factor the numerator or the denominator, simplify, and then substitute the value c into the new expression.

- Rationalize the numerator or the denominator by using the conjugate, simplify, and then substitute the value c into the new expression.

- Simplify the complex fraction, and then substitute the value c into the new expression.

MODEL PROBLEMS

1. Evaluate $\lim\limits_{x \to 3} \frac{x+2}{x}$.

(A) $\frac{5}{3}$

(B) 2

(C) $\frac{1}{3}$

(D) $\frac{3}{5}$

Solution

Substitute $x = 3$ into the expression $\frac{x+2}{x}$. The value of the limit is $\frac{5}{3}$.

Choice (A) is correct.

2. Evaluate $\lim\limits_{x \to 4} \frac{x^2 - 16}{x - 4}$.

(A) 4

(B) 0

(C) 8

(D) The limit is an indeterminate form.

Solution

We substitute $x = 4$ into the expression and are left with $\frac{0}{0}$, which is an indeterminate form. Try factoring the expression prior to substitution to determine the limit here.

3. Evaluate $\lim\limits_{x \to 1} \frac{3x^2 - 4x + 1}{x^2 - 1}$.

(A) 2

(B) 1

(C) 0.5

(D) 2.5

Solution

We see right away simple substitution is not going to work in this problem either. Since the numerator is a trinomial and the denominator is the difference of squares, simplification by factoring is a good strategy to try.

FR **4.** Evaluate $\lim\limits_{x \to 25} \dfrac{\sqrt{x} - 5}{x - 25}$.

Solution

Recall from previous math classes that you can rationalize numerators as well as denominators. Since substitution will result in an indeterminate form again, rationalizing the numerator is a good first step. Once complete, you can factor.

FR **5.** Evaluate $\lim\limits_{x \to a} \dfrac{\sqrt{x} - \sqrt{a}}{x - a}$.

Solution

What strategies reviewed in this lesson make a good first step for this problem?

FR **6.** Evaluate $\lim\limits_{x \to 3} \dfrac{x - 3}{\frac{1}{x} - \frac{1}{3}}$.

Solution

Simple substitution of 3 for x will give us a 0 denominator. There is no rationalization here, so instead we multiply through by $3x$ to simplify the complex fraction. Then, $\left(\dfrac{3x}{3x}\right) \cdot \left(\dfrac{x - 3}{\frac{1}{x} - \frac{1}{3}}\right) = \dfrac{3x(x - 3)}{3x\left(\frac{1}{x}\right) - 3x\left(\frac{1}{3}\right)} = \dfrac{3x(x - 3)}{3 - x}$.

Now we must find $\lim\limits_{x \to 3} \dfrac{3x(x - 3)}{3 - x}$. How should we proceed?

Explain: Trigonometric Limits and the Squeeze Theorem

Trigonometric Limits   In Lesson 1, we stated that $\lim\limits_{\theta \to 0} \dfrac{\sin \theta}{\theta} = 1$ and we showed the table generated by graphing $y = \dfrac{\sin x}{x}$, repeated below.

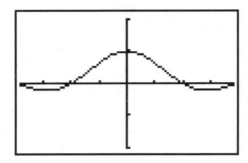

We can evaluate limits similar to $\lim\limits_{x \to 0} \dfrac{\sin x}{x} = 1$ by replacing the symbol x with another expression as long as that expression also approaches 0. For example, suppose that we replace x by $2x$ so we want to find $\lim\limits_{x \to 0} \dfrac{\sin 2x}{2x}$. This limit is the same as $\lim\limits_{x \to 0} \dfrac{\sin x}{x}$, since as $x \to 0$, so does $2x \to 0$.

If x in $\lim\limits_{x \to 0} \dfrac{\sin x}{x}$ is replaced by $\dfrac{1}{y}$, then

$$\lim_{\frac{1}{y} \to 0} \frac{\sin\left(\frac{1}{y}\right)}{\frac{1}{y}} = \lim_{y \to \infty} y \sin\left(\frac{1}{y}\right),$$

since as $\dfrac{1}{y} \to 0, y \to \infty$. Therefore,

$$\lim_{y \to \infty} y \sin\left(\frac{1}{y}\right) = 1.$$

Remember to always look carefully at the limits. For example, to evaluate $\lim\limits_{x \to \frac{\pi}{2}} \dfrac{\sin x}{x}$, the limit is $\dfrac{\sin\frac{\pi}{2}}{\frac{\pi}{2}} = \dfrac{1}{\frac{\pi}{2}} = \dfrac{2}{\pi}$.

MODEL PROBLEMS

1. Evaluate $\lim\limits_{x \to 0} \dfrac{\sin 4x}{x}$.

(A) 1

(B) 4

(C) $\dfrac{1}{4}$

(D) 2

Solution

For this problem we can see that $\lim\limits_{x \to 0} 4\left(\dfrac{\sin 4x}{x}\right) = 4 \cdot \lim\limits_{x \to 0} \dfrac{\sin 4x}{4x}$.

Then, $\lim\limits_{x \to 0} \dfrac{\sin 4x}{x} = 4$. The correct answer is (B).

2. Evaluate $\lim\limits_{x \to 0} \dfrac{\sin ax}{bx}$.

(A) a

(B) b

(C) $\dfrac{a}{b}$

(D) $\dfrac{b}{a}$

Solution

We can use a strategy similar to what we used in Model Problem #1 to solve this question. In that problem, we multiplied both sides by 4. For this problem, by what term should we multiply each side?

3. Evaluate $\lim\limits_{x \to 0} \dfrac{1 - \cos^2 x}{x}$.

(A) 0

(B) 1

(C) $\dfrac{1}{2}$

(D) 2π

Solution

Here we must rely on our knowledge of trigonometric identities. Recall that $\sin^2 x = 1 - \cos^2 x$. We can rewrite the problem as $\lim\limits_{x \to 0} \dfrac{\sin^2 x}{x}$. You solve from here.

The Squeeze Theorem

Consider three functions: $f(x)$, $g(x)$, and $h(x)$. If $g(x)$ is squeezed between both $f(x)$ and $h(x)$ near the value a, and if $f(x)$ and $h(x)$ have the same limit, L, at a, then g also has a limit of L.

The Squeeze Theorem: If $f(x) \le g(x) \le h(x)$ when x is near a, except possibly at the value a, and $\lim\limits_{x \to a} f(x) = \lim\limits_{x \to a} h(x) = L$, then $\lim\limits_{x \to a} g(x) = L$.

This theorem is also known as the pinching theorem and the sandwich theorem.

MODEL PROBLEMS

TT 1. Use the squeeze theorem to show that $\lim\limits_{x \to 0} x^2 \sin \dfrac{1}{x} = 0$.

Solution

From trigonometry, we know that $-1 \le \sin \dfrac{1}{x} \le 1$, so $-x^2 \le x^2 \sin \dfrac{1}{x} \le x^2$. For this limit, $f(x) = -x^2$, $g(x) = \sin \dfrac{1}{x}$, and $h(x) = x^2$. Then, from the limit laws, $\lim\limits_{x \to 0} x^2 = 0$ and $\lim\limits_{x \to 0} (-x^2) = 0$. Using the squeeze theorem,

$\lim\limits_{x \to 0} \sin \dfrac{1}{x} = 0$ and $\lim\limits_{x \to 0} x^2 \sin \dfrac{1}{x} = \lim\limits_{x \to 0} x^2 \cdot \lim\limits_{x \to 0} \sin \dfrac{1}{x} = 0 \cdot 0 = 0$.

2. Use the squeeze theorem to evaluate $\lim\limits_{x \to 0} x^2 \cos \dfrac{1}{x}$.

(A) -1

(B) 1

(C) $\dfrac{1}{2}$

(D) 0

Solution

This problem is quite similar to Model Problem #1. Start by identifying the function being squeezed, and then determine the limit of each function that is squeezing.

Explain: Limits at Infinity and Beyond

As we learned in Lesson 1, finding the limit of a rational function over a required interval can mean finding the location of the function's asymptotes. While Lesson 1 primarily focused on locating asymptotes, in this lesson we move to evaluating the limits of these functions.

The limit of a rational function as x approaches infinity gives the value that identifies the horizontal asymptote. If a function $f(x)$ is not a rational function, it may be possible to evaluate the limit as x approaches infinity. One method is to graph the function and make a table of values for increasingly large x-values and increasingly small x-values to see if the values of $f(x)$ appear to approach a finite number.

Another method is to consider the rate at which exponential, polynomial, and logarithmic functions increase as x increases without bound. In general, exponential functions increase most rapidly, polynomial functions increase less rapidly, and logarithmic functions increase least rapidly as x increases without bound.

MODEL PROBLEMS

1. Evaluate $\lim\limits_{x\to\infty} \dfrac{3x - 1}{2x + 1}$.

   (A) $\dfrac{3}{2}$

   (B) 0

   (C) 1

   (D) $\dfrac{2}{3}$

   Solution

   Since this is a rational function, and the numerator and denominator have the same degree, the limit is the ratio of the leading coefficients, 3:2. This is the same as finding the horizontal asymptote. Thus the limit is $\dfrac{3}{2}$.

   The correct answer is (A).

2. Evaluate $\lim\limits_{x\to\infty} \dfrac{2x^2 + x + 1}{5x^2 - x + 5}$.

   (A) $\dfrac{5}{2}$

   (B) 0

   (C) $\dfrac{2}{5}$

   (D) 2

   Solution

   Consider what type of expression we are evaluating. What do you know about evaluating limits of this type?

3. Evaluate $\lim\limits_{x\to\infty} \dfrac{x^2 + x + 4}{5x^3 + 7x}$.

(A) $\dfrac{2}{3}$

(B) 1

(C) 0

(D) $\dfrac{3}{2}$

Solution

In this case, the degree of the numerator is less than the degree of the denominator. What does this mean for the value of the limit?

4. Evaluate $\lim\limits_{x\to\infty} \dfrac{6x^3}{7x^2 + 1000x - 9}$.

(A) ∞

(B) 1

(C) 0

(D) $-\infty$

Solution

The degree of the denominator is greater than the degree of the numerator. How does this fact impact the value of the limit?

FR **5.** Evaluate $\lim\limits_{x\to\infty} \dfrac{\sin x}{x}$.

Solution

The functions contained in the numerator and denominator are not polynomials, so we cannot use the degrees to determine the limit. We also cannot factor or otherwise simplify the expression. Our only other option at this point is the squeeze theorem. As before, we know that $-1 \le \sin x \le 1$ and so $-\dfrac{1}{x} \le \dfrac{\sin x}{x} \le \dfrac{1}{x}$. Now we need to figure out $\lim\limits_{x\to\infty}\left(-\dfrac{1}{x}\right)$ and $\lim\limits_{x\to\infty}\left(\dfrac{1}{x}\right)$. If we mentally substitute ∞ for x in each limit, we have a small integer being divided by a very, very large number. When you divide a relatively small number by a very, very large number, the limit approaches 0. Thus, $\lim\limits_{x\to\infty}\left(-\dfrac{1}{x}\right)$ and $\lim\limits_{x\to\infty}\left(\dfrac{1}{x}\right)$ are equal to 0 and $\lim\limits_{x\to\infty}\dfrac{\sin x}{x} = 0$.

FR **6.** Evaluate $\lim\limits_{x\to\infty} \dfrac{1 - \cos x}{x + 5}$.

Solution

Examine the process we used to solve Model Problem #1 on page 65 and Model Problem #5 above. How can you use this information to start solving this question?

A **piecewise-defined function,** or **split function,** has two or more pieces, each of which is defined on a specific domain. When evaluating the limit of a piecewise-defined function, first consider whether x is approaching a value where the function splits.

To find the limit of the function as x approaches a value where the function does not split:

- Evaluate the limit of the function as before, using the piece of the function that has that value of x in its domain.

To find the limit of the function as x approaches a value where the function does split:

- Since there are two distinct pieces on either side of this value, evaluate a left-hand limit using the piece of the function defined on the left of the value. Evaluate a right-hand limit using the piece of the function defined on the right of the value.

- If the left-hand limit and the right-hand limit are the same, then this is the limit of the function. If the left-hand limit and the right-hand limit are not the same, then the limit of the function does not exist at this value in the domain.

MODEL PROBLEMS

FR **1.** For the function $f(x) = \begin{cases} x - 1, & x \geq 0 \\ x^2, & x < 0 \end{cases}$ find:

(a) $\lim\limits_{x \to -1} f(x)$

(b) $\lim\limits_{x \to 0} f(x)$

Solution

Consider the graph of $f(x)$.

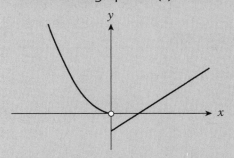

(a) The split occurs at $x = 0$. To find the limit as $x \to -1$, find the value of

$$\lim_{x \to -1} f(x) = \lim_{x \to -1} x^2 = 1.$$

(b) Since the split occurs at $x = 0$, to find the limit as $x \to 0$, find

$$\lim_{x \to 0^+} f(x) = \lim_{x \to 0^+} (x - 1) = -1, \text{ and}$$

$$\lim_{x \to 0^-} f(x) = \lim_{x \to 0^-} x^2 = 0.$$

Since $\lim\limits_{x \to 0^+} f(x) \neq \lim\limits_{x \to 0^-} f(x)$, $\lim\limits_{x \to 0} f(x)$ does not exist.

FR 2.

(a) Graph $f(x) = \begin{cases} x + 2, & x < 0 \\ \sqrt{x} + 2, & 0 \le x < 4. \\ \ln x, & x \ge 4 \end{cases}$

(b) Use the graph to determine

- $f(0)$

- $\lim\limits_{x \to 0} f(x)$

- $f(4)$

- $\lim\limits_{x \to 4} f(x)$

Solution

(a) The graph of the piecewise-defined function is

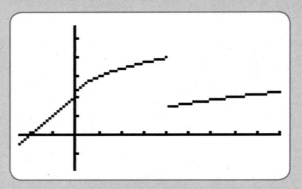

Now use the graph and the function's definition to determine the answers to question (b).

AP Calculus Exam-Type Questions

Multiple Choice Questions
No calculator permitted for these questions.

1. Evaluate $\lim\limits_{x \to -1} \dfrac{x^2 - 5x - 6}{x^2 - 1}$.

(A) 1

(B) 3

(C) $\dfrac{7}{2}$

(D) 12

2. Evaluate $\lim\limits_{x \to \infty} \dfrac{x - 5}{2x^2 + 1}$.

(A) -5

(B) $-\dfrac{1}{2}$

(C) 0

(D) $\dfrac{1}{2}$

3. Evaluate $\lim\limits_{x \to 0} \dfrac{\sin 7x}{x}$.

(A) 0

(B) $\dfrac{1}{7}$

(C) 1

(D) 7

4. If $2x \le g(x) \le x^4 - x^2 + 2$ for all x, what is $\lim\limits_{x \to 1} g(x)$?

(A) 2

(B) 0

(C) 3

(D) $\dfrac{1}{2}$

5. Evaluate $\lim\limits_{x \to \infty} \dfrac{x^2 - 5}{2x^2 + 1}$.

(A) -5

(B) $\dfrac{1}{2}$

(C) 1

(D) 2

6. Evaluate $\lim\limits_{x \to \infty} \dfrac{x^2 - 5}{2x + 1}$.

(A) $\dfrac{1}{2}$

(B) 1

(C) 2

(D) ∞

7. Evaluate $\lim\limits_{x \to \infty} \dfrac{\cos^2(2x)}{3 - 2x}$.

(A) ∞

(B) 1

(C) 0

(D) $-\infty$

8. Evaluate $\lim\limits_{x \to 0} \dfrac{x - 1}{x^2 - 1}$.

(A) $-\dfrac{1}{2}$

(B) $\dfrac{1}{4}$

(C) $\dfrac{1}{2}$

(D) 1

9. Evaluate $\lim\limits_{x \to 0^-} x^3 \cos\left(\dfrac{3}{x}\right)$.

(A) 0

(B) 1

(C) -1

(D) indeterminate

10. Evaluate $\lim\limits_{x \to 0} \dfrac{\sin x}{7x}$.

(A) 0

(B) $\dfrac{1}{7}$

(C) 1

(D) 7

11. Evaluate $\lim\limits_{x \to 7} \dfrac{\sqrt{x + 2} - 3}{x - 7}$.

(A) 3

(B) 0

(C) 6

(D) $\dfrac{1}{6}$

Exercises 12 – 14:

Use $f(x) = \begin{cases} x + 3, & x < 0 \\ x - 3, & x \geq 0 \end{cases}$.

12. $\lim\limits_{x \to 0^-} f(x) =$

(A) -3

(B) 0

(C) 1

(D) 3

13. $\lim\limits_{x \to 0^+} f(x) =$

(A) -3

(B) 0

(C) 1

(D) 3

14. $\lim\limits_{x \to 1} f(x) =$

(A) -2

(B) -1

(C) 0

(D) 1

15. Evaluate $\lim\limits_{x \to 2} \dfrac{x - 2}{\dfrac{1}{x} - \dfrac{1}{2}}$.

(A) -4

(B) -2

(C) 0

(D) 2

16. Find the value of $\lim\limits_{x \to \pi} \dfrac{\sin x}{x}$.

(A) $-\pi$

(B) -1

(C) 0

(D) 1

17. Evaluate $\lim\limits_{x \to 0} \dfrac{\sin 7x}{7x}$.

(A) 0

(B) $\dfrac{1}{7}$

(C) 1

(D) 7

18. Evaluate $\lim\limits_{x\to\infty} \dfrac{100x}{x^2-1}$.

(A) -1

(B) 0

(C) 1

(D) 100

Free Response Questions

A graphing calculator is required for some questions.

1. Using the graph of $f(x)$ shown, find:

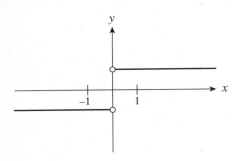

(a) $\lim\limits_{x\to-1} f(x)$

(b) $\lim\limits_{x\to0^+} f(x)$

(c) $\lim\limits_{x\to0^-} f(x)$

(d) $\lim\limits_{x\to0} f(x)$

2. Sketch a graph of the greatest integer function, $f(x) = \lfloor x \rfloor$, and evaluate:

(a) $\lim\limits_{x\to\frac{1}{2}} f(x)$

(b) $\lim\limits_{x\to1} f(x)$

(c) $\lim\limits_{x\to n} f(x)$, where n is an integer.

3. (a) Graph $f(x) = \dfrac{x}{x^2-1}$.

(b) Use the graph to determine:

• $\lim\limits_{x\to1^+} f(x)$

• $\lim\limits_{x\to1^-} f(x)$

• $\lim\limits_{x\to-1^+} f(x)$

• $\lim\limits_{x\to-1^-} f(x)$

• $\lim\limits_{x\to-\infty} f(x)$

4. Use the special trigonometric limits to find the value of each of the following:

(a) $\lim\limits_{x\to0} \dfrac{\tan x}{x}$

(b) $\lim\limits_{x\to0} \dfrac{\sin^2 x}{x}$

(c) $\lim\limits_{x\to0} \dfrac{\cos^2 x}{x}$

(d) $\lim\limits_{x\to0} \dfrac{x^2}{\sin x}$

5. Sketch $f(x) = \begin{cases} x, & x < 0 \\ \sin x, & x \geq 0 \end{cases}$, and find:

(a) $\lim\limits_{x\to-3} f(x)$

(b) $\lim\limits_{x\to0} f(x)$

6. Prove that $\lim\limits_{x\to0} \dfrac{1-\cos x}{x} = 0$ using $\lim\limits_{x\to0} \dfrac{\sin x}{x} = 1$ and a Pythagorean identity.

7. Sketch a function $f(x)$ that has all of the following properties:

• $f(0) = 1$

• $\lim\limits_{x\to1^+} f(x) = \infty$

• $\lim\limits_{x\to1^-} f(x) = \infty$

• $\lim\limits_{x\to\infty} f(x) = 1$

• $\lim\limits_{x\to-\infty} f(x) = 1$

8. Graph $f(x) = \dfrac{x}{e^x-1}$ and make a table of values to find $\lim\limits_{x\to0} f(x)$.

9. Sketch the graph of a function $f(x)$ that has all of the following properties:

• continuous for all $x \neq 3$

• has a hole at $x = -1$

• $\lim\limits_{x\to3} f(x) = -\infty$

• $\lim\limits_{x\to\infty} f(x) = 0$

• $\lim\limits_{x\to-\infty} f(x) = -\infty$

Lesson 3: Special Limits

- Limits of Unbounded Functions
- Left- and Right-Hand Limits
- Limits of Oscillating Functions

Explain: Limits of Unbounded Functions

A function, $f(x)$, is unbounded when $f(x)$ approaches either positive infinity or negative infinity as x increases toward positive infinity or toward negative infinity. At such points, the limit does not exist since the function does not tend to a specific finite number. Depending on the situation, we express these limits as

Case 1	$\lim\limits_{x \to \infty} f(x) = \infty$
Case 2	$\lim\limits_{x \to -\infty} f(x) = \infty$
Case 3	$\lim\limits_{x \to \infty} f(x) = -\infty$
Case 4	$\lim\limits_{x \to -\infty} f(x) = -\infty$

The first and second cases are common with quadratic functions, while the first and the last are common with cubic and linear functions. The second and third limits could describe a linear function with negative slope.

It is important to note here that a function is also unbounded when it approaches a vertical asymptote. If the equation of the vertical asymptote is $x = c$, the limit of the function $f(x)$ as x approaches c can be:

$$\lim\limits_{x \to c} f(x) = \infty \text{ or } \lim\limits_{x \to c} f(x) = -\infty$$

MODEL PROBLEMS

1. Find the limit of the function $f(x) = -3x + 1$ as x approaches $-\infty$.

(A) ∞

(B) -3

(C) $-\infty$

(D) 0

Solution

When the value of x is negative, the function is positive. When x decreases in value without bound, the function increases in value without bound; hence, no finite value is arrived at and $\lim\limits_{x \to -\infty} (-3x + 1) = \infty$. The correct option is (A).

2. Evaluate $\lim_{x \to \infty}(x^3 + 4x + 2)$.

(A) ∞

(B) -3

(C) $-\infty$

(D) 0

Solution

What happens to the value of the dependent variable in cubic functions when the independent variable increases without bound? Does the function tend toward a finite real number or does it also increase without bound?

FR **3.** Evaluate $\lim_{x \to 1} \dfrac{2x}{x-1}$ and explain your answer.

Solution

From our previous knowledge we know that this function has a vertical asymptote at $x = 1$. What does that mean for the limit of this function as x approaches 1?

Explain: Left- and Right-Hand Limits

Model Problem #3, immediately above, brings up an important concept we have used but have not yet formally defined. For a limit to exist, the function's limit as we approach an x-value from the left must be the same value as the limit of the function as we approach from the right. We often abbreviate "left-hand limit" as LHL and "right-hand limit" as RHL. The function $f(x) = \dfrac{2x}{x-1}$ is an example where the

LHL ≠ RHL and so the limit itself does not exist (DNE) at that point. What other types of functions typically display this behavior?

If a function increases or decreases suddenly from one constant value to the next, we say that function is a step function. We show the graphs of two steps functions below.

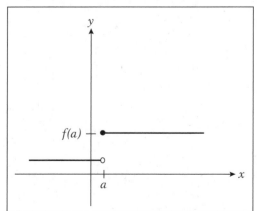
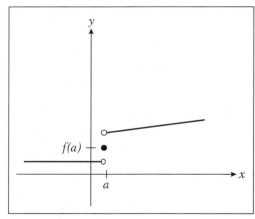

In the graph on the left, there is step at $x = a$, and the output value of the function at a is the closed dot on the upper line on the graph. In the graph on the right, the value of the function at $x = a$ is neither on the first part

nor the last part of the function but at some value that is isolated from the two main sub-functions. In both of these cases, the LHL does not equal the RHL and the limit of the function as x approaches a DNE.

MODEL PROBLEMS

1. Evaluate the limit $\lim\limits_{x \to 1} f(x)$ if $f(x) = \begin{cases} -x + 2, & x \leq 1 \\ x - 1, & x > 1 \end{cases}$.

(A) -1

(B) 2

(C) 0

(D) DNE (Does not exist)

Solution

We graph the function and evaluate what is happening in $f(x)$ as we approach $x = 1$ from both the left- and right-hand sides. The left-hand side limit is $\lim\limits_{x \to 1^-} f(x) = \lim\limits_{x \to 1^-} (-x) + 2 = -1 + 2 = 1$. We see this is true by examining the graph. On the right-hand side, $\lim\limits_{x \to 1^-} f(x) = \lim\limits_{x \to 1^-} (x - 1) = 1 - 1 = 0$. These two limits are not equal, so $\lim\limits_{x \to 1} f(x)$ DNE and the correct answer is (D).

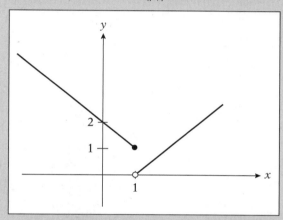

FR 2. Evaluate the limit $\lim\limits_{x \to 0} f(x)$ if $f(x) = \begin{cases} 2x + 2, & x < 0 \\ (x + 2)^2, & x \geq 0 \end{cases}$.

Solution

Here we are interested in what happens to $f(x)$ as x approaches 0. We start by graphing the function.

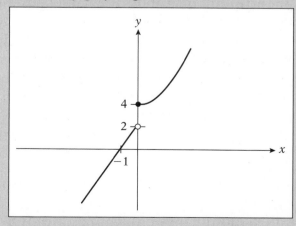

It doesn't look like the LHL will agree with the RHL, but we must show it is true algebraically. Show the limits are unequal algebraically to complete the problem.

3. Evaluate the limit $\lim_{x\to 0} f(x)$ if $f(x) = \begin{cases} x + 3, & x < 0 \\ 2, & x = 0 \\ x^2, & x > 0 \end{cases}$.

Solution

Instead of drawing the graph for this function, try to visualize what is happening based on the sub-equations. We have a linear function from $-\infty < x < 0$, then a point at $(0, 2)$, and part of a quadratic function where $x > 0$. What does this mean for the limit of $f(x)$ as x approaches 0?

Explain: Limits of Oscillating Functions

The functions sine and cosine are periodic trigonometric functions. Both of these functions have output values that repeat every 2π units. Periodic functions can **oscillate**, which can be problematic when they are composed with other functions. Let's consider the graph of $f(x) = \sin\left(\frac{1}{x}\right)$ around $x = 0$. We can see that the output values do not converge to a specific value, so the function's limit at $x = 0$ does not exist.

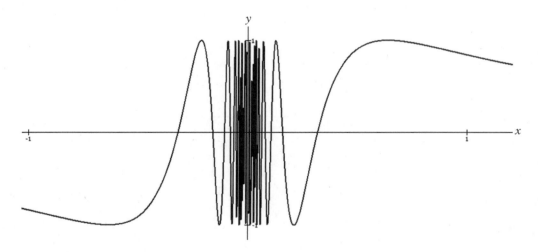

These types of oscillations occur at points where the argument function, $u(x)$, which is the input function of the periodic functions $\sin(u(x))$ or $(\cos(u(x)))$, approaches infinity, where $u(x)$ is a rational function.

We see a similar phenomenon with the function $f(x) = \cos\left(\frac{1}{x}\right)$. This function's limit also does not exist at $x = 0$.

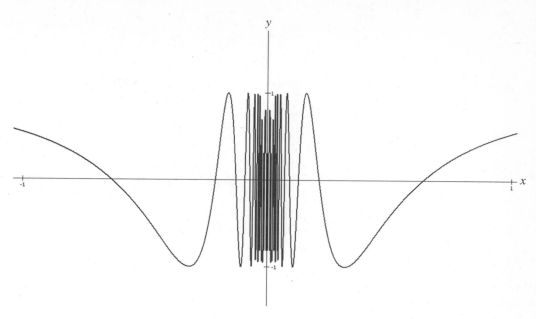

To summarize, if $f(x) = \sin(u(x))$ or $f(x) = \cos(u(x))$, where $u(x) = \dfrac{p(x)}{q(x)}$, then the function oscillates very quickly at $x = s$ where $q(s) = 0$. The result is that $\lim\limits_{x \to s} f(x)$ does not exist where $f(x) = \cos(u(x))$ or $f(x) = \sin(u(x))$.

MODEL PROBLEMS

1. Evaluate $\lim\limits_{x \to 0} \cos\left(\dfrac{1}{x^2}\right)$.

(A) 0

(B) 1

(C) DNE (Does not exist)

(D) −1

Solution

We can use our graphing calculator to create this graph, but look at the function's structure. The input of the periodic function, $\cos u$, is $u(x) = \dfrac{1}{x^2}$. We already know that $\lim\limits_{x \to 0} u(x) = \lim\limits_{x \to 0} \dfrac{1}{x^2} = \infty$, so the function $\cos u$ has very quick oscillations as $x = 0$. Therefore, $\lim\limits_{x \to 0} \cos\left(\dfrac{1}{x^2}\right)$ does not exist and the correct answer is (C).

FR **2.** Find the value(s) of c such that $\lim\limits_{x \to c} \sin\left(\dfrac{1}{x^2 - 1}\right)$ does not exist.

Solution

The input of the periodic function is $u(x) = \dfrac{1}{x^2 - 1}$ and $\sin\left(u(x)\right)$ will oscillate quickly when $x = \pm 1$. Thus, the value(s) of c such that $\lim\limits_{x \to c} \sin\left(\dfrac{1}{x^2 - 1}\right)$ does not exist are $c = -1$ and $c = 1$.

3. Find the value of a such that $\lim\limits_{x \to a} \cos\left(\dfrac{x + 3}{x^2 - x - 2}\right)$ does not exist.

(A) $a = 0$

(B) $a = -3$

(C) $a = -1$

(D) $a = -1$ and $a = 2$

Solution

This question is very similar to Model Problem #2 on page 75. What is the input of the periodic function? How can we use that information to determine the values of a?

AP Calculus Exam-Type Questions

Multiple Choice Questions
No calculator permitted for these questions.

1. Evaluate $\lim\limits_{x \to \infty} x^2$.

(A) ∞

(B) 0

(C) 1

(D) $-\infty$

2. Evaluate $\lim\limits_{x \to \infty} \sqrt{x - 1}$.

(A) ∞

(B) $-\infty$

(C) 1

(D) 0

3. Find a value of c such that $\lim\limits_{x \to c} \cos\left(\dfrac{1}{x^2 - 4}\right)$ does not exist.

(A) 0

(B) 4

(C) 1

(D) -2

4. Evaluate $\lim\limits_{x \to 0} f(x)$ if $f(x) = \begin{cases} x & x < 0 \\ 1 - x & x \geq 0 \end{cases}$.

(A) 1

(B) -1

(C) DNE (Does not exist)

(D) 0

5. Find the value of a such that $\lim\limits_{x \to a} \cos\left(\dfrac{3}{x - 2}\right)$ does not exist.

(A) 0

(B) 2

(C) 3

(D) -2

6. Evaluate $\lim\limits_{x \to \infty} (1 - x - x^2)$.

(A) $-\infty$

(B) 0

(C) ∞

(D) 1

7. Evaluate $\lim\limits_{x \to 0^+} g(x)$ using the graph of g shown below.

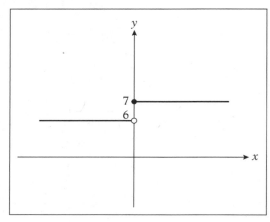

(A) 0

(B) DNE (Does not exist)

(C) 7

(D) 6

8. Find the value of a such that $\lim\limits_{x \to a} \sin\left(\dfrac{1}{x^2}\right)$ does not exist.

(A) 0

(B) 1

(C) -1

(D) ∞

9. Which of the following best describes the function whose graph is shown below?

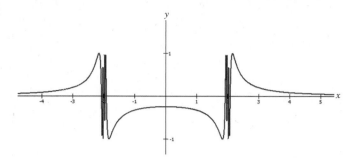

(A) $f(x) = \cos\left(\dfrac{1}{x-2}\right)$

(B) $f(x) = \cos\left(\dfrac{1}{x^2-4}\right)$

(C) $f(x) = \sin\left(\dfrac{1}{x-2}\right)$

(D) $f(x) = \sin\left(\dfrac{1}{x^2-4}\right)$

10. Evaluate $\lim\limits_{x\to-\infty}(6x^3 - 3x + 2)$.

(A) $-\infty$

(B) 0

(C) 5

(D) ∞

11. Evaluate $\lim\limits_{x\to3^-} f(x)$ if $f(x) = \begin{cases} x+3, & x \le 3 \\ 2x, & x > 3 \end{cases}$.

(A) -6

(B) 5

(C) 6

(D) DNE (Does not exist)

12. Evaluate $\lim\limits_{x\to-3}\dfrac{1}{x+3}$.

(A) 1

(B) 0

(C) 6

(D) DNE (Does not exist)

13. Evaluate $\lim\limits_{x\to-1^+} f(x)$ if $f(x) = \begin{cases} x-3, & x > -1 \\ -2x, & x > -1 \end{cases}$.

(A) -4

(B) 2

(C) -2

(D) DNE (Does not exist)

14. Consider the figure below, which shows the graph of $f(x)$. Evaluate the limit $\lim\limits_{x\to5^-} f(x)$.

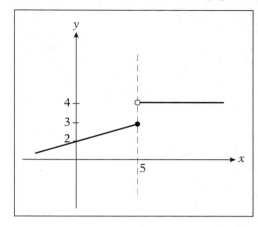

(A) DNE (Does not exist)

(B) 4

(C) 5

(D) 3

15. Which of the following best describes the function whose graph is shown below?

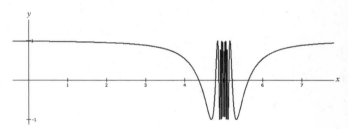

(A) $f(x) = \cos\left(\dfrac{1}{x-5}\right)$

(B) $f(x) = \cos\left(\dfrac{1}{x+5}\right)$

(C) $f(x) = \sin\left(\dfrac{1}{x-5}\right)$

(D) $f(x) = \sin\left(\dfrac{1}{x^2-25}\right)$

16. Evaluate $\lim\limits_{x\to-1}\dfrac{1}{x+1}$.

(A) -1

(B) 0

(C) 1

(D) DNE (Does not exist)

17. Evaluate $\lim_{x \to \infty} (x^5 + x^3 + 1)$.

(A) ∞

(B) 1

(C) -1

(D) 0

18. Evaluate $\lim_{x \to 0^+} f(x)$ if $f(x) = \begin{cases} -4, & x \le 0 \\ x + 4, & x > 0 \end{cases}$.

(A) 4

(B) -4

(C) 0

(D) DNE (Does not exist)

Free Response Questions

A graphing calculator is required for some questions.

1. Evaluate $\lim (2 - 80x^2)$.

2. From the graph of the function $g(x)$, shown below, find

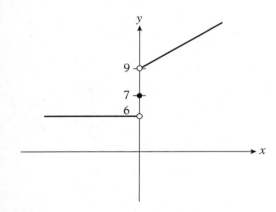

(a) $\lim_{x \to 0^-} g(x)$

(b) $\lim_{x \to 0^+} g(x)$

(c) $\lim_{x \to 0} g(x)$

3. Given that $f(x) = \sin\left(\dfrac{4}{2x + 1}\right)$, find the value of a such that $\lim_{x \to a} f(x)$ DNE.

4. Given $f(x) = \begin{cases} x^2 + 1, & x \le 0 \\ 2 - 3x, & x > 0 \end{cases}$, evaluate the following

(a) $\lim_{x \to 0^-} f(x)$

(b) $\lim_{x \to 0^+} f(x)$

(c) $\lim_{x \to 0} f(x)$

5. Given that $f(x) = \cos\left(\dfrac{x - 1}{x^2 - 9}\right)$, find the value of a such that $\lim_{x \to a} f(x)$ DNE.

6. From the graph of the function $g(x)$ shown below, find

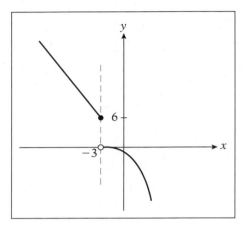

(a) $\lim_{x \to -3^-} g(x)$

(b) $\lim_{x \to -3^+} g(x)$

(c) $\lim_{x \to 3} g(x)$

7. Evaluate $\lim_{x \to -\infty} (7x^2 + 4)$.

8. Given that $f(x) = \sin\left(\dfrac{3}{5x}\right)$, find the value of a such that $\lim_{x \to a} f(x)$ DNE.

9. Write a function that describes the graph shown below.

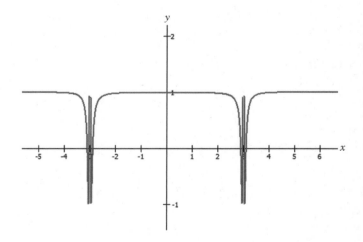

Lesson 4: Continuity

- Continuity Definition
- Continuity of Different Function Families
- Discontinuities
- Theorems Related to Function Continuity

Explain: Continuity Definition

Continuity is a property of a function. An intuitive definition of a continuous function is a function whose graph can be drawn without lifting the pencil from the paper. A continuous function has no breaks or holes in its graph.

> **By definition, a function $f(x)$ is continuous at $x = c$ if all of the following conditions exist:**
>
> 1. The function has a value at $x = c$; that is, $f(c)$ exists.
> 2. $\lim\limits_{x \to c} f(x)$ exists.
> 3. $\lim\limits_{x \to c} f(x) = f(c)$.

By this definition, a function is continuous at c if the function is defined at c, has a limit as x approaches c, and if the limit as x approaches c is equal to $f(c)$.

A function is *everywhere continuous* if it is continuous at each point of its domain. A function is *continuous on an interval* if it is continuous at every point in that interval.

MODEL PROBLEM

FR 1. Discuss the continuity of the function $f(x) = x^3 - 2x + 1$ at $x = -1$.

Solution

For this question, $c = -1$. By conditions of continuity, $f(c) = f(-1)$ $= (-1)^3 - 2(-1) + 1 = 2$, and the function has a finite value at that point so $\lim\limits_{x \to c} f(x) = \lim\limits_{x \to -1} (x^3 - 2x + 1)$. Since the function is a polynomial, we simply carry out the substitution. Then $\lim\limits_{x \to c} f(x) = \lim\limits_{x \to -1} (x^3 - 2x + 1)$ $= (-1)^3 - 2(-1) + 1 = 2$, and $\lim\limits_{x \to c} f(x) = 2 = f(c)$.

FR 2. Discuss the continuity of the figures below at $x = 0$.

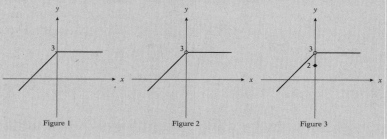

Figure 1   Figure 2   Figure 3

Solution

For Figure 1, we see that the function exists at $x = 0$ and that $f(0) = 3$. Since the graph is defined differently on each side of 0, we will evaluate both the LHL and the RHL. For the LHL, as we move along the left-hand side of the x-axis towards zero, the value of the function tends to 3. Thus $\lim\limits_{x \to 0^-} f(x) = 3$. Is the limit the same on the right-hand side? Moving along the right side of the x-axis toward 0, the value of the function is 3 and $\lim\limits_{x \to 0^+} f(x) = 3$. Since $\lim\limits_{x \to 0^-} f(x) = 3 = \lim\limits_{x \to 0^+} f(x)$, the limit exists and $\lim\limits_{x \to 0} f(x) = 3$. We also note that $\lim\limits_{x \to 0} f(x) = 3 = f(0)$ so all the conditions for continuity are met at $x = 0$. You try Figures 2 and 3.

FR **3.** Is $f(x)$ continuous at $x = 1$?

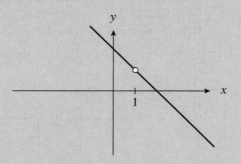

Solution

Use the definition of continuity. Is this function everywhere continuous?

FR **4.** Is $f(x)$ continuous at $x = 1$?

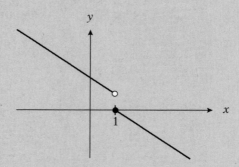

Solution

Using the definition of continuity from page 79, does this function meet all three conditions? Can you show that one or more of the conditions is unsatisfied?

FR **5.** Is $f(x)$ continuous at $x = 1$?

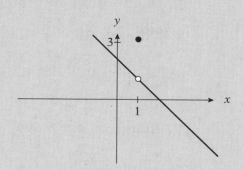

Solution

Carefully consider if this function meets all the conditions for continuity.

Explain: Continuity of Different Function Families

As we've seen, not all functions are everywhere continuous. Here we review the basic function families and their continuity along the real number line.

Function Family	Form	Continuity
Polynomial	$f(x) = ax^2 + bx + c$	Everywhere continuous.
Rational	$f(x) = \dfrac{p(x)}{q(x)}$	Everywhere continuous.
Power	$f(x) = ax^b$	Everywhere continuous.
Exponential	$f(x) = ar^{bx}$	Everywhere continuous.
Logarithmic	$f(x) = a\log_b rx$	Everywhere continuous.
Trigonometric (sine, cosine, tangent)	$f(x) = \sin(x)$ $f(x) = \cos(x)$ $f(x) = \tan(x)$	Sine and cosine functions are everywhere continuous. The tangent function is not continuous at $\pm\dfrac{n\pi}{2}$ where $n = 1, 3, 5, 7, \ldots$.

MODEL PROBLEM

FR **1.** Is the function $f(x) = \dfrac{x+1}{x^2-1}$ continuous at $x = -1$?

Solution

When $x = -1$, we find $f(-1) = \dfrac{-1+1}{(-1)^2-1} = \dfrac{0}{0}$ and a hole exists at that point. Hence, the function is not continuous at $x = -1$.

Questions 2 – 4: Use the function $f(x) = \dfrac{1}{1+\sin x}$.

2. Find $f\left(-\dfrac{\pi}{2}\right)$.

(A) 0

(B) 1

(C) −1

(D) Undefined

Solution

We are asked to evaluate $f\left(-\dfrac{\pi}{2}\right) = \dfrac{1}{1+\sin\left(-\dfrac{\pi}{2}\right)}$. What do we know about the sine function at multiples of $\dfrac{\pi}{2}$?

3. What is $\lim\limits_{x \to -\frac{\pi}{2}} f(x)$?

(A) 0

(B) 1

(C) 2

(D) DNE (Does not exist)

Solution

Based on your answer to Model Problem #2 above, how does the value of the function relate to the limit of the function at that same value? Is there a line of algebraic reasoning you can use to prove your answer is correct?

FR **4.** Is this function continuous at $x = -\dfrac{\pi}{2}$? Justify your answer.

Solution

For this question, you need to compare your answers to Model Problems #2 and #3. How does the value of a function at a certain input relate the the limit of the function at that same input? And how do those two pieces of information relate to a function's continuity at that point?

Explain: Discontinuities

When a function is not continuous at a particular point, we say it is discontinuous at that particular point. There are four different types of discontinuities: jump discontinuities, removable discontinuities, infinite discontinuities, and essential discontinuities, which we briefly outline below.

Jump Discontinuity   A function has a jump discontinuity if there is a break between the portions of the functions at a given point. A function $f(x)$ has this type of discontinuity at $x = a$ if $\lim_{x \to a^-} f(x)$ and $\lim_{x \to a^+} f(x)$ exist but they are unequal.

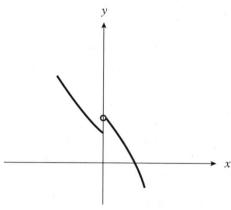

Jump Discontinuity

Removable Discontinuity   A removable discontinuity exists at $x = a$ if a function has a hole at that particular value. Thus, the limits $\lim_{x \to a^-} f(x)$ and $\lim_{x \to a^+} f(x)$ exist and are equal but $f(a) \neq \lim_{x \to a^-} f(x) = \lim_{x \to a^+} f(x)$. In most cases, this situation is corrected by defining the value of the function at that point to be equal to the limit. When we do this, the discontinuity is said to have been removed.

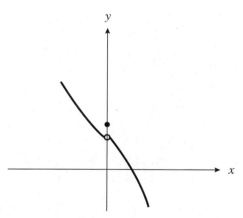

Removable Discontinuity

Infinite Discontinuity   A function has an infinite discontinuity at $x = a$ if the function approaches the line $x = a$ asymptotically. Thus, this happens at a point where a function has a vertical asymptote.

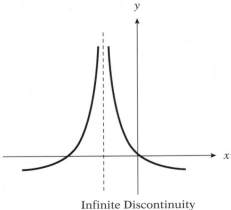

Infinite Discontinuity

Essential Discontinuity   Essential discontinuities happen when a function oscillates very quickly, as seen in Lesson 3 of this Main Idea. Many of the functions that display this discontinuity are trigonometric functions where the argument is a rational expression.

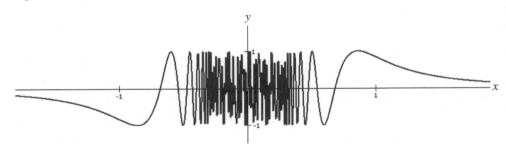

Essential Discontinuity

MODEL PROBLEMS

FR **1.**   Identify all the locations and types discontinuities of the function $f(x) = \frac{x-2}{x^2-4}$.

Solution

It is helpful to first identify the function family for $f(x)$. This is a rational function. It will be discontinuous where the denominator is equal to 0. Using basic algebra, we find that the function has discontinuities at $x = \pm 2$. But what types of discontinuities will they be? We simplify the given function and find $f(x) = \frac{x-2}{x^2-4} = \frac{x-2}{(x-2)(x+2)} = \frac{1}{x+2}$. There will be a vertical asymptote and an infinite discontinuity at $x = -2$. There is a hole at $x = 2$, so that discontinuity is removable.

2. Classify the discontinuity of $f(x) = \dfrac{2}{3x - 2}$.

(A) Jump discontinuity

(B) Essential discontinuity

(C) Removable discontinuity

(D) Infinite discontinuity

Solution

This problem is similar to what we showed in Model Problem #1 on page 84. Consider if there are points excluded from the domain of this function and what is happening, graphically, at those points.

3. Identify where the function $g(x) = \dfrac{4x}{x^2 - 6x}$ has a removable discontinuity.

(A) $x = 4$

(B) $x = 0$

(C) $x = 6$

(D) This function does not have a removable discontinuity.

Solution

A removable discontinuity appears when both the numerator and denominator of a rational function have a common factor. Does this function contain a discontinuity that fits this definition? If so, does it exist at one of the given answer choices?

FR **4.** $f(x) = \begin{cases} 2x - 3, & x \neq 2 \\ 0, & x = 2 \end{cases}$ has a removable discontinuity. Redefine $f(x)$ so that it is continuous at $x = 2$.

Solution

This question is slightly different than from those we saw above. We are told where the discontinuity exists and what type it is. We need to redefine $f(x)$ to be continuous at $x = 2$. This means we need to figure out the value of the function's limit as x approaches 2. To accomplish this, use the function $f(x) = 2x - 3$ and evaluate its LHL and its RHL.

Explain: Theorems Related to Function Continuity

There are several important theorems that make use of the ideas of continuity, including the Intermediate Value Theorem and the Extreme Value Theorem. The Mean Value Theorem and Rolle's Theorem are also important consequences of continuity; however, we will discuss those theorems when we cover differentiation.

The **Intermediate Value Theorem** guarantees that as long as a function is continuous within an interval, there will be an input for each output selected from that range. Specifically, the theorem states if a function $f(x)$ is continuous on a closed interval $[a, b]$ where a and b are real numbers, then for any number, K, such that $f(a) \leq K \leq f(b)$ there is a number c, $a \leq c \leq b$ where $f(c) = K$. For example, if we allow $K = 0$, then $f(c) = 0$ implies that c is a zero of the function.

The **Extreme Value Theorem** guarantees the existence of an absolute maximum and absolute minimum of a function between any two points. However, it does not provide any means of determining where these points occur. The theorem states that if a function $f(x)$ is continuous on a closed interval $[a, b]$, then there exist numbers h and k, $a \leq h, k \leq b$ such that between $f(h)$ and $f(k)$, one is the absolute maximum while the other is the function's absolute minimum.

MODEL PROBLEM

FR **1.** Use the Intermediate Value Theorem to show that the function $f(x) = \dfrac{2x - 5}{x^2 - 4x + 3}$ has a zero in the interval $[0, 5]$.

Solution

First we need to determine if the function is continuous on $[0, 5]$. If the function is not continuous over this interval, the Intermediate Value Theorem does not apply. We know the function will not be defined when $x^2 - 4x + 3 = 0$, so we factor and find that the function is not defined when $x = 1$ or when $x = 3$. This means the function is not defined at those points, which are in the interval $[0, 5]$. Because the function is not continuous over the entire interval, the Intermediate Value Theorem does not apply.

FR **2.** Use the Intermediate Value Theorem to show $f(x) = x^2 - 7x$ has a zero in the interval $[-1, 4]$.

Solution

The given function is a polynomial, so is it continuous everywhere and we can use the Intermediate Value Theorem. We're being asked if there is a number, c, such that $f(c) = 0$ somewhere in the given interval.

FR **3.** Consider the function $f(x) = x^2 + 2$ on the interval $[-2, 2]$. Can we apply the Extreme Value Theorem to this function? Why? What does this mean for the absolute minimum and maximum values over this interval?

Solution

What type of function is $f(x)$? Will this function be continuous in the given interval?

AP Calculus Exam-Type Questions:

Multiple Choice Questions
No calculator permitted for these questions.

Questions 1 – 4: Use the function

$$f(x) = \begin{cases} e^x, & x < 1 \\ \ln x, & x \geq 1 \end{cases}.$$

1. $f(1) =$

   (A) 0
   (B) 1
   (C) 2
   (D) e

2. $\lim\limits_{x \to 1^-} f(x) =$

   (A) 0
   (B) 1
   (C) 2
   (D) e

3. $\lim\limits_{x \to 1^+} f(x) =$

   (A) 0
   (B) 1
   (C) 2
   (D) e

4. $\lim\limits_{x \to 1} f(x) =$

   (A) 0
   (B) 1
   (C) e
   (D) Does not exist

5. $f(x) = \begin{cases} x^2 + 1, & x < 2 \\ 4, & x > 2 \end{cases}, \lim\limits_{x \to 2^-} f(x) =$

   (A) 0
   (B) 2
   (C) 4
   (D) 5

6. The domain of $y = \ln x - 1$ is

   (A) $\{x \geq 0\}$
   (B) $\{x \leq 0\}$
   (C) $\{x \neq 0\}$
   (D) $\{x \geq 1\}$

7. For what value(s) of x is $f(x) = \dfrac{x-1}{x^2-1}$ discontinuous?

   (A) $x = 0$
   (B) $x = 1$
   (C) $x = -1$
   (D) $x = 1$ and $x = -1$

8. $f(x) = \dfrac{1}{x^2}$ is continuous for all real numbers. except

   (A) $x = 0$
   (B) $x = 1$ only
   (C) $x = 1$ and $x = -1$
   (D) $x = -1$ only

9. $\lim\limits_{x \to 0} \dfrac{\sin 2x}{x \cos x} =$

   (A) 0
   (B) 2
   (C) 1
   (D) DNE (Does not exist)

10. Find $f(2)$ for $f(x) = \begin{cases} x^2 + 4, & x < 0 \\ 3 - x, & x \geq 0 \end{cases}.$

    (A) 8
    (B) 0
    (C) 1
    (D) Not defined

11. At which point(s) is $f(x) = \dfrac{x}{5x - x^2}$ not continuous?

    (A) 5
    (B) 0
    (C) 5 and 0
    (D) 1

12. Which of the following graphs shows a function that is continuous for all real numbers?

(A)
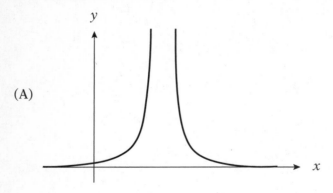

(B)
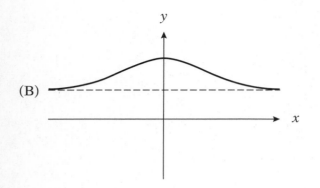

(C)
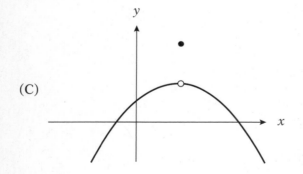

(D)
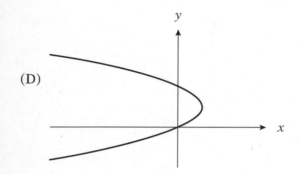

Questions 13 – 16: Given that $f(x) = \frac{x+1}{\cos x}$,

13. find $f(0)$.

   (A) 0
   (B) 1
   (C) −1
   (D) DNE (Does not exist)

14. find $\lim\limits_{x \to 0^-} f(x)$.

   (A) 1
   (B) 0
   (C) −1
   (D) DNE (Does not exist)

15. find $\lim\limits_{x \to 0^+} f(x)$.

   (A) 0
   (B) −1
   (C) 1
   (D) DNE (Does not exist)

16. find $\lim\limits_{x \to 0} f(x)$.

   (A) 0
   (B) 1
   (C) −1
   (D) DNE (Does not exist)

17. Identify the kind of discontinuity in $f(x) = \frac{2}{x}$.

   (A) Infinite discontinuity
   (B) Essential discontinuity
   (C) Removable discontinuity
   (D) Jump discontinuity

18. The function $g(x) = \begin{cases} x \text{ if } x < -1 \\ x^3 \text{ if } x > -1 \end{cases}$ has a removable discontinuity. Define $g(-1)$ so that the function is continuous at the point of discontinuity.

   (A) $g(-1) = 1$
   (B) $g(-1) = -1$
   (C) $g(-1) = 0$
   (D) $g(x)$ cannot be continuous.

Free Response Questions

A graphing calculator is required for some questions.

1. For the function $f(x) = \begin{cases} kx + 1, & x \leq 1 \\ x^2, & x \geq 1 \end{cases}$

   (a) find the value of k so that $f(x)$ is continuous at $x = 1$.

   (b) using the value of k found in part (a), sketch the graph of $f(x)$.

2. For the function $g(x) = \begin{cases} x^2 + 2, & x \leq -1 \\ x - p, & x \geq -1 \end{cases}$

   (a) find the value of p so that $f(x)$ is continuous at $x = -1$.

   (b) using the value of p found in part (a), sketch the graph of $f(x)$.

3. (a) Write a function $f(x)$ that has a removable discontinuity.

   (b) Write a function $g(x)$ that has a non-removable discontinuity.

4. Use the graph of $f(x)$ shown below to find the following limits:

   - $\lim\limits_{x \to -1} f(x)$
   - $\lim\limits_{x \to 1} f(x)$
   - $\lim\limits_{x \to 2} f(x)$

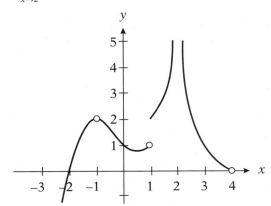

5. Find the zeros, holes, and vertical / horizontal asymptotes of $f(x) = \dfrac{3x - 6}{x + 5}$.

6. Sketch a function $f(x)$ with all of the following properties:

   - $f(x)$ is odd.
   - $f(1) = 2$
   - The x-axis is a horizontal asymptote.

7. Identify the discontinuity in the function $f(x) = \sin\left(\dfrac{2}{x - 1}\right)$.

8. Identify the discontinuities in $g(x) = \dfrac{4x - 1}{16x^2 - 1}$.

9. Is $f(x) = \begin{cases} x - 3 & \text{if } x < 1, \\ -2 & \text{if } x = 1, \\ 2 - 4x & \text{if } x > 1 \end{cases}$ continuous?

   Justify your answer.

Lesson 5: Comparing Functions Using Limits

- Relative Rate of Growth
- The Dominant Term
- Relative Rate of Decay

Explain: Relative Rate of Growth

Many functions we work with in calculus have larger and larger outputs as x grows without bound. This means that for many common functions, $\lim\limits_{x \to +\infty} f(x) = +\infty$. Beyond the limit itself, sometimes we'd like to know how quickly the function is growing. This is where the function's relative rate of growth comes into play.

A function's relative rate of growth is the rate at which a function approaches infinity with respect to another function. For polynomial functions, we can use the degree of the polynomial to get a general comparison. For instance, the function $f(x) = x^3$ grows faster than the function $g(x) = x$. Stated another way, the function of degree 3 grows more quickly than the function of degree 1. To formally compare the rate of growth of polynomials, as well as other functions, we consider the limit of their quotient.

If $f(x)$ and $g(x)$ are functions defined over the real numbers where $\lim\limits_{x \to \infty} |f(x)| = \lim\limits_{x \to \infty} |g(x)| = \infty$, then $f(x)$ grows more quickly than $g(x)$ when

$$\lim_{x \to \infty} \left| \frac{f(x)}{g(x)} \right| = \infty$$

Additionally, $f(x)$ approaches infinity more slowly than $g(x)$ when

$$\lim_{x \to \infty} \left| \frac{f(x)}{g(x)} \right| = 0$$

Finally, if $f(x)$ approaches infinity at the same rate as $g(x)$, then

$$\lim_{x \to \infty} \left| \frac{f(x)}{g(x)} \right| = M \neq 0$$

where M is a finite, non-zero number.

We summarize the growth of three categories of functions: exponential, power, and logarithmic. Other function types require the use of L'Hôpital's rule, which we have not yet reviewed.

For two functions, $f(x)$ and $g(x)$, of identical type (for example, two exponential, two power, or two logarithmic),

Exponential	$f(x) = a^x$ approaches infinity faster than $g(x) = b^x$ when $a > b > 0$, $a \neq 1$.
Power	$f(x) = x^a$ approaches infinity faster than $g(x) = x^b$ when $a > b$ and a and b are positive integers.
Logarithmic	Logarithmic functions approach infinity at the same rate.

MODEL PROBLEMS

1. Describe the relative rate of growth of $f(x)$ with respect to $g(x)$ for $f(x) = 2x^2 + 1$ and $g(x) = x + 2$.

(A) The function $g(x)$ grows more quickly than $f(x)$.

(B) The function $g(x)$ grows more slowly than $f(x)$.

(C) The functions grow at the same rate.

(D) Cannot be determined.

Solution

$\lim\limits_{x \to \infty} \dfrac{2x^2 + 1}{x + 2}$	To answer this question, we need to determine $\lim\limits_{x \to \infty}\left\|\dfrac{f(x)}{g(x)}\right\|$. Start by substituting in the functions.
$\lim\limits_{x \to \infty} \dfrac{2 + \dfrac{1}{x^2}}{\dfrac{1}{x} + \dfrac{2}{x^2}}$	Divide all the terms by the highest power present.
$\lim\limits_{x \to \infty} \dfrac{1}{x} = \lim\limits_{x \to \infty} \dfrac{2}{x^2} = \lim\limits_{x \to \infty} \dfrac{1}{x^2} = 0$	We can ignore the constant, 2.

$\lim\limits_{x \to \infty} \dfrac{2x^2 + 1}{x + 2} = \dfrac{2}{0}$ which results in a limit of positive infinity, so the correct answer is (B).

2. Describe the relative rate of growth of $f(x)$ with respect to $g(x)$ for $f(x) = -x^3 + 6x + 3$ and $g(x) = 4x^3 + 2x^2 - 7x + 3$.

(A) The function $g(x)$ grows more quickly than $f(x)$.

(B) The function $g(x)$ grows more slowly than $f(x)$.

(C) The functions grow at the same rate.

(D) Cannot be determined.

Solution

This problem is very similar to Model Problem #1. We can use the same process for solving. When you divide through by the highest power present, what does the result imply about the limit of each term?

3. Describe the relative rate of growth of $f(x)$ with respect to $g(x)$ for $f(x) = 8 + 3x - 9x^2$ and $g(x) = 5 - 4x^4$.

(A) The function $g(x)$ grows more quickly than $f(x)$.

(B) The function $g(x)$ grows more slowly than $f(x)$.

(C) The functions grow at the same rate.

(D) Cannot be determined.

Solution

Again, use the same solving process as in Model Problems #1 and #2. Interpret your results.

4. $\lim\limits_{x\to\infty} \dfrac{x^2 + 2}{e^{2x}}$ is

(A) ∞

(B) 2

(C) 1

(D) 0

Solution

Compare the growth rates of these two functions. Which one is growing more quickly and what does that mean for the limit?

Explain: The Dominant Term

You may have noticed that comparing growth rates of polynomial functions is simply the process of taking the limit of a rational function. As such, we can consider using **dominant terms**. Recall that the dominant term is the term with the highest power in any function. Rather than evaluating the limit of each numerator term and each denominator term, simply evaluate the limit of the dominant terms. For example, in Model Problem #3, on page 91, the dominant terms are $-4x^4$ and $-9x^2$. So, the limit is

$$\lim_{x\to\infty} \left|\frac{g(x)}{f(x)}\right| = \lim_{x\to\infty} \frac{5 - 4x^4}{8 + 3x - 9x^2} = \lim_{x\to\infty} \frac{-4x^4}{-9x^2} = \lim_{x\to\infty} \frac{-4}{-9}x^2 = \infty$$

MODEL PROBLEMS

1. $\lim\limits_{x\to\infty} \dfrac{1 - x^2}{5x^2 + 3x + 7}$ is

(A) 0

(B) $\dfrac{1}{5}$

(C) ∞

(D) $-\dfrac{1}{5}$

Solution

Evaluate the limit of the dominant terms to find $\lim\limits_{x\to\infty} \dfrac{-x^2}{5x^2} = \lim\limits_{x\to\infty} \dfrac{-1}{5} = -\dfrac{1}{5}$. The correct option is (D).

2. $\lim\limits_{x\to\infty} \dfrac{3x^3 - 2x^2 + x + 1}{3x^4 + 5x^3 - 9}$ is

(A) 3

(B) 0

(C) ∞

(D) $-\infty$

Solution

The dominant terms for the numerator and the denominators are $3x^3$ and $3x^4$, respectively. What is the limit of their quotient?

3. $\lim\limits_{x\to\infty} \dfrac{\log_3 x^2 + 3}{8x^2 + 2x - 5}$ is

(A) $\dfrac{3}{8}$

(B) ∞

(C) 0

(D) $-\infty$

Solution

Here we do not have the quotient of two polynomials. Nevertheless, we can use dominant terms. In this problem, the dominant terms are $\log_3 x^2$ and $8x^2$. Consider using a graph to compare these dominant terms.

4. $\lim\limits_{x\to\infty} \dfrac{\log_2 x + x^2}{2 - 9x}$ is

(A) $-\infty$

(B) 0

(C) ∞

(D) $-\dfrac{1}{9}$

Solution

Compare this problem to Model Problem #2 on page 92. Would the dominant term of the numerator be $\log_2 x$ or would you use x^2? Which has the faster growth rate: a logarithmic function or a power function? Can you use a graph to help solve this problem?

Explain: Relative Rate of Decay

The rate of decay refers to how quickly or slowly a function approaches 0. Here we want to compare the rate at which functions that have a higher degree in the denominator approach zero. For example, since x^2 has a greater degree than x, the function $\dfrac{1}{x^2}$ decays faster than the function $\dfrac{1}{x}$. We look at the cases of relative rate of decay. If $f(x)$ and $g(x)$ are functions defined on real numbers and $\lim\limits_{x\to\infty}|f(x)| = \lim\limits_{x\to\infty}|g(x)| = 0$, then $f(x)$ approaches 0 more quickly than $g(x)$ if

$$\lim_{x\to\infty} \left|\frac{f(x)}{g(x)}\right| = 0$$

If $f(x)$ approaches 0 more slowly than $g(x)$, then

$$\lim_{x\to\infty} \left|\frac{f(x)}{g(x)}\right| = \infty$$

When $f(x)$ and $g(x)$ approach 0 at the same rate, then

$$\lim_{x\to\infty} \left|\frac{f(x)}{g(x)}\right| = M \neq 0$$

where M is a finite, non-zero number.

MODEL PROBLEMS

FR **1.** Evaluate $\lim\limits_{x \to \infty} \dfrac{h(x)}{g(x)}$ when $h(x) = \dfrac{10}{x}$ and $g(x) = \dfrac{13}{x^2}$.

Solution

$\lim\limits_{x \to \infty} \dfrac{h(x)}{g(x)} = \lim\limits_{x \to \infty} \dfrac{\frac{10}{x}}{\frac{13}{x^2}}$	Begin by substituting the functions into the limit expression.
$\lim\limits_{x \to \infty} \dfrac{10\,x^2}{13x} = \lim\limits_{x \to \infty} \left(\dfrac{10x}{13}\right) = \infty$	Simplify.

2. Describe rate of decay of $h(x)$ with respect to $g(x)$ if $h(x) = \dfrac{1}{e^x} + 1$ and $g(x) = \dfrac{2}{x^2}$.

(A) Cannot be determined.

(B) The functions $h(x)$ and $g(x)$ approach 0 at the same rate.

(C) The function $h(x)$ approaches 0 more slowly than the function $g(x)$.

(D) The function $h(x)$ approaches 0 more quickly than the function $g(x)$.

Solution

We substitute to find $\lim\limits_{x \to \infty} \dfrac{h(x)}{g(x)} = \dfrac{\frac{1}{e^x} + 1}{\frac{2}{x^2}}$. Well, that's a mess. Consider how the function in the numerator decays. The limit of $\dfrac{1}{e^x}$ as x goes to positive infinity is 0. To that we add 1, so the limit of the numerator is 1. The limit of the denominator will be 0 as x goes to positive infinity. The correct answer is (C).

3. $\lim\limits_{x \to \infty} \dfrac{e^{-x}}{6\,x^{-2}}$ is

(A) ∞

(B) 0

(C) $\dfrac{e}{6}$

(D) $-\infty$

Solution

Examine the function in the numerator and the function in the denominator. What is $\lim\limits_{x \to \infty} e^{-x}$? What is $\lim\limits_{x \to \infty} 6\,x^{-2}$? What does that mean for the rate of decay?

4. $\lim\limits_{x \to \infty} \cos\left(\dfrac{1}{x^2 - 1}\right)$ is

(A) 1

(B) ∞

(C) -1

(D) 0

Solution

What happens to the denominator of the argument as the value of x approaches infinity?

AP Calculus Exam-Type Questions:

Multiple Choice Questions
No calculator permitted for these questions.

For Questions 1 – 6, use $f(x) = \dfrac{1}{x^2 + 7x + 6}$ and $g(x) = \dfrac{3}{x^2}$.

1. $\displaystyle\lim_{x \to \infty} \dfrac{1}{x^2 + 7x + 6}$ is
   - (A) ∞
   - (B) 0
   - (C) 1
   - (D) $-\infty$

2. $\displaystyle\lim_{x \to \infty} \dfrac{3}{x^2}$ is
   - (A) $-\infty$
   - (B) 3
   - (C) ∞
   - (D) 0

3. $\displaystyle\lim_{x \to \infty} \dfrac{g(x)}{f(x)}$ is
   - (A) 1
   - (B) 0
   - (C) 3
   - (D) $\dfrac{1}{3}$

4. Describe the relative rate of $g(x)$ with respect to $f(x)$ as x approaches ∞.
   - (A) The function $g(x)$ approaches ∞ at the same rate as the function $f(x)$.
   - (B) The function $g(x)$ approaches 0 at a slower rate than the function $f(x)$.
   - (C) The functions $g(x)$ and $f(x)$ approach 0 at the same rate.
   - (D) The function $g(x)$ approaches 0 more quickly than the function $f(x)$.

5. $\displaystyle\lim_{x \to \infty} \dfrac{f(x)}{g(x)}$ is
   - (A) $\dfrac{1}{3}$
   - (B) 3
   - (C) 0
   - (D) ∞

6. Describe the relative rate of $f(x)$ with respect to $g(x)$ as x approaches ∞.
   - (A) The function $f(x)$ approaches ∞ at the same rate as the function $g(x)$.
   - (B) The function $f(x)$ approaches 0 at a slower rate than the function $g(x)$.
   - (C) The functions $f(x)$ and $g(x)$ approach 0 at the same rate.
   - (D) The function $f(x)$ approaches 0 more quickly than the function $g(x)$.

7. $\displaystyle\lim_{x \to \infty} \dfrac{4x + 3}{x}$ is
   - (A) 0
   - (B) 7
   - (C) 4
   - (D) ∞

8. $\displaystyle\lim_{x \to \infty} \dfrac{-2}{1 - x^3}$ is
   - (A) 0
   - (B) $-\infty$
   - (C) ∞
   - (D) -2

9. $\displaystyle\lim_{x \to \infty} \dfrac{\log_3 x - x}{\log_4 x}$ is
   - (A) ∞
   - (B) 0
   - (C) $\dfrac{3}{4}$
   - (D) $\dfrac{4}{3}$

10. $\displaystyle\lim_{x \to \infty} \dfrac{6x^2 + e^{9x}}{e^{2x} - x}$ is
    - (A) ∞
    - (B) 0
    - (C) 6
    - (D) e

For Questions 11 – 15, use $f(x) = e^{-2x}$ and $g(x) = \dfrac{1}{x} + e^{-x}$.

11. $\displaystyle\lim_{x \to \infty} f(x)$ is
    - (A) 0
    - (B) 1
    - (C) e
    - (D) ∞

12. $\lim\limits_{x\to\infty} g(x)$ is

(A) ∞

(B) 1

(C) e

(D) 0

13. Identify the dominant term of $g(x)$.

(A) $\frac{1}{x}$

(B) x

(C) e^{-x}

(D) 1

14. $\lim\limits_{x\to\infty} \dfrac{f(x)}{g(x)}$ is

(A) ∞

(B) 0

(C) 1

(D) e

15. Describe the rate of change of $f(x)$ with respect to $g(x)$ as x approaches ∞.

(A) The function $f(x)$ approaches ∞ more slowly than the function $g(x)$.

(B) The function $f(x)$ approaches 0 more quickly than the function $g(x)$.

(C) The function $f(x)$ approaches 0 more slowly than the function $g(x)$.

(D) The function $f(x)$ approaches ∞ more quickly than the function $g(x)$.

For Questions 16 – 17, use $g(x) = x^5 - 5x^2 + 2$ and $h(x) = -x + 6x^3 - 5x^5$.

16. $\lim\limits_{x\to\infty} \dfrac{h(x)}{g(x)}$ is

(A) -5

(B) 0

(C) ∞

(D) 5

17. Describe the rate of change of $f(x)$ with respect to $g(x)$ as x approaches ∞.

(A) The function $f(x)$ approaches ∞ more slowly than the function $g(x)$.

(B) The function $f(x)$ approaches 0 at the same rate as the function $g(x)$.

(C) The function $f(x)$ approaches ∞ more quickly than the function $g(x)$.

(D) The function $f(x)$ approaches ∞ at the same rate as the function $g(x)$.

Free Response Questions

A graphing calculator is required for some questions.

1. Identify the dominant term in $f(x) = x^2 + 10 + e^{x^2}$.

2. Given that $f(x) = x^{-3} + 2x^{-1}$ and

$$g(x) = \frac{1}{\log_3 x},$$

(a) find $\lim\limits_{x\to\infty} f(x)$.

(b) find $\lim\limits_{x\to\infty} g(x)$.

(c) find $\lim\limits_{x\to\infty} \dfrac{f(x)}{g(x)}$.

(d) describe the rate of change of $f(x)$ with respect to $g(x)$ as x approaches ∞.

3. Evaluate $\lim\limits_{x\to\infty} \dfrac{2x^3 + x - 4}{x^2 + 6x + 2}$.

4. Evaluate $\lim\limits_{x\to\infty} \dfrac{7x^2 + 4x + 4x^5 - 3}{3x^3 + x^2 - 8x^6 + 9}$.

5. If $g(x) = -6x^4$,

(a) find $\lim\limits_{x\to\infty} |g(x)|$.

(b) describe the rate of change of $|g(x)|$ with respect to its limit as $x \to \infty$.

6. If $f(x) = xe^x$ and $g(x) = -3x^3$,

(a) evaluate $\lim\limits_{x\to\infty} \dfrac{f(x)}{g(x)}$.

(b) describe the rate of change of $f(x)$ in relation to $g(x)$ as x approaches infinity.

7. Evaluate $\lim\limits_{x\to\infty} \dfrac{e^{-3x} + x^2}{x^3}$.

CALCULUS AB/BC

SECTION I, Part A
Time – 60 minutes
Number of problems – 30

A graphing calculator is not permitted for these problems.

1. $\lim\limits_{x \to 2} \dfrac{x}{x-2} =$

   (A) -1

   (B) 1

   (C) 2

   (D) Does not exist

2. $\lim\limits_{x \to 5} \dfrac{x-5}{x^2-25} =$

   (A) 0

   (B) $\dfrac{1}{10}$

   (C) 1

   (D) Does not exist

3. $\lim\limits_{x \to \frac{\pi}{2}} \dfrac{\sin x}{x} =$

   (A) 0

   (B) $\dfrac{2}{\pi}$

   (C) $\dfrac{\pi}{2}$

   (D) Does not exist

4. $\lim\limits_{x \to 0} \dfrac{\sin 2x}{x \cos x} =$

   (A) 0

   (B) 1

   (C) 2

   (D) Does not exist

5. $f(x) = \begin{cases} x^2 + 1, & x < 2 \\ 4, & x > 2 \end{cases}$

   $\lim\limits_{x \to 2^-} f(x) =$

   (A) 0

   (B) 2

   (C) 4

   (D) 5

6. Evaluate $\lim\limits_{x \to \infty} \dfrac{x^2-5}{2x^2+1}$.

   (A) $\dfrac{1}{2}$

   (B) 1

   (C) 2

   (D) ∞

7. Evaluate $\lim\limits_{x \to \infty} \dfrac{x^2-5}{2x+1}$.

   (A) $\dfrac{1}{2}$

   (B) 1

   (C) 2

   (D) ∞

8. Evaluate $\lim\limits_{x \to \infty} \dfrac{x-5}{2x^2+1}$.

   (A) $-\dfrac{1}{2}$

   (B) 0

   (C) $\dfrac{1}{2}$

   (D) ∞

9. Evaluate $\lim\limits_{x\to\infty} \dfrac{100x}{x^2-1}$.

(A) -1

(B) 0

(C) 1

(D) 100

10. Find the value of $\lim\limits_{x\to\pi} \dfrac{\sin x}{x}$.

(A) -1

(B) 0

(C) 1

(D) π

11. The vertical asymptote of $f(x) = \dfrac{x}{x-1}$ has equation

(A) $x = 0$

(B) $x = 1$

(C) $y = 0$

(D) $y = 1$

12. The horizontal asymptote of $f(x) = \dfrac{x}{x-1}$ is

(A) $x = 0$

(B) $x = 1$

(C) $y = 0$

(D) $y = 1$

13. The vertical asymptote of $f(x) = \dfrac{4}{x+1}$ is

(A) $x = -1$

(B) $x = 0$

(C) $y = -1$

(D) $y = 0$

14. The horizontal asymptote of $f(x) = \dfrac{4}{x+1}$ is

(A) $x = -1$

(B) $x = 0$

(C) $y = -1$

(D) $y = 0$

15. For what value(s) of x is $f(x) = \dfrac{x-1}{x^2-1}$ discontinuous?

(A) $x = 0$

(B) $x = 1$

(C) $x = -1$

(D) $x = 1$ and $x = -1$

16. $f(x) = \dfrac{1}{x^2}$ is continuous for all real numbers except

(A) $x = 0$

(B) $x = 1$ only

(C) $x = 1$ and $x = -1$

(D) $x = -1$ only

17. $\lim\limits_{x\to\frac{\pi}{3}} \dfrac{1-\cos x}{x} =$

(A) $\dfrac{\pi}{3}$

(B) $\dfrac{3}{\pi}$

(C) $\dfrac{3}{2\pi}$

(D) $\dfrac{3(1-\sqrt{3})}{2\pi}$

18. $\lim\limits_{x\to 0} \dfrac{\sin 3x}{7x} =$

(A) $\dfrac{3}{7}$

(B) $\dfrac{7}{3}$

(C) 3

(D) 7

19. $\lim\limits_{x\to 2} \dfrac{2-x}{x^2-4} =$

(A) $-\dfrac{1}{2}$

(B) $-\dfrac{1}{4}$

(C) $\dfrac{1}{4}$

(D) $\dfrac{1}{2}$

20. $\lim\limits_{x\to\infty} \dfrac{x^2-4x+4}{4x^2-1} =$

(A) $\dfrac{1}{4}$

(B) 1

(C) 4

(D) 8

21. Find the equation of the vertical asymptote of $f(x) = \dfrac{x}{4x + 8}$.

(A) $y = \dfrac{1}{4}$

(B) $y = -2$

(C) $x = -2$

(D) $x = 2$

22. Find the equation of the horizontal asymptote of $y = \dfrac{x^2}{2x^2 - 2}$.

(A) $y = 0$

(B) $x = \dfrac{1}{2}$

(C) $y = \dfrac{1}{2}$

(D) $x = 1$

23. $\displaystyle\lim_{x \to \infty} \dfrac{\sqrt{x} - 2}{x - 2} =$

(A) -2

(B) 0

(C) 1

(D) 2

24. $\displaystyle\lim_{x \to 3} \dfrac{\dfrac{1}{x} - \dfrac{1}{3}}{x - 3} =$

(A) $-\infty$

(B) $-\dfrac{1}{3}$

(C) $-\dfrac{1}{9}$

(D) 0

25. Which of the following graphs shows a function that is continuous for all real numbers?

(A)

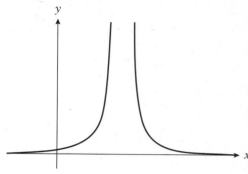

(B)

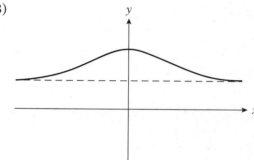

(C)

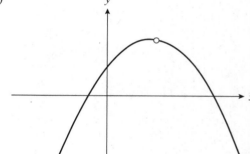

(D)

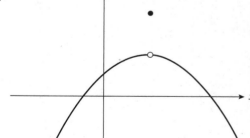

26. $\lim\limits_{x \to 0^-} \left(x^3 + \dfrac{1}{x} \right) =$

(A) 0

(B) $-\infty$

(C) ∞

(D) Does not exist

27. $\lim\limits_{x \to 0^+} \left(x^3 + \dfrac{1}{x} \right) =$

(A) 0

(B) $-\infty$

(C) ∞

(D) Does not exist

28. $\lim\limits_{x \to 0} \cos\dfrac{1}{x} =$

(A) 0

(B) 1

(C) -1

(D) Does not exist

29. $\lim\limits_{x \to 0} x^3 \cos\left(\dfrac{1}{x} \right) =$

(A) 0

(B) 1

(C) -1

(D) Does not exist

30. If $\lim\limits_{x \to \infty} \dfrac{f(x)}{g(x)} = \infty$, then for sufficiently large values of x,

(A) $f(x) \gg g(x)$

(B) $g(x) \gg f(x)$

(C) $\lim\limits_{x \to \infty} f(x) = \lim\limits_{x \to \infty} g(x) = \infty$

(D) None of the above

CALCULUS AB/BC

SECTION I, Part B

Time – 45 minutes
Number of problems – 15

A graphing calculator is required for these problems.

For Questions 1–4, use $f(x) = \begin{cases} x^2, & x \neq 2 \\ 2, & x = 2 \end{cases}$.

1. $f(2) =$

   (A) 0

   (B) 1

   (C) 2

   (D) 4

2. $\lim\limits_{x \to 2^-} f(x) =$

   (A) 0

   (B) 1

   (C) 2

   (D) 4

3. $\lim\limits_{x \to 2^+} f(x) =$

   (A) 0

   (B) 1

   (C) 2

   (D) 4

4. $\lim\limits_{x \to 2} f(x) =$

   (A) 0

   (B) 1

   (C) 2

   (D) 4

For Questions 5–8, use $f(x) = \begin{cases} e^x, & x < 1 \\ \ln x, & x \geq 1 \end{cases}$

5. $f(1) =$

   (A) 0

   (B) 1

   (C) e

   (D) Does not exist

6. $\lim\limits_{x \to 1^-} f(x) =$

   (A) 0

   (B) 1

   (C) e

   (D) Does not exist

7. $\lim\limits_{x \to 1^+} f(x) =$

   (A) 0

   (B) 1

   (C) e

   (D) Does not exist

8. $\lim\limits_{x \to 1} f(x) =$

   (A) 0

   (B) 1

   (C) e

   (D) Does not exist

For Questions 9–13, use $f(x) = \begin{cases} x + 3, & x < 0 \\ x - 3, & x \geq 0 \end{cases}$.

9. $\lim\limits_{x \to 0^-} f(x) =$

   (A) -3

   (B) 0

   (C) 1

   (D) 3

10. $\lim\limits_{x \to 0^+} f(x) =$

   (A) -3

   (B) 0

   (C) 1

   (D) 3

11. $\lim\limits_{x \to 0} f(x) =$

(A) -3

(B) 0

(C) 1

(D) Does not exist

12. $\lim\limits_{x \to 1} f(x) =$

(A) -2

(B) -1

(C) 1

(D) Does not exist

13. $\lim\limits_{x \to -2} f(x) =$

(A) -3

(B) 0

(C) 3

(D) Does not exist

14. Evaluate $\lim\limits_{x \to 0} \dfrac{\sin x}{7x}$.

(A) 0

(B) $\dfrac{1}{7}$

(C) 1

(D) 7

15. Find the value of $\lim\limits_{x \to 2^-} \dfrac{2x}{x - 2}$.

(A) $-\infty$

(B) $\dfrac{1}{2}$

(C) 1

(D) 2

CALCULUS AB/BC

SECTION II, Part A

Time – 30 minutes
Number of problems – 2

A graphing calculator is required for these problems.

1. (a) Graph $f(x) = \begin{cases} x + 2, & x < 0 \\ \sqrt{x} + 2, & 0 \le x < 4. \\ \ln x, & x \ge 4 \end{cases}$

   (b) Use the graph to determine

   - $f(0)$
   - $\lim\limits_{x \to 0} f(x)$
   - $f(4)$
   - $\lim\limits_{x \to 4} f(x)$

2. (a) Graph $f(x) = \dfrac{x + 3}{x - 3}$.

   (b) Use ⬛TABLE⬛ to find:

   - $\lim\limits_{x \to 3^-} f(x)$
   - $\lim\limits_{x \to 3^+} f(x)$
   - $\lim\limits_{x \to \infty} f(x)$
   - $\lim\limits_{x \to -\infty} f(x)$

   (c) State the zeros and asymptotes of $f(x)$.

   (d) Is $f(x)$ even, odd, or neither? Use your calculator to determine the answer.

   (e) Does $f(x)$ have an inverse? If yes, find the inverse and graph it. If not, explain why.

Main Idea 1: Limits
Summary Assessment

A graphing calculator is not permitted for these problems.

1. $f(x) = \begin{cases} kx + 1, x < 1 \\ x^2, \quad x \geq 1 \end{cases}$

   (a) Find the value of k so that $f(x)$ is continuous at $x = 1$.

   (b) Using the value of k found in part (a), sketch the graph of $f(x)$.

2. Use the special trigonometric limits to find the value of each of the following:

   (a) $\lim\limits_{x \to 0} \dfrac{\tan x}{x}$

   (b) $\lim\limits_{x \to 0} \dfrac{\sin^2 x}{x}$

   (c) $\lim\limits_{x \to 0} \dfrac{\cos^2 x}{x}$

   (d) $\lim\limits_{x \to 0} \dfrac{x^2}{\sin x}$

3. (a) Graph $f(x) = \dfrac{x}{x^2 - 1}$.

   (b) Use the graph to determine:

   - $\lim\limits_{x \to 1^+} f(x)$

   - $\lim\limits_{x \to 1^-} f(x)$

   - $\lim\limits_{x \to -1^+} f(x)$

   - $\lim\limits_{x \to -1^-} f(x)$

   - $\lim\limits_{x \to \infty} f(x)$

   - $\lim\limits_{x \to -\infty} f(x)$

4. Find all the zeros, holes, and vertical and horizontal asymptotes of $f(x) = \dfrac{3x - 6}{x + 5}$.

CORRELATION CHART

Use the given charts to mark the questions you missed. Then go back and review the suggested lesson(s) to improve your understanding of the concepts.

Section I, Part A (No Calculator Allowed)

Missed?	Question Number	Review the information in...
	1	Lesson 2
	2	Lesson 2
	3	Lesson 2, Lesson 3
	4	Lesson 2, Lesson 3
	5	Lesson 3, Lesson 4
	6	Lesson 2
	7	Lesson 2
	8	Lesson 2
	9	Lesson 2
	10	Lesson 2, Lesson 3
	11	Lesson 1
	12	Lesson 1
	13	Lesson 1
	14	Lesson 1
	15	Lesson 4
	16	Lesson 4
	17	Lesson 2, Lesson 3
	18	Lesson 2, Lesson 3
	19	Lesson 2
	20	Lesson 1, Lesson 2, Lesson 5
	21	Lesson 1
	22	Lesson 1
	23	Lesson 2, Lesson 5
	24	Lesson 2, Lesson 5
	25	Lesson 4
	26	Lesson 3
	27	Lesson 3
	28	Lesson 2, Lesson 3
	29	Lesson 3, Lesson 5
	30	Lesson 5

Section I, Part B (Calculator Required)

Missed?	Question Number	Review the information in...
	1	Lesson 4
	2	Lesson 4
	3	Lesson 4
	4	Lesson 3, Lesson 4
	5	Lesson 4
	6	Lesson 4
	7	Lesson 4
	8	Lesson 3, Lesson 4
	9	Lesson 4
	10	Lesson 4
	11	Lesson 3, Lesson 4
	12	Lesson 3, Lesson 4
	13	Lesson 3, Lesson 4
	14	Lesson 2, Lesson 3
	15	Lesson 2

Section II, Part A (Calculator Required)

Missed?	Question Number	Review the information in...
	1(a)	Lesson 3, Lesson 4
	1(b)	
	2(a)	Lesson 1, Lesson 2, Lesson 3
	2(b)	
	2(c)	
	2(d)	
	2(e)	

Section II, Part B (No Calculator Allowed)

Missed?	Question Number	Review the information in...
	1(a)	Lesson 4
	1(b)	
	2(a)	Lesson 2
	2(b)	
	2(c)	
	2(d)	
	3(a)	Lesson 1, Lesson 3
	3(b)	
	4	Lesson 1

Main Idea 2
Derivatives

Lesson 1: Average and Instantaneous Rates of Change

- The Average Rate of Change of a Function on an Interval
- Instantaneous Rate of Change of a Function and the Definition of a Derivative

You've been calculating averages since the time you knew how to add and divide. In fact, as a student, finding averages is key to determining your course grades, the score you must earn on a test to maintain or raise your current grade, and so on. But averages play an important role in the foundation of calculus. We know from previous math courses that we can calculate the average rate of change of a function over a given interval, which we will review below. But how do we calculate the instantaneous rate of change? For example, if an object is moving at a certain speed over a given time interval, how quickly is the object moving at exactly time t? We explore this idea and other related concepts in this Main Idea.

Explain: Calculating and Interpreting Average Rate of Change

The **average rate of change** of a function $f(x)$ on an interval $[a, b]$ is found by computing the slope of the line joining the endpoints of the function on that interval, as pictured on the top of the next page.

The average rate of change of $f(x)$ on $[a, b] = \dfrac{f(b) - f(a)}{b - a}$.

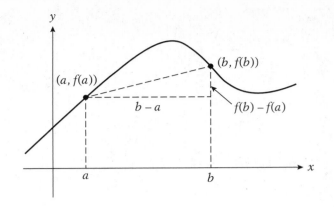

MODEL PROBLEMS

FR **1.** Find the average rate of change of $f(x) = x^2$ on the interval $[-1, 2]$.

Solution

$$\frac{f(2) - f(-1)}{2 - (-1)} = \frac{4 - 1}{2 + 1} = \frac{3}{3} = 1$$

We calculate using the formula on page 107.

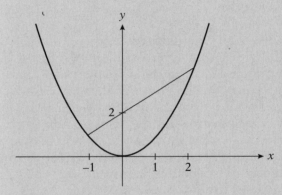

Note that the average rate of change is positive over the given interval. This means the function must be increasing at some values in the interval.

2. Find the average rate of change of $g(x) = x^3$ on the interval $[-2, 2]$.

(A) 8

(B) 0

(C) 4

(D) −16

Solution

This question is very similar to Model Problem #1. Calculate the average rate of change using the formula.

Explain: Instantaneous Rate of Change of a Function and the Definition of a Derivative

In the last section, we defined the average rate of change of a function over an interval as $\dfrac{f(b) - f(a)}{b - a}$. There are two other equivalent means by which we may express this idea:

$$\frac{f(a + h) - f(a)}{h}$$

and

$$\frac{f(x) - f(a)}{x - a}.$$

But what if we'd like to know exactly how quickly a function is changing at a specific point, say $x = a$? That is the **instantaneous rate of change** of $f(x)$ at $x = a$. To calculate this value, we take the limit of either formula given above.

$$\lim_{h \to 0} \frac{f(a + h) - f(a)}{h}$$

or

$$\lim_{x \to a} \frac{f(x) - f(a)}{x - a}.$$

When we find the limit of a function using these formulas, we are finding the derivative of the function, which is denoted $f'(a)$. We practice applying this derivative definition to several different types of functions below.

MODEL PROBLEMS

1. Use the definition of the derivative to find a formula for the derivative of $f(x) = x^2$.

(A) $f'(x) = x^3$

(B) $f'(x) = 2x + h$

(C) $f'(x) = 2x$

(D) $f'(x) = 2x^3 + h$

Solution

$f'(a) = \lim\limits_{h \to 0} \dfrac{f(a + h) - f(a)}{h}$	Use the definition of the derivative.
$f'(x) = \lim\limits_{h \to 0} \dfrac{(x + h)^2 - x^2}{h}$	Substitute.
$f'(x) = \lim\limits_{h \to 0} \dfrac{x^2 + 2xh + h^2 - x^2}{h}$	Expand.

$f'(x) = \lim_{h \to 0} \dfrac{2xh + h^2}{h}$ $f'(x) = \lim_{h \to 0} \dfrac{\cancel{h}(2x + h)}{\cancel{h}}$ $f'(x) = \lim_{h \to 0}(2x + h) = 2x$	Simplify. The derivative of $f(x) = x^2$ is $f'(x) = 2x$. The correct answer is (C).

2. Find the derivative of $f(x) = 3x^2$ using the limit definition.

(A) $f'(x) = 3x^3$

(B) $f'(x) = 6x + h$

(C) $f'(x) = 6x^2 + h$

(D) $f'(x) = 6x$

Solution

This is very similar to Model Problem #1. Be careful with your substitutions, expansions, and simplifications as you move through your calculations.

FR 3. Find the derivative of $f(x) = x^2 + x$ using the limit definition.

Solution

The correct substitution is $\lim_{h \to 0} \dfrac{(x + h)^2 + x + h - (x^2 + x)}{h}$. You try solving from here.

FR 4. Find the derivative of $f(x) = \sin x$ using the limit definition.

Solution

$\lim_{h \to 0} \dfrac{\sin(x + h) - \sin(x)}{h}$	Substitute.
$\lim_{h \to 0} \dfrac{[\sin(x)\cos(h) + \cos(x)\sin(h)] - \sin(x)}{h}$	Utilize the angle-sum identity (you didn't forget that, did you?).
$\lim_{h \to 0} \dfrac{\cos(x)\sin(h) - \sin(x) + \sin(x)\cos(h)}{h}$	Do a bit of rearranging.
$\lim_{h \to 0} \dfrac{\cos(x)\sin(h) - \sin(x) \cdot (1 - \cos(h))}{h}$	Factor.

See if you can continue solving from this point. Consider that we are only concerned with the limit of the function as h goes to 0, not as both x and h go to 0.

FR 5. Find the derivative of $f(x) = \cos x$ using the limit definition.

Solution

The process to solve this problem is very similar to how Model Problem #4 was solved. Follow that model to determine the derivative of the trigonometric function using the limit definition.

6. Let g be the piecewise-defined linear function shown below. Which, if any, of the given statements are true?

$$g(x) = \begin{cases} 3x - 1 & \text{for } x < 2 \\ 3x - 4 & \text{for } x \geq 2 \end{cases}$$

I. $\lim\limits_{h \to 0^-} \dfrac{f(2 + h) - f(2)}{h} = 2$

II. $\lim\limits_{h \to 0^+} \dfrac{f(2 + h) - f(2)}{h} = 2$

III. $f'(2) = 2$

(A) None

(B) I only

(C) II only

(D) I, II, and III

Solution

Since this is a piecewise-defined function, we need to consider both the LHL and the RHL to see if they are the same. If they are, then the limit exists at that point and a derivative will also exist at that point. Use the limit definition of the derivative to determine which of the statements, if any, are true.

AP Calculus Exam-Type Questions

Multiple Choice Questions
No calculator permitted for these questions.

1. The average rate of change of $f(x) = 4x - x^2$ on the interval $[1, 3]$ is

(A) 2

(B) 1

(C) 0

(D) -1

2. The average rate of change of $f(x) = mx + b$ on the interval $[a, c]$ is

(A) 0

(B) 1

(C) m

(D) $\dfrac{mc - ma + 2b}{c - a}$

3. If $f(x) = 5, f'(x) =$

(A) 0

(B) 1

(C) 5

(D) $5x$

4. If $f(x) = 5x, f'(x) =$

(A) 0

(B) $\dfrac{1}{5}$

(C) 1

(D) 5

5. If $f(x) = 5x + 5$, then $f'(x) =$

   (A) -1

   (B) 0

   (C) 1

   (D) 5

6. What is the instantaneous rate of change at $x = 2$ of the function f given by $f(x) = \dfrac{x^2 - 2}{x - 1}$?

   (A) -2

   (B) $\dfrac{1}{6}$

   (C) $\dfrac{1}{2}$

   (D) 2

7. Find the value of $\displaystyle\lim_{h \to 0} \dfrac{\tan\left(\frac{\pi}{4} + h\right) - \tan\left(\frac{\pi}{4}\right)}{h}$.

   (A) -1

   (B) 0

   (C) 1

   (D) 2

8. What is $\displaystyle\lim_{h \to 0} \dfrac{8\left(\frac{1}{2} + h\right)^8 - 8\left(\frac{1}{2}\right)^8}{h}$?

   (A) 0

   (B) $\dfrac{1}{2}$

   (C) 1

   (D) 2

9. $\displaystyle\lim_{x \to \frac{\pi}{4}} \dfrac{\sin\left(x - \frac{\pi}{4}\right)}{x - \frac{\pi}{4}}$ is

   (A) 0

   (B) $\dfrac{1}{\sqrt{2}}$

   (C) 1

   (D) $\dfrac{\pi}{4}$

10. If $f(x) = 2 + |x - 3|$ for all x, then the value of the derivative of $f(x)$ at $x = 3$ is

   (A) -1

   (B) Does not exist

   (C) 0

   (D) 2

11. If $f(x) = x + \sin x$, then $f'(x) =$

   (A) $1 + \cos x$

   (B) $1 - \cos x$

   (C) $\cos x$

   (D) $\sin x + \cos x$

12. If $f(x) = \dfrac{x - 1}{x + 1}$ for all $x \neq -1$, then $f'(1) =$

   (A) $-\dfrac{1}{2}$

   (B) -1

   (C) $\dfrac{1}{2}$

   (D) 0

Free Response Questions

A graphing calculator is required for some questions.

1. (a) Sketch the graph of $f(x) = 4x - x^2$ on $[0, 4]$.

   (b) Complete the following table by estimating the slope of the tangent to $f(x)$ at each of the values of x.

x	0	1	2	3	4
Slope					

   (c) Plot the points in the table and sketch a curve that connects the points.

2. (a) Find the average rate of change of $f(x) = 4x - x^2$ on each of the following intervals.

    i. $[0, 2]$

    ii. $[1, 3]$

    iii. $[2, 4]$

   (b) Find an approximate value of x so that the slope of the tangent to $f(x)$ at $(x, f(x))$ has the same value as your answers to i, ii, and iii.

3. Use the definition of the derivative to find $f'(x)$ if $f(x) = 5x^2$.

4. Use the definition of the derivative to find $f'(x)$ if $f(x) = 5x^2 + 5x + 5$.

Lesson 2: Derivative Notation and Basic Calculation

- Notation
- Basic Derivative Rules
- Derivative Rules for Exponential and Logarithmic Functions
- Trigonometric and Inverse Trigonometric Rules
- Rules for Deriving Sums, Products, and Quotients

Explain: Notation

In Lesson 2.1, we explained that the derivative is the instantaneous rate of change of a function at a given value. We can also describe the derivative as the limit of the difference quotient. There are several notations we can use to indicate the derivative, which are listed below.

$f'(x)$	We read this as "f prime of x."
$\dfrac{dy}{dx}$	This notation is read as "the derivative of y with respect to x," and is also known as **Leibniz notation.**
y'	Read this notation as "y-prime."

In most cases, we can use notations interchangeably.

Explain: Basic Derivative Rules

For the remainder of this lesson, we review the rules for finding the derivatives of different types of functions (for direct practice with the chain rule and implicit differentiation, see Lesson 2.3). To be successful on the AP exam you should memorize these rules for finding derivatives.

Constant Rule   If $f(x) = c$, a constant, then $f'(x) = 0$

Power Rule $(x^n)' = nx^{n-1}$

Sum and Difference Rule $(f(x) \pm g(x))' = f'(x) \pm g'(x)$

Generalized Power Rule   Let $P(x)$ be a function. Then,

$$\left((P(x))^n\right)' = nP(x)^{n-1} \cdot P'(x)$$

The generalized power rule is an extension, sometimes called special case, of the chain rule (Lesson 2.3). It is very useful for finding the derivative of a function that is raised to the nth power.

MODEL PROBLEMS

1. Find the derivative of $f(x) = (2x^2)^3$.

(A) $12x^4$

(B) $8x^6$

(C) $48x^5$

(D) $36x^6$

Solution

There are two different ways we can solve this question.

Method 1   Simplify and apply the Power Rule.

$$f(x) = (2x^2)^3$$

$$f(x) = 8x^6$$

$$f'(x) = 48x^5$$

Method 2   Apply the Generalized Power Rule.

$$f(x) = (2x^2)^3$$

$$f'(x) = 3(2x^2)^2 \cdot f'(2x^2)$$

$$f'(x) = 12x^4 \cdot 4x$$

$$f'(x) = 48x^5$$

Using either method, the correct answer is (C).

2. Find the derivative of $f(x) = (x^5 + 3x)^8$.

(A) $8(x^5 + 3x)^7 \cdot (5x^4 + 3)$

(B) $8(x^5 + 3x)^8 \cdot (5x^4 + 3x)$

(C) $(8x^5 + 3x)^7 \cdot (5x^4 + 3x)$

(D) $(8x^5 + 3x^7)^7 \cdot (5x + 3)$

Solution

For this problem you must use the Generalized Power Rule. Follow the formula given and solve.

3. Find the derivative of $f(x) = \dfrac{1}{x+1}$.

(A) $-\ln(x + 1)$

(B) $-\dfrac{1}{x+1}$

(C) $-\dfrac{1}{(x+1)^3}$

(D) $-(x+1)^{-2}$

Solution

Consider rewriting the given function as $(x + 1)^{-1}$. Now which rule can you apply to find the derivative?

Explain: Derivative Rules for Exponential and Logarithmic Functions

Here are the rules for finding the derivatives of exponential and logarithmic functions.

Exponential Rules

$(e^x)' = e^x$

$(e^{f(x)})' = e^{f(x)} \cdot f'(x)$

$(a^x)' = a^x \ln a$

$(a^{f(x)})' = a^{f(x)} \cdot f'(x) \ln a$

Logarithmic Rules

$(\ln x)' = \dfrac{1}{x}$

$(\ln f(x))' = \dfrac{1}{f(x)} \cdot f'(x)$

$(\log_a x)' = \dfrac{1}{x \ln a}$

$(\log_a f(x))' = \dfrac{1}{f(x) \ln a} \cdot f'(x)$

MODEL PROBLEMS

1. What is the derivative of $f(x) = 6^{3x+2}$?

(A) $f'(x) = (\ln 6) \cdot 6^3$

(B) $f'(x) = 3(\ln 6) \cdot 6^{3x+2}$

(C) $f'(x) = (\ln 6) \cdot 6^{3x+2}$

(D) $f'(x) = 18 (\ln \cdot 6)^{3x+2}$

Solution

$(a^{f(x)})' = a^{f(x)} \cdot f'(x) \ln a$	We look at the Exponential Rules to see which one fits our function. In this case $f(x) = 3x + 2$ and $a = 6$.
$f'(x) = 6^{3x+2}(3x + 2)' \cdot \ln 6$	Substitute.
$f'(x) = 6^{3x+2}(3) \cdot \ln 6$ $f'(x) = 3(\ln 6) \cdot 6^{3x+2}$	Simplify and rewrite. The correct answer is (B).

2. Find the derivative of $f(x) = e^{x^2}$.

(A) e^{x^2}

(B) $2xe^{x^2}$

(C) $e^{x^2} \cdot \ln 2$

(D) $x^2 e^{x^2}$

Solution

Examine the Exponential Rules on page 115. Which of them most closely matches the given function? Use that rule to solve for the derivative.

3. Find the derivative of $f(x) = \log_2(4x - 9)$.

(A) $f'(x) = \dfrac{1}{4x - 9}$

(B) $f'(x) = \dfrac{4}{4x - 9}$

(C) $f'(x) = \dfrac{1}{4x + 9 \cdot \ln 2}$

(D) $f'(x) = \dfrac{4}{(4x - 9) \cdot \ln 2}$

Solution

Although this derivative involves a logarithm rather than an exponential function, we use the same process to determine how to find its derivative. Of the Logarithmic Rules on page 115, which most closely matches the given function?

4. What is the derivative of $f(x) = \ln(x^2 + x)$?

(A) $\dfrac{1}{x^2 + x}$

(B) $\dfrac{1}{(x^2 + x) \cdot \ln e}$

(C) $\dfrac{2x + 1}{x^2 + x}$

(D) $\dfrac{1}{2x \cdot \ln e}$

Solution

Be sure to use the correct logarithmic rule.

Explain: Trigonometric and Inverse Trigonometric Rules

The following are the rules for finding the derivative of both trigonometric and inverse trigonometric functions. It is important to recall that all trigonometric functions have an argument. For example, in $\sin(3x)$, $3x$ is the argument. In $\tan(x^2)$, x^2 is the argument. When taking trigonometric derivatives, it helps to remember that the argument always stays the same.

Trigonometric Rules

$(\sin x)' = \cos x$

$(\sin f(x))' = \cos f(x) \cdot f'(x)$

$(\cos x)' = -\sin x$

$(\cos f(x))' = -\sin f(x) \cdot f'(x)$

$(\tan x)' = \sec^2 x$

$(\tan f(x))' = \sec^2 f(x) \cdot f'(x)$

$(\cot x)' = -\csc^2 x$

$(\cot f(x))' = -\csc^2 f(x) \cdot f'(x)$

$(\sec x)' = \sec x \tan x$

$(\sec f(x))' = \sec f(x) \tan f(x) \cdot f'(x)$

$(\csc x)' = -\csc x \cot x$

$(\csc f(x))' = -\csc f(x) \cot (x) \cdot f'(x)$

Inverse Trigonometric Rules

$$(\arcsin x)' = \dfrac{1}{\sqrt{1 - x^2}}$$

$$(\arctan x)' = \dfrac{1}{1 + x^2}$$

MODEL PROBLEMS

1. Find the derivative of $f(x) = \sin(3x)$.

(A) $3\cos(3x)$

(B) $\cos(3x)$

(C) $-3\cos(3x)$

(D) $3\cos^2(3x)$

Solution

$f'(x) = \cos(3x) \cdot (3x)'$ $f'(x) = \cos(3x) \cdot 3$ $f'(x) = 3\cos(3x)$	The derivative of $\sin(f(x))$ is $\cos(f(x)) \cdot f'(x)$. We substitute and simplify. The correct answer is (A).

2. What is the derivative of $f(x) = \sec(e^x)$?

(A) $f'(x) = e^x \sec(e^x) \cdot \tan(e^x)$

(B) $f'(x) = e^x \sec^2(e^x)$

(C) $f'(x) = \sec(e^x) \cdot \tan(e^x)$

(D) $f'(x) = e^x \tan(e^x)$

Solution

The derivative of $\sec(f(x))$ is $\sec f(x) \tan f(x) \cdot f'(x)$. In this case, $f(x) = e^x$, which has a very simple derivative. You try solving from here.

3. The derivative of $f(x) = \tan(x^2)$ is

(A) $f'(x) = \sec^2(x^2)$

(B) $f'(x) = 2x\sec^2(x^2)$

(C) $f'(x) = 2x\csc^2(x^2)$

(D) $f'(x) = \tan^2(x^2)$

Solution

Which rule from page 116 should you use here?

Explain: Rules for Deriving Sums, Products, and Quotients

The last set of rules presented is the sum, product, and quotient rules for general functions. Many times, we will need to use these rules in conjunction with other derivative rules.

Sum and Difference Rule $(f(x) \pm g(x))' = f'(x) \pm g'(x)$

Product Rule $(f(x) \cdot g(x))' = f(x)g'(x) + g(x)f'(x)$

Quotient Rule $\left(\dfrac{f(x)}{g(x)}\right)' = \dfrac{g(x)f'(x) - f(x)g'(x)}{(g(x))^2}$

MODEL PROBLEMS

1. The derivative of $f(x) = x + \ln x$ is

(A) $f'(x) = \dfrac{1}{x}$

(B) $f'(x) = 1$

(C) $f'(x) = 1 + \dfrac{1}{x}$

(D) $f'(x) = \dfrac{1}{x + \ln x}$

Solution

$f'(x) = (x)' + (\ln x)'$ $f'(x) = 1 + \dfrac{1}{x}$	We will need to use the Sum Rule and a Logarithmic Rule. The answer is (C).

2. What is the derivative of $f(x) = x \ln x$?

(A) $f'(x) = 1$

(B) $f'(x) = 1 + \ln x$

(C) $f'(x) = \dfrac{1}{x}$

(D) $f'(x) = \dfrac{1}{x + \ln x}$

Solution

This problem is very similar to Model Problem #1. You will need to use the Product Rule and a Logarithmic Rule to solve for the derivative.

3. Find the derivative of $f(x) = \dfrac{\sin(x)}{x}$.

(A) $f'(x) = \dfrac{\cos(x) - x\sin(x)}{x^2}$

(B) $f'(x) = \dfrac{x\sin(x) - \cos(x)}{x^2}$

(C) $f'(x) = \dfrac{\cos(x) + \sin(x)}{x^2}$

(D) $f'(x) = \dfrac{x\cos(x) - \sin(x)}{x^2}$

AP Calculus Exam-Type Questions

Multiple Choice Questions
No calculator is allowed for these questions.

1. Find the derivative of $y = (x^3 + x)^5$.

   (A) $3x^2 + 1$

   (B) $5(x^3 + x)^4$

   (C) $(15x^2 + 5)(x^3 + x)^4$

   (D) $5(3x^2 + 1)$

2. Find the derivative of $y = 6\ln\left(\dfrac{1}{x^2}\right)$.

   (A) -6

   (B) $-\dfrac{12}{x^3}$

   (C) $\dfrac{6}{x}$

   (D) $-\dfrac{12}{x}$

3. Find the derivative of $f(x) = \ln(x^2 + 2x + 1)$.

   (A) $\dfrac{2x}{x^2 + 2x + 1}$

   (B) $\dfrac{2}{x + 1}$

   (C) $\dfrac{1}{x^2 + 2x + 1}$

   (D) $\dfrac{1}{x + 1}$

4. Find the derivative of $y = \sin(x^2)$.

   (A) $2\sin x \cos x$

   (B) $2x \sin(x^2)$

   (C) $2x \sin x$

   (D) $2x \cos(x^2)$

5. If $y = \ln(\tan x)$, then $y' =$

   (A) $\dfrac{2}{\sin 2x}$

   (B) $\sec^2 x$

   (C) $\dfrac{1}{x \tan x}$

   (D) $\cot x$

6. If $y = e^{5x+5}$, then $y'(0) =$

   (A) e^5

   (B) 1

   (C) $5e^5$

   (D) 5

7. Find the derivative of $y = e^x \sin x$.

   (A) $e^x \cos x$

   (B) $e^x + \cos x$

   (C) $e^x(\sin x + \cos x)$

   (D) $\ln(\sin x)$

8. If $y = \sqrt{x^2 - 2x}$, then $y' =$

   (A) $\dfrac{1}{2}(x^2 - 2x)$

   (B) $\dfrac{1}{2}(x^2 - 2x)^{-\frac{1}{2}}$

   (C) $(x^2 - 2x)^{-\frac{1}{2}}(x - 1)$

   (D) $x - 1$

9. If $f(x) = \cos x$ and $g(x) = \sqrt{x}$, the derivative of $f \circ g(x)$ is equal to

(A) $-\sin \sqrt{x}$

(B) $\sin \sqrt{x}$

(C) $-\dfrac{\sin x}{2\sqrt{x}}$

(D) $-\dfrac{\sin \sqrt{x}}{2\sqrt{x}}$

10. Find the derivative of $y = \tan(x^2)$ is

(A) $\sec^2(x^2)$
(B) $2x \sec^2(x^2)$
(C) $2x \sec(x^2)$
(D) $\sec(x^2)$

11. If $y = \ln e^{\tan^2 x}$, find $y'\left(\dfrac{\pi}{4}\right)$.

(A) 1
(B) 2
(C) $2\sqrt{2}$
(D) 4

12. $(\arctan(3x))' =$

(A) $\dfrac{3}{1 + 3x^2}$

(B) $\dfrac{3}{1 + x^2}$

(C) $\dfrac{3}{1 + 9x^2}$

(D) $\dfrac{1}{1 + 9x^2}$

13. $\dfrac{d}{dx}(\arcsin(x^2)) =$

(A) $\dfrac{x^2}{\sqrt{1 - x^4}}$

(B) $\dfrac{2x}{\sqrt{1 - x^4}}$

(C) $\dfrac{2x}{\sqrt{1 - x^2}}$

(D) $\dfrac{1}{\sqrt{1 - x^4}}$

Free Response Questions

A graphing calculator is required for some questions.

1. (a) Enter $Y_1 = \sqrt{x^2 + 2x + 1}$ in $\boxed{Y=}$ on a graphing calculator, and sketch the graph. Note that on the **TI-*nspire***, the square root icon can be accessed using $\boxed{\text{CTRL}} + \boxed{x^2}$ or press the equation template button and select the square root icon.

(b) Write another name for this function.

(c) Enter the derivative of Y_1 into Y_2 and graph as follows:
TI–83: $Y_2 = \boxed{\text{MATH}}$ 8 nDeriv(Y_1, x, x).
Change $\boxed{\text{MODE}}$ from Connected to Dot and graph in $\boxed{\text{ZOOM}}$ 4.
TI–89: $Y_2 = d(Y_1(x), x)$. In $\boxed{Y=}$, change F6: Style to Dot.
TI-*nspire*: The derivative template is located in the equation template.

(d) Explain the relationship between the graph of Y_1 and graph of Y_2.

2. Sketch the derivative of
$$f(x) = \begin{cases} x^2 + 2x, & x < 1 \\ 4x, & x \geq 1 \end{cases}$$

(a) by hand.
(b) on the graphing calculator.
(c) Is $f'(x)$ continuous at $x = 1$? Explain why or why not.

3. Find the derivative of $y = (x^2 + 1)(x^3 + 1)$

(a) by using the Product Rule.
(b) by multiplying first.
(c) Compare the results of parts (a) and (b).

Lesson 3: The Chain Rule, Implicit Differentiation, and L'Hôpital's Rule

- The Chain Rule
- Inverse Functions and Their Derivatives
- Implicit Differentiation
- Finding Limits Using L'Hôpital's Rule

Explain: The Chain Rule

We open this lesson with the formal definition of the chain rule. Suppose that we have two functions, $f(x)$ and $g(x)$, which are both differentiable. If $F(x) = (f \circ g)(x)$ then $F'(x) = f'(g(x)) \cdot g'(x)$. In less mathematical terms, we say that the derivative of a function composition is the derivative of the outer function, evaluated at the inner function, multiplied by the derivative of the inner function. Most students find the chain rule somewhat cumbersome to understand and work with. The key to using the chain rule successfully lies with identifying a function composition and then determining which function is the inner function and which is the outer function. We demonstrate in the model problems below.

MODEL PROBLEMS

1. What is the derivative of $h(x) = \sin(4x^2 + 2x)$?

(A) $h'(x) = \cos(4x^2 + 2x) \cdot (8x + 2)$

(B) $h'(x) = \cos(8x + 2) \cdot (8x + 2)$

(C) $h'(x) = \sin(8x + 2) \cdot (8x + 2)$

(D) $h'(x) = \sin(8x + 2) \cdot (4x^2 + 2x)$

Solution

First, recognize that this is a composition of the sine function and $4x^2 + 2x$. In this case, the outer function is the sine function and the inner function is the binomial. So,

$f(x) = \sin(x) \qquad g(x) = 4x^2 + 2x$ $f'(x) = \cos(x) \qquad g'(x) = 8x + 2$	We find the derivative of both the inner and outer functions.
$h'(x) = f'(g(x)) \cdot g'(x)$ $h'(x) = \cos(4x^2 + 2x) \cdot (8x + 2)$	Substitute the expressions into the definition of the chain rule. The correct option is (A).

2. Find the derivative of $f(t) = e^{t^3 + 2t^2 - 3}$.

(A) $f'(t) = (3t^2 + 4t)(e^{3t^2 + 4t})$

(B) $f'(t) = (t^3 + 2t^2 - 3)(e^{3t^2 + 4t})$

(C) $f'(t) = (3t^2 + 4t)(e^{t^3 + 2t^t - 3})$

(D) $f'(t) = 3t^2(e^{t^3 + 2t^t - 3})$

Solution

This is a composition of functions, where the inside function is $t^3 + 2t^2 - 3$ and the outside function is e^x. You try finding the derivative from this point.

3. The derivative of $g(x) = \ln(x^{-2} + x^2)$ is

(A) $g'(x) = \dfrac{x^{-2} + x^2}{-2x^{-3} + 2x}$

(B) $g'(x) = \dfrac{1}{x^{-2} + x^2}$

(C) $g'(x) = \dfrac{2x^{-3} - 2x}{x^{-2} + x^2}$

(D) $g'(x) = \dfrac{-2x^{-3} + 2x}{x^{-2} + x^2}$

Solution

Because we are practicing the chain rule, we can be confident this is a composition of functions. Identify the inner and outer functions and find the derivative.

FR **4.** If $F(x) = \sin\big(\ln(x^2 + 3x - 4)\big)$, what is $F'(x)$?

Solution

For this question, you will need to utilize the chain rule more than once.

You may have noticed the chain rule extensions of the power rule, exponential rule, logarithmic rule, and trigonometric rules presented without comment in Lesson 2.2. While some students find it simpler to memorize chain rule extensions, other students find it easier to understand the chain rule itself, and then apply it as needed to different function compositions. We chose to present the chain rule in this manner to allow students the freedom to choose the method that will be most helpful to them, not only on the AP exam, but also throughout their ongoing study of calculus.

Explain: Inverse Functions and Their Derivatives

Recall from previous math courses that if $f(x)$ and $g(x)$ are inverse functions then $f(g(x)) = x$. Suppose that we take the derivative of each side of this equation. Then,

$$\frac{d}{dx} f(g(x)) = \frac{d}{dx}(x)$$

and, using the chain rule,

$$f'(g(x)) \cdot g'(x) = 1.$$

From this, we can conclude that $g'(x) = \dfrac{1}{f'(g(x))}$.

MODEL PROBLEMS

TI **1.** $f(x) = \sqrt{x-4}$ and $g(x)$ is the inverse of $f(x)$. Find $g'(1)$.

(A) $\dfrac{1}{3}$

(B) 2

(C) 5

(D) $\dfrac{1}{2}$

Solution

There are several ways we can find $g'(1)$. We will apply the formula above: $g'(1) = \dfrac{1}{f'(g(1))}$. Since we know that $f(x)$ and $g(x)$ are inverses, $g(1)$ is the value in the domain of $f(x)$ that makes $f(x) = 1$. Thus, $g(1) = 5$ and $g'(1) = \dfrac{1}{f'(5)}$. We solve for $f'(x) = \dfrac{1}{2\sqrt{x-4}}$ and $f'(5) = \dfrac{1}{2}$. Therefore $g'(1) = \dfrac{1}{\frac{1}{2}} = 2$. The correct answer is (B).

2. $f(x)$ and $g(x)$ are inverses, and $f(x) = \sqrt{x^3 + 1}$. Find $g'(3)$.

(A) $\dfrac{1}{4}$

(B) 2

(C) 4

(D) $\dfrac{1}{2}$

Solution

Set up this problem similarly to how we solved Model Problem #1. In this case, $g'(3) = \dfrac{1}{f'(g(3))}$.

3. $f(x) = \tan x$. If $g(x)$ is the inverse of $f(x)$, find $g'(1)$.

(A) $\dfrac{1}{5}$

(B) 2

(C) 5

(D) $\dfrac{1}{2}$

Solution

You are looking to find the value $g'(1) = \dfrac{1}{f'(g(1))}$. In this problem, you need to pay attention to the domain of the tangent function, which is restricted to the interval $\left(-\dfrac{\pi}{2}, \dfrac{\pi}{2}\right)$.

Explain: Implicit Differentiation

Most of the functions in calculus are given in the form $f(x) =$ or $y = $. These functions are *explicit* functions of the variable. However, we often study equations that do not have an explicit form and may not even be functions. For example, we study the equation of a circle centered at the origin with standard form $x^2 + y^2 = r^2$. In this example, y is related to x *implicitly*. This means that given a value x, we can find the corresponding y-value(s), but we cannot always solve for y as an explicit function of x. When y is an implicit function of x, we use **implicit differentiation** to find y' or $\dfrac{dy}{dx}$.

At this point, we want to note that the chain rule is the basis for implicit differentiation and can be used in place of implicit differentiation. The chain rule allows us to differentiate functions within functions while implicit differentiation is a way to find the derivative of a term with respect to a given variable without having to solve the equation for that variable. We do this by treating the second variable as a function of the first variable. We illustrate this concept with the model problems that follow.

MODEL PROBLEMS

FR 1. Find $\dfrac{dy}{dx}$ for the equation $x^2 + y^2 = r^2$.

Solution

In this case, we will use the notation $\dfrac{d}{dx}$ to be clear that we are differentiating with respect to x.

$\dfrac{d}{dx}\left(x^2 + y^2\right) = \dfrac{d}{dx}\left(r^2\right)$	We find the derivative of each side of the equation.
$\dfrac{d}{dx}\left(x^2\right) + \dfrac{d}{dx}\left(y^2\right) = 0$	Expand on the left-hand side and recall that r^2 is a constant.
$2x + \dfrac{d}{dx}\left(y^2\right) = 0$	We easily differentiate x^2, but what is $\dfrac{d}{dx}\left(y^2\right)$?
$\dfrac{d\left(y^2\right)}{dx} \cdot \dfrac{dy}{dx} = 2y\dfrac{dy}{dx} = $	Multiply the y^2 term by $\dfrac{dy}{dx}$.
$2x + 2y\dfrac{dy}{dx} = 0$ $\dfrac{dy}{dx} = -\dfrac{x}{y}$	Put it all together and then solve for $\dfrac{dy}{dx}$, which is in terms of both x and y.

Note that we could have solved this problem using the chain rule by solving the original equation for y such that $y = \pm\sqrt{r^2 - x^2}$ and then taking the derivative. However, unless you enjoy cumbersome algebra, implicit differentiation is a better solution strategy.

Explain: Finding Limits Using L'Hôpital's Rule

In Lesson x.x, we briefly touched on indeterminate forms of limits such as

$$\frac{0}{0}, \frac{\infty}{\infty}, -\frac{\infty}{\infty}, 0 \cdot \infty, \text{ or } \infty - \infty$$

and we stated that we could not find the limit of these functions at the given points using the methods discussed. It turns out, though, that we can find the limit of some of these functions using L'Hôpital's rule.

L'Hôpital's Rule

If

$$\lim_{x \to a} \frac{f(x)}{g(x)} = \frac{0}{0}, \frac{\infty}{\infty}, \text{ or } -\frac{\infty}{\infty}.$$

Then

$$\lim_{x \to a} \frac{f(x)}{g(x)} = \lim_{x \to a} \frac{f'(x)}{g'(x)}.$$

Tips for Using L'Hôpital's Rule

- Apply L'Hôpital's Rule ONLY when taking the limit of a quotient. If the expression is an indeterminate form, but not in the form of a quotient, it must first be rewritten in quotient form.

- Remember to take the derivative of the numerator and the derivative of the denominator when applying L'Hôpital's Rule. Do not use the quotient rule!

- Be sure to recheck each time L'Hôpital's Rule is applied to see if the result is still indeterminate. L'Hôpital's Rule may be applied more than once, but only if the limit results in an indeterminate form each time.

MODEL PROBLEMS

FR 1. Evaluate $\lim\limits_{x \to 5} \dfrac{x^2 - 5x}{x - 5}$.

Solution

In Lesson 1.2, we simply factored the numerator and then simplified to find the limit. But, since $\lim\limits_{x \to 5} \dfrac{5^2 - 25}{5 - 5} = \dfrac{0}{0}$, we can apply L'Hôpital's rule instead:

$\lim\limits_{x \to 5} \dfrac{2x - 5}{1} = 5$ Find the derivative of both the numerator and the denominator. The limit is 5.

2. Find the value of $\lim\limits_{x \to 0} \dfrac{2e^x - 2}{x}$.

(A) 0

(B) 2

(C) 1

(D) $\dfrac{1}{2}$

Solution

Substituting the value $x = 0$ into the limit gives the result $\dfrac{0}{0}$. Since this is an indeterminate form, we can apply L'Hôpital's rule. Find the derivative of both the numerator and the denominator and then evaluate the limit at $x = 0$.

3. Evaluate the limit of $\lim\limits_{x \to \infty} \dfrac{\ln x}{x}$, if it exists.

(A) 1

(B) $\dfrac{1}{2}$

(C) 0

(D) 2

Solution

Both $\ln x$ and x approach ∞ as $x \to \infty$, so the limit has the indeterminate form $\dfrac{\infty}{\infty}$. Apply L'Hôpital's rule to find the value of the limit.

4. Find $\lim\limits_{x \to 0^+} x^x$.

(A) 2

(B) $\dfrac{1}{2}$

(C) 1

(D) 0

Solution

In this case, the indeterminant form is 0^0. In order to apply L'Hôpital's rule, the limit must be written in the form of a quotient. We use the fact that $x^x = \lim_{x \to 0^+} e^{\ln x^x} = e^{x \ln x}$. So, $\lim_{x \to 0^+} x^x = \lim_{x \to 0^+} e^{x \ln x} = \lim_{x \to 0^+} e^{\lim_{x \to 0^+} x \ln x}$. The second piece of the equality uses the fact that e^x is a continuous function. Now,

$$\lim_{x \to 0^+} x \ln x = \lim_{x \to 0^+} \frac{\ln x}{\frac{1}{x}} = -\frac{\infty}{\infty} \qquad \text{Express } x \ln x \text{ as a quotient.}$$

Now that we have the indeterminant limit in quotient form, we can apply L'Hôpital's rule. You continue solving from here.

5. Find $\lim_{x \to \infty} \dfrac{x}{\sqrt{x^2 - 1}}$.

(A) 0

(B) 1

(C) 2

(D) ∞

Solution

Evaluating the limit as it is yields the indeterminant form $\frac{\infty}{\infty}$, so we apply L'Hôpital's rule.

$$\lim_{x \to \infty} \frac{x}{\sqrt{x^2 - 1}} =$$

$$\lim_{x \to \infty} \frac{\frac{1}{x}}{\sqrt{x^2 - 1}} = \lim_{x \to \infty} \frac{\sqrt{x^2 - 1}}{x}$$

Applying L'Hôpital's rule does not result in a numerical answer. Instead, we ended up with the reciprocal of the original expression. If we were to apply L'Hôpital's rule a second time, the result would be the original expression. We need to try another method.

$$\lim_{x \to \infty} \frac{x}{\sqrt{x^2 - 1}} =$$

Divide the numerator and denominator of the original expression by x.

$$\lim_{x \to \infty} \frac{\frac{x}{x}}{\frac{\sqrt{x^2 - 1}}{x}} = \lim_{x \to \infty} \frac{1}{\sqrt{\frac{x^2 - 1}{x^2}}} = 1$$

This model problem demonstrates that L'Hôpital's rule does not always give an answer for every indeterminate form. Sometimes we must also try algebraic methods of determining limits.

AP Calculus Exam-Type Questions

Multiple Choice Questions
No calculator allowed for these problems.

1. If $f(x) = \cos x$ and $g(x) = x^4$, the derivative of $g(f(x))$ is

   (A) $4 \sin x \cos^3 x$

   (B) $-4 \cos^3 x \sin x$

   (C) $4 \sin^3 x \cos x$

   (D) $-4 \sin^3 x \cos^2 x$

2. What is the derivative of $f(x) = \csc(2x)$?

   (A) $-2\sec(2x)$

   (B) $-2\csc(2x)\cot(2x)$

   (C) $-2\cot(2x)$

   (D) $-2\sec(2x)\cot(2x)$

3. The derivative of $e^{1-\cos(x)}$ is

   (A) $\sin(x)e^{1-\cos(x)}$

   (B) $\sin(x)e^{1-\sin(x)}$

   (C) $\cos(x)e^{1-\cos(x)}$

   (D) $-\sin(x)e^{1-\cos(x)}$

4. Find the derivative of $h(x) = x^2\ln(x^3)$.

   (A) $\ln(x^3) + 3x$

   (B) $-2x\ln(x^3)$

   (C) $2x\ln(x^3) + 3x$

   (D) $-\ln(x^3) + 6x$

5. If $f(x) = x^3$, where $x > 0$ and $g(x)$ is the inverse of $f(x)$, find $g'(-27)$.

   (A) $\frac{1}{9}$

   (B) 27

   (C) $\frac{1}{27}$

   (D) -27

6. If $f(x) = \ln x$ and $g(x)$ is the inverse of $f(x)$, find $g'(1)$.

   (A) 0

   (B) 1

   (C) e

   (D) $\frac{1}{e}$

7. $f(x) = \arcsin x$ and $g(x) = f^{-1}(x)$. Find $g'(0)$.

   (A) 0

   (B) 1

   (C) $\frac{\pi}{2}$

   (D) $\frac{2}{\pi}$

8. $g(x) = -\sqrt{x}$ and $f(x) = g^{-1}(x)$. Find $f'(-1)$.

   (A) -2

   (B) $-\frac{1}{2}$

   (C) $\frac{1}{2}$

   (D) 2

9. Find $\dfrac{dy}{dx}$ if $x^2 + y^2 = -2xy$.

   (A) 1

   (B) -1

   (C) $\dfrac{x - y}{x + y}$

   (D) $\dfrac{x + y}{x - y}$

10. Find the slope of the line tangent to the graph of $2xy^2 + xy = y$ when $y = 1$.

(A) $-\dfrac{9}{2}$

(B) $-\dfrac{2}{9}$

(C) $\dfrac{2}{9}$

(D) $\dfrac{1}{3}$

11. Evaluate $\lim\limits_{x \to 2} \dfrac{2x^2 - 8}{x - 2}$.

(A) 0

(B) 2

(C) 4

(D) 8

12. Find $\lim\limits_{x \to 1} \dfrac{x - 1}{1 - \sqrt{x}}$.

(A) -2

(B) $-\dfrac{1}{2}$

(C) $\dfrac{1}{2}$

(D) 2

13. Find the value of $\lim\limits_{x \to \infty} \dfrac{\sin x}{x}$.

(A) 0

(B) 1

(C) 2π

(D) ∞

14. If $f(x) = x^{1/x}$, find $\lim\limits_{x \to \infty} f(x)$.

(A) 0

(B) 1

(C) e

(D) ∞

Free Response Questions

A graphing calculator is required for some questions.

1. $f(x) = \sin x$.

(a) State the domain of $f(x)$ so that $f(x)$ has an inverse.

(b) Write an expression for $g(x) = f^{-1}(x)$, and state the domain and range of $g(x)$.

(c) Write an expression for $g'(x)$, and use it to show that $g'(x) = \dfrac{1}{f'(g(x))}$ for $x = \dfrac{1}{2}$.

2. $f(x) = 2x^2 - 3$ for $x \geq 0$.

(a) Is $f(x)$ one-to-one?

(b) If $g(x)$ is the inverse of $f(x)$, use the formula $g'(x) = \dfrac{1}{f'(g(x))}$ to find $g'(0)$.

(c) Find an algebraic expression for $g(x)$ and use it to confirm the answer in part (b).

3. Use the process of implicit differentiation to find $\dfrac{dy}{dx}$ for the equation $x^2 + y^2 + xy = 5$.

4. Evaluate each of the following limits:

i. $\lim\limits_{x \to \infty} \dfrac{x^{100}}{e^x}$

ii. $\lim\limits_{x \to \infty} \dfrac{e^x}{4^x}$

iii. $\lim\limits_{x \to \infty} \dfrac{\ln (100x)}{x}$

iv. $\lim\limits_{x \to \infty} \dfrac{x}{\sqrt{e^x}}$

Lesson 4: Derivatives and Their Graphs

- Determining and Understanding Increasing or Decreasing Behavior of Graphs
- Determining and Understanding Critical Values

Explain: Determining and Understanding Increasing or Decreasing Behavior of Graphs

Now that we have a handle on calculating derivatives, we turn to the interpretation of their graphs and compare those graphs to graphs of the original function. What can the value of the derivative tell us about the behavior of the function itself?

The derivative of a function describes the behavior of the function. On the graph of $y = f(x)$, the **derivative** of the function at x is the slope of the line tangent to the graph at the point $(x, f(x))$.

Recall that a line with a positive slope rises or increases (from left to right), and that a line with a negative slope falls or decreases (from left to right).

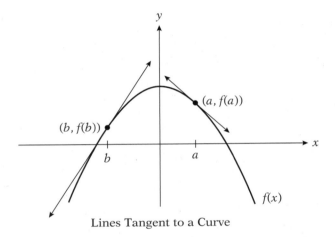

Lines Tangent to a Curve

Since the derivative of a function is the slope of the line tangent to the graph of the function, we can ascertain the following:

- If the derivative is positive at a value, the function is increasing.

- If the derivative is negative at a value, the function is decreasing.

- If the derivative is zero or undefined at a value, this value is called a **critical value** of the function.

- If the derivative equals zero, the tangent line at that value of the function is horizontal.

- If the derivative is undefined, there may be a vertical tangent or no tangent to the graph of the function at that value.

MODEL PROBLEMS

FR **1.** (a) Sketch the graph of the function $f(x) = x^2 - 2x$.

(b) State whether the following are positive, negative, or zero: the slope of the line tangent to the graph of $f(x)$

   i. at $x = 1$.

   ii. for $x < 1$.

   iii. for $x > 1$.

(c) Sketch the graph of the derivative.

Solution

(a)	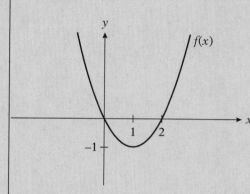	We sketch the graph of $f(x)$. It is a parabola with a vertex at the point $(1, -1)$.
(b)	i. $m = 0$	i. Since the vertex is located at $(1, -1)$, the slope of the tangent line at $x = 1$ is 0.
	ii. The slope is negative.	ii. The function is decreasing where $x < 1$.
	iii. The slope is positive.	iii. The function is increasing where $x > 1$.
(c)	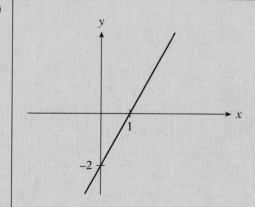	Based on the behavior of $f(x)$, we know that $f'(x)$ crosses the x-axis at $x = 1$, is below the x-axis for $x < 1$, and exists above the x-axis where $x > 1$. Note that the graph of the derivative of a quadratic function is linear.

FR **2.** (a) Sketch the graph of $f(x) = \sin(x)$ on the interval $[0, 2\pi]$.

(b) At what value(s) of x is the slope of the line tangent to the graph of $f(x)$ positive? At what value(s) is it negative? At what value(s) is it zero?

(c) Write a brief description of the graph of the derivative of $f(x)$ and sketch it.

Solution

(a)

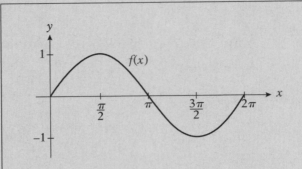

We sketch the graph of $f(x)$.

(b) The sine curve has two turning points on $[0, 2\pi]$, a high point at $x = \frac{\pi}{2}$ and a low point at $x = \frac{3\pi}{2}$. Thus, the slope of the tangent of $f(x)$ is zero at $x = \frac{\pi}{2}$ and at $x = \frac{3\pi}{2}$.

The slope of the tangent is positive at any point in the interval $\left(0, \frac{\pi}{2}\right)$ and at any point in the interval $\left(\frac{3\pi}{2}, 2\pi\right)$, where the function is increasing.

The slope of the tangent is negative at any point in the interval $\left(\frac{\pi}{2}, \frac{3\pi}{2}\right)$, where the function is decreasing.

(c) The graph of the derivative of $\sin x$ will cross the x-axis at $x = \frac{\pi}{2}$ and at $x = \frac{3\pi}{2}$. What is the graph's behavior below the x-axis? Above the x-axis?

FR **3.** (a) Sketch the graph of $f(x) = x^3$.

(b) At what value(s) of x is the slope of the line tangent to the graph of $f(x)$ positive? At what value(s) is it negative? At what value(s) is it zero?

(c) Write a brief description and sketch the graph of the derivative.

Solution

Use your knowledge of cubic functions and finding the derivative of a polynomial to answer this question. Be sure your graphs are appropriately labeled and easy to read.

Explain: Determining and Understanding Critical Values

We have seen that when the first derivative of a function is positive, the function is increasing, and when the first derivative of a function is negative, the function is decreasing. Note that the converse of this statement is not true.

If a function is increasing, its first derivative may be positive or it may be zero. For example, by the definition of an increasing function, $f(x) = x^3$ is strictly increasing. Yet its derivative is zero when $x = 0$.

Critical values are values in the domain of a function where its derivative is zero or is undefined. Critical values are candidates for the x-coordinates of the high and low points on the function. The corresponding y-coordinates of these points may be the **relative maxima** (the high points) or **relative minima** (the low points) of the function. Together these y-values are called **relative extrema** of the function.

Once the critical values have been found, use the following procedure to determine whether each critical number is a relative maximum, a relative minimum, or neither. Draw a number line, mark it f', and put the critical numbers on it. Next to the number line, make a table of values of x and f'. The x-values in the table are values to the left of, in between, and to the right of the critical numbers on the number line. The corresponding values in the f' column can be found by hand or by using TABLE in the calculator.

Using the numbers in the f' column, find the sign changes for each critical number. These sign changes determine the nature of each critical number. This is called the **First Derivative Test.**

The First Derivative Test

- If the sign of f' changes from positive to negative at a critical value, then f has a relative maximum at that value of x.

- If the sign of f' changes from negative to positive at a critical value, then f has a relative minimum at that value of x.

- If f' does not change sign at a critical value, then there is neither a relative minimum nor a relative maximum at that value of x.

After drawing the number line and completing the table of values of x and f', use the First Derivative Test to write a statement that identifies each critical value as a relative maximum, a relative minimum, or neither. This written statement is an important step in the justification of an answer.

MODEL PROBLEMS

FR **1.** (No calculator)

(a) Find the critical values of $f(x) = x^3 + 3x^2 + 4$, and identify each as a relative maximum, a relative minimum, or neither. Justify your answer.

(b) State the intervals where f is increasing.

Solution

(a)

$f(x) = x^3 + 3x^2 + 4$ $f'(x) = 3x^2 + 6x$ $3x^2 + 6x = 0$ $3x(x + 2) = 0$ $x = 0$ or $x = -2$	To find the critical values, find the derivative, set the derivative equal to zero, and solve for the variable. The critical values are $x = 0$ and $x = -2$.
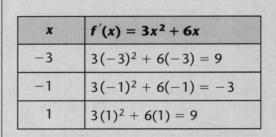 <table><tr><th>x</th><th>f'(x) = 3x² + 6x</th></tr><tr><td>−3</td><td>3(−3)² + 6(−3) = 9</td></tr><tr><td>−1</td><td>3(−1)² + 6(−1) = −3</td></tr><tr><td>1</td><td>3(1)² + 6(1) = 9</td></tr></table>	Next, we place the critical values on a number line labeled f', and then choose values of x for the table that are to the left of, in between, and to the right of the critical values. We use those values to calculate $f'(x)$.
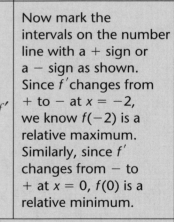	Now mark the intervals on the number line with a + sign or a − sign as shown. Since f' changes from + to − at $x = -2$, we know $f(-2)$ is a relative maximum. Similarly, since f' changes from − to + at $x = 0$, $f(0)$ is a relative minimum.

(b) Since f' is positive on the intervals to the left of -2 and to the right of 0, f is increasing on the intervals $(-\infty, -2)$ and $(0, \infty)$.

FR **2.** (a) The graph shown below is of f', the derivative of f. Using the graph, find the critical values of f, and identify each as a relative maximum, a relative minimum, or neither. Justify your answer.

(b) Use the graph of f' to state the intervals where f is increasing.

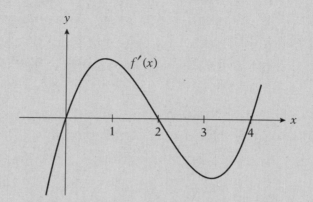

Solution

(a)
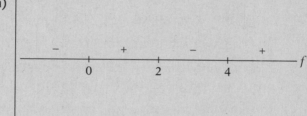

From the graph we can see that $f'(x) = 0$ at $x = 0$, $x = 2$, and $x = 4$. These are the critical values of $f(x)$.

(b) From the first derivative test, we conclude that:

Since f' changes from $-$ to $+$ at $x = 0$, $f(0)$ is a relative minimum.

Since f' changes from $+$ to $-$ at $x = 2$, $f(2)$ is a relative maximum.

Since f' changes from $-$ to $+$ at $x = 4$, $f(4)$ is a relative minimum.

Since f' is positive on the intervals between 0 and 2, and to the right of 4, f' is increasing on the intervals $(0, 2)$ and $(4, \infty)$.

FR **3.** (a) Given the graph of f' below, find the critical values of f and identify each as a relative maximum, a relative minimum, or neither. Justify your answer.

(b) Use the graph of f' to find the intervals where the graph of f is increasing.

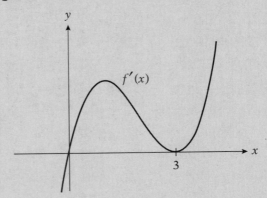

Solution

Remember that the critical values lie where the first derivative is equal to zero. In this case, the critical values are $x = 0$ and $x = 3$. Now determine if the graph is increasing or decreasing in those intervals and answer the questions.

FR **4.** (No calculator)

(a) Find the critical values of $f(x) = \sin(x) + \cos(x)$ on the interval $[0, 2\pi]$.

(b) Identify each critical value as a relative maximum, a relative minimum, or neither. Justify your answer.

(c) State the intervals where f is increasing on the interval $[0, 2\pi]$.

(d) Find the absolute maximum and the absolute minimum of $f(x)$ on $[0, 2\pi]$.

Solution

The derivative of this function is $f'(x) = \cos(x) - \sin(x)$. Remember that you are only looking for the critical values in the interval $[0, 2\pi]$. For part (d), recall that to solve for the absolute minimum and the absolute maximum, you need to find the $f(x)$ value for the critical points and the endpoints.

FR **5.** (No calculator)

(a) Find the critical values of $f(x) = e^x - x$.

(b) Identify each critical value as a relative maximum, a relative minimum, or neither. Justify your answer.

(c) State the intervals where f is increasing.

Solution

Follow the examples in the previous model problems to complete this question. Note that it is possible for a function to have only a single critical value.

AP Calculus Exam-Type Questions

Multiple Choice Questions

A graphing calculator is required for some questions.

1. Match the graphs of the functions I, II, and III to the graphs of their derivatives A, B and C.

I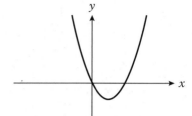

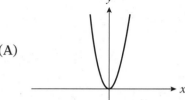

(A)

II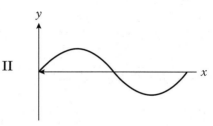

(B)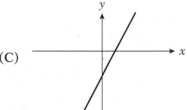

III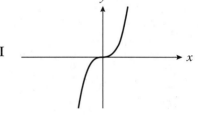

(C)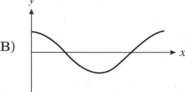

For questions 2 – 5, refer to the figure below.

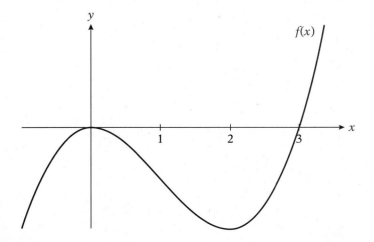

2. On what interval is $f(x)$ positive?

   (A) $(0, \infty)$

   (B) $[1, \infty)$

   (C) $[2, \infty)$

   (D) $(3, \infty)$

3. On what interval(s) is the slope of the tangent to the graph of $f(x)$ positive?

   (A) $(-\infty, 0)$ and $(2, \infty)$

   (B) $(-\infty, 0)$

   (C) $(0, 2)$

   (D) $(2, \infty)$

4. The critical value(s) of $f(x)$ is (are) $x =$

(A) 2

(B) 0 and 2

(C) 0

(D) 0 and 3

5. The graph of the derivative of $f(x) = 2x + 3$ is

(A) a horizontal line.

(B) a vertical line.

(C) a line with a positive slope.

(D) a line with a negative slope.

6. The derivative of $f(x) = -\frac{1}{2}x + 5$ has the equation

(A) $x = 0$

(B) $y = 0$

(C) $x = -\frac{1}{2}$

(D) $y = -\frac{1}{2}$

7. The graph of the derivative of $f(x) = x^2$ is

(A) a horizontal line.

(B) a vertical line.

(C) a line with positive slope.

(D) a line with negative slope.

8. The critical values of $f(x) = 9x^4 + 16x^3 + 6x^2 +$ are at $x =$

(A) 0 only.

(B) -1 and 0.

(C) -1 and $-\frac{1}{3}$.

(D) -1, $-\frac{1}{3}$, and 0.

9. The function $f(x) = e^x - x + 2$ has

(A) a relative minimum at $(0, 3)$.

(B) a relative minimum at $(0, 0)$.

(C) a relative maximum at $(0, 3)$.

(D) two critical values.

10. The relative minimum of the function $f(x) = 2x^3 - \frac{5}{2}x^2 - 4x + 2$ on the interval $[-1, 2]$ is at $x =$

(A) -1

(B) $-\frac{1}{2}$

(C) $\frac{4}{3}$

(D) $\frac{5}{3}$

11. On the interval $[-\pi, \pi]$, the function $f(x) = 2 \cos x - \sin 2x$ has

(A) one relative maximum and one relative minimum.

(B) one relative maximum and two relative minimums.

(C) two relative maxima and one relative minimum.

(D) only a relative maximum.

12. The number of critical points of the function $f(x) = -x \sin x$ on $[-6, 6]$ is

(A) 2

(B) 3

(C) 4

(D) 5

Free Response Questions

A graphing calculator is required for some questions.

1. Sketch the graph of the derivative of each function.

(a) $y = x$

(b) $y = 2$

2. Sketch the graph of the derivative of $y = |x - 1|$.

3. Sketch the graph of the derivative of

$$f(x) = \begin{cases} x + 2, x \leq 1 \\ x - 2, x > 1 \end{cases}.$$

4. A function $f(x)$ with domain all real numbers has critical values at $x = 1, 2,$ and 3. The number line shows the sign of $f'(x)$ on intervals between and outside these critical values. Use the number line to answer the following questions. Justify your conclusions.

(a) At what value(s) of x does $f(x)$ have a relative maximum? a relative minimum?

(b) On what intervals is $f(x)$ increasing? decreasing?

5. For $f(x) = x^{2/3} - 1$ on the interval $[-1, 8]$,

(a) find the critical values.

(b) at which critical values in $[-1, 8]$ does $f(x)$ have a relative maximum? A relative minimum?

(c) find the absolute maximum and absolute minimum of $f(x)$ on $[-1, 8]$.

Lesson 5: Tangent Lines

- The Equation of a Tangent Line
- Continuity vs. Differentiability

As stated in Lesson 2.4, a function's derivative describes the behavior of the function itself. We also reiterated that the derivative of a function at x is the slope of the line tangent to the graph at the point $(x, f(x))$. In this lesson, we describe how to find the equation of that tangent line. We also touch on continuity as it relates to derivatives.

Explain: The Equation of a Tangent Line

Using the formula for the derivative of a function, find the value of the derivative at the given point to find the slope of the tangent line. To find the equation of the tangent line use one of the forms of the equation of a line. The point-slope form is usually the easiest to use.

MODEL PROBLEMS

1. Find the equation of the line tangent to $f(x) = 2x^2 + 5x$ at the point $(1, 7)$.

   (A) $y - 7 = 9(x - 1)$

   (B) $y = 16x - 9$

   (C) $y = 9x - 16$

   (D) $y + 3 = 9(x - 1)$

   Solution

$f(x) = 2x^2 + 5x$ $f'(x) = 4x + 5$	Begin by finding the derivative of $f(x)$.
$f'(1) = 4(1) + 5 = 9$	Find the value of $f'(1)$.
$y - 7 = 9(x - 1)$	Use the point-slope form for the equation of a line. This is the equation of the tangent line at this point. The equation may be left in this form in a free-response question on the AP exam. The correct answer choice is (A).

2. Find the equation of the line tangent to $f(x) = 6 - x^3$ at $x = 1$.

   (A) $y + 5 = 3(x - 1)$

   (B) $y = -3x - 2$

   (C) $y - 5 = -3(x - 1)$

   (D) $y = 3x - 8$

Solution

We take this opportunity to explain how to use graphing calculator technology to determine the equation of the tangent line. Although it is not necessary for this simple function, it can be useful for more complex derivatives.

By the definition of the derivative, the slope of the line tangent to $f(x)$ at $x = 1$ will be equal to the $f'(1)$. This value can be found by graphing the derivative and using the CALC function.

Enter Y_2 = MATH 8 VARS Y-VARS ENTER ENTER ⏵ X,T,Θ,n ⏵ X,T,Θ,n ⏵.

Press GRAPH to see a graph of the function $f(x)$ and its derivative $f'(x)$.

Press 2nd CALC ENTER and enter $x = 1$. Use the ⏶ ⏷ keys to move the cursor to the graph of the derivative. Press ENTER to calculate the y-coordinate -3, which is also the slope of the tangent to $f(x)$ at $x = 1$.

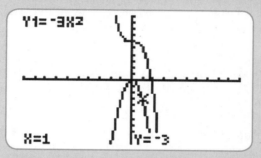

By moving the cursor to the graph of $f(x)$, we can determine also that $f(1) = 5$. We can then use the point-slope form with the point $(1, 5)$ and slope -3 to get the equation $y - 5 = -3(x - 1)$.

Using the TI-*n*spire

Access the graphing screen and TAB to the entry line. Type $6 - x^3$ in $f1(x)$. Then enter the following in $f2(x)$: $\frac{d}{dx}(f1(x))|x = 1$. Remember that $\frac{d}{dx}$ is

found in the equation editor. The "|" symbol can be located in the catalog. Press ENTER. The calculator will graph a horizontal line through $y = -3$. This is the value of the derivative at $x = 1$ and it is the slope of the tangent line. Now graph $-3(x - 1) + 5$ in $f3(x)$. This is the equation of the line tangent to $f1(x)$ at $x = 1$. Answer (C) is correct.

3. Find the slope of the tangent line to $f(x) = 3 + x + x^2$ at $x = 1$.

(A) $y = x + 5$

(B) $y = x - 2$

(C) $y - 1 = (x - 3)$

(D) $y - 5 = 3(x - 1)$

Solution

Use Model Problems #1 and #2 to help you solve this problem.

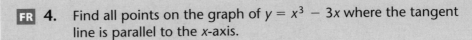

FR **4.** Find all points on the graph of $y = x^3 - 3x$ where the tangent line is parallel to the *x*-axis.

Solution

Lines that are parallel to the *x*-axis have a slope of 0. Find the derivative of *y* and set that expression equal to 0. Then solve for *x*.

5. Find the *y*-intercept of the line tangent to $f(x) = \tan(x) - x$ at $x = \frac{\pi}{4}$.

(A) $x - \frac{\pi}{4}$

(B) $1 - \frac{\pi}{2}$

(C) $1 + \frac{\pi}{2}$

(D) $\frac{\pi}{6}$

Solution

First find the equation of the line tangent to the given *x*-coordinate. Express the line in slope-intercept form so the *y*-intercept is clearly visible.

FR **6.** Find the coordinates of the point on the curve $f(x) = xe^{2x} + 1$ where the tangent line is horizontal.

Solution

What is the slope of the tangent line if it is horizontal? This is similar to Model Problem #4.

Explain: Continuity vs. Differentiability

If a function is differentiable at a given *x*-value, then there is a line of tangency that can be drawn through that point. What else is true about that *x*-value?

If a function is differentiable at a value of *x*, then the function is continuous at that value of *x*.

Be careful to use the statement above correctly, since the *converse* is NOT true. A function that is continuous at a value of *x* may or may not be differentiable at *x*.

There are many examples of functions that are continuous but NOT differentiable. A standard example is $f(x) = |x|$. The absolute value of *x* is continuous for all values of *x*, but its derivative does not exist at $x = 0$.

Another example is $f(x) = x^{2/3}$. This function is continuous for all values of *x*, but it does not have a derivative at $x = 0$.

All polynomial functions, $\sin(x)$, $\cos(x)$, e^x, and $\ln x$ are differentiable at every value in their domains, so it follows that they are continuous at every value in their domains.

If a question asks to verify the continuity of a function, check each of the three conditions in the definition of continuity. (See Lesson x.x for the definition of continuity.)

If a question asks to verify whether or not a function has a derivative (that is, if the function is differentiable), first check to see if the function is continuous. If it is continuous, then check to see if the derivative exists.

MODEL PROBLEMS

FR 1. For $f(x) = \begin{cases} x^2, & x < 1 \\ 2x^2, & x \geq 1 \end{cases}$, is $f(x)$ differentiable at $x = 1$?

Solution

First we use the definition of continuity to see if $f(x)$ is continuous at $x = 1$.

1. Is $f(x)$ is defined at $x = 1$? Yes.

2. Does $\lim\limits_{x \to 1} f(x)$ exist?

$\lim\limits_{x \to 1^-} f(x) = \lim\limits_{x \to 1^-} x^2 = 1$ and

$\lim\limits_{x \to 1^+} f(x) = \lim\limits_{x \to 1^+} 2x = 2$.

Since $\lim\limits_{x \to 1^-} f(x) \neq \lim\limits_{x \to 1^+} f(x)$, $\lim\limits_{x \to 1} f(x)$ does not exist and $f(x)$ is not continuous at $x = 1$. Since $f(x)$ is not continuous at $x = 1$, it is not differentiable at $x = 1$.

2. For what values of x is $f(x) = |x + 1|$ differentiable?

(A) For all $x \geq 1$

(B) For all real numbers

(C) For all $x \neq 1$

(D) For all $x \neq -1$

Solution

Consider looking at the graph of the absolute value function. Is there a point where you know the function is not differentiable?

AP Calculus Exam-Type Questions

Multiple Choice Questions

A graphing calculator is required for some questions.

1. Find the equation of the line tangent to $f(x) = 2x + 2e^x$ at $x = 0$.

    (A) $y = 4x + 2$

    (B) $y = 2x + 2$

    (C) $y = 4x$

    (D) $y = 4x - 2$

2. Find the equation of the line perpendicular to the line tangent to $f(x) = \ln(3 - 2x)$ at $x = 1$.

    (A) $y = -2x + 1$

    (B) $y = \frac{1}{2}x + 1$

    (C) $y = \frac{1}{2}(x - 1)$

    (D) $y = \frac{1}{2}(x + 1)$

3. Find the slope of the line tangent to
$f(x) = \dfrac{1}{x^2 + 1}$ at $x = -1$.

(A) -2

(B) $\dfrac{1}{2}$

(C) 1

(D) 2

4. The y-intercept of the line tangent to
$y = x \sin x$ at $x = \pi$ is

(A) $-\pi$

(B) π

(C) $-\pi^2$

(D) π^2

5. $f(x) = \dfrac{1}{\ln x}$ is continuous and differentiable
on which interval(s)?

(A) $(0, 1)$ or $(1, \infty)$

(B) $(0, \infty)$

(C) $(-\infty, \infty)$

(D) $[0, \infty)$

6. Every polynomial is continuous and differentiable:

(A) for all $x \geq 0$.

(B) for all real x.

(C) for all $x > 0$.

(D) for $0 < x < 1$.

7. $f(x) = \begin{cases} 4, & x < 2 \\ x^2, & x \geq 2 \end{cases}$ is differentiable for

(A) all real numbers.

(B) $x \neq 2$.

(C) $x > 2$.

(D) $x \geq 2$.

Free Response Questions

A graphing calculator is required for some questions.

1. (a) Find the equations of the tangent lines at the zeros of $f(x) = x^2 - 2x - 3$, and find their point of intersection.

   (b) Repeat part (a) for $f(x) = \sin x$ on the interval $[0, 2\pi]$.

2. (a) Sketch the graph of $f(x) = x^3 - 13x + 12$ on the calculator by setting x-range from -8 to 8 and y-range from -15 to 35.

   (b) Use the calculator to find the equations of the tangent lines at the following values of x, and complete the table below. Sketch each tangent line on the graph from part (a).

x	Equation of tangent line	Is tangent line above or below graph?
-3		
-1		
2		
3		

   (c) At what value of x does the tangent line appear to change from being above the curve to below the curve?

3. Write a function that is continuous for all real numbers and differentiable except at $x = 1$.

4. The graph of $f(x)$ is shown in the figure.

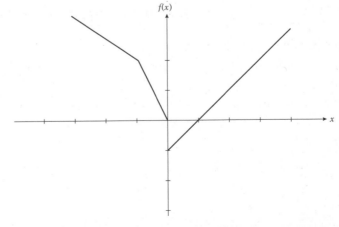

   (a) For what values of x is $f(x)$ continuous?

   (b) Sketch the graph of the derivative of $f(x)$.

Lesson 6: Higher Order Derivatives

- Second and Higher Order Derivatives
- Applying the Second Derivative
- Curve Sketching

Explain: Second and Higher Order Derivatives

As you may have guessed, we can take the derivative of a function more than once. In Lesson 2.2, we reviewed common derivative notation, such as y' and $\frac{dy}{dx}$. In calculus, we present higher order derivatives in prime notation using an increasing number of primes. For example, y'' is the second-order derivative of y. Beyond the second or third derivative, though, all those primes get messy, so we often express the order of the derivative as a numeral superscript; for example, the ninth derivative of $f(x)$ with respect to x is written as $f^{(9)}(x)$. To express higher order derivatives in **Leibnitz notation** we use

$$\left(\frac{d}{dx}\right)^n f(x) = \frac{d^n y}{dx^n}$$

MODEL PROBLEMS

1. Find y'' of $y = 4x^6 + 3x^5 - 8x^3 + 6x^2 + 15$.

(A) $y'' = 24x^5 + 15x^4 - 24x^2 + 12x$

(B) $y'' = 24x^4 + 60x^3 - 48x^2 + 12$

(C) $y'' = 120x^4 + 60x^3 - 48x + 12$

(D) $y'' = 120x^5 + 15x^3 - 48x + 12$

Solution

This is a straightforward polynomial function. To find the second derivative, we will find the first derivative, and then find the derivative of that derivative.

$y' = 24x^5 + 15x^4 - 24x^2 + 12x$ Find the first derivative using the power rule.

$y'' = 120x^4 + 60x^3 - 48x + 12$ Find the derivative of y'. We again apply the power rule. The correct answer is (C).

2. What is $\frac{d^2 y}{dx^2}$ when $y = \cos(2x^3 - 9x)$?

(A) $-9(2x^2 - 3)^2 \cdot \cos(2x^3 - 9x) - 12x \cdot \sin(2x^3 - 9x)$

(B) $-9(2x^2 - 3)^2 \cdot \sin(2x^3 - 9x) - 12x \cdot \cos(2x^3 - 9x)$

(C) $-9(2x^2 - 3)^2 \cdot \sin(2x^3 - 9x) - 12x \cdot \sin(2x^3 - 9x)$

(D) $-9(2x^2 - 3)^2 \cdot \cos(2x^3 - 9x) - 12x \cdot \cos(2x^3 - 9x)$

Solution

Begin by noting that we are being asked for the second derivative of $h(x)$. This means we will need to take the derivative twice. The first derivative in this case is $h'(x) = -\sin(2x^3 - 9x) \cdot (6x^2 - 9)$. You finish solving from here.

3. Find $y^{(4)}$ when $y(x) = 3x^3 + 2x^2 - x + 9$.

(A) $18x$

(B) 9

(C) 0

(D) $9x^2 + 4$

Solution

For this problem, we need to determine the fourth derivative of $y(x)$. We can take the derivative four times or we can consider what happens to the function when you find a derivative that has a higher degree than the function itself.

4. Find the second derivative of y when $2x^4 + y^2 = 1 - 6y^2$.

(A) $12x^2 5y$

(B) $-12x^2 y$

(C) $\dfrac{12x^2 \cdot 7y}{5}$

(D) $-\dfrac{12x^2}{7y}$

Solution

We need to find the second derivative of y, but we will need to use implicit differentiation to do so. Refer to Lesson 2.3, if needed. The first derivative of y is $y' = -\dfrac{4x^3}{7y}$. You solve the problem from here.

Explain: Applying the Second Derivative

Second derivatives are useful for more than just complicated algebra. Just as the first derivative can tell us information about the graph of the function, the second derivative test can tell us about the shape of $f(x)$, specifically, about its **concavity**.

Consider the two curves on the following page. In the figure on the left, the slopes of the tangent lines change from negative to zero to positive (looking from left to right). Thus, the slope of the tangent, which is the derivative of $f(x)$, is increasing. When a function is increasing, its derivative is positive. That is, when $f'(x)$ is increasing, the derivative of $f'(x)$, $f''(x)$, is positive. This type of shape is called **concave up.** Even if we see only a small part of this graph, the shape is still called concave up.

Concave Up   Concave Down

In the figure on the right, the slopes of the tangent lines change from positive to zero to negative (looking from left to right). Thus, the slope of the tangent, which is $f'(x)$, is decreasing. When a function is decreasing, its derivative is negative. That is, when $f'(x)$ is decreasing, the derivative of $f'(x)$, or $f''(x)$, is negative. This type of shape is called **concave down.** Even if we see only a small part of this graph, the shape is still called concave down.

For graphs that are *concave up*, tangent lines lie *below* the graph. For graphs that are *concave down*, tangent lines lie *above* the graph.

Looking at the curve on the left, we see that this curve has a relative minimum. In the graph on the right, there is a relative maximum. This is the essence of the second derivative test.

The Second Derivative Test

If c is a critical number of $f(x)$, and
   $f''(c) > 0$, then there is a relative minimum at c.
   $f''(c) < 0$, then there is a relative maximum at c.
   $f''(c) = 0$, then there is no conclusion possible.

The Second Derivative Test is easy to use, but it is also limiting since there is no conclusion when the second derivative is zero. In that case, use the First Derivative Test, which can be applied in every case.

Points of Inflection   Points where the concavity of a function changes are called **points of inflection**. Points of inflection are at values in the domain of the function where the second derivative changes sign from + to − or from − to +.

To find points of inflection, find the second derivative and solve for the values of x where the second derivative is either zero or undefined. Call these x-values possible points of inflection (PPI's). Next draw a number line and put these values of x on it. Then make a table of values of x and $f''(x)$. Choose values of x on the number line that are to the left of, between, and to the right of the PPI's, and list them in the table. The corresponding values of $f''(x)$ can be found by hand or by using the TABLE in the calculator. If the sign of f'' changes around the x-values on the number line, then that value of x is a point of inflection.

MODEL PROBLEMS

1. Find the a possible point of inflection of $f(x) = x^3 + 3x^2 + 4$.

(A) $(0, 0)$

(B) $(-2, 8)$

(C) $(0, 4)$

(D) $(-1, 6)$

Solution

To find a possible point of inflection, find the function's second derivative, set it equal to 0, and then solve for the variable.

$f'(x) = 3x^2 + 6x$	Use the power rule to find the first derivative.
$f''(x) = 6x + 6$	Apply the power rule again to determine the second derivative.
$6x + 6 = 0$ $x = -1$	Set the second derivative equal to 0. This is the x-value of the possible point of inflection.
$f(-1) = (-1)^3 + 3(-1)^2 + 4$ $f(-1) = 6$	Solve $f(-1)$. This is the y-value of the possible point of inflection. The correct answer is (D).

FR **2.** Find the x-coordinates of the points of inflection of $f(x)$ given the graph of $f'(x)$ shown below.

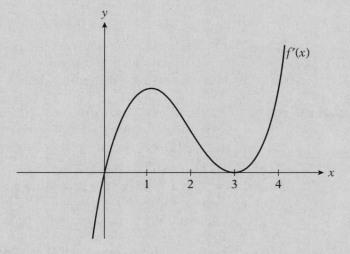

Solution

The x-coordinates of the possible points of inflection of $f(x)$ are the value(s) of x where $f''(x) = 0$ or where $f''(x)$ is undefined. Using the graph of $f'(x)$, these are the points where $f'(x)$ is zero or is undefined. In addition, we need to see that the sign of $f''(x)$ changes at those points, meaning that the sign of the slope of $f'(x)$ changes at those points. We leave the rest to you.

3. Find the coordinates of the points of inflection of $f(x) = \sin(x) + \cos(x)$ for values of x in the interval $[0, 2\pi]$.

(A) $\left(\frac{11\pi}{4}, 0\right)$ and $\left(\frac{15\pi}{4}, 0\right)$

(B) $\left(\frac{3\pi}{4}, 0\right)$ and $\left(\frac{11\pi}{4}, 0\right)$

(C) $\left(\frac{3\pi}{4}, 0\right)$ and $\left(\frac{7\pi}{4}, 0\right)$

(D) $\left(\frac{7\pi}{4}, 0\right)$ and $\left(\frac{11\pi}{4}, 0\right)$

Solution

To find the *x*-coordinates of the possible points of inflection, find the solutions to $f''(x) = 0$ and check whether the sign of $f''(x)$ changes at each point. Remember that you are only concerned with the interval $[0, 2\pi]$.

FR **4.** Find the coordinates of the points of inflection of $f(x) = e^x - x$.

Solution

We need to find $f''(x)$. It is easy to see that $f'(x) = e^x - 1$ and $f''(x) = e^x$. But $e^x = 0$ has no solutions so there are no points of inflection for this function. This means that the given function is either always concave up or always concave down. The second derivative is always positive, so $f(x)$ is always concave up.

Explain: Curve Sketching

With the introduction of the graphing calculator, the focus of curve sketching on the AP Calculus exam has changed. In the past, students were given a function and they found its first and second derivatives, its critical values, its relative extrema, and its points of inflection, and then used this information to sketch the graph of the function. We summarize how these ideas are connected to the graph of $f(x)$ below.

Function	Setting the function equal to 0,	Positive (1)	Negative (2)
$f(x)$	gives the zero(s) of $f(x)$.	The function is above the *x*-axis.	The function is below the *x*-axis
$f'(x)$	reveals the critical values of $f(x)$. These are the possible maximum or minimum values of $f(x)$. The values are confirmed by using the 1st or 2nd derivative test.	Where $f'(x)$ is positive, $f(x)$ is increasing.	Where $f'(x)$ is negative, $f(x)$ is decreasing.
$f''(x)$	reveals the possible points of inflection.	Where $f''(x)$ is positive, $f(x)$ is concave up.	Where $f''(x)$ is negative, $f(x)$ is concave down.

On the current AP Calculus exam, however, students first graph the function in their graphing calculator, and then they find its first and second derivatives, its critical values, its relative extrema, and its points of inflection to algebraically support what they see on the screen.

It may seem that graphing a function first leaves little else to be done, but a graph is only one representation of a function. The graphing calculator is a tool, and being able to use it effectively requires an understanding of the theorems and procedures that are fundamental to the study of calculus. Furthermore, the calculator does not always show the true function, and may even mislead or give erroneous information about a function. These calculator discrepancies emphasize the fact that the graph does not stand alone: the mathematical processes that truly describe a function, ones that use the first and second derivatives, must support it. The developers of AP Calculus Examination questions are aware of this. While the calculator is required on about half of the exam, students earn credit by demonstrating an understanding of mathematics, not for their ability to press buttons.

MODEL PROBLEMS

FR **1.** Graph $y = x\sqrt{4 - x}$ in different windows, and use the graph to find its x-intercepts.

Solution

In the TI-83/84, graph y in ZOOM 4 and ZOOM 6 windows.

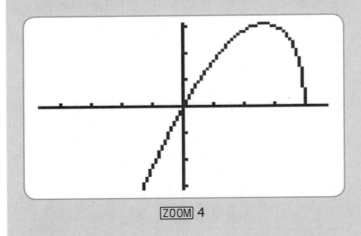

ZOOM 4

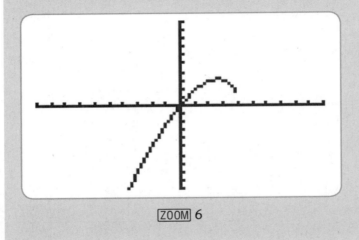

ZOOM 6

In $\boxed{\text{ZOOM}}$ 4, the graph appears to touch the x-axis at $x = 4$, while in $\boxed{\text{ZOOM}}$ 6, the graph does not appear to touch the x-axis at $x = 4$. This disparity is easily resolved by looking at the function and solving for the x-intercepts. Solving $y = 0$, the x-intercepts are $x = 0$ and $x = 4$. Thus, $x = 4$ is one of the x-intercepts though the calculator may not show this.

In the TI-89, the graph does not appear to touch the x-axis at $x = 4$ using either $\boxed{\text{ZOOM}}$ 4 or $\boxed{\text{ZOOM}}$ 6.

When using the **TI-*nspire***, graphing with a standard window shows the function above the x-axis at $x = 4$. Using $\boxed{\text{MENU}}$, **Window/Zoom, Data**, the graph does appear to touch the x-axis at $x = 4$. To be sure of the intercepts, use the key sequence $\boxed{\text{MENU}}$, **Analyze Graph, Zero**.

Standard Window:

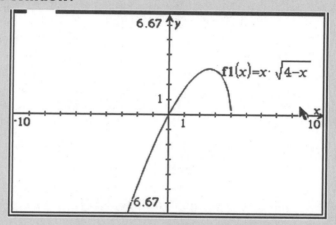

Zoom Data:

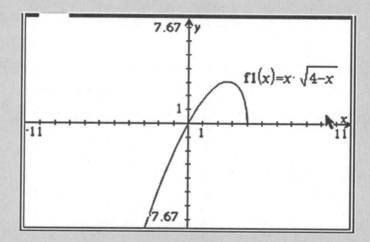

Calculator Note

The different appearances of the graphs in Model Problem #1 are due to the number of pixels in the screen of the calculator. In $\boxed{\text{ZOOM}}$ 4, or $\boxed{\text{ZOOM}}$ Decimal, the pixels are located at decimal values of x. Since 4 is equal to 4.0, this value appears on the graph in $\boxed{\text{ZOOM}}$ 4. In $\boxed{\text{ZOOM}}$ 6, the pixels are not located at decimal values of x. Thus $x = 4$ does not appear on the graph.

FR 2. Find the derivative of $y = |x|$ at $x = 0$.

Solution

Since this is the absolute value function, we already know the derivative does not exist when $x = 0$. But what happens when we try to use our calculators to determine the derivative?

On the TI-83/84, use the numerical derivative nDeriv (press MATH 8) to find the derivative of $|x|$ at $x = 0$. The syntax for nDeriv is nDeriv (function, variable, value). Thus, the numerical derivative of $|x|$ at $x = 0$ should be nDeriv ($|x|$, x, 0). The TI-83 gives the value 0, which is incorrect.

So the TI-83/84 calculators will return an incorrect result for this problem. What about other calculator models?

Using the TI-89, calculate the derivative by pressing F3 and then selecting 1: d(differentiate. Enter d(abs(x), x) and the calculator will return the value "sign(x)", which means the answer depends on the sign of the argument, x. This indicates the values of the limit from the left- and right-hand sides are unequal. Therefore, there is no limit and hence no value for the derivative of $y = |x|$ at $x = 0$.

To compute the numerical value of a derivative at a given point using the **TI-*nspire***, begin by accessing the scratchpad. Enter $\frac{d}{dx} |x| | x = 0$.

The value returned is "undefined," meaning that the derivative of the function does not exist at this point.

Two TI calculators discussed here will return a correct result. This model problem serves as a reminder that your graphing calculator is a powerful tool, but it does have limitations.

FR 3. Sketch the graph of a function with the following properties:

- a vertical asymptote at $x = 1$
- a horizontal asymptote at $y = 2$
- $f'(x) < 0$ for $x < 1$
- $f'(x) < 0$ for $x > 1$

Solution

To solve this problem, begin by sketching the asymptotes. Recall that the asymptotes guide the end behavior of the function.

AP Calculus Exam-Type Questions

Multiple Choice Problems

A graphing calculator is required for some questions.

1. The second derivative of $f(x) = \ln(x)$ at $x = 3$ is

   (A) $-\frac{1}{3}$

   (B) $-\frac{1}{9}$

   (C) $\frac{1}{9}$

   (D) $\frac{1}{3}$

2. If $f(x) = \sqrt{x - 16}$, what is $f'''(x)$?

   (A) $\dfrac{1}{(x - 16)^{\frac{5}{2}}}$

   (B) $\dfrac{3}{8(x - 16)^{\frac{5}{2}}}$

   (C) $(x - 16)^{\frac{5}{2}}$

   (D) $8(x - 16)^{\frac{5}{2}}$

3. A function g is defined by $g(x) = 3e^{3x}$. What is $g''(2)$?

   (A) $\dfrac{1}{9e^3}$

   (B) $27e^3$

   (C) $9e^3$

   (D) $27e^6$

4. On what interval is $f(x) = x^3 + x$ concave down?

   (A) $(-\infty, \infty)$

   (B) $(0, \infty)$

   (C) $(-\infty, 0)$

   (D) $(0, 1)$

5. The x-coordinate(s) of the point(s) of inflection of $f(x) = \dfrac{x}{x^2 + 1}$ is (are)

   (A) 0

   (B) ± 1

   (C) $\pm\sqrt{3}$

   (D) 0 and $\pm\sqrt{3}$

6. On what parts of the interval $[-2, 2]$ is the graph of $f(x) = x \sin x^2$ concave up?

   (A) $(0, 0.994)$

   (B) $(-1, 1)$

   (C) $(-0.994, 0.994)$

   (D) $(0, 0.994)$ and $(-2, -0.994)$

7. On what interval is the graph of $f(x) = \ln(x^2 + 1)$ concave up?

   (A) $(0, 1)$

   (B) $(-1, 1)$

   (C) $(-0.5, 0.5)$

   (D) $\left(-\dfrac{\sqrt{3}}{3}, \dfrac{\sqrt{3}}{3}\right)$

8. The graph of $y = \ln(x + 2)$ has an asymptote with the equation

   (A) $x = -2$

   (B) $y = -2$

   (C) $x = 0$

   (D) $x = 2$

9. $y = e^{x-2} - 2$ has which of the following as an asymptote?

   (A) $x = -2$

   (B) $y = -2$

   (C) $x = 0$

   (D) $x = 2$

Questions 10 and 11 refer to the graph of the function $f(x) = x^2\sqrt{4 - x^2}$.

10. The critical values of $f(x)$ are

    (A) 0 only

    (B) $0, \pm 2$

    (C) 2 only

    (D) $0, \pm 2, \pm \dfrac{2\sqrt{6}}{3}$

11. The range of $f(x)$ is

    (A) $[0, 3]$

    (B) $(0, 3.072)$

    (C) $[0, 3.072]$

    (D) $[0, 3.079]$

Free Response Questions

A graphing calculator is required for some questions.

1. Sketch $f(x) = |x^2 - 2x|$ and

   (a) identify critical values of the function.

   (b) find the relative extrema and justify your conclusion.

   (c) find the intervals where the function is concave up and concave down.

2. Sketch $f(x) = e^{-x^2}$ and state

   (a) the domain and range.

   (b) asymptotes.

   (c) whether the function is even, odd, or neither.

   (d) the critical values.

   (e) relative extrema.

   (f) absolute extrema.

   (g) points of inflection.

   (h) intervals where the graph is concave up.

3. Draw the graph of a function that has the following properties:

   - the function is continuous for all real numbers
   - the function is odd
   - there are at least 2 points of inflection
   - $y = 0$ is a horizontal asymptote
   - the relative maximum = the absolute maximum
   - the relative minimum = the absolute minimum

4. (a) Sketch a function $f(x)$ that is always increasing, is always concave up, and has $f(0) = 1$.

   (b) Sketch a function $f(x)$ that is decreasing and concave down on the interval $[0, 1]$, is decreasing and concave up on the interval $[1,2]$, and has $f(0) = 1$.

   (c) Sketch a function $f(x)$ that is always increasing, is concave up on the interval $(0, 1)$, is concave down on the interval $(0, 2)$, and has $f(0) = 1$.

---

5. A function $f(x)$ and its first and second derivatives have values as described in the table below. Sketch the graph of $f(x)$.

x	0	(0, 1)	1	(1, 2)	2	(2, 3)	3	(3, 4)	4
f	0		1		0		−1		0
f'		+	undef.	−	0	−	undef.	+	0
f''		+		+	0	−		−	

Lesson 7: Applications of the Derivative, Part 1

- Particle Motion, Speed, Velocity, and Acceleration
- Related Rates
- Optimization

The derivative has several real-world applications, which we will explore in this lesson. Here we focus on rectilinear motion, related rates, and optimization. Lesson 8 will review BC Exam only topics such as vector-valued functions, parametric functions, and functions in polar coordinates.

Explain: Particle Motion, Speed, Velocity, and Acceleration

In questions about particle motion, the particle may be moving in one dimension along a line, usually the x-axis (though it could also be moving along the y-axis). The particle may also be moving in two dimensions, in which case it may be referred to as a freely falling object.

The **position** of the particle at time t, usually denoted $x(t)$ or $s(t)$, is its location on the number line if it moves in one dimension, or its height if it moves in two dimensions. Position is expressed in linear units such as meters or feet.

The **velocity** $v(t)$ of the particle is the rate of change of position with respect to time, or the derivative of position. Velocity is calculated using $v(t) = x'(t)$ or $s'(t)$. Velocity has magnitude and direction: it tells how fast and in what direction the particle is moving. Velocity can be positive, negative, or zero. When the velocity is zero, the particle is at rest. When the velocity is positive, the particle is moving to the right (or moving up). When the velocity is negative, the particle is moving to the left (or moving down). Velocity is expressed as a ratio of linear units and time units, such as m/s (meters per second) or ft/s (feet per second).

The **speed** of the particle tells us only how fast the particle is moving. Speed can be positive or zero. Speed is the absolute value of velocity.

Particle Velocity	
$v(t) = 0$	Particle at rest.
$v(t) > 0$	Particle moves right (or up).
$v(t) < 0$	Particle moves left (or down).
Sign of $v(t)$ changes	Particle changes direction.

The **acceleration**, $a(t)$, of the particle is the rate of change of velocity with respect to time, or the derivative of velocity. Since velocity is the first derivative of position, acceleration is the second derivative of position. Acceleration is calculated using $a(t) = v'(t) = x''(t)$ or $s''(t)$. Acceleration can be positive, negative, or zero and is expressed as a ratio of linear units and time units squared, such as m/s^2 or ft/s^2.

MODEL PROBLEMS

FR **1.** Suppose a particle is moving along a line with its position at time t given by $s(t) = t^3 - 3t + 2$, for $t \geq 0$. (t is in seconds and s is in feet).

(a) Find the velocity function.

(b) Find $v(0)$ and $v(2)$.

(c) When is the velocity zero? Where is the particle at that time?

(d) Draw a number line indicating the position and the velocity of the particle at $t = 0$, $t = 1$, and $t = 2$.

(e) Refer to the number line to write a description of the motion of the particle from $t = 0$ to $t = 2$.

Solution

(a)	$s'(t) = 3t^2 - 3$	Find the first derivative of $s(t)$ since $v(t) = s'(t)$.
(b)	$v(0) = 3(0)^2 - 3 = -3\,\text{feet/second}$ $v(2) = 3(2)^2 - 3 = 9 \text{ feet/second}$	Calculate.
(c)	$3t^2 - 3 = 0$ $3(t^2 - 1) = 0$ $t = \pm 1$	To find when the velocity is 0, solve the equation $s'(t) = 0$. Since this function is defined for $t \geq 0$, the only solution is $t = 1$. At $t = 1$, $s(1) = 0$.

(d)

We create a number line and table.

Particle Motion				
Time	t	0	1	2
Position	$s(t) = t^3 - 3t - 2$	2	0	4
Velocity	$v(t) = s'(t) = 3t^2 - 3$	−3 ft/sec	0 ft/sec	9 ft/sec

(e) As seen in the number line and the table, at $t = 0$, the particle is at $s = 2$ and is moving to the left at 3 ft/sec. One second later at $t = 1$, the particle is at $s = 0$ and is at rest. The particle then turns and at $t = 2$, and at $s = 4$, the particle is moving to the right at 9 ft/sec.

2. A particle moves along a number line with position function $s(t) = t - \ln t$, for $t \geq 1$.

(a) Find the velocity and the acceleration functions.

(b) Find $s(1)$, $s(5)$, $v(2)$, and $v(4)$.

(c) Is there a value of t that makes the velocity zero? If yes, find the value of t. If no, explain why not.

(d) As t increases, does the velocity increase or decrease? Explain your answer in a complete sentence. (What value does the velocity approach as t gets larger; that is, find $\lim_{t \to \infty} v(t)$.)

(e) Is the acceleration positive or negative for $t \geq 1$? Explain your answer in a complete sentence.

(f) Draw a number line indicating the position and velocity for $t = 1$, $t = 3$, and $t = 5$.

(g) Refer to the number line and your answers to parts (c), (d), and (e) to write a description of the motion of the particle.

Solution

(a) This part of the question asks you to determine the first and second derivatives of the given function.

(b) Now evaluate at the given values. You may need to round your answers to the nearest thousandth.

(c) You'll need to set the velocity function equal to 0 and solve for this part of the question.

(d) Use the hint given in the problem to help you with this part.

(e) Are the output values for t^2 always positive, always negative, or does the output value depend on the sign of the input value? How does this affect the acceleration?

(f) Create a drawing and table similar to Model Problem #1(d).

(g) Describe the motion of the particle.

The motion of an object, such as a ball being dropped from a height or thrown up into the air, can be modeled by an equation that gives the position of the object as a function of time. The general equation that describes this kind of motion is

$$s(t) = \frac{1}{2}at^2 + v_0 t + s_0,$$

where t is time, a is the acceleration due to gravity, v_0 is the initial velocity, and s_0 is the initial height.

> If the height is in feet and time is in seconds, then $a = -32$ ft/sec^2.
>
> If the height is in meters and time is in seconds, then $a = -9.8$ m/sec^2.

MODEL PROBLEMS

FR **1.** Suppose a ball is dropped from a window 20 feet above the ground.

(a) Find the height of the ball after 1 second.

(b) Find the velocity of the ball after 1 second.

(c) When will the ball hit the ground? What is its speed at that moment?

Solution

(a)	$s(t) = \frac{1}{2}(-32t^2) + 0t + 20$ $s(t) = -16t^2 + 20$	Determine the motion equation. The ball was dropped from a height of 20 ft, so $v_0 = 0$ ft/s and $s_0 = 20$ ft.
	$s(1) = -16(1)^2 + 20 = 4$ feet	The height of the ball after 1 second is the value of $s(1)$.
(b)	$s'(t) = -32t$ $s'(1) = -32(1) = -32$ ft/second	The velocity is $v(t) = s'(t)$ evaluated at $t = 1$.
(c)	$-16t^2 + 20 = 0$ $t = \frac{\sqrt{5}}{2} \approx 1.12$ seconds	The ball will hit the ground when $s(t) = 0$. Solve this equation for t.
	$\|v(t)\| = \|s'(t)\| = \|-32t\|$ $= \left\|-32\left(\frac{\sqrt{5}}{2}\right)\right\| \approx 35.78$ feet/second	Now determine the speed of the ball at that time. Recall that speed $= \|v(t)\|$.

FR 2. A ball is thrown upward from the hand of a player. When the ball leaves the player's hand, it is at a height of 2 meters and traveling at a speed of 5 meters per second. Round all answers to the nearest hundredth, as needed.

(a) What is the speed of the ball one second later?

(b) When is the ball 3 meters above the ground? 1.5 meters above the ground?

(c) When does the ball hit the ground?

(d) When is the ball at its highest point?

Solution

(a) Begin by determining the equation of motion for distance measured in meters. What are the values of s_0 and v_0? Once you have the equation, the solution to part (a) is the value of $\|v(1)\|$.

(b) The ball is 3 meters above the ground when $s(t) = 3$. It will be 1.5 meters above the ground when $s(t) = 1.5$.

(c) The ball will hit the ground when $s(t) = 0$. Keep in mind that you will have two solutions to this part, but only one will be meaningful.

(d) The ball will be at its highest point when $v(t) = 0$.

Explain: Related Rates

There are several different types of related rate problems, but generally these problems involve finding the rate at which some quantity changes by relating that quantity to other quantities whose **rates** of change are known. We usually measure rates of change with respect to time. All related rate problems are applications of implicit differentiation (see Lesson 2.3 if needed). We begin with particle motion, which is generally tested on the AP exam.

Suppose a particle starts from the origin and moves along the curve $y = x^2$ in the first quadrant. As it moves, both the x-coordinate and the y-coordinate of its position change. If the rate of change of the x-coordinate is $\frac{1}{2}$ unit/s, that is, $\frac{dx}{dt} = \frac{1}{2}$ unit/s, then the rate of change of the y-coordinate can be calculated as:

$$\frac{dy}{dt} = \frac{dy}{dx} \cdot \frac{dx}{dt}.$$

Since $y = x^2$, $\frac{dy}{dt} = 2x \cdot \frac{dx}{dt} = 2x\left(\frac{1}{2}\right) = x$.

The rate of change of the y-coordinate at a point on the curve is equal to the value of the x-coordinate at that point. For example, at the point $(1, 1)$, $\frac{dy}{dt} = 1$ unit/s, and at the point $(3, 9)$, $\frac{dy}{dt} = 3$ units/s.

Thus, for a function $y = f(x)$, the rates of change of the x-coordinate and the y-coordinate are related by the equation

$$\frac{dy}{dt} = \frac{dy}{dx} \cdot \frac{dx}{dt}.$$

MODEL PROBLEMS

FR 1. A particle moves along the curve $y = 3x^2 - 6x$ so that the rate of change of the x-coordinate, $\frac{dx}{dt}$, is 2 units/s. Find the rate of change of the y-coordinate, $\frac{dy}{dt}$, when the particle is at the origin.

Solution

$\frac{dy}{dx} = y' = 6x - 6$	The relationship between $\frac{dx}{dt}$ and $\frac{dy}{dt}$ is given by the equation $\frac{dy}{dt} = \frac{dy}{dx} \cdot \frac{dx}{dt}$. Determine $\frac{dy}{dx}$.
$\frac{dy}{dt} = (6x - 6)(2)$ $= 12x - 12$	Substitute known values in to the equation $\frac{dy}{dt} = \frac{dy}{dx} \cdot \frac{dx}{dt}$.
$12(0) - 12 = -12$ units per second.	At the origin $x = 0$, so $\frac{dy}{dx}$ is -12 units per second.

FR 2. Suppose a particle moves along a circle with equation $x^2 + y^2 = 25$. If the particle is at the point $(-4, 3)$ and the y-coordinate is increasing so that $\frac{dy}{dt} = 2$ units/s, find the rate of change of x-coordinate $\frac{dy}{dx}$.

Solution

$$\frac{d}{dt}(x^2 + y^2) = \frac{d}{dt}(25)$$

$$\frac{d}{dt}(x^2) + \frac{d}{dt}(y^2) = \frac{d}{dt}(25)$$

$$\frac{d}{dt}(x^2) \cdot \frac{dx}{dt} + \frac{d(y^2)}{dt} \cdot \frac{dy}{dt} = 0$$

To find the rates of change of the x-coordinate $\frac{dx}{dt}$ and the y-coordinate $\frac{dy}{dt}$, find the derivative of the equation with respect to t. You continue solving from this point.

3. Air is pumped into a spherical balloon so that its volume increases at a rate of 10 cm³/s. How fast is the radius of the balloon increasing when its diameter is 10 cm?

(A) $\frac{1}{100\pi}$ cm/s

(B) $\frac{1}{10\pi}$ cm/s

(C) 20π cm/s

(D) 10π cm/s

Solution

Keep in mind that rates of change are derivatives, so we can express the increasing volume as $\frac{dV}{dt} = 10$ cm³/s. The unknown rate is $\frac{dr}{dt}$ when $r = 5$ cm. Recall that the formula for the volume of a sphere is $V = \frac{4}{3}\pi r^3$; this is the equation we will need to differentiate with respect to t. Once you have differentiated this equation, solve for the unknown quantity, $\frac{dr}{dt}$. Leave your answer in terms of π.

Explain: Optimization

We can also use derivatives to solve optimization problems. These types of problems often involve finding the largest or smallest values of a function, such as area, perimeter, volume, length, or time. As with all functions, the domain is vital to determining the solution.

> **Typical optimization problems ask:**
>
> • How large a rectangular area can be enclosed with a fixed amount of fencing?
> *In this case, the dimensions of the region are non-negative quantities.*
>
> • What is the largest volume that can be enclosed by making a box from a rectangular piece of material?
> *In this case, the dimensions of the box are non-negative quantities.*
>
> • What is the minimum distance from a given point to a curve?
> *In this case, the domain of the distance function is restricted to the domain of the curve given.*

MODEL PROBLEMS

1. A rectangular vegetable garden is to be enclosed by 60 feet of fencing. Find the length and width of the rectangle that will give the maximum area.

(A) 30 feet by 10 feet

(B) 20 feet by 20 feet

(C) 15 feet by 10 feet

(D) 15 feet by 15 feet

Solution

$2x + 2y = 60$ $y = 30 - x$	Let x represent the length of the garden and let y represent the garden's width. Solve the equation for y. This is the width of the garden in terms of x.
$A(x) = x(30 - x)$ $A(x) = 30x - x^2$	Write the equation for the area of the garden in terms of x.
Here we point out that the dimensions of the rectangle must be non-negative quantities. Since $y = 30 - x$ and $y \geq 0$, this means that $x \leq 30$. The domain of $A(x)$ is $\{0 \leq x \leq 30\}$.	
$A'(x) = 30 - 2x$ $x = \dfrac{-b}{2a}$ $x = \dfrac{-30}{-2} = 15$ feet	There is more than one way to solve this problem. Since the function is a quadratic that opens down, we find the vertex of $A'(x)$. Calculate the x-coordinate.
$y = 30 - 15 = 15$ feet.	Calculate the y-coordinate. The maximum area of the garden is 15 feet by 15 feet. This is choice (D).

2. A store constructs a box from a square sheet of cardboard 20 inches on a side by cutting out squares of the same size from each of the four corners of the box. Once the squares are removed a salesperson folds up the sides of the box. How long should the side of a cut square be so that the box has the maximum possible volume when the sides are folded up?

(A) $\dfrac{10}{3}$ inches

(B) 2.5 inches

(C) 10 inches

(D) $\dfrac{8}{3}$ inches

Solution

Start by defining x = length of the side of a square that is cut out. The volume of a rectangular box is $V = lwh$, and in this case, length and width are equal to $20 - 2x$. So the volume of this box must be $V = x(20 - 2x)(20 - 2x)$. Try solving from here.

3. A cylindrical can must hold 1 liter of oil. Find the dimensions of the can that will minimize the cost of the material used to manufacture the can.

(A) $r = \dfrac{250}{\pi}$, $h = 2r$

(B) $r = \sqrt{\dfrac{500}{\pi}}$, $h = r$

(C) $r = \sqrt[3]{\dfrac{500}{\pi}}$, $h = 2r$

(D) $r = \sqrt[3]{\dfrac{250}{\pi}}$, $h = 2r$

Solution

The surface area for a cylinder is $A = 2\pi r^2 + 2\pi rh$ and the volume of a cylinder is given by the formula $V = \pi r^2 h$. We know the volume of the can must be 1 liter, which is equivalent to 1,000 cm³. Then $1000 = \pi r^2 h$, which we solve for h. This expression can be substituted back into the formula for surface area to determine the function to be minimized. Pay attention to the domain of the function.

AP Calculus Exam-Type Questions

Multiple Choice Questions

A graphing calculator is required for some questions.

For Questions 1–6, consider a particle whose motion is represented by the position equation $s(t) = t^2 - t$, $t \geq 0$, where s is feet and t is seconds.

1. The velocity of the particle after two seconds is

(A) 0 ft/s

(B) 1 ft/s

(C) 2 ft/s

(D) 3 ft/s

2. The accelaration of the particle after two seconds is:

(A) 0 ft/sec²

(B) 1 ft/sec²

(C) 2 ft/sec²

(D) 3 ft/sec²

3. What is the position of the particle at $t = 2$?

(A) 0 ft

(B) 1 ft

(C) 2 ft

(D) 3 ft

4. At what value(s) of t does the particle change direction?

(A) $t = \dfrac{1}{2}$

(B) $t = 1$

(C) $t = 1$ and $t = 2$

(D) $t = 2$

5. Find the distance traveled by the particle in the first two seconds.

(A) 1.75 ft

(B) 2 ft

(C) 2.25 ft

(D) 2.5 ft

6. The particle moves to the right when

   (A) $t > 0$

   (B) $t > \frac{1}{2}$

   (C) $t > 1$

   (D) $t > 2$

For Questions 7 and 8 consider a particle moving along $s(t) = t^3 - 3t$, $t \geq 0$.

7. The particle moves to the left for

   (A) $0 < t < 1$

   (B) $0 < t < 2$

   (C) $1 < t < 2$

   (D) $0 < t < 3$

8. Find the distance traveled by the particle in the first two seconds.

   (A) 0

   (B) 2

   (C) 4

   (D) 6

For Questions 9–12, the position of a freely falling object is given by $s(t) = -16t^2 + v_0 t + s_0$, where s is feet and t is seconds. The initial position is s and the initial velocity is v_0.

9. A ball is thrown upward from the top of a building 100 feet high at initial velocity of 20 ft/s. How long will it take until the ball hits the ground?

   (A) 1.952 s

   (B) 2.5 s

   (C) 3.2 s

   (D) 3.8 s

10. A ball is dropped from the top of a building 200 feet high. It hits the ground after

   (A) 2 s

   (B) 2.5 s

   (C) 3 s

   (D) 3.536 s

11. A pebble is thrown into a pond forming ripples whose radius increase at the rate of 4 in./s. How fast is the area of the ripple changing when the radius is one foot?

   (A) 2π in.^{2}/s

   (B) 24π in.^{2}/s

   (C) $\frac{2\pi}{3}$ ft^2/s

   (D) 2π ft^2/s

12. A piece of ice cut in the shape of a cube melts uniformly so that its volume decreases at 3 cm^3/s. How fast is its surface area decreasing when the edge of the cube is 5 cm?

   (A) $\frac{12}{25}$ cm^2/s

   (B) 2.4 cm^2/s

   (C) 3 cm^2/s

   (D) 6 cm^2/s

13. A 20-foot ladder leans against the wall of a building. The ladder starts sliding down the wall so that the top of the ladder moves down at the rate of 0.5 ft/s. How fast is the foot of the ladder moving away from the wall when the foot of the ladder is 12 feet from the wall?

   (A) 0.5 ft/s

   (B) $\frac{5}{8}$ ft/s

   (C) $\frac{2}{3}$ ft/s

   (D) $\frac{4}{3}$ ft/s

14. A spherical balloon is filled with air at 8 in.^{3}/s. How fast is the diameter of the balloon increasing when the volume of the balloon is 36π in.^{3}?

   (A) $\frac{4}{9\pi}$ in./s

   (B) $\frac{2}{3\pi}$ in./s

   (C) $\frac{2}{9\pi}$ in./s

   (D) $\frac{8}{27\pi}$ in./s

15. Two positive numbers have a sum of 10. Find their largest possible product.

(A) 5

(B) 10

(C) 25

(D) 50

16. Find the x-coordinate of the point on the graph of $4x + 3y = 7$ that is closest to the origin.

(A) 0

(B) 1

(C) 1.120

(D) 1.960

17. A rectangle is inscribed in the semicircle $y = \sqrt{4 - x^2}$. Find its largest possible area.

(A) 1.4

(B) $\sqrt{3}$

(C) $2\sqrt{3}$

(D) 4

18. Squares of equal size are cut off the corners of an 8 inches by 10 inches piece of cardboard. The sides are then turned up to form an open box. What is the largest possible volume of the box?

(A) 52.51 inches^3

(B) 52.50 inches^3

(C) 23.99 inches^3

(D) 1.5 inches^3

Free Response Questions

A graphing calculator is required for some questions.

1. A particle travels on a number line with position given by $s(t) = t \sin t$ for t in the interval $[0, 2\pi]$.

(a) Find the velocity and acceleration functions.

(b) For what value(s) of t is the particle at rest?

(c) Draw the path of the particle on a number line and show the direction of increasing t.

(d) Is the distance traveled by the particle greater than 10? Explain your answer.

Questions 2 and 3 provide practice with two techniques of using the graphing calculator in parametric mode to illustrate the motion of a particle on a number line.

- Set the MODE 1 to Par.
- In Y=, enter: $X_{1T} = t^2 - 4t$ and $Y_{1T} = 2$.
- In WINDOW, set Tmin = 0, Tmax = 5, and Tstep = 0.03. Set Xmin = −6, Xmax = 8, Ymin = −2, and Ymax = 5.

The bigger the value of Tstep, the faster the particle moves. When you press GRAPH, you will see the particle moving along a number line two units above the x-axis. Press TRACE and hold down ▶ to see the particle moving again. As it moves, you can see the values of t, x, and y at the bottom of the screen.

Using the TI-*n*spire

- To change the calculator to parametric mode, press MENU, then select **Graph Type**, **Parametric**.
- Tab to enter the following equations: $x1(t) = t^2 - 4t$, $y1(t) = t$ and change the parameters to $0 \le t \le 5$, tstep = 0.03.
- Alter the window settings to XMin = −6, XMax = 8, YMin = −2, and YMax = 5.
- Select MENU, **Trace, Graph Trace,** and use the arrows to see the particle move along the line.

2. Use the calculator to answer the following:

(a) When is the particle at rest?

(b) Describe the behavior of the particle as its position moves left toward −4.

(c) Describe the behavior of the particle as it moves to the right away from $x = -4$.

(d) Make a number line and draw the path of the particle showing the direction of increasing t.

3. In Y=, deselect X_{1T} and Y_{1T}, and enter $X_{2T} = 2t - 4$ and $Y_{2T} = 4$. Change Tstep to 0.01 and press GRAPH. Describe the motion of the particle and explain how this second function relates to the motion in #2.

4. A ball is thrown upward from the top of a building that is 80 feet tall toward a 6-foot-tall friend standing on the ground who reaches up to catch it. With what initial velocity must the ball be thrown upward to reach the friend's hand in 3 seconds?

5. A conical paper cup (vertex down) is being filled with water at the rate of 3 cm³/s. If the depth of the water is always twice the radius at the surface, find the following:

(a) How fast is the radius increasing when the water is 2 cm deep?

(b) How fast is the area of the surface of the water increasing when the water is 2 cm deep?

6. A coffee maker has a filter in the shape of a cone with radius 5 cm. 500 cm³ of water are poured. Brewed coffee drips out of the cone at the rate of 20 cm³/min into a cylindrical coffee pot that has the same radius as the filter holder.

(a) Find a formula for the rate of change of the depth of the coffee in the coffee pot.

(b) What is the final depth of the coffee in the coffee pot?

7. A rectangle is inscribed above the x-axis in the parabola $y = a^2 - x^2$ as shown below. Find the area of the largest possible rectangle.

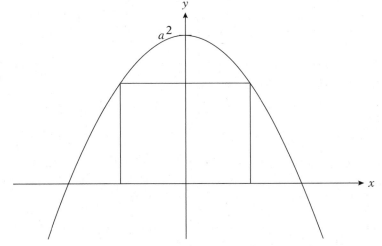

8. A rectangular plot is to be fenced in using the side of an existing barn that is 50 feet long as one side of the plot. Two hundred feet of fencing are available for the other three sides of the plot. Find the largest possible area that can be enclosed.

9. Twenty feet of wire are to be used to create a wire sculpture that consists of a square and a circle. Find the largest number of square feet of area that can be enclosed by the square and the circle.

Lesson 8: Applications of the Derivative, Part 2 (BC Exam Only)

- Derivatives of Parametric Functions
- Derivatives of Vector-Valued Functions
- Tangent Lines of Polar Equations

This lesson discusses derivatives with parametric, vector-valued, and polar functions. These topics are found only on the AP Calculus BC exam, so if you are sitting for the AB exam, you may skip this lesson.

Explain: Derivatives of Parametric Functions

In systems of parametric equations, the x- and y-coordinates of a point are given in terms of another variable called the parameter, often denoted by the letter t. To find the derivative $\frac{dy}{dx}$, use the formula $\frac{dy}{dx} = \frac{\frac{dy}{dt}}{\frac{dx}{dt}}$. The derivative $\frac{dy}{dx}$ is defined for values of t where $\frac{dx}{dt}$ exists, and t can denote time. The components of the velocity vector are $(x'(t), y'(t))$.

MODEL PROBLEMS

FR **1.** $x(t) = 3t^2 - 2t$, $y(t) = 6t + 2$. Find $\frac{dy}{dx}$ at $t = 1$ and the velocity vector at $t = 1$.

Solution

$\frac{dy}{dx} = \frac{\frac{dy}{dt}}{\frac{dx}{dt}} = \frac{6}{6t - 2}$	We use the given formula.
$\frac{dy}{dx} = \frac{6}{4} = \frac{3}{2}$	Evaluate at $t = 1$.
The velocity vector is $(6t - 2, 6)$. When $t = 1$, the vector is $(4, 6)$.	

2. What is $\frac{dy}{dx}$ when $x(t) = 2\cos t$ and $y(t) = 2\sin t$?

(A) $2\sec t$

(B) $-\cot t$

(C) $\tan t$

(D) $-2\tan t$

Solution

Use the formula $\dfrac{dy}{dx} = \dfrac{\frac{dy}{dt}}{\frac{dx}{dt}}$ to determine the derivative of this parametric function. Don't forget to completely simplify your answer.

3. If $x(t) = t + \cos t$ and $y(t) = \sin t$, find the first derivative of this parametric function.

(A) $\sin t$

(B) $1 - \cos t$

(C) $\dfrac{t}{\sec t}$

(D) $\dfrac{\cos t}{1 - \sin t}$

Solution

Again we need to use the formula to find the derivative and completely simplify our final answer.

4. The position of a particle moving in the xy-plane is given by the parametric equations $x(t) = \dfrac{4t}{t+2}$ and $y(t) = \dfrac{-6}{t^2+9}$. What is the slope of the line tangent to the path of the particle at $t = 1$?

(A) $\dfrac{3}{4}$

(B) $\dfrac{1}{2}$

(C) $\dfrac{27}{200}$

(D) There is no tangent line at $t = 1$.

Solution

Here we must find the derivative of the given parametric equations and then determine the value at $t = 1$. This question is similar in structure to the question in Model Problem #1 on page 166.

Explain: Derivatives of Vector Valued Functions

A vector-valued function is one such that its domain is a subset of the real numbers and its range is a vector. Suppose that $r(t) = (f(t), g(t), h(t))$ is a vector-valued function. Its derivative, then, is

$$r'(t) = \big(f'(t), g'(t), h'(t)\big)$$

We simply take the derivative of each vector component.

MODEL PROBLEMS

FR **1.** What is $r'(t)$ if $r(t) = \big(\cos(t^2),\ e^{t^3}, \ln t\big)$?

Solution

Mathematically, all we need to do is find the derivative of each component of the vector. So $r'(t) = \left(-2t\sin(t^2),\ 3t^2 e^{t^3}, \dfrac{1}{t}\right)$.

2. An object is moving in a plane such that its position vector is $r(t) = (t^3, t^2)$. Find its velocity vector when $t = 2$.

(A) $(12, 4)$

(B) $(8, 4)$

(C) $(12, 8)$

(D) $(8, 6)$

Solution

$r'(t) = (3t^2, 2t)$	Find the derivative.
$r'(2) = (3(2)^2, 2(2)) = (12, 4)$	Evaluate at $t = 2$. The correct answer is (A).
Note that we can find the acceleration vector of the particle by taking the derivative of $r'(t)$ and then evaluating at $t = 2$.	
$r''(t) = (6t, 2)$	Determine the derivative of $r'(t)$.
$r''(2) = (6(2), 2) = (12, 2)$	This is the acceleration vector.

FR 3. Find the velocity and acceleration vectors of a particle whose position vector is $r(t) = (t^3, e^t, te^t)$.

Solution

Here we are not given a value of t, so we are just looking for the velocity and acceleration vectors, which will both be functions of t. Find the first and second derivatives of $r(t)$.

Explain: Tangent Lines of Polar Equations

We can find the tangent line to a polar curve defined as $r = f(\theta)$ when we regard θ as a parameter. The parametric equations are then

$$x = r\cos(\theta) = f(\theta)\cos(\theta) \text{ and}$$

$$y = r\sin(\theta) = f(\theta)\sin(\theta),$$

and we know that $\dfrac{dy}{dx} = \dfrac{\frac{dy}{d\theta}}{\frac{dx}{d\theta}} = \dfrac{\frac{dr}{d\theta}\sin\theta + r\cos\theta}{\frac{dr}{d\theta}\cos\theta - r\sin\theta}$. We can locate the

horizontal tangent of a polar curve by finding the points where $\dfrac{dy}{d\theta} = 0$

(provided that $\dfrac{dx}{d\theta} \neq 0$) and vertical tangents are located where $\dfrac{dx}{d\theta} = 0$

(provided that $\dfrac{dy}{d\theta} \neq 0$). Note that if we are looking for tangents at a pole,

then we know that $r = 0$ and the derivative equation simplifies to $\dfrac{dy}{dx} = \tan(\theta)$

if $\dfrac{dr}{d\theta} \neq 0$.

MODEL PROBLEMS

FR **1.** Find the equation of the tangent line for the curve $r = 1 + \cos(\theta)$ at $\theta = \frac{\pi}{3}$.

Solution

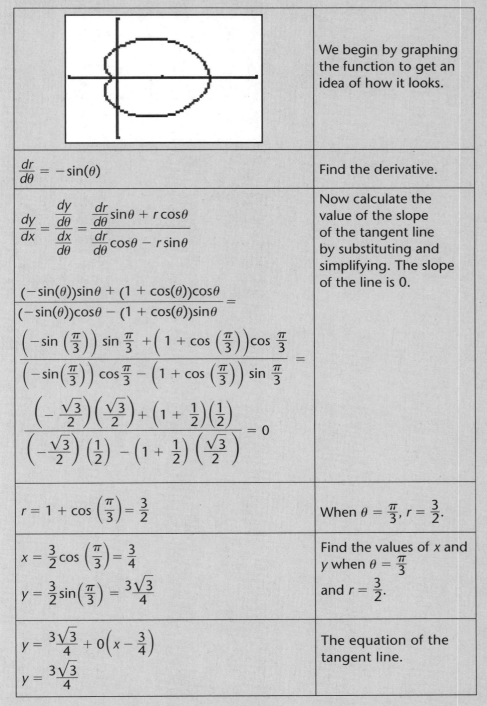	We begin by graphing the function to get an idea of how it looks.
$\dfrac{dr}{d\theta} = -\sin(\theta)$	Find the derivative.
$\dfrac{dy}{dx} = \dfrac{\dfrac{dy}{d\theta}}{\dfrac{dx}{d\theta}} = \dfrac{\dfrac{dr}{d\theta}\sin\theta + r\cos\theta}{\dfrac{dr}{d\theta}\cos\theta - r\sin\theta}$ $\dfrac{(-\sin(\theta))\sin\theta + (1+\cos(\theta))\cos\theta}{(-\sin(\theta))\cos\theta - (1+\cos(\theta))\sin\theta} =$ $\dfrac{\left(-\sin\left(\frac{\pi}{3}\right)\right)\sin\frac{\pi}{3} + \left(1+\cos\left(\frac{\pi}{3}\right)\right)\cos\frac{\pi}{3}}{\left(-\sin\left(\frac{\pi}{3}\right)\right)\cos\frac{\pi}{3} - \left(1+\cos\left(\frac{\pi}{3}\right)\right)\sin\frac{\pi}{3}} =$ $\dfrac{\left(-\frac{\sqrt{3}}{2}\right)\left(\frac{\sqrt{3}}{2}\right) + \left(1+\frac{1}{2}\right)\left(\frac{1}{2}\right)}{\left(-\frac{\sqrt{3}}{2}\right)\left(\frac{1}{2}\right) - \left(1+\frac{1}{2}\right)\left(\frac{\sqrt{3}}{2}\right)} = 0$	Now calculate the value of the slope of the tangent line by substituting and simplifying. The slope of the line is 0.
$r = 1 + \cos\left(\frac{\pi}{3}\right) = \frac{3}{2}$	When $\theta = \frac{\pi}{3}$, $r = \frac{3}{2}$.
$x = \frac{3}{2}\cos\left(\frac{\pi}{3}\right) = \frac{3}{4}$ $y = \frac{3}{2}\sin\left(\frac{\pi}{3}\right) = \frac{3\sqrt{3}}{4}$	Find the values of x and y when $\theta = \frac{\pi}{3}$ and $r = \frac{3}{2}$.
$y = \frac{3\sqrt{3}}{4} + 0\left(x - \frac{3}{4}\right)$ $y = \frac{3\sqrt{3}}{4}$	The equation of the tangent line.

FR **2.** Find the equation of the tangent line for the curve $r = 2 + 6\sin(\theta)$ at $\theta = \frac{\pi}{6}$.

Solution

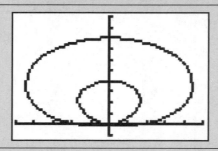	Graph the function.
$\dfrac{dr}{d\theta} = 6\cos(\theta)$	Find the function's derivative.

Now find the slope of the tangent line by substituting into

$$\frac{dy}{dx} = \frac{\dfrac{dy}{d\theta}}{\dfrac{dx}{d\theta}} = \frac{\dfrac{dr}{d\theta}\sin\theta + r\cos\theta}{\dfrac{dr}{d\theta}\cos\theta - r\sin\theta} \quad \text{and simplifying.}$$

AP Calculus Exam-Type Questions

Multiple Choice Questions
A graphing calculator is required for some questions.

For Questions 1 and 2, the motion of the particle is $x(t) = 3t^2 - 3$, $y(t) = 2t + 1$, when $t \geq 0$.

1. Find the slope of the tangent at $t = 1$.

    (A) $\dfrac{1}{3}$

    (B) 1

    (C) 2

    (D) 3

2. Find the speed of the particle at $t = 1$.

    (A) 0.333

    (B) 2.828

    (C) 6.164

    (D) 6.325

3. Find the speed of a particle at $t = 3$ for the system with parametric equations $x(t) = 3t^3 - 1$ and $y(t) = t - 1$.

    (A) $\dfrac{1}{27}$

    (B) 9

    (C) $\dfrac{1}{9}$

    (D) 81

4. The position of a particle moving the xy-plane is given by $r(t) = \left(\ln(t^2 + 2t), 2t^2\right)$ when time $t > 0$. What is the particle's velocity vector at time $t = 2$?

    (A) $\left(\dfrac{3}{4}, 8\right)$

    (B) $\left(\dfrac{3}{4}, 4\right)$

    (C) $\left(\dfrac{1}{8}, 8\right)$

    (D) $\left(\dfrac{1}{8}, 4\right)$

5. In the xy-plane, a particle is moving so that when $t > 0$, its x-coordinate is $t^3 - t$ and its y-coordinate is $(2t - 1)^3$. What is the acceleration vector when $t = 3$?

    (A) $(24, 125)$

    (B) $(26, 125)$

    (C) $(18, 120)$

    (D) $(28, 120)$

6. When $t \geq 0$, the position of a particle in the xy-plane is $x(t) = t^2 + 1$ and $y(t) = \ln(2t + 6)$. What is the particle's acceleration vector?

    (A) $\left(2, (t + 3)^{-1}\right)$

    (B) $\left(2, -(t + 3)^{-2}\right)$

    (C) $\left(2t, -(t + 3)^{-2}\right)$

    (D) $\left(2t, (t + 3)\right)$

Free Response Questions
A graphing calculator is required for some questions.

1. Sketch the graph of the system of parametric equations:

    $x(t) = 3\sin t - 3$, $y(t) = t - 1$ for $0 \leq t \leq 2\pi$.

    (a) Sketch the path of the particle, indicating the direction of increasing t.

    (b) Find the position of the particle at $t = 3$.

    (c) Find the velocity of the particle at $t = 3$.

    (d) Find the speed of the particle at $t = 3$.

    (e) Find the slope of the line tangent to the graph at $t = 3$.

2. Find the equations of the tangent lines to the curve $r = 1 - 2\sin(\theta)$ at $(0, 0)$.

Lesson 9: Slope Fields

- Defining and Drawing Slope Fields
- Differential Equations and Their Slope Fields

In Lesson 3.9 we will review how to solve **differential equations**, which are simply equations whose terms include the derivative(s) of a function with respect to an independent variable. Such equations are to be solved for an unknown function. We can and will work such problems analytically, but in this lesson we introduce the concept of slope fields. Generally, a slope field is a graphical representation of the family of solutions of a first-order differential equation. These representations are useful because they allow us to visualize solutions to differential equations as well as numerically approximate them.

Explain: Defining and Drawing Slope Fields

Imagine the coordinate plane and all the points (x, y). Suppose that $\frac{dy}{dx} = f(x)g(y)$ is a differential equation, where f and g are given functions of their indicated variables. A solution would be a function $y = y(x)$ whose first derivative equals the product of f and g. Now suppose that we calculate the value of $\frac{dy}{dx}$ at every point in the plane and then draw a tiny line segment at each point with slope equal to $\frac{dy}{dx}$. The resulting set of tiny line segments is the slope field. Since drawing a line segment at every point on the coordinate plane is simply not possible, we are usually given a finite number of points at which to draw the slope field.

MODEL PROBLEM

1. Draw the slope field for the differential equation $\frac{dy}{dx} = \frac{x}{y}$ at each point (x, y) where x and y are the integers $-1 \leq x \leq 1$ and $-1 \leq y \leq 1$.

Solution

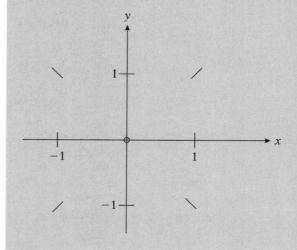

We are creating a slope field for the equation in the given interval.

Calculator Note

The graphing calculator can be used to draw slope fields. There is a program that can be entered into the TI-83/84 to draw slope fields, but the TI-89 is tailor-made for drawing slope fields since it has a built-in slope fields program and a better display window than the TI-83/84. Slope fields may also be easily graphed on the **TI-nspire**.

The instructions that follow are for the TI-89.

Press MODE. On the first line scroll right on Graph → DIFF EQUATIONS. Then press ENTER twice (once to make the choice and the second time to lock it into the calculator's memory). Now access the Y= screen. When using the TI-89 it is important to note that y is a function of t so to input the differential equation $\dfrac{dy}{dx} = 2xy$, we would enter 2t × y1.

Press Zoom 4 and the slope field will appear on the screen. To see the slope field below, press ◆ WINDOW and set Xmin = −5 and Xmax = 5.

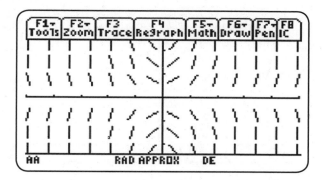

Recall a slope field shows the family of solutions to a given differential equation. To determine which specific solution we are after, we are usually given an **initial condition**, abbreviated IC. The symbol y_i1 on the equation entry screen allows us to enter an IC. We can also enter an IC by pressing 2ND F3 when in the graph screen. We can enter more than IC at a time so we can see what properties the solutions have in common.

So, in other words, initial conditions are values of the solution and/or its derivative(s) at specific points. As we will see eventually, solutions to sufficiently nice differential equations are unique and hence only one solution will meet the given conditions.

MODEL PROBLEMS

FR **1.** Graph the slope field for $\frac{dy}{dx} = 2xy$ using your calculator and then enter the initial conditions $t = 0$, $y1 = 2$ and $t = 0$, $y1 = -1$. Sketch what you see.

Solution

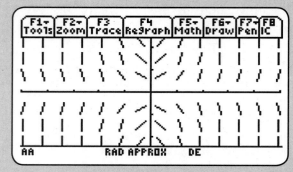

We graph the slope field.

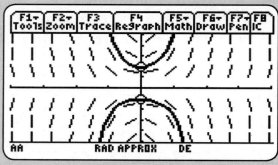

We graph the initial conditions.

2. The slope field for the differential equation $\frac{dy}{dx} = x^2$

(A) has all line segments symmetric to the y-axis.

(B) shows that the solution to the differential equation are even functions.

(C) shows that the graphs of the solutions are increasing for increasing x.

(D) shows that all the solutions have a horizontal asymptote.

Solution

The derivative of a function gives its slope. So we are looking to analyze what happens when the slope of y with respect to x is x^2. The line segments will not all be symmetric to the y-axis, so choice (A) is incorrect. Which of the remaining three choices makes sense?

Explain: Differential Equations and Their Slope Fields

A common task on the AP Calculus exam is to match a differential equation to its slope field. Below we outline some common features you can look for on slope field graphs to identify their differential equations.

Differential Equation Type	Slope Field
$\frac{dy}{dx}$ is equal to a constant, such as in $\frac{dy}{dx} = \frac{1}{2}$. For these types of differential equations the slope is constant no matter what point you consider. Notice that all the lines in the slope field have a slope of $\frac{1}{2}$.	
Suppose that the differential equation has only an x-term as in $\frac{dy}{dx} = x + 2$. We can see that the all the slope lines with the same x-coordinate have the same slope.	
What about a differential equation that has only a y-term as in $\frac{dy}{dx} = 3y$? We can see that the all the slope lines with the same y-coordinate have the same slope.	

When a differential equation contains both an *x*- and a *y*-term, we must look for points that have the same slope to determine the equation.

MODEL PROBLEMS

1.

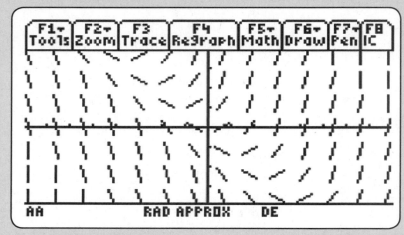

Shown above is a slope field for which of the following differential equations?

(A) $\dfrac{dy}{dx} = x + y$

(B) $\dfrac{dy}{dx} = -\dfrac{x}{y}$

(C) $\dfrac{dy}{dx} = -y + 1$

(D) $\dfrac{dy}{dx} = x + xy$

Solution

Examination of the slope field reveals this is not the graph of a constant, or of an equation containing just an *x*- or *y*-term. This eliminates choice (C). We make table to try to see the differential equation.

x	y	$\dfrac{dy}{dx}$
0	−1	−1
−1	0	−1
1	2	3
2	1	3
2	2	4

From our table we see that if we sum the *x*- and *y*-terms, the result is $\dfrac{dy}{dx}$. Thus, $\dfrac{dy}{dx} = x + y$ and the correct answer is (A).

2.

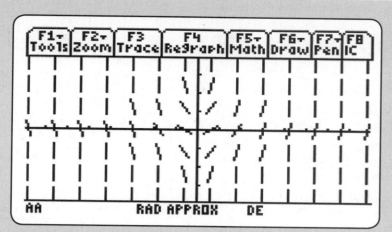

Shown above is a slope field for which of the following differential equations?

(A) $\dfrac{dy}{dx} = \dfrac{y^2}{x}$

(B) $\dfrac{dy}{dx} = -y + 1$

(C) $\dfrac{dy}{dx} = -\dfrac{x}{y}$

(D) $\dfrac{dy}{dx} = x + xy^2$

Solution

Clearly this is not the graph of a constant. Move to analyzing the slopes of the *x*-coordinates. Do all the points with the same *x*-coordinate have the same slope? We can see they do not. The same is true for the *y*-coordinates, so the correct differential equation has both an *x*- and *y*-term. Eliminate choice (B). Try using a chart as we did in Model Problem #1 and solve from here.

AP Calculus Exam-Type Questions

Multiple Choice Questions

A graphing calculator is required for some questions.

1. In a slope field, the line segments are

   (A) part of the graph of the solution to the differential equation.

   (B) parts of the lines tangent to the graphs of the solutions to the differential equation.

   (C) asymptotes to the graph of the solution of the differential equation.

   (D) lines of the symmetry of the graph of the solution to the differential equation.

2. Drawing a slope field

   (A) provides a way of visualizing the solutions to a differential equation.

   (B) can help find horizontal asymptotes to the graphs of the solutions of the differential equation.

   (C) can serve as a check to the solutions of a differential equation.

   (D) All of the above.

3. The slope field for the differential equation $\dfrac{dy}{dx} = x$

    (A) has line segments symmetric to the y-axis.
    (B) shows that the solutions to the differential equation are odd functions.
    (C) shows that the solutions to the differential equation are straight lines.
    (D) shows that the solutions to the differential equation are decreasing for increasing x.

4. The slope field for $\dfrac{dy}{dx} = y$ shows that the solutions to the differential equation

    (A) have y-intercept (0, 1).
    (B) have a positive y-intercept.
    (C) have a horizontal asymptote.
    (D) are even functions.

5. Which is the slope field for the differential equation $\dfrac{dy}{dx} = 2y - 4$?

    (A)

    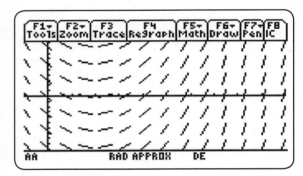

    (B)

    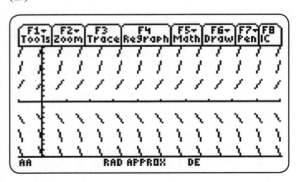

(C)

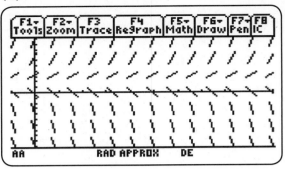

(D)

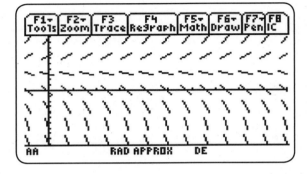

6. Which graph shows a slope field with a solution to the differential equation $\dfrac{dy}{dx} = y^2$?

    (A)

    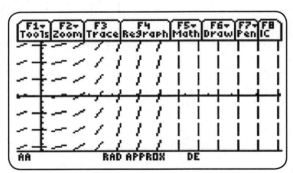

    (B)

    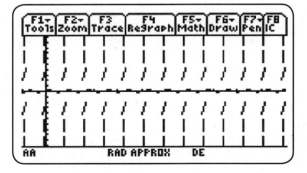

(C)

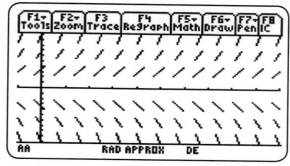

(D)

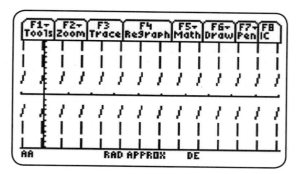

7. Of the four curves *A, B, C,* and *D,* on the slope field shown, which graphs the function that is the solution to the equation $\dfrac{dy}{dx} = -\dfrac{x}{y}$ with initial condition $y(0) = 4$?

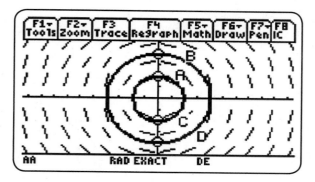

(A) *A*

(B) *B*

(C) *C*

(D) *D*

8. The solution to $\dfrac{dy}{dx} = -x$ with initial condition $y(0) = 1$

(A) is always concave up.

(B) is always concave down.

(C) is undefined at $x = 0$.

(D) is always increasing.

Free Response Question

A graphing calculator is required.

1. Given the differential equation $\dfrac{dy}{dx} = \dfrac{2x}{y}$,

(a) find the value of $\dfrac{dy}{dx}$ at the points (x, y) where x and y are integers such that $-2 \le x \le 2$ and $-2 \le y \le 2$.

(b) On graph paper, draw a tiny line segment at each of the points above with slope equal to the value of $\dfrac{dy}{dx}$ at that point.

(c) In which quadrants is $\dfrac{dy}{dx} > 0$? In which quadrants is $\dfrac{dy}{dx} < 0$?

(d) For what values of x and y is $\dfrac{dy}{dx} = 0$? For what values is $\dfrac{dy}{dx}$ undefined?

Lesson 10: Mean Value Theorem and Rolle's Theorem

- Mean Value Theorem
- Rolle's Theorem

Explain: Mean Value Theorem

The **Mean Value Theorem** is one of the most important theorems in calculus. It states that if a function, $f(x)$, is continuous on the closed interval $[a, b]$ and is differentiable on the open interval (a, b), then there is at least one number, c, in the interval (a, b) such that $f'(c) = \dfrac{f(b) - f(a)}{b - a}$.

Consider the graph below. If we draw line AB to join the endpoints $(a, f(a))$ and $(b, f(b))$, then by the Mean Value Theorem, there must be at least one value in (a, b), called c, where the tangent line at $(c, f(c))$ is parallel to line AB.

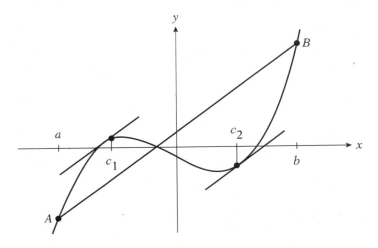

MODEL PROBLEMS

FR **1.** Show that $f(x) = x^2 - 2x$ satisfies the conditions of the Mean Value Theorem on the closed interval $[-1, 2]$.

Solution

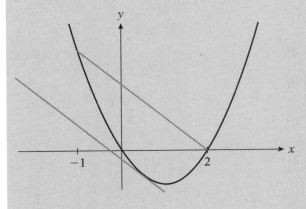

To satisfy the conditions of the Mean Value Theorem, the function must be continuous on the closed interval $[-1, 2]$ and differentiable on the open interval $(-1, 2)$. Both of these conditions are satisfied by a quadratic function.

FR **TT** **2.** Find the value of c guaranteed by the Mean Value Theorem for $f(x) = \ln x$ on the closed interval $[1, e^2]$.

Solution

To use the Mean Value Theorem, we must make sure the given function is continuous on the closed interval and differentiable on the open interval. In both cases the answer is yes, so we can go ahead with the problem as we are guaranteed that such a value exists.

$f'(c) = \dfrac{f(b) - f(a)}{b - a}$	There exists a value, c, such that this is true.
$\dfrac{1}{c} = \dfrac{\ln(e^2) - \ln(1)}{e^2 - 1}$	Substitute.
$\dfrac{1}{c} = \dfrac{2}{e^2 - 1}$ $c = \dfrac{e^2 - 1}{2} \approx 3.195$	Solve for c. The solution is in the open interval $(1, e^2)$.

3. Find the value(s) of c guaranteed by the Mean Value Theorem for $f(x) = 3x^3 - 4x^2 + x - 1$ on the interval $[0, 2]$.

(A) $c = -0.357, 1.25$

(B) $c = 1.25$

(C) $c = 1$

(D) This function does not satisfy the conditions of the Mean Value Theorem.

Solution

This problem is very similar to Model Problem #2. First check and make sure you can use the Mean Value Theorem for this function. If so, proceed to determine the value of c. Be sure to pay attention to the interval.

Explain: Rolle's Theorem

Rolle's Theorem is a special case of the Mean Value Theorem. Suppose that a function is continuous on the closed interval $[a, b]$ and has a derivative on the open interval (a, b), but the values of $f(a)$ and $f(b)$ are equal. Then there must be at least one value, c, between a and b such that the function has a horizontal tangent.

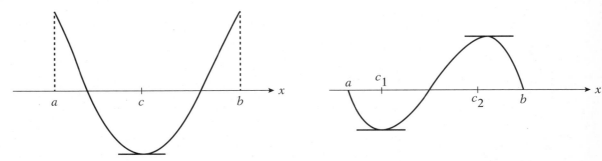

MODEL PROBLEMS

1. Find the value of c guaranteed by Rolle's Theorem for $f(x) = 1 - x^2$ in the interval $[-1, 1]$.

(A) $c = \dfrac{1}{2}$

(B) $c = -2$

(C) $c = 0$

(D) This function does not satisfy the conditions of Rolle's theorem.

Solution

First check to make sure the function is continuous on the given closed interval and differentiable on the open interval. As it is, we can proceed. Now, is $f(-1) = f(1)$? Both $f(-1)$ and $f(1) = 0$ so this function satisfies the conditions of Rolle's theorem. We are guaranteed a value c in the open interval where $f'(c) = 0$.

$0 = -2c$ $0 = c$	Solve for c.
Since $c = 0$ lies in the given open interval, the correct answer is (C).	

2. Find the value of c guaranteed by Rolle's Theorem for $f(x) = x^3 - 3x^2 + 2$ in the interval $[0, 3]$.

(A) $c = 1, 2$

(B) $c = 0, 2$

(C) $c = 2$

(D) This function does not satisfy the conditions of Rolle's theorem.

Solution

Check to make sure the given function satisfies all the conditions of Rolle's Theorem. If so, solve for the value of c, paying close attention to the interval.

AP Calculus Exam-Type Questions

Multiple Choice Questions

A graphing calculator is required for some questions.

1. Which of the following functions satisfy the assumptions of Rolle's Theorem on the interval [0, 2]?

   I. $f(x) = \dfrac{1}{|x - 1|}$.

   II. $f(x) = |x - 1|$.

   III. $f(x) = x^2 - 2x$.

   (A) I only

   (B) II only

   (C) III only

   (D) II and III

2. Which of the following functions satisfy the hypotheses of the Mean Value Theorem on the interval [0, 2]?

   I. $f(x) = \sin \pi x + \cos 2x$.

   II. $f(x) = \sqrt[3]{x - 8}$.

   III. $f(x) = |x^2 - 2x|$.

   (A) II only

   (B) III only

   (C) I and II

   (D) I, II, and III

3. At what value(s) of x in the interval [0, 2] is the slope of the line tangent to $f(x) = x^3 - 3x^2$ equal to the slope of the line joining $(0, f(0))$ and $(2, f(2))$?

   (A) 0.423

   (B) 1.577

   (C) 2

   (D) 0.423 and 1.577

4. How many values of c satisfy the conclusion of the Mean Value Theorem for $f(x) = x^3 + 1$ on the interval [-1, 1]?

   (A) 0

   (B) 1

   (C) 2

   (D) 3

5. How many values of c are guaranteed by Rolle's Theorem for the function $f(x) = \dfrac{\sin x}{x}$ on the interval [-10, 10]?

   (A) 5

   (B) 6

   (C) 7

   (D) The theorem does not apply this this function.

6. A function f is continuous on the closed interval [-1, 0] with $f(-1) = 0$ and $f(0) = 3$. Which of the following additional conditions guarantees that there is a number c in the open interval (-1, 0) such that $f'(c) = 0$?

   (A) No additional conditions are necessary.

   (B) f has a relative extremum on the open interval (-1, 0).

   (C) f is differentiable on the open interval (-1, 0).

   (D) The limit of f exists at $x = 2$.

Free Response Questions

A graphing calculator is required for some questions.

For each of Questions 1–4:

(a) Determine if the function satisfies the two hypotheses of the Mean Value Theorem on the indicated interval.

(b) If the function satisfies the hypotheses of the Mean Value Theorem, find the value of $f'(c)$ guaranteed by the theorem on the indicated interval.

1. $f(x) = \dfrac{1}{x}$ on [1, 3]

2. $f(x) = \dfrac{x}{x - 2}$ on [1, 3]

3. $f(x) = |x - 2|$ on [1, 3]

4. $f(x) = x^{2/3}$ on $[0, 1]$

5. Find the value(s) of c guaranteed by Rolle's Theorem for $f(x) = x \sin x$ on the interval $[-3, 3]$.

6. (a) Find the value of c guaranteed by the Mean Value Theorem for $f(x) = e^x - x$ on the interval $[-2, 2]$.

(b) Using the DRAW menu on the calculator ([2nd] DRAW 5: Tangent), draw a line tangent to the graph of $f(x) = e^x - x$ at the value of c found in part (a). Then go to [2nd] DRAW 2: Line, and draw a line joining $(-2, f(-2))$ and $(2, f(2))$. Sketch what you see.

CALCULUS AB/BC

SECTION I, Part A

Time – 60 minutes
Number of problems – 30

A graphing calculator is not permitted for these problems.

1. Find the value(s) of x for which $f(x) = e^x$ is increasing.

   (A) $x > 0$
   (B) All real numbers
   (C) $x < 0$
   (D) $x = 0$

2. For what values of x is $f(x) = -x^2 + 2x$ increasing?

   (A) $x > 0$
   (B) $x < 1$
   (C) $x > 2$
   (D) $x < 2$

3. Find the average rate of change of $y = \dfrac{x}{1 + x^2}$ on the interval $[1, 2]$.

   (A) 0.35
   (B) 0.15
   (C) 0.50
   (D) 0.85

4. $f(x) = \ln(\sin x)$. Find $f'\left(\dfrac{\pi}{4}\right)$.

   (A) $-\dfrac{1}{2}\ln 2$
   (B) $\dfrac{\sqrt{2}}{2}$
   (C) 0
   (D) 1

5. $y = \sin 2x - x$. Find $y'\left(\dfrac{\pi}{2}\right)$.

   (A) -3
   (B) -1
   (C) 0
   (D) 1

6. $y = \ln\left(e^{x^2-1}\right)$. Find $y'(1)$

   (A) 0
   (B) $\dfrac{1}{2}$
   (C) 1
   (D) 2

7. $y = e^{x^3}$. Find $y'(1)$.

   (A) $3e^2$
   (B) $3e$
   (C) e
   (D) e^3

8. For what values of x is $f(x) = \sqrt{(\ln x)^2}$ differentiable?

   (A) $x > 0$
   (B) $x \geq 1$
   (C) $x \neq 0$
   (D) $x > 0$ and $x \neq 1$

9. Find $\dfrac{dy}{dx}$ for $xy + x - y = 2$ when $x = 0$.

   (A) -2
   (B) -1
   (C) 0
   (D) 1

10. Find the derivative of $f(x) = x^2 - \ln x$.

    (A) $2x - 1$
    (B) $2x - \ln x$
    (C) $2x - \dfrac{1}{x}$
    (D) $x - \dfrac{1}{x}$

11. Find the second derivative of $\sqrt{(x^2 + 1)}$.

(A) $(x^2 + 1)^{-3/2}$

(B) $(x^2 + 1)^{-1/2}$

(C) $x(x^2 + 1)^{-1/2}$

(D) $2x(x^2 + 1)^{-3/2}$

12. Find y'' for $y = x \ln x - 3x$.

(A) $\frac{1}{x} - 3$

(B) $1 + \ln x$

(C) $\ln x - 2$

(D) $\frac{1}{x}$

13. Find the slope of the tangent to the graph of $y = \sqrt{(x + 2)}$ at $x = -1$.

(A) $-\frac{\sqrt{2}}{2}$

(B) $-\frac{1}{2}$

(C) $\frac{1}{2}$

(D) $\frac{\sqrt{2}}{2}$

14. Write the equation of the line tangent to the graph of $x = y^2 + 4$ at the point $(5, 1)$.

(A) $2y = x - 2$

(B) $2y = x - 3$

(C) $2y = x + 9$

(D) $2y = x - 7$

15. Write the equation of the line tangent to the graph of $f(x) = \frac{1}{(x^2 + 2)}$ at $x = 0$.

(A) $y = \frac{1}{2}$

(B) $x = \frac{1}{2}$

(C) $y = -\frac{16}{81}x + \frac{1}{2}$

(D) $y = -\frac{1}{2}$

16. Which of the following is a condition for Rolle's Theorem that is not satisfied by $f(x) = \frac{2}{x - 1}$ on the interval $[3, 5]$?

(A) f is continuous on $[3, 5]$.

(B) f is differentiable on $(3, 5)$.

(C) $f(3) = f(5)$

(D) $f'(c) = 0$

17. Which of the following could be the slope field for the differential equation $\frac{dy}{dx} = y^2 - 4$?

(A)

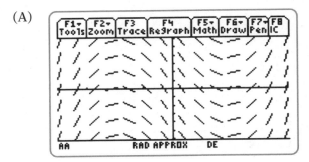

(B)

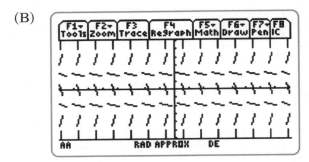

(C)

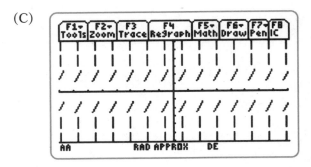

(D)

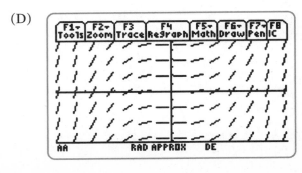

Questions 18–19: Use $x(t) = 2t^2$ and $y(t) = 4t - 1$.

BC **18.** Find the slope of the line tangent to the curve at $t = 1$.

(A) -4

(B) $\dfrac{1}{4}$

(C) 1

(D) 4

BC **19.** Find the equation of the line tangent to the curve at $t = 1$.

(A) $y = x + 1$

(B) $y = 4x - 5$

(C) $y = \dfrac{1}{4}x + \dfrac{5}{2}$

(D) $y = -4x + 11$

20. Find $\dfrac{dy}{dx}$ if $x^2 + y^2 = -2xy$.

(A) 1

(B) -1

(C) $\dfrac{x - y}{x + y}$

(D) $\dfrac{x + y}{x - y}$

21. Find the slope of the line tangent to the graph of $2xy^2 + xy = y$ when $y = 1$.

(A) $-\dfrac{9}{2}$

(B) $-\dfrac{2}{9}$

(C) $\dfrac{2}{9}$

(D) $\dfrac{1}{3}$

22. The equation of the tangent line to the graph of $x \cos y + y = x^2$ at the point $(1, 0)$ is

(A) $y = 2x$

(B) $y = x$

(C) $y = x - 1$

(D) $y = -x + 1$

For Questions 23–26, consider a particle whose motion is represented by the position equation $s(t) = t^2 - t$, $t \geq 0$, where s is in feet and t is in seconds.

23. The velocity of the particle after two seconds is

(A) $0\,\text{ft/s}$

(B) $1\,\text{ft/s}$

(C) $2\,\text{ft/s}$

(D) $3\,\text{ft/s}$

24. The acceleration of the particle after two seconds is

(A) $0\,\text{ft/s}^2$

(B) $1\,\text{ft/s}^2$

(C) $2\,\text{ft/s}^2$

(D) $3\,\text{ft/s}^2$

25. What is the position of the particle at $t = 2$ seconds?

(A) $0\,\text{ft}$

(B) $1\,\text{ft}$

(C) $2\,\text{ft}$

(D) $3\,\text{ft}$

26. At what value(s) of t does the particle change direction?

(A) $t = \dfrac{1}{2}$

(B) $t = 1$

(C) $t = 1$ and $t = 2$

(D) $t = 2$

27. Find the interval(s) where $f(x) = -x^4 + 3x^2 - 2$ is greater than 0.

(A) $(-\infty, -1.225) \cup (0, 1.225)$

(B) $\left(-\infty, -\dfrac{\sqrt{6}}{2}\right) \cup \left(0, \dfrac{\sqrt{6}}{2}\right)$

(C) $\left(-\sqrt{2}, -1\right) \cup \left(1, \sqrt{2}\right)$

(D) $(-1.414, -1) \cup (1, 1.414)$

28. Over what interval is the graph of $y = x^3 + 3x^2 - 2x + 1$ concave up?

(A) $(-\infty, -1)$

(B) $(-1, \infty)$

(C) $\left(-1 - \dfrac{\sqrt{15}}{3}, \infty\right)$

(D) $\left(-\infty, -1 + \dfrac{\sqrt{15}}{3}\right)$

29. Where does $f'(x)$ not exist for $f(x) = \sqrt[3]{x - 2}$?

(A) $x < 2$

(B) $x = 2$

(C) $x > 2$

(D) $x \geq 2$

30. Find y'' for $y = \cos(x^2 + 2)$.

(A) $-2x \sin(2x)$

(B) $-2x \sin(x^2 + 2)$

(C) $-4x^2 \cos(x^2 + 2) - 2 \sin(x^2 + 2)$

(D) $4x^2 \cos(x^2 + 2) + 2 \sin(x^2 + 2)$

CALCULUS AB/BC

SECTION I, Part B

Time – 45 minutes
Number of problems – 15

A graphing calculator is required for these problems.

1. For what part of the interval $[-\pi, \pi]$ is $y = -2\sin x$ decreasing?

   (A) $\left[-\frac{\pi}{2}, \frac{\pi}{2}\right]$

   (B) $\left[-\frac{\pi}{3}, \frac{\pi}{3}\right]$

   (C) $\left[-\frac{\pi}{4}, \frac{\pi}{4}\right]$

   (D) $[-\pi, 0]$

2. Find the number of horizontal asymptotes of $y = 2 - \ln x$.

   (A) 0

   (B) 1

   (C) 2

   (D) 3

3. Find the value of $\lim\limits_{h \to 0} \dfrac{\tan\left(\frac{\pi}{4} + h\right) - \tan\left(\frac{\pi}{4}\right)}{h}$.

   (A) -1

   (B) 0

   (C) 1

   (D) 2

4. If $f(x) = x^4 - 4x$, evaluate $\lim\limits_{x \to -1} \dfrac{f(x) - f(-1)}{x + 1}$.

   (A) -8

   (B) 0

   (C) 1

   (D) 2

5. $f(x) = \frac{1}{2}(x - 1)^3$. Find $f'(0)$.

   (A) -3

   (B) $-\frac{3}{2}$

   (C) $-\frac{1}{2}$

   (D) $\frac{3}{2}$

6. $y = 3\tan^2\left(\frac{x}{3}\right)$. Find $y'(\pi)$.

   (A) 1

   (B) $\frac{8\sqrt{3}}{3}$

   (C) 9

   (D) $8\sqrt{3}$

7. For what values of x is $f(x) = \frac{\sin x}{x}$ continuous?

   (A) $x \neq 0$

   (B) $x > 0$

   (C) $x > 1$

   (D) $x \geq 1$

8. A particle moves along the y-axis with a motion defined by the equation $s(t) = \frac{\ln t}{t}$ for $t > 0$. Find the velocity at $t = 2$.

   (A) 0

   (B) 0.0767

   (C) 0.693

   (D) 1

9. Find the equation of the line tangent to $y = \arctan x$ at $x = 1$.

(A) $x - 2y = 1 - \pi$

(B) $2x - 4y = 2 - \pi$

(C) $2x - 4y = \pi - 2$

(D) $4x - 4y = 4 - \pi$

10. $f(x) = \dfrac{1}{x^2}$, $x > 0$. If $g(x)$ is the inverse of $f(x)$, find $g'(2)$.

(A) $-4\sqrt{2}$

(B) $-\dfrac{1}{\sqrt{2}}$

(C) $-\sqrt{2}$

(D) $-\dfrac{\sqrt{2}}{8}$

11. If $f(x) = -x^4 + 3x^2 - 2$, find the interval(s) where $f'(x)$ is greater than 0.

(A) $(-\infty, -1.225) \cup (0, 1.225)$

(B) $\left(-\infty, -\dfrac{\sqrt{6}}{2}\right) \cup \left(0, \dfrac{\sqrt{6}}{2}\right)$

(C) $\left(\sqrt{2}, -1\right) \cup \left(1, \sqrt{2}\right)$

(D) $(-1.414, -1) \cup (1, 1.414)$

12. Which of the following are true for the function $f(x) = 3x^3 - x$?

I. $f(x)$ is an odd function.

II. $f(x)$ has one relative maximum and one relative minimum.

III. Its point of inflection is at $x = 0$.

(A) II and III only

(B) I and II only

(C) I and III only

(D) I, II, and III

13. A ball is dropped from the top of a building 100 feet high. After how many seconds does the ball hit the ground?

(A) 1.952 s

(B) 2.5 s

(C) 3.202 s

(D) 5 s

14. A ball is dropped from the top of a building 200 feet high. It hits the ground after

(A) 2 s

(B) 2.5 s

(C) 3 s

(D) 3.536 s

15. Antonia has 50 feet of fencing to enclose a rectangular area for her vegetable garden. If a wall of her garage will serve as one side of the garden, what is the maximum area she can enclose?

(A) 277.8 ft^2

(B) 312.5 ft^2

(C) 325 ft^2

(D) 625 ft^2

CALCULUS AB/BC

SECTION II, Part A
Time – 30 minutes
Number of problems – 2

A graphing calculator is required for these problems.

1. $f(x) = 2x^2 - 3$ for $x \geq 0$

    (a) Is $f(x)$ one-to-one?

    (b) If $g(x)$ is the inverse of $f(x)$, use the formula $g'(x) = \dfrac{1}{f'(g(x))}$ to find $g'(0)$.

    (c) Find an algebraic expression for $g(x)$ and use it to confirm the answer in part (b).

    (d) Sketch the graphs of $f(x)$ and $g(x)$.

2. A particle travels on a number line with position given by $s(t) = t \sin t$ for t in the interval $[0, 2\pi]$.

    (a) Find the velocity and acceleration functions.

    (b) For what value(s) of t is the particle at rest?

    (c) Draw the path of the particle on a number line and show the direction of increasing t.

    (d) Is the distance traveled by the particle greater than 10? Explain your answer.

CALCULUS AB/BC

SECTION II, Part B
Time – 60 minutes
Number of problems – 4

A graphing calculator is not permitted for these problems.

1. (a) Find $\dfrac{dy}{dx}$ if $x^2y + y^2 = 2x$.

 (b) Find the point(s) on the graph of $\dfrac{dy}{dx}$ where there is a horizontal tangent.

 (c) Find the point(s) on the graph of $\dfrac{dy}{dx}$ where there is a vertical tangent.

2. For the function $f(x) = x^3 - 4x^2 - 4x + 16$,

 (a) find the critical value(s) of the function.

 (b) find the point(s) of inflection of the function to the nearest thousandth.

 (c) find the value of c guaranteed by the Mean Value Theorem on the interval $[0, 2]$.

 (d) find the absolute extrema on the interval $[0, 4]$ to the nearest thousandth.

3. What is the minimum initial velocity needed so that a ball thrown upwards from the ground reaches the top of a building 40 feet high?

4. A cylindrical terrarium hanging from the ceiling leaks sand at the rate of 5 cm³/minute. The sand falls to the floor, forming a conical pile. The radius and the height of the cone are in the ratio 3:2. How fast is the height of the pile increasing when the radius is 9 cm?

CORRELATION CHART

Use the given charts to mark the questions you missed. Then go back and review the suggested lesson(s) to improve your understanding of the concepts.

Section I, Part A (No Calculator Allowed)

Missed?	Question Number	Review the information in...
	1	Lesson 4
	2	Lesson 4
	3	Lesson 1
	4	Lesson 2, Lesson 3
	5	Lesson 2, Lesson 3
	6	Lesson 2, Lesson 3
	7	Lesson 2, Lesson 3
	8	Lesson 2, Lesson 3
	9	Lesson 3
	10	Lesson 2, Lesson 3
	11	Lesson 6
	12	Lesson 6
	13	Lesson 1, Lesson 5
	14	Lesson 1, Lesson 5
	15	Lesson 1, Lesson 5
	16	Lesson 10
	17	Lesson 9
	18	Lesson 8 (BC Exam Only)
	19	Lesson 8 (BC Exam Only)
	20	Lesson 3
	21	Lesson 5
	22	Lesson 5
	23	Lesson 7
	24	Lesson 7
	25	Lesson 7
	26	Lesson 7
	27	Lesson 4, Lesson 6
	28	Lesson 6
	29	Lesson 5
	30	Lesson 6

Section I, Part B (Calculator Required)

Missed?	Question Number	Review the information in...
	1	Lesson 4
	2	Lesson 6
	3	Lesson 1
	4	Lesson 1
	5	Lesson 1, Lesson 2, Lesson 3
	6	Lesson 2, Lesson 3
	7	Lesson 5
	8	Lesson 7
	9	Lesson 5
	10	Lesson 2
	11	Lesson 6
	12	Lesson 4, Lesson 6
	13	Lesson 7
	14	Lesson 7
	15	Lesson 7

Section II, Part A (Calculator Required)

Missed?	Question Number	Review the information in...
	1(a)	Lesson 2, Lesson 4, Lesson 6
	1(b)	
	1(c)	
	1(d)	
	2(a)	Lesson 7
	2(b)	
	2(c)	
	2(d)	

Section II, Part B (No Calculator Allowed)

Missed?	Question Number	Review the information in...
	1(a)	Lesson 3, Lesson 6
	1(b)	
	1(c)	
	2(a)	Lesson 4, Lesson 6, Lesson 10
	2(b)	
	2(c)	
	2(d)	
	3	Lesson 7
	4	Lesson 7

Main Idea 3

Integrals and the Fundamental Theorem of Calculus

Lesson 1: Antiderivatives

- Antiderivatives Introduction and Rules
- Techniques for Finding Antiderivatives
- Integration by Change of Variable (u-Substitution Method)
- Integration by Parts (BC Exam Only)
- Integration by the Method of Partial Fractions (BC Exam Only)

Explain: Antiderivatives Introduction and Rules

The antiderivative of a function $f(x)$ is any function, or family of functions, $F(x)$, whose derivative is $f(x)$. The function $F(x)$ is also referred to as the **indefinite integral** of $f(x)$. Generally, finding antiderivatives is a more complex task than finding derivatives.

Vocabulary Notes
- The process of finding an antiderivative is called **antidifferentiation** or **integration.**
- The **antiderivative** is also called the **indefinite integral.**

Formulas for antiderivatives involve a function called the integrand and a symbol indicating the variable with respect to which we are taking the derivative. In the expression $\int f(x)\, dx$, the symbol $\int$ is an integral sign; $f(x)$ is the integrand, which is the function that is to be integrated; and dx indicates that x is the variable of integration.

The Power Rule In the power rule for antiderivatives, x^n is the integrand and dx indicates that the antiderivative is with respect to x. The power rule has two parts:

   1. For $n \neq -1$,

$$\int x^n\, dx = \frac{x^{n+1}}{n+1} + c.$$

   Note: Since the denominator, $n + 1$, cannot be equal to zero, this formula is restricted to values of n other than -1.

   2. For $n = -1$,

$$\int \frac{1}{x}\, dx = \ln|x| + c.$$

The Constant, c The derivative of x^2 is $2x$; thus, the antiderivative of $2x$ should be x^2. This is almost correct, but observe that the derivative of $x^2 + 2$ is also $2x$, and the derivative of $x^2 - 20$ is again $2x$. Therefore, $2x$ is really the derivative of $x^2 + c$, where c is a constant and the antiderivative of $2x$ is $x^2 + c$, where c is a constant. The antiderivative of $2x$ is described as a family of functions of the form $F(x) = x^2 + c$, where c is a constant.

MODEL PROBLEMS

1. What is $\int x^3\, dx$?

(A) $\frac{4x^4}{4} + c$

(B) $\frac{x^4}{4} + c$

(C) $4x^4 + c$

(D) $\frac{x^4}{4}$

Solution

We apply the power rule. In this problem $n = 3$, so $\int x^3\, dx$ becomes $\frac{x^{3+1}}{3+1} + c = \frac{x^4}{4} + c$. The correct answer is (B).

2. Find $\int 6\, dx$.

(A) $6 + c$

(B) $\frac{6}{x} + c$

(C) $6x + c$

(D) $\frac{x}{6} + c$

Solution

Although there is no variable in the integrand, we can use the power rule. What is n equal to in this problem?

3. $\int \frac{1}{x^2} dx$ is

(A) $-\frac{1}{x} + c$

(B) $-x + c$

(C) $x^2 + c$

(D) $\frac{2}{x} + c$

Solution

Consider that you can equivalently express the integrand as $\int x^{-2} dx$, and apply the power rule.

4. Find $\int \sqrt{x} \, dx$.

(A) $\frac{2}{3} x^{3/2} + c$

(B) $2x + c$

(C) $\frac{3}{2} x^{3/2} + c$

(D) $\frac{2}{3} x^{1/2} + c$

Solution

How might you express the function $\sqrt{x}$ so you can use the power rule?

The Addition-Subtraction Rule and the Constant Rule

When a function $h(x)$ consists of two functions that are joined by addition or subtraction, we can find the antiderivative of $h(x)$ by finding the antiderivative of each function.

$$\int (f(x) \pm g(x)) \, dx = \int f(x) \, dx \pm \int g(x) \, dx$$

When a function is multiplied by a constant, that constant can be pulled in front of the integral.

$$\int cf(x) \, dx = c \int f(x) \, dx$$

MODEL PROBLEMS

1. $\int \frac{2 + 7 x^2}{2 x^2}$ is

(A) $-\frac{1}{x} + \frac{2}{7} x + c$

(B) $\frac{1}{x} - \frac{7}{2} x + c$

(C) $-\frac{1}{x} + \frac{7}{2} x + c$

(D) $-\frac{1}{x} + \frac{7}{2} + c$

Solution

There are several ways we can go about solving this problem. We will use a combination of the rules we have reviewed thus far.

$$\int \frac{2 + 7x^2}{2x^2} = \int \frac{2}{2x^2}\,dx + \int \frac{7x^2}{2x^2}\,dx$$ Addition-Subtraction Rule.

$$\int \frac{2}{2x^2}\,dx + \int \frac{7x^2}{2x^2}\,dx = \int \frac{1}{x^2}\,dx + \int \frac{7}{2}\,dx$$ Simplify each integrand.

$$-\frac{1}{x} + \frac{7}{2}\int dx$$

Substitute the antiderivative for $\int \frac{1}{x^2}\,dx$, since we previously calculated this integral. We also apply the constant rule.

$$-\frac{1}{x} + \frac{7}{2}x + c$$

Find the antiderivative of 1 and multiply it by the constant. This is the final answer, so the correct choice is (C).

FR **2.** Find $\int (2x + 5)^2\,dx$.

Solution

For this type of problem, we can expand the binomial and then find the antiderivative of each term.

Explain: Techniques for Finding Antiderivatives

There are formulas for finding antiderivatives of certain types of functions, which correspond to the formulas for derivatives. The differentiation rules provide the foundation for finding antiderivatives and were used to derive the formulas for finding antiderivatives. These antiderivative formulas are part of the Calculus AB curriculum. There are several additional methods of finding antiderivatives of other types of functions, which are part of the Calculus BC curriculum. Finally, there are some functions whose antiderivatives either are difficult to find or do not exist in a standard form. In these cases, methods of approximating the solution to the antiderivative are used.

Other Antiderivative Rules

Exponential Rules

$$\int e^x\,dx = e^x + c$$

$$\int a^x\,dx = \frac{a^x}{\ln a} + c, \text{ where } a \text{ is a positive constant, } a \neq 1$$

Trigonometric Rules

$$\int \sin x\,dx = -\cos x + c \qquad \int \sec x \tan x\,dx = \sec x + c$$

$$\int \cos x\,dx = \sin x + c \qquad \int \csc x \cot x\,dx = -\csc x + c$$

$$\int \sec^2 x\,dx = \tan x + c \qquad \int \tan x\,dx = -\ln|\cos x| + c = \ln|\sec x| + c$$

$$\int \csc^2 x\,dx = -\cot x + c \qquad \int \cot x\,dx = \ln|\sin x| + c$$

$$\int \sec x\,dx = \ln|\sec x + \tan x| + c \quad \int \csc x\,dx = \ln|\csc x - \cot x| + c$$

MODEL PROBLEMS

1. What is $\int \cos(x)\, dx$?

(A) $-\cos(x) + c$

(B) $\sin(x) + c$

(C) $\tan(x) + c$

(D) $\sin(x + c)$

Solution

To find the antiderivative of a trigonometric function, we simply read the given table. Note that the correct answer is (B), which is different from the incorrect answer (D). The constant c should be added to the function itself, not just to the argument. Although it's a bit of a chore, memorizing the trigonometric integrals will be quite helpful to you on the AP exam.

2. $\int \sin(x)\, dx$ is

(A) $-\cos(x) + c$

(B) $\sin(x) + c$

(C) $\tan(x) + c$

(D) $-\cos(x + c)$

Solution

Here we simply use the trigonometric rules as shown on page 198.

Explain: Integration by Change of Variable (u-Substitution Method)

There are rules for finding antiderivatives of many functions, but additional methods are required to find the antiderivatives of many other integrands. Suppose we needed to evaluate $\int x\sqrt{x + 2}\, dx$. Since a function whose derivative is $x\sqrt{x+2}$ does not easily come to mind, we need another method of integration.

The only other method of integration required in the AP Calculus AB curriculum is the change of variable method, often called the u-substitution method. The **u-substitution method** involves using the variable u to replace part of a complicated function. For example, if $u = x + 2$, then $x = u - 2$. We can then proceed by making these substitutions in the original integral:

$$\int x\sqrt{x + 2}\, dx \text{ becomes } \int (u - 2)\sqrt{u}\, du = \int (u^{3/2} - 2u^{1/2})\, du.$$

While there are other methods of integration required in the BC curriculum, the u-substitution method is one of the most powerful tools for finding antiderivatives since it applies to so many different situations where the antiderivative is not obvious.

> **The most important things to remember in using the**
> **u-substitution method are:**
> - Choose an appropriate quantity for the variable u.
> - Find du.
> - Express all parts of the integrand in terms of u.

In choosing a quantity to substitute for u, look for the expression inside parentheses or under a radical sign. Then mentally take the derivative and check to see if the derivative is part of the integrand. Don't worry if the coefficients are not the same; you can always adjust for a constant.

MODEL PROBLEMS

FR **1.** Find $\int 2x(x^2 - 5)^4 \, dx$.

Solution

It would be a tedious task to expand $(x^2 - 5)^4$, multiply each term by $2x$, and find the antiderivative of each term of this polynomial function. Instead let $u = x^2 - 5$. Then $\frac{du}{dx} = 2x$, or $du = 2x \, dx$. The integrand $\int 2x(x^2 - 5)^4 \, dx$ can be rewritten as

$$\int (x^2 - 5)^4 (2x \, dx) = \int u^4 \, du.$$

This antiderivative is easily found using the Power Rule as $\frac{u^5}{5} + c$.

The final step for evaluating this indefinite integral is to replace u with $x^2 - 5$, giving the final answer $\frac{(x^2 - 5)^5}{5} + c$.

FR **2.** Find $\int x\sqrt{4x^2 + 9} \, dx$.

Solution

By the method of u-substitution, choose $u = 4x^2 + 9$. Then $\frac{du}{dx} = 8x$, or $du = 8x \, dx$. The integrand can be rewritten as $\sqrt{4x^2 + 9} \, (x \, dx)$.

To find an expression to substitute for $x \, dx$, multiply both sides of the equation $du = 8x \, dx$ by $\frac{1}{8}$ to get $\frac{1}{8} du = x \, dx$.

The integrand is then replaced in terms of u by $\sqrt{u}\left(\frac{1}{8} du\right) = \frac{1}{8}\sqrt{u} \, du$.

To find $\int \frac{1}{8}\sqrt{u} \, du$, rewrite the integral as

$$\frac{1}{8} \int \sqrt{u} \, du = \frac{1}{8} \int u^{1/2} \, du,$$

and use the Power Rule. The result is

$$\frac{1}{8} u^{3/2}\left(\frac{2}{3}\right) + c = \frac{1}{12} u^{3/2} + c.$$

Replacing u with $4x^2 + 9$, the final answer is $\frac{1}{12}(4x^2 + 9)^{3/2} + c$.

FR 3. Find $\int \cos(4x)\, dx$.

Solution

Here we can let $u = 4x$. Then $\dfrac{du}{dx} = 4$ and $du = 4\, dx$. You finish solving from here.

FR 4. Find $\int 2x e^{3x^2}\, dx$.

Solution

In this case, $u = 3x^2$. This means that $\dfrac{du}{dx} = 6x$ and $du = 6x\, dx$. Once the u-substitution is taken care of, there are several ways to solve this problem.

FR 5. Find $\int \dfrac{x}{x^2 + 2}\, dx$.

Solution

In this problem, what should u stand for? Don't forget to calculate $\dfrac{du}{dx}$.

Explain: Integration by Parts (BC Exam Only)

Integration by parts is a method of transforming an integral that is impossible to evaluate into an integral that is possible to evaluate. The method of integration by parts comes from the product rule for derivatives. If u and v are functions of x, then the derivative of uv is

$$\frac{d(uv)}{dx} = u\frac{dv}{dx} + v\frac{du}{dx}, \text{ or } d(uv) = u\, dv + v\, du.$$

Thus,

$$u\, dv = d(uv) - du.$$

Taking the antiderivative of both sides, we get

$$\int u\, dv = uv - \int v\, du,$$

which is the formula for integration by parts.

To apply the formula for integration by parts:

1. Identify the two parts, u and dv, in the integrand.
2. Integrate dv to find v and differentiate u to find du.
3. Substitute v and du into the integration by parts formula.

Skillful use of integration by parts can change a difficult problem into an easy one. An integral that cannot be found is traded for an integral that can be found. If the correct trade is made, then the integration by parts method works.

Integration by parts is often effective when the integrand is the product of two functions that are unrelated, such as a polynomial and an exponential function, a polynomial and a logarithmic function, a trigonometric and an exponential function, or a polynomial and a trigonometric function.

MODEL PROBLEMS

FR **1.** Find the antiderivative $\int x \sin x\, dx$.

Solution

Since the integrand is the product of a polynomial and a trigonometric function, integration by parts is a possible method of solution.

Use the formula for integration by parts: $\int u\, dv = uv - \int v\, du$.

Let

$u = x$ and $dv = \sin x\, dx$.

Then

$du = dx$ and $v = \int \sin x\, dx = -\cos x$.

By the formula, the integrand becomes

$$\int x \sin x\, dx = -x \cos x - \int -\cos x\, dx = -x \cos x + \sin x + c.$$

The method of integration by parts traded $\int x \sin x\, dx$ for $\int \cos x\, dx$, which is an antiderivative that can be found more easily.

Note: It is not necessary to add a constant of integration in finding v, the antiderivative of dv, as long as one constant of integration, c, is included at the end.

FR **2.** Find the antiderivative $\int x \sin x\, dx$ by letting $u = \sin x$ and $dv = x\, dx$. Is it possible to solve this problem this way?

Solution

If we use the suggestion in the problem, $du = \cos x\, dx$ and $v = \frac{x^2}{2}$. Then,

$$\int x \sin x\, dx = \frac{x^2}{2} \sin x - \int \frac{x^2}{2} \cos x\, dx.$$

In this case, the $\int x \sin x\, dx$, which cannot be found, was traded for $\int \frac{x^2}{2} \cos x\, dx$, which also cannot be found. This was not a good trade since it led to an integrand with a higher power of x, which cannot be solved by elementary methods.

FR **3.** Find the antiderivative $\int \ln x\, dx$.

Solution

The integrand is the product of $\ln x$ and dx.

Use the formula for integration by parts: $\int u\, dv = uv - \int v\, du$.

Let

$u = \ln x$ and $dv = dx$.

Then

$du = \frac{1}{x}\, dx$ and $v = x$.

You continue solving from this point.

FR **4.** Find the antiderivative $\int \arctan x\, dx$.

Solution

Use the formula for integration by parts: $\int u\, dv = uv - \int v\, du$.

Let $u = \arctan x$ and $dv = dx$. Then $du = \dfrac{1}{1 + x^2}\, dx$ and $v = x$. Solve from here.

Explain: Integration by the Method of Partial Fractions (BC Exam Only)

Adding fraction arithmetically involves finding the least common denominator, rewriting equivalent fractions with the same denominator, and then adding the numerators. The **method of partial fractions** uses the same understanding of fractions to transform an integrand that is a rational function into an integrand that is easier to evaluate. The objective of this method is to find the factors of the denominator, and rewrite the rational function as a sum of fractions in which each denominator is a factor of the given denominator. The antiderivative is then determined by finding the antiderivatives of the individual, simpler fractions. Breaking a rational function down into its component fractions can be a tedious algebraic process.

MODEL PROBLEMS

FR **1.** Rewrite $\dfrac{1}{x^2 - x}$ as a sum of its component fractions.

Solution

The denominator can be factored as $x^2 - x = x(x - 1)$. Thus the fraction $\dfrac{1}{x^2 - x}$ can be written as the sum of $\dfrac{A}{x}$ and $\dfrac{B}{x - 1}$, where A and B are constants.

$$\frac{1}{x^2 - x} = \frac{A}{x} + \frac{B}{x - 1}.$$

To find the values of A and B, multiply the equation by $x^2 - x$:

$$(x^2 - x)\frac{1}{x^2 - x} = \frac{A}{x} + \frac{B}{x - 1}(x^2 - x)$$

$$1 = A(x - 1) + Bx.$$

To solve for A and B, choose appropriate values of x and substitute into the equation above. The values of x chosen in this model problem are $x = 1$ and $x = 0$. These are values for which the original equation is undefined.

When $x = 1$, the equation $1 = A(x - 1) + Bx$ becomes

$$1 = A(1 - 1) + B(1)$$
$$1 = B$$

Thus, $B = 1$.

When $x = 0$, the equation $1 = A(x - 1) + Bx$ becomes

$$1 = A(0 - 1) + B(0)$$
$$1 = A(-1)$$

Thus, $A = -1$.

Using these values of A and B, the fraction can be written

$$\frac{1}{x^2 - x} = \frac{-1}{x} + \frac{1}{x - 1}.$$

FR **2.** Find the antiderivative $\int \frac{1}{x^2 - x} dx$.

Solution

Note that we are being asking to find the antiderivative of the fraction we worked with in Model Problem #1. We really need to find $\int \left(\frac{-1}{x} + \frac{1}{x - 1} \right) dx$, which is $-\ln|x| + \ln|x - 1| + c$. Using the properties of the ln function, we can rewrite $-\ln|x| + \ln|x - 1|$ as $\ln\left|\frac{x - 1}{x}\right|$ and the antiderivative is $\ln\left|\frac{x - 1}{x}\right| + c$.

FR **3.** Find the antiderivative $\int \frac{1}{x^3 - x} dx$.

Solution

Find the factors of the denominator, and use them to rewrite the fraction $\frac{1}{x^3 - x}$ as the sum of its component fractions. The factors of $x^3 - x$ are x, $x + 1$, and $x - 1$. Find the values of A, B, and C such that

$$\frac{1}{x^3 - x} = \frac{A}{x} + \frac{B}{x + 1} + \frac{C}{x - 1}.$$

Multiply this equation by $x^3 - x$ to get

$$1 = A(x + 1)(x - 1) + Bx(x - 1) + Cx(x + 1).$$

Choose values of x that make the factors x, $x + 1$, and $x - 1$ equal to zero.

$x = 0$: $1 = A(1)(-1)$, and $A = -1$

$x = -1$: $1 = B(-1)(-2)$, and $B = \frac{1}{2}$

$x = 1$: $1 = C(1)(2)$, and $C = \frac{1}{2}$ You finish solving from here.

If the integrand is a rational function for which the degree of the numerator is greater than or equal to the degree of the denominator, then we must use long division to rewrite the integrand as

quotient $+ \frac{\text{remainder}}{\text{divisor}}$. Then, if necessary, proceed to rewrite the term with $\frac{\text{remainder}}{\text{divisor}}$ as the sum of its component fractions.

4. Find the antiderivative $\int \dfrac{x^2 - x + 1}{x^2 - x} dx$.

Solution

Since the degree of the numerator is greater than or equal to the degree of the denominator, we must use long division.

$$
\begin{array}{r}
1 \\
x^2 - x \overline{)\ x^2 - x + 1} \\
\underline{-x^2 - x} \\
1
\end{array}
$$

We find that the quotient $= 1$ and the remainder $= 1$. Thus,

$\dfrac{x^2 - x + 1}{x^2 - x} = 1 + \dfrac{1}{x^2 - x}$. Does this expression look familiar? Use your

prior knowledge to complete the problem.

AP Calculus Exam-Type Questions

1. Evaluate the integrals.

(a) $\int (e^x + x)\, dx =$

(b) $\int \dfrac{\sin x - 1}{\cos x}\, dx =$

2. Evaluate the integrals.

(a) $\int \dfrac{\sqrt{x} + \sqrt[3]{x}}{x}\, dx =$

(b) $\int \dfrac{x^4 - 3x^2 + 2}{x^2 - 2}\, dx =$

Multiple Choice Questions
No calculator permitted for these questions.

3. $\int \dfrac{x + 1}{3x^2}\, dx =$

(A) $-\dfrac{1}{3x^2} - \dfrac{2}{3x^3} + c$

(B) $\dfrac{1}{x} + \dfrac{1}{x^2} + c$

(C) $\dfrac{1}{3}\ln|x| - \dfrac{1}{3x} + c$

(D) $\dfrac{1}{6x} + c$

4. $\int 2x^{-3}\, dx =$

(A) $-\dfrac{1}{x^2} + c$

(B) $-\dfrac{1}{2x^4} + c$

(C) $2 \ln x^3 + c$

(D) $-\dfrac{1}{8x^2} + c$

5. $\int (\sqrt{x} + 5)^2\, dx =$

(A) $\dfrac{x^2}{2} + 25x + \dfrac{20}{3}x^{3/2} + c$

(B) $\dfrac{(\sqrt{x} + 5)^3}{3} + c$

(C) $(\sqrt{x} + 5) + c$

(D) $1 + \dfrac{5}{\sqrt{x}} + c$

6. $\int \dfrac{e^{2x} - e^{3x}}{e^x} dx =$

(A) $\dfrac{1}{2}e^{-x} + c$

(B) $e^{-2x} + c$

(C) $e^x - 2e^{2x} + c$

(D) $e^x - \dfrac{1}{2}e^{2x} + c$

6. $\int \dfrac{10^x}{\ln 10} dx =$

(A) $10^x + c$

(B) $\dfrac{10^x}{(\ln 10)^2} + c$

(C) $\dfrac{x}{\ln 10} + c$

(D) $\dfrac{x(10^{x-1})}{\ln 10} + c$

7. Find $\int \dfrac{2x}{\sqrt{x^2 + 6}} dx$.

(A) $(x^2 + 6)^{1/2} + c$

(B) $2(x^2 + 6)^{1/2} + c$

(C) $\ln(x^2 + 6) + c$

(D) $\dfrac{2}{3}(x^2 + 6)^{3/2} + c$

8. Find $\int x^2(x^3 - 1)^5 dx$.

(A) $\dfrac{(x^3 - 1)^6}{18} + c$

(B) $\dfrac{(x^3 - 1)^6}{6} + c$

(C) $\dfrac{(x^3 - 1)^6}{2} + c$

(D) $6(x^3 - 1)^6 + c$

9. Find $\int \dfrac{2x + 2}{(x^2 + 2x)^5} dx$.

(A) $\dfrac{1}{4(x^2 + 2x)^4} dx$

(B) $-\dfrac{1}{4(x^2 + 2x)^4} + c$

(C) $-\dfrac{1}{2(x^2 + 2x)^4} + c$

(D) $-\dfrac{1}{8(x^2 + 2x)^4} + c$

10. Find $\int \dfrac{x^3}{x^4 + 1} dx$.

(A) $\dfrac{3(x^4 + 1)^2}{2} + c$

(B) $\dfrac{(x^4 + 1)^2}{2} + c$

(C) $\ln(x^4 + 1) + c$

(D) $\dfrac{\ln(x^4 + 1)}{4} + c$

11. Find $\int \dfrac{e^x}{e^x + 4} dx$.

(A) $e^x \ln(e^x + 4) + c$

(B) $x + \dfrac{1}{4}e^x + c$

(C) $\dfrac{(e^x + 4)^{-2}}{-2} + c$

(D) $\ln(e^x + 4) + c$

12. Find $\int \dfrac{e^x + 4}{e^x} dx$.

(A) $\dfrac{(e^x + 4)^2}{2} + c$

(B) $4e^{-x} + c$

(C) $\ln(e^x + 4) + c$

(D) $x - 4e^{-x} + c$

13. Find $\int \dfrac{e^{-x}+4}{e^x}\,dx$.

(A) $-\dfrac{1}{2}(e^{-2x}+4e^{-x})+c$

(B) $-\dfrac{1}{2}(e^{-2x}+8e^{-x})+c$

(C) $-2e^{-2x}+4e^{-x}+c$

(D) $\dfrac{(e^{-x}+4)^2}{2}+c$

The remaining multiple choice questions test objectives unique to the BC exam. If you are taking the AB exam, you may omit these questions.

14. $\int x^3 e^{x^2}\,dx =$

(A) $\dfrac{1}{2}e^{x^2}(x^2-1)+c$

(B) $\dfrac{1}{2}e^{x^2}(x^2+1)+c$

(E) $3x^2 e^{x^2}+c$

(D) $x^2 e^{x^2}(2x^2+3)+c$

15. $\int \arcsin x\,dx =$

(A) $(1-x^2)^{-1/2}+c$

(B) $x\arcsin x + \sqrt{1-x^2}+c$

(C) $x\arcsin x + \dfrac{1}{2}\sqrt{1-x^2}+c$

(D) $x\arcsin x - \sqrt{1-x^2}+c$

16. $\int x\cos(x^2)\,dx =$

(A) $x\,\sin(x^2)+c$

(B) $\dfrac{1}{2}\sin(x^2)+c$

(C) $-\dfrac{1}{2}\sin(x^2)+c$

(D) $\cos(x^2)+c$

17. $\int \dfrac{x^2+5x}{x^2+5x+6}\,dx =$

(A) $-6\ln\left|\dfrac{x+2}{x+3}\right|+c$

(B) $x-6\ln\left|\dfrac{x+2}{x+3}\right|+c$

(C) $-5\ln\left|\dfrac{x+2}{x+3}\right|+c$

(D) $-\ln\left|\dfrac{x+2}{x+3}\right|+c$

18. $\int \dfrac{(x+2)^3}{x^2+2x}\,dx =$

(A) $4\ln|x|+c$

(B) $\dfrac{1}{2}x^2+4x+\ln|x|+c$

(C) $\dfrac{1}{2}x^2+2x+4\ln|x|+c$

(D) $\dfrac{1}{2}x^2+4x+4\ln|x|+c$

Free Response Questions

There are no free response questions for this lesson.

Lesson 2: Riemann Sums and The Trapezoidal Rule

- Area Under the Curve: Rieman Sums
- The Trapezoidal Rule

Explain: Area Under the Curve: Riemann Sums

In Lesson 1, we discussed algebraic techniques for finding the antiderivatives for different types of functions. In this lesson we review Riemann sums and their connection to antiderivatives and definite integrals.

Ancient Greek mathematicians such as Eudoxus and Archimedes studied the problem of finding the area inside a closed curve. One method of finding a formula for the area of a circle involves inscribing a regular polygon with n sides.

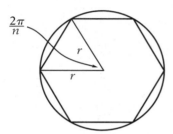

Each triangle has two sides of length r and an included angle with measure $\frac{2\pi}{n}$. The area of each triangle is $\frac{1}{2}r^2 \sin\left(\frac{2\pi}{n}\right)$. Thus, the area of the polygon is $n \cdot \frac{1}{2}r^2 \sin\left(\frac{2\pi}{n}\right)$.

The area of the circle is the limit of the area of the polygon as n increases without bound. So, the area of the circle is $\lim_{n\to\infty} \left(n \cdot \frac{1}{2}r^2 \sin\left(\frac{2\pi}{n}\right)\right)$. Using the special trigonometric limit presented in Lesson 1.2, we can evaluate this limit as

$$\lim_{n\to\infty} \frac{1}{2}r^2 \frac{\sin\left(\frac{2\pi}{n}\right)}{\frac{1}{n}} = \frac{1}{2}r^2(2\pi) = \pi r^2.$$

Using a similar method to that described above, we can evaluate the area between a curve and the x-axis. Consider the region enclosed by the curve $y = x^2$, the x-axis, and the line $x = 2$, as shown on the next page. This area is called R.

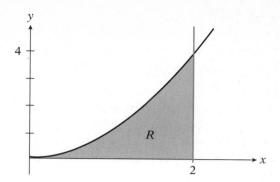

If the interval $[0, 2]$ is divided into n equal subintervals, the length of each subinterval is $\frac{2}{n}$. The x-coordinates of the partitions are $\frac{0}{n}, \frac{2}{n}, \frac{4}{n}, \frac{6}{n}, \ldots, \frac{2n}{n}$. To approximate R, we can draw rectangles with bases of length $\frac{2}{n}$ and heights equal to the value of the function $y = x^2$ at the right endpoint of each subinterval, as shown below.

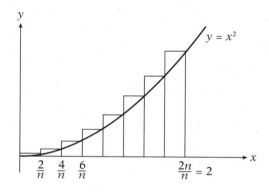

The sum of the areas of these rectangles is

$$\frac{2}{n}\left(\left(\frac{2}{n}\right)^2 + \left(\frac{4}{n}\right)^2 + \left(\frac{6}{n}\right)^2 + \cdots + \left(\frac{2n}{n}\right)^2\right).$$

This expression can be rewritten as

$$\frac{2}{n}\left(\frac{2^2}{n^2} + \frac{4^2}{n^2} + \frac{6^2}{n^2} + \cdots + \frac{(2n)^2}{n^2}\right)$$

$$= \frac{2}{n^3}(2^2 + 4^2 + 6^2 + \cdots + (2n)^2)$$

$$= \frac{2}{n^3} \cdot 2^2 (1^2 + 2^2 + 3^2 + \cdots + n^2).$$

Now, using a formula for the sum of the first n squares,

$$1^2 + 2^2 + 3^2 + \cdots + n^2 = \frac{n(n + 1)(2n + 1)}{6},$$

the sum of the rectangles is

$$\frac{2}{n^3} \cdot 2^2 \cdot \frac{n(n + 1)(2n + 1)}{6} = \frac{4}{3n^2}(2n^2 + 3n + 1).$$

Taking the limit of this expression as n approaches ∞, the area of region R is

$$\text{Area} = \lim_{n \to \infty} \frac{4}{3n^2}(2n^2 + 3n + 1) = \frac{8}{3}.$$

If the same subintervals were used to partition the interval $[0, 2]$, but the height of each rectangle was the value of the function $y = x^2$ at the left endpoint of each subinterval, the process described above would give the same answer. The rectangles would then be inscribed in the region R as shown below.

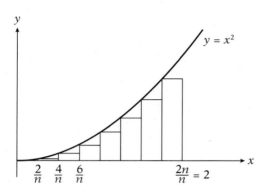

The sum of the areas of these rectangles is

$$\frac{2}{n}\left(\left(\frac{0}{n}\right)^2 + \left(\frac{2}{n}\right)^2 + \left(\frac{4}{n}\right)^2 + \left(\frac{6}{n}\right)^2 + \cdots + \left(\frac{2(n-1)}{n}\right)^2\right),$$

which can be rewritten as

$$\frac{2}{n}\left(\frac{0^2}{n^2} + \frac{2^2}{n^2} + \frac{4^2}{n^2} + \frac{6^2}{n^2} + \cdots + \frac{2^2(n-1)^2}{n^2}\right),$$

or $\dfrac{2}{n^3} \cdot 2^2(1^2 + 2^2 + 3^2 + \cdots + (n-1)^2)$.

Using the formula for the sum of the first $(n-1)$ squares

$$1^2 + 2^2 + 3^2 + \cdots + (n-1)^2 = \frac{(n-1)n(2n-1)}{6},$$

the sum of these rectangles inscribed in region R is

$$\frac{2}{n^3} \cdot 2^2 \cdot \frac{(n-1)n(2n-1)}{6} \quad \text{or} \quad \frac{4}{3n^2}(2n^2 - 3n + 1).$$

Taking the limit of this expression as n approaches ∞, the area of region R is

$$\text{Area} = \lim_{n \to \infty} \frac{4}{3n^2}(2n^2 - 3n + 1) = \frac{8}{3}.$$

If the same partition of $[0, 2]$ is used but the height of each rectangle is the value of the function $y = x^2$ at the midpoint of each subinterval, the process described would give the same answer for the area of region R. In this case, however, the rectangles are neither above the curve nor inscribed in the region, but partly above and partly under the curve, as shown on the next page.

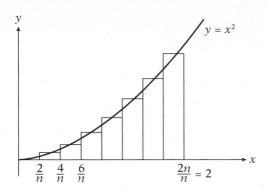

The base of each rectangle is still $\frac{2}{n}$, but the midpoints have x-coordinates $\frac{1}{n}, \frac{3}{n}, \frac{5}{n}, \ldots, \frac{2n-1}{n}$. The sum of areas of the rectangles, using the midpoints of each subinterval, is

$$\frac{2}{n}\left(\left(\frac{1}{n}\right)^2 + \left(\frac{3}{n}\right)^2 + \left(\frac{5}{n}\right)^2 + \cdots + \left(\frac{2(n-1)}{n}\right)^2\right).$$

This sum can be rewritten as

$$\frac{2}{n^3}(1^2 + 3^2 + 5^2 + \cdots + (2n-1)^2).$$

Using the formula for the sum of odd integers from 1 to $(2n-1)$, the sum is equal to

$$\frac{2}{n^3} \cdot \frac{(2n-1)(2n)(2n+1)}{6} \text{ or } \frac{2}{3n^2}(4n^2 - 1).$$

Taking the limit of this expression as n approaches ∞, the area of region R is

$$\text{Area} = \lim_{n \to \infty} \frac{2}{3n^2}(4n^2 - 1) = \frac{8}{3}.$$

Vocabulary Notes

The sum using the right-hand endpoints of each subinterval is called a **right-hand sum.** The sum using the left-hand endpoints of each subinterval is called a **left-hand sum.** The sum using the midpoints of each subinterval is called a **midpoint sum.** Since the function $y = x^2$ is increasing on the interval $[0, 2]$, the left-hand sum is also a **lower sum,** and the right-hand sum is also an **upper sum.**

The graphing calculator can be useful in finding a lower or an upper sum for any function. We provide instructions for entering the data into a list on either the TI-89 or the TI-83. There are also programs that calculate upper and lower sums.

On the AP exam, whether you are using a program or entering the data into a calculator yourself, be sure to follow the instructions given in the problem. In many cases, work must be shown to receive full credit. The answer alone is generally not acceptable.

Calculator Notes

The graphing calculator can be used to find left-hand, right-hand, and midpoint sums. For the previous example, first enter the function $y = x^2$ into Y=. Using five subdivisions on the interval [0, 2], the partition points are 0, 0.4, 0.8, 1.2, 1.6, and 2, and the length of the subinterval is 0.4.

Using the TI-89

To find the left-hand sum, go to APPS 6: Data/Matrix Editor 3: New. For Type: Data ▶ List ENTER. Variable x ENTER ENTER. The word LIST should appear in the upper left corner.

Use arrows to highlight c_1, and type in the entry line:

$$c_1 = 0.4 \times y_1 \ (\text{seq}(x, x, 0, 1.6, 0.4)).$$

Now press HOME and type into the entry line: sum (x). The answer should be 1.92.

To find the right-hand sum, enter APPS 6: Data/Matrix Editor 1: Current.

Use arrows to highlight c_1, and type into the entry line:

$$c_1 = 0.4 \times y_1 \ (\text{seq}(x, x, 0.4, 2, 0.4)).$$

Now press HOME and type into the entry line: sum (x). The answer should be 3.52.

To find the midpoint sum, enter APPS 6: Data/Matrix Editor 1: Current.

Use arrows to highlight c_1, and type into the entry line:

$$c_1 = 0.4 \times y_1 \ (\text{seq}(x, x, 0.2, 1.8, 0.4)).$$

Now press HOME and type into the entry line: sum(x). The answer should be 2.64.

Using the TI-83/84

To find the left-hand sum, enter the function $y = x^2$ into Y=. Go to STAT EDIT. Highlight L1. Use the following keystrokes to type L1 = $0.4Y_1$(seq(x, x, 0, 1.6, 0.4)) into the entry line:

0.4 VARS Y-VARS ENTER ENTER (2nd LIST OPS 5 X,T,Θ,n , X,T,Θ,n , 0 , 1.6 , 0.4)).

Press ENTER.

Press 2nd QUIT, and then type into the home screen: 2nd STAT MATH 5.

The screen prompt sum(will appear. Enter sum(L1) by pressing 2nd L1) ENTER. The answer should be 1.92.

To find the right-hand sum, go to STAT EDIT. Highlight L1. Use the following keystrokes to type L1 = $0.4Y_1$(seq(x, x, 0.4, 2, 0.4)) into the entry line:

0.4 VARS Y-VARS ENTER ENTER (2nd LIST OPS 5 X,T,Θ,n , X,T,Θ,n , 0.4 , 2 , 0.4)).

Press ENTER.

Press 2nd QUIT, and then type into the home screen: 2nd STAT MATH 5.

The screen prompt sum(will appear. Enter sum(L1) by pressing 2nd L1) ENTER. The answer should be 3.52.

To find the midpoint sum, go to STAT EDIT. Highlight L1. Use the following keystrokes to type L1 = 0.4Y₁ (seq(x, x, 0.2, 1.8, 0.4)) into the entry line:

0.4 [VARS] Y-VARS [ENTER] [ENTER] [(] [2nd] LIST OPS 5 [X,T,Θ,n] [,] [X,T,Θ,n] [,] 0.2 [,] 1.8 [,] 0.4 [)] [)].

Press [ENTER].

Press [2nd] QUIT, and then type into the home screen: [2nd] [STAT] MATH 5.

The screen prompt sum(will appear. Enter sum(L1) by pressing [2nd] L1 [)] [ENTER]. The answer should be 2.64.

The left-hand, right-hand, and midpoint sums are all examples of a more general approach to finding areas called Riemann sums. In a **Riemann sum,** a function and an interval are given, the interval is partitioned, and the height of each rectangle can be the value of the function at any point in the subinterval. In fact, even the subintervals do not necessarily need to be the same length. All you need to remember is that a Riemann sum uses rectangles to find the area between a curve and the x-axis; the left-hand, right-hand, and midpoint sums are all examples of a Riemann sum.

In the case of the left-hand sum, the height of each rectangle is the value of the function at the left point in each subinterval. For a right-hand sum, the height of the rectangle is the value of the function at the right point in each subinterval. Finally, in a midpoint sum, the height of the rectangle is the value of the function at the midpoint of each subinterval. The function $y = x^2$ is increasing on the interval $[0, 2]$, so the left-hand sum is the lowest estimate of the area of region R, the right-hand sum is the highest estimate of the area of region R, and the midpoint sum is between the two.

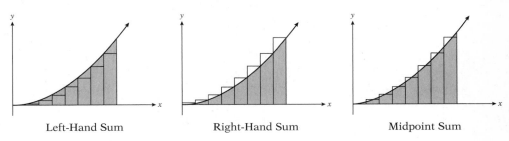

| Left-Hand Sum | Right-Hand Sum | Midpoint Sum |

The actual area of region R lies between the lower sum and the upper sum. As the number of subintervals, n, increases, the lower sum increases, while the upper sum decreases. For any value of n,

lower sum $\leq$ area of the region $\leq$ upper sum

In the function $y = x^2$ on the interval $[0, 2]$, the limit of the lower sum $= \frac{8}{3} =$ the limit of the upper sum. Since the actual area of region R is sandwiched between the lower and upper sums for every value of n, and since the limits of both the lower and upper sums are the same, the area of region R is also $\frac{8}{3}$.

The essential part of the process of finding the area between a curve and the x-axis is to start with a function $f(x)$ on a closed interval $[a, b]$, and create rectangles on the subintervals. In a general Riemann sum, a rectangle may be drawn using any value x_i in each of the n subintervals, and the subintervals are not necessarily of equal length. The height of the rectangle is then $f(x_i)$, and the length of the rectangle is Δx_i. The sum of the areas of the rectangles may be written using the summation symbol, as $\sum_{i=1}^{n} f(x_i) \Delta x_i$, and the area under the curve is the limit of this sum

$$\lim_{n \to \infty} \sum_{i=1}^{n} f(x_i) \Delta x_i.$$

MODEL PROBLEMS

1. The left-hand sum of $f(x) = \sqrt{x}$ on the interval $[0, 1]$ with four equal subintervals is

(A) 0.25

(B) 0.518

(C) 0.667

(D) 0.768

Solution

We graph the function with lower sums to get a clear picture of what is happening in this problem.

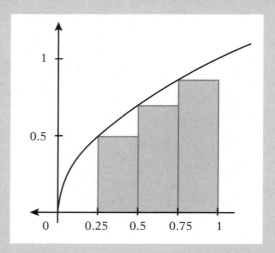

To solve, we need to apply the limit, $\lim_{n \to \infty} \sum_{i=1}^{n} f(x_i) \Delta x_i$. Keep in mind that this is a lower limit (also called a left-hand limit). In this case, $n = 4$, $\Delta x_i = 0.25$, and $f(x_i) = \sqrt{x}$. We calculate $\lim_{n \to \infty} \sum_{i=1}^{4} f(\sqrt{x}) \cdot 0.25 = f(0) \cdot 0.25 + f(0.50) \cdot 0.25 + f(0.75) \cdot 0.25 \approx 0.518$. The correct answer is (B).

Explain: The Trapezoidal Rule

The **Trapezoidal Rule** is used to approximate the value of a definite integral, particularly a definite integral whose antiderivative is difficult or impossible to evaluate. A trapezoidal approximation gives a more accurate estimate than a lower or upper sum, and may be found using subintervals of equal or unequal length. If an interval $[a, b]$ is partitioned into equal subintervals, then the process of finding an approximation to the definite integral is called the Trapezoidal Rule. This is the same process as was used to find upper and lower sums. The difference here is that instead of rectangles, connect the points on the graph of $f(x)$ to form trapezoids.

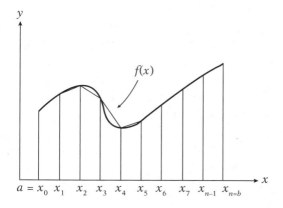

Trapezoidal Rule

Each subinterval has length $\frac{b-a}{n}$. If the partition points are $a = x_0, x_1, x_2,$ ..., $x_{n-1}, x_n = b$, the values of the function are $f(a) = f(x_0), f(x_1),$ $f(x_2), ..., f(x_{n-1}), f(x_n) = f(b)$.

The Trapezoidal Rule approximates the definite integral as

$$\frac{b-a}{2n} \left[f(x_0) + 2f(x_1) + 2f(x_2) + ... + 2f(x_{n-1}) + f(x_n) \right].$$

Error in the Trapezoidal Rule

If $f(x)$ has a continuous second derivative, the error, E, in approximating the definite integral of $f(x)$ on the interval $[a, b]$ is

$$E \le \frac{(b-a)^3}{12n^2} \max \left| f''(x) \right|.$$

MODEL PROBLEMS

FR **1.** Use the Trapezoidal Rule with five subintervals to approximate the area under the curve $y = x^2$ on the interval $[0, 1]$. Then find the actual value of the area and find the error.

Solution

$\frac{b-a}{2n}[f(x_0) + 2f(x_1) + 2f(x_2) + \cdots + 2f(x_{n-1}) + f(x_n)]$	The Trapezoidal Rule states that the area under the curve can be calculated using this formula.
$\frac{b-a}{n} = \frac{1-0}{5} = 0.2$	We begin by dividing the interval into five equal parts.
$f(x_0) = (0)^2 = 0$ $f(x_1) = (0.2)^2 = 0.04$ $f(x_2) = (0.4)^2 = 0.16$ $f(x_3) = (0.6)^2 = 0.36$ $f(x_4) = (0.8)^2 = 0.64$ $f(x_5) = (1)^2 = 1$	Find the value of the function at each of 0, 0.2, 0.4, 0.6, 0.8, and 1.0.
$\frac{1-0}{2(5)}[0 + 2(0.04) + 2(0.16) + 2(0.36) +$ $2(0.64) + 1] = 0.34$	Substitute. The area is approximately equal to 0.34.

The actual value of the definite integral $\int_0^1 x^2\, dx = \frac{1}{3}$, which is a difference of about 0.0067.

Calculator Note

For a large number of terms, the trapezoidal approximation can be performed on a graphing calculator as follows. In Model Problem #1, above, the approximation can be rewritten as

$$\frac{1}{10}[0 + 1 + 2((0.2)^2 + (0.4)^2 + (0.6)^2 + (0.8)^2)].$$

First enter x^2 into Y= Y_1.

Then find the sum of the sequence by entering the following in the home screen: 1 ÷ 10 ((0 + 1 + 2 (.

To get the sum term, enter 2nd STAT MATH 5.

To get the sequence term, enter 2nd STAT OPS 5.

Then enter VARS Y-VARS 1 1 ((X,T,Θ,n)) , X,T,Θ,n , 0.2 , 0.8 , 0.2))).

Pressing ENTER will give the following result:

```
1/10(0+1+2(sum(s
eq(Y1(X),X,.2,.8
,.2)))
                 .34
■
```

In the calculator screen, the last three numbers in the parentheses indicate where the sequence starts, where the sequence ends, and the increment from one term in the sequence to the next. This is one way to add the terms in the formula for the Trapezoidal Rule and is especially useful as the number of subintervals increases.

FR **2.** (a) Use the Trapezoidal Rule with ten subintervals to approximate the area under the curve $y = \frac{1}{x}$ on the interval $[1, 2]$.

(b) Compute the error bound, E.

Solution

(a)

$\frac{b-a}{n} = \frac{2-1}{10} = 0.1$	Divide the interval into 10 subintervals.

Find the value of the function at each point and then substitute those values into the Trapezoidal Rule to finish out this part of the question.

(b) Using the graphing calculator, enter $Y_1 = \frac{1}{x}$, and the trapezoidal approximation can be rewritten as

$$\frac{1}{20}\left[1 + \frac{1}{2} + 2(\text{sum(seq}(Y_1(x), x, 1.1, 1.9, 0.1)))\right].$$

The error bound $E \leq \frac{1}{1,200} \max \left|\frac{2}{x^3}\right|$ on $[1, 2]$.

$$E \leq \frac{1}{1,200}(2) = \frac{1}{600} = 0.00167$$

FR **3.** Use the Trapezoidal Rule with five subintervals to approximate the area under the curve $y = \sin x$ on the interval $\left[0, \frac{\pi}{2}\right]$.

Solution

For this question, make sure to choose the correct values for n and $(b - a)$ to determine the partition points. You can then calculate the value of the function $y = \sin(x)$ at each of those points and solve problem.

AP Calculus Exam-Type Questions

Multiple Choice Questions

A graphing calculator is required for some of these questions.

1. The limit of the right-hand sum

$$\lim_{n\to\infty} \frac{1}{n}\left[\left(\frac{n+1}{n}\right)^3 + \left(\frac{n+2}{n}\right)^3 \right.$$

$$\left. + \left(\frac{n+3}{n}\right)^3 + \cdots + \left(\frac{n+n}{n}\right)^3\right]$$

represents the area of which function on which interval?

(A) $f(x) = x^3$ on $[0, 1]$

(B) $f(x) = \frac{1}{x^3}$ on $[0, 1]$

(C) $f(x) = x^3$ on $[1, 2]$

(D) $f(x) = x^3$ on $[0, 2]$

2. The lower sum of $f(x) = -(x-1)^2 + 1$ on the interval $[0, 2]$ with four equal subintervals is

(A) $\frac{1}{2}$

(B) $\frac{3}{4}$

(C) $\frac{4}{3}$

(D) $\frac{3}{2}$

3. The left-hand sum for $f(x) = x^5$ on the interval $[-1, 1]$ using four equal subintervals is

(A) -1

(B) $-\frac{1}{2}$

(C) 0

(D) $\frac{1}{2}$

4. Which of the following is true for $f(x) = \cos x$ on the interval $\left[-\frac{\pi}{2}, \frac{\pi}{2}\right]$ using four equal subintervals?

(A) right-hand sum < left-hand sum

(B) midpoint sum < left-hand sum

(C) midpoint sum = left-hand sum

(D) left-hand sum = right-hand sum

5. Which value of n gives the largest upper sum for $f(x) = 2x^2$ on the interval $[-1, 1]$?

(A) $n = 4$

(B) $n = 10$

(C) $n = 20$

(D) $n = 30$

6. Which of the following is true for the left-hand sum of $f(x) = \frac{1}{x}$ on the interval $[1, 2]$ for any number of subintervals?

(A) left-hand sum > ln 2

(B) left-hand sum $\geq \frac{1}{2}$

(C) left-hand sum = ln 2

(D) left-hand sum = $\frac{1}{2}$

7. Which of the following expressions is the Trapezoidal Rule approximation for $y = x^2$ on the interval $[0, 2]$ with 10 equal subintervals?

(A) $\frac{1}{20}\left[(0.2)^2 + 2(0.4)^2 + \cdots + 2(1.8)^2 + 2^2\right]$

(B) $\frac{1}{10}\left[2(0.2)^2 + 2(0.4)^2 + \cdots + 2(1.8)^2 + 2^2\right]$

(C) $\frac{1}{5}\left[2(0.2)^2 + 2(0.4)^2 + \cdots + 2(1.8)^2 + 2^2\right]$

(D) $\frac{1}{20}\left[2(0.2)^2 + 2(0.4)^2 + \cdots + 2(1.8)^2 + 2^2\right]$

8. Which of the following statements is true about the graph of $y = \ln x$ on the interval $[1, e]$ with 10 equal subintervals?

(A) the trapezoidal approximation < the area under the curve

(B) the trapezoidal approximation = the left-hand sum

(C) the trapezoidal approximation = the right-hand sum

(D) the trapezoidal approximation > the area under the curve

9. Which of the following is the trapezoidal approximation for $f(x) = \frac{1}{x}$ on the interval $[1, 3]$ with n equal subintervals?

(A) $\dfrac{1}{n}\left[1 + \dfrac{2}{1 + \frac{2}{n}} + \dfrac{2}{1 + \frac{4}{n}} + \dfrac{2}{1 + \frac{6}{n}} + \cdots \right.$

$\left. + \dfrac{2}{1 + \frac{2(n-1)}{n}} + \dfrac{1}{3}\right]$

(B) $\dfrac{2}{n}\left[1 + \dfrac{2}{1 + \frac{2}{n}} + \dfrac{2}{1 + \frac{4}{n}} + \dfrac{2}{1 + \frac{6}{n}} + \cdots \right.$

$\left. + \dfrac{2}{1 + \frac{2(n-1)}{n}} + \dfrac{1}{3}\right]$

(C) $\dfrac{2}{n}\left[1 + \dfrac{2}{1 + \frac{1}{n}} + \dfrac{2}{1 + \frac{2}{n}} + \dfrac{2}{1 + \frac{3}{n}} + \cdots \right.$

$\left. + \dfrac{2}{1 + \frac{n-1}{n}} + \dfrac{1}{3}\right]$

(D) $\dfrac{2}{n}\left[1 + \dfrac{1}{1 + \frac{2}{n}} + \dfrac{1}{1 + \frac{4}{n}} + \dfrac{1}{1 + \frac{6}{n}} + \cdots \right.$

$\left. + \dfrac{1}{1 + \frac{2(n-1)}{n}} + \dfrac{1}{3}\right]$

10. Which of the following is true about the trapezoidal approximation for the graph of $f(x) = e^{-x}$ on the interval $[-1, 1]$ with n equal subintervals?

(A) Using $n = 5$ gives a closer approximation to the area under the curve than $n = 10$.

(B) The trapezoidal approximation on the interval $[-1, 0]$ is equal to the trapezoidal approximation on the interval $[0, 1]$,

(C) The trapezoidal approximation is greater than the area under the curve.

(D) The trapezoidal approximation is greater than the upper sum.

Free Response Questions

A graphing calculator is required for some questions.

1. During a recent snowfall, several students monitored the accumulation of snow on the flat roof of their school. The table records the data they collected for the 12-hour period of the snowfall.

Number of Hours	Rate of Snowfall (in./hour)
0	0
2	1.5
3	2.1
4.5	2.4
6.5	2.8
8	2.2
10.5	1.8
12	1.6

(a) Use a right-hand sum to approximate the total depth of snow in the 12-hour period.

(b) Using the right-hand sum approximation, estimate the average rate of snowfall in the 12-hour period.

2. A car slows down as it approaches a red light at an intersection. When the light turns green, the velocity of the car increases as shown in the table.

Time t (sec)	Velocity v (ft/s)
0	8
2	14
4	22
6	30
8	40
10	45

(a) Find the average rate of change of the velocity v on the interval $[0, 10]$.

(b) Approximate the distance traveled in the first ten seconds using five equal subintervals.

(c) Approximate the acceleration of the car at $t = 6$.

3. (a) Use the Trapezoidal Rule with ten subintervals to approximate

$$\int_0^2 (x^2 + 1)\, dx.$$

(b) Compare the approximation with the actual value of the antiderivative.

4. (a) Use the Trapezoidal Rule with ten subintervals to approximate $\int_0^2 (x^2 - 2)\, dx.$

(b) Compare the approximation with the actual value of the antiderivative.

5. (a) Use the Trapezoidal Rule with ten subintervals to approximate $\int_{-1}^1 \cos x\, dx.$

(b) Compare the approximation with the actual value of the antiderivative.

6. Based on the comparisons between the actual and approximated values in Questions 3–6, write an explanation of why some approximations are greater than the actual value and why some are less.

Lesson 3: The Fundamental Theorem of Calculus

- The Fundamental Theorem of Calculus: Part One
- The Fundamental Theorem of Calculus: Part Two

Explain: The Fundamental Theorem of Calculus: Part One

In Lesson 3.2, we used Riemann sums to approximate the area of a region. This is an important step in understanding how calculus is used to find the area that lies between the x-axis and the graph of a function, $f(x)$, over a given interval.

Now that we have reviewed how to use Riemann sums to find areas, we are in a position to formally define the relationship between the antiderivative of a function and the area under the graph of that function. We have seen that they are the same! This relationship is the basis for the Fundamental Theorem of Calculus, which has two parts.

> **The Fundamental Theorem of Calculus: Part One**
>
> If $f(x)$ has an antiderivative called $F(x)$, then
>
> $$\int_a^b f(x)\, dx = F(b) - F(a).$$

Part One of the theorem is used to compute the area under a curve. Since area is a nonnegative quantity, if $f(x)$ is positive on the interval $[a, b]$, then the definite integral $\int_a^b f(x)\, dx$ represents the area between the graph of $f(x)$ and the x-axis on the interval $[a, b]$. If $f(x)$ is negative on the interval $[a, b]$, then the absolute value of $\int_a^b f(x)\, dx$ represents the area between the curve and the x-axis. If $f(x)$ crosses the x-axis on the interval $[a, b]$, then the area between the curve and the x-axis is calculated by breaking the interval $[a, b]$ into the parts where $f(x)$ is positive and where $f(x)$ is negative. The area is then the sum of the absolute values of the integrals.

Another method of computing the area between the graph of $f(x)$ and the x-axis is to find $\int_a^b \left| f(x) \right| dx$.

This part of the Fundamental Theorem is also used to find the area between two curves. If $f(x) \geq g(x)$ on an interval $[a, b]$, then the area between the two curves is found using the formula

$$\int_a^b (f(x) - g(x))\, dx.$$

This formula works for $f(x)$ and $g(x)$ whether they are above or below the x-axis. To find the area of the region under the curve $y = x^2$ on the interval $[0, 2]$, simply take the antiderivative of x^2, and evaluate it as follows:

$$\text{area of the region} = \int_0^2 x^2\, dx = \left. \frac{x^3}{3} \right|.$$

The limits of integration on the top and bottom of the integral symbol, $\int$, indicate that

this is a **definite integral.** Now evaluate the antiderivative $\frac{x^3}{3}$ at the limits: substitute the upper limit 2 for x, then substitute the lower limit 0 for x. Subtract the value at the lower limit from the value at the upper limit to find the area. The area of the region $= \frac{8}{3} - \frac{0}{3} = \frac{8}{3}$, which is exactly the same value we calculated using Riemann sums!

MODEL PROBLEMS

1. Find the area under the curve $y = x^2$ on the interval $[0, 3]$.

(A) 2

(B) 9

(C) 27

(D) 3

Solution

Use the Power Rule to find the antiderivative, and then substitute in the upper and lower limits.

$$\int_0^3 x^2\,dx = \frac{x^3}{3}\Big|_0^3 = \frac{3^3}{3} - \frac{0^3}{3} = \frac{27}{3} - 0 = 9.$$

The correct answer choice is (B).

2. Find the area under the curve $y = 4 - x^2$ on the interval $[-1, 1]$.

(A) 22

(B) $\frac{16}{3}$

(C) $\frac{22}{3}$

(D) 3

Solution

Use the Power Rule and the Addition-Subtraction Rule to find the antiderivative, and then substitute in the upper and lower limits.

$$\int_{-1}^1 (4 - x^2)\,dx = \left(4x - \frac{x^3}{3}\right)\Big|_{-1}^1$$

You finish solving from here.

3. Find the area under the curve $y = e^x$ on the interval $[0, \ln 2]$.

(A) 2

(B) ln 2

(C) 1

(D) 4

Solution

Use the Exponential Function Rule to find the antiderivative, and then substitute in the upper and lower limits. Continue solving the problem from this point.

TT **4.** Find the area under the curve $y = \frac{1}{x}$ on the interval $[1, 4]$.

(A) ln 4

(B) ln 2

(C) 4

(D) 2

Solution

Set up this problem using an integral over the interval $[1, 4]$. The function requires the use of the Log Function Rule in order to solve.

5. Find the area between the graphs of $f(x) = 4 - x^2$ and $g(x) = x^2 + 1$ on the interval $[-1, 1]$.

(A) 6

(B) 0

(C) 4

(D) 2

Solution

Since over the entire interval $f(x) = 4 - x^2 \geq g(x) = x^2 + 1$, the area between $f(x)$ and $g(x)$ on the interval $[-1, 1]$ is calculated using the integral

$$\int_{-1}^{1} (f(x) - g(x))\, dx = \int_{-1}^{1} ((4 - x^2) - (x^2 + 1))\, dx.$$

You finish solving from here.

FR **6.** Find the area under the curve $f(x) = 2x^2 + 1$ on the interval $[0, 1]$.

Solution

This problem is a simple integration over the interval $[0, 1]$. You set up the problem and solve. Express your answer as an improper fraction.

FR **7.** Find the area between the curve $f(x) = x^2 - 1$ and the x-axis.

Solution

For this problem, we must find the interval to integrate over. Consider that you need to find the points where $f(x)$ intersects the x-axis, which will create a bounded region over which to integrate.

Note: $\int_{a}^{b} f(x)\, dx$ may be positive or negative. It is only when you are asked to find the *area* that your answer must be positive.

Explain: The Fundamental Theorem of Calculus: Part Two

The second part of the Fundamental Theorem says that the derivative of the antiderivative is the original function.

> **The Fundamental Theorem of Calculus: Part Two**
>
> $$\frac{d}{dx}\int_{a}^{x} (f(t)\,dt) = f(x)$$

Part Two may seem obvious, but it reveals an important fact. It says that the rate at which the area between the graph of a function and the horizontal axis is changing will be equal to the height of the function at that value of x. To make this clear, two variables, t and x, are used, but f is the same function. The following model problems will clarify the second part of the Fundamental Theorem by stepping through the process for several functions, $f(t)$.

MODEL PROBLEMS

FR 1. Find $\dfrac{d}{dx}\displaystyle\int_{3}^{x} (t^2 + t)\,dt$.

Solution

In this example, $f(t) = t^2 + t$, and $a = 3$. According to the first part of the Fundamental Theorem, $\dfrac{d}{dx}\displaystyle\int_{3}^{x}(t^2 + t)\,dt = x^2 + x$. We can check this ourselves. Use the first part of the Fundamental Theorem to find the antiderivative on the interval $[3, x]$:

$$\int_{3}^{x} (t^2 + t)\,dt = \left[\frac{t^3}{3} + \frac{t^2}{2}\right]_{3}^{x} = \frac{x^3}{3} + \frac{x^2}{2} - \left(\frac{3^3}{3} - \frac{3^2}{2}\right) = \frac{x^3}{3} + \frac{x^2}{2} - \frac{9}{2}.$$

The antiderivative here is the area between the graph of f and the t-axis from $t = a$ to $t = x$. The area depends on the upper limit, x.

Now find the derivative of the result with respect to x:

$$\frac{d}{dx}\left(\frac{x^3}{3} + \frac{x^2}{2} - \frac{9}{2}\right) = x^2 + x = f(x), \text{ the height of the curve at } x.$$

The derivative here is the rate at which the area found above is changing with respect to x.

FR 2. Find $\dfrac{d}{dx}\displaystyle\int_{1}^{5x} e^t\,dt$.

Solution

Calculating the antiderivative of e^t yields e^t. Use the first part of the Fundamental Theorem to evaluate e^t on the interval $[1, 5x]$. The result is $e^{5x} - e$. Now take the derivative of $e^{5x} - e$ with respect to x, and the result is $5e^{5x}$.

Model Problem #2 above illustrates a further complexity of the second part of the Fundamental Theorem. When one of the limits of the integral is not just x, but a function of x, in this case $5x$, not only is the variable t in the integrand replaced by $5x$, but since the Chain Rule is applied, the result is also multiplied by the derivative, 5. Therefore, the final answer is $5e^{5x}$.

3. Find $\dfrac{d}{dx}\displaystyle\int_x^4 \sin t\, dt$.

(A) $\cos x$

(B) $\tan x$

(C) $-\sin x$

(D) $-\cos x$

Solution

The variable is at the lower limit of the integral, so use this property of integrals (p. 231) to switch the limits of the integral:

For any real numbers a and b, $\displaystyle\int_a^b f(x)\, dx = -\int_b^a f(x)\, dx$.

The integral now follows the form of the Fundamental Theorem of Calculus Part 2 and can be easily solved.

Model Problems #1-3 use integrands for which we can find the antiderivative. In Model Problems #4 and 5, below, we apply the second part of the Fundamental Theorem of Calculus to integrands for which the antiderivatives are difficult or impossible to find.

FR **4.** Find $\dfrac{d}{dx}\displaystyle\int_2^x \sqrt{t^3+1}\, dt$.

Solution

We could use go the long route and find the antiderivative of $\sqrt{t^3+1}$ with a complex computation. That doesn't sound like what we'd like to do. Instead, we'll apply the second part of the Fundamental Theorem. The derivative with respect to the antiderivative of $\sqrt{t^3+1}$ replaces the variable t with x and the result is $\sqrt{x^3+1}$.

FR **5.** Find $\dfrac{d}{dx}\displaystyle\int_1^{2x} \sin(t^2)\, dt$.

Solution

By the second part of the Fundamental Theorem, replace the variable t in $\sin(t^2)$ with $2x$. Since the derivative of $2x$ is 2, apply the Chain Rule and finish solving.

AP Calculus Exam-Type Questions

Multiple Choice Questions

A graphing calculator is required for some questions.

1. Find the area under the graph of $y = x + 2$ on the interval $[1, 3]$.

(A) 2

(B) 3

(C) 5

(D) 8

2. Find the area between the x-axis and the graph of $y = |x|$ on the interval $[-10, 10]$.

(A) 10

(B) 20

(C) 50

(D) 100

3. Find the area between the x-axis and the graph of $y = 3 - |x|$ on the interval $[0, 6]$.

(A) 0

(B) $\dfrac{9}{2}$

(C) 9

(D) 18

4. Find the area bounded by the graph of $f(x) = \sqrt{16 - x^2}$ and the x-axis.

(A) π

(B) 2π

(C) 4π

(D) 8π

5. Which of the following graphs shows a shaded region whose area is represented by

$$\int_{-1}^{2} 2 \, dx?$$

(A)

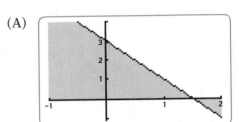

(B)

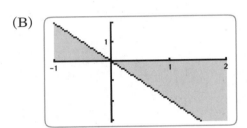

(C)

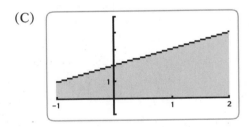

(D)

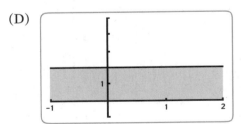

6. $\displaystyle\int_{-1}^{1} (e^x - 1) \, dx =$

(A) -2

(B) 0

(C) $\dfrac{e^2 - 2e - 1}{e}$

(D) $\dfrac{e^2 - 2e + 1}{e}$

7. Find the area bounded by the graphs of $y = x^2 - 4x$ and $y = x$.

(A) $\dfrac{25}{3}$

(B) 10

(C) 12.5

(D) $\dfrac{125}{6}$

8. The area enclosed by the graphs of $y = e^x$, $y = x$, the y-axis, and the line $x = 2$ is equal to

(A) e^2

(B) $e^2 - 1$

(C) $e^2 + 1$

(D) $e^2 - 3$

9. Find the area bounded by the curve $y = \cos x$ and the x-axis from $x = -\pi$ to $x = \pi$.

(A) –2

(B) 0

(C) 2

(D) 4

10. Find the area bounded by the graphs of $y = x + 2$, $y = -x + 4$, and the x-axis.

(A) 4.5

(B) 6

(C) 7

(D) 9

11. Find the area enclosed by the graphs of $y = \sqrt{x}$ and $y = x^3$.

(A) $\dfrac{1}{4}$

(B) $\dfrac{1}{3}$

(C) $\dfrac{5}{12}$

(D) $\dfrac{2}{3}$

Free Response Questions

A graphing calculator is required for Questions 1 – 3.

1. Find the value of k so that the line $x = k$ divides into two equal areas the region enclosed by the graph of $y = x^2$, the line $x = 2$, and the x-axis.

2. Region R is enclosed by the graph of $f(x) = \dfrac{1}{x^2}$, the lines $x = 1$ and $x = 2$, and the x-axis. The lines $x = p$ and $x = q$ divide R into three regions of equal area. Find the values of p and q.

3. For what value of k does the line $x = k$ divide the region bounded by the graphs of $y = e^x$, $y = -x$, the y-axis, and the line $x = 2$ so that the area of the region on the interval $[0, k]$ is 50% of the area of the region on the interval $[k, 2]$?

No calculator is allowed for Questions 4 and 5.

4. Sketch the graph of a function $f(x)$ so that $f(x) > 0$ on the closed interval $[-2, 2]$ and
$$\int_{-2}^{2} f(x)\, dx = 5.$$

5. The graph of f is a semicircle and two line segments. Find the area between the graph of f on the interval $[-8, 8]$ and the x-axis.

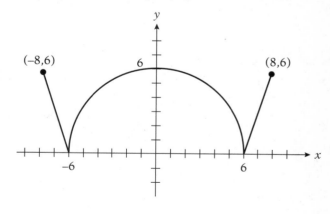

Lesson 4: More on Definite Integrals

- Evaluation and Approximation of Definite Integrals Using Various Methods
- Properties and Extensions of Definite Integrals

Explain: Evaluation and Approximation of Definite Integrals Using Various Methods

The graph of the function f is shown below.

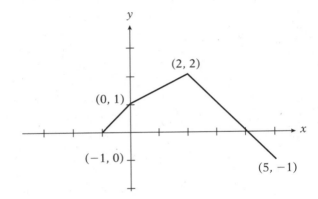

We can see that the graph of f consists of three line segments.

If

$$g(x) = \int_0^x f(t)\,dt,$$

Then

Part Two of the Fundamental Theorem can be used to determine:

- where $g(x)$ is increasing or decreasing.
- the values of x where $g(x)$ has a relative maximum or a relative minimum.
- where $g(x)$ is concave up or concave down.
- the values of x that are points of inflection of g.

The function $g(x)$ is called the **accumulation function** because it accumulates the area under the graph of f as x increases. By the second part of the Fundamental Theorem, $g'(x) = f(x)$.

Since $g'(x) = f(x)$, $g' > 0$ means g is increasing and $g' < 0$ means g is decreasing. Thus when $f > 0$, g is increasing and when $f < 0$, g is decreasing. Looking at the graph of f, $f > 0$ on the interval $(-1, 4)$ and $f < 0$ on the interval $(4, 5)$. Therefore, g is increasing on the interval $(-1, 4)$ and decreasing on the interval $(4, 5)$.

We can find the critical values by analyzing the values of x for which $g'(x) = 0$ or $g'(x)$ is undefined. Additionally, each critical value can be identified as a relative maximum or a relative minimum.

When $g'(x) = 0$, then $f(x) = 0$ and when $g'(x)$ is undefined, that means that $f(x)$ is undefined.

In this case, $f(x)$ is always defined on $[-1, 5]$, so $f(x) = 0$ at $x = -1$ and $x = 4$.

Since $x = -1$ is an endpoint of the interval, only $x = 4$ can be a relative maximum or minimum. We illustrate this on the number line below:

By the First Derivative Test, since g' changes sign from $+$ to $-$ at $x = 4$, $g(4)$ is a relative maximum. To find the absolute maximum and the absolute minimum values of $g(x)$ on the interval $[-1, 5]$, find the value of g at the endpoints and the value of $g(4)$ by using basic geometry to evaluate the definite integral $\int_{0}^{x} f(t)\, dt$ as follows:

$$g(-1) = \int_{0}^{-1} f(t)\, dt = -\int_{-1}^{0} f(t)\, dt = -\frac{1}{2}$$

$$g(4) = \int_{0}^{4} f(t)\, dt = \int_{0}^{2} f(t)\, dt + \int_{2}^{4} f(t)\, dt = 3 + 2 = 5$$

(using the formula for the area of a triangle and the area of a trapezoid)

$$g(5) = \int_{0}^{5} f(t)\, dt = \int_{0}^{4} f(t)\, dt + \int_{4}^{5} f(t)\, dt = 5 + \left(-\frac{1}{2}\right) = 4.5$$

Since $g(4) = 5$, $g(-1) = -\frac{1}{2}$, and $g(5) = 4.5$, the absolute maximum of g is 5 and the absolute minimum of g is $-\frac{1}{2}$.

The second derivative of g, $g''(x)$, can be found by taking the derivative of $g'(x) = f(x)$. Thus $g''(x) = f'(x)$. To find the points of inflection of g, find the values of x where $g''(x) = 0$ or $g''(x)$ is undefined. Since $g''(x) = f'(x)$, find the values of x where $f'(x) = 0$ or $f'(x)$ is undefined. There are no values of x where $f'(x) = 0$, but $f'(x)$ is undefined at $x = 0$ and $x = 2$. Putting these values on a number line, indicates where $g''(x)$ is positive or negative.

Since $g''(x)$ changes sign at $x = 2$, there is a point of inflection on the graph of g at $x = 2$. Additionally, g is concave up on the intervals $(-1, 0)$ and $(0, 2)$ and concave down on the interval $(2, 5)$.

Using the information about the graph of $g(x)$, it is possible to sketch the graph.

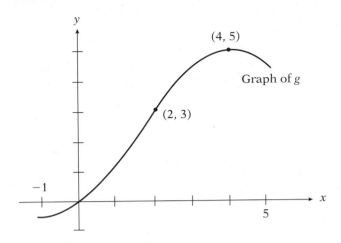

MODEL PROBLEMS

1. Integrate $f(x) = -x^2 + 4$ from $[-1, 1]$.

(A) 6 units squared

(B) $\frac{22}{3}$ units squared

(C) 0 units squared

(D) 13 units squared

Solution

Begin by graphing the function. We are only concerned with the graph from -1 to 1, so we draw lines and shade the area of interest.

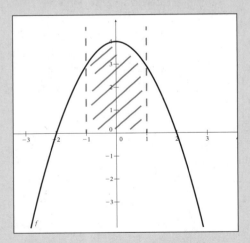

$$\int_a^b f(x)\,dx = \int_{-1}^1 (-x^2 + 4)\,dx$$

Now we set up the integral.

$$\int_{-1}^1 (-x^2 + 4)\,dx = -\frac{1}{3}x^3 + 4x$$

Calculate the integral using rules of integration. Note that here we did not add a constant, as that will cancel out in the end.

$$\int_{-1}^1 f(x)\,dx = F(1) - F(-1)$$

$$\int_{-1}^1 f(x)\,dx = \left[-\frac{1}{3}(1)^3 + 4(1)\right] - \left[-\frac{1}{3}(-1)^3 + 4(-1)\right]$$ Integrate over $[-1, 1]$.

$$\left[-\frac{1}{3} + 4\right] - \left[\frac{1}{3} - 4\right] = \frac{22}{3}$$

The area under the curve from -1 to 1 is $\frac{22}{3}$ units squared. The correct option is (B).

Explain: Properties and Extensions of Definite Integrals

Integrals have several properties, which we formally state below:

Properties of Integrals

1. For any real number a, $\displaystyle\int_a^a f(x)\,dx = 0$.

2. For any real numbers a and b, $\displaystyle\int_a^b f(x)\,dx = -\int_b^a f(x)\,dx$.

3. For real numbers a, b, and c, where $a < b < c$, $\displaystyle\int_b^a f(x)\,dx + \int_a^c f(x)\,dx = \int_a^b f(x)\,dx$.

4. If $f(x)$ is an even function, $\displaystyle\int_{-a}^a f(x)\,dx = 2\int_0^a f(x)\,dx$.

5. If $f(x)$ is an odd function, $\displaystyle\int_{-a}^a f(x)\,dx = 0$.

There are also properties by which we can reverse the limits of integration or find the integral of a function over two adjacent intervals. In this section, we also discuss integrating functions with removable or jump discontinuities.

We often utilize the reversal of the limits of integration with double integrals, which is not part of the Calculus AB or BC curriculum. However, we can review and practice the process of bound reversal using single integrals.

Suppose that you have a function, $f(x)$, whose antiderivative is $F(x)$. Then, we know from Lesson 3.3 that

$$\int_a^b f(x)\,dx = F(b) - F(a)$$

which is the same as

$$-\big(F(b) - F(a)\big) \int_a^b f(x)\,dx$$

We can see that reversing the limits of integration will lead to a solution with the opposite sign.

MODEL PROBLEMS

1. The solution of $\int_{1}^{4} x + 1^2\, dx$ is 39. What is the solution of $\int_{4}^{1} x + 1^2\, dx$?

(A) $\dfrac{117}{3}$

(B) 125

(C) $\dfrac{98}{3}$

(D) -39

Solution

From the explanation on page 231, we know that integrating the same function over a reversed interval leads to an answer with the opposite sign. The answer is (D).

2. Consider the integral $\int_{2}^{7} \sqrt{x + 2}\, dx$. What is $\int_{7}^{2} \sqrt{x + 2}\, dx$?

(A) $\dfrac{3}{38}$

(B) 3

(C) -38

(D) $-\dfrac{38}{3}$

Solution

Consider that it may be easier to determine the definite integral

$\int_{2}^{7} \sqrt{x + 2}\, dx$ and then use $-\big(F(a) - F(b)\big) = -\int_{a}^{b} fx\, dx$.

Up to this point, we have integrated a given function over the entire required interval. We take this opportunity to note that there are times when it is easier to integrate a function over two adjacent intervals rather than over the entire interval at once.

If we have a function, $f(x)$, that is continuous over the interval $[a, c]$, then, as stated on page 231,

$$\int_{a}^{b} f(x)\, dx = \int_{a}^{c} f(x)\, dx + \int_{c}^{b} f(x)\, dx$$

This idea is especially helpful for functions with removable and jump discontinuities.

Consider the function $f(x) = \frac{\sin x}{x}$, which is undefined for $x = 0$. If we

change $f(x)$ to $\begin{cases} \frac{\sin x}{x} & \text{for } x \neq 0 \\ 0 & \text{for } x = 0 \end{cases}$, we have defined a value for $f(0)$ and now f

(x) is continuous. We show the graph on the next page. Notice that $\lim\limits_{x \to 0^-} f(x)$

$= \lim\limits_{x \to 0^+} f(x) = 1$, so we know that $\lim\limits_{x \to 0} f(x) = 1$.

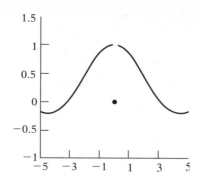

Formally, if a function has a removable discontinuity at $x = b$ in the open interval (a, c), but it is continuous everywhere else in the closed interval $[a, c]$, then we can apply the adjacent intervals property as such

$$\int_a^c f(x)\, dx = \int_a^b f(x)\, dx + \int_b^c f(x)\, dx = \lim_{r \to b^-} \int_a^r f(x) + \lim_{r \to b^+} \int_r^c f(x)$$

We can apply a similar idea to integrating functions with jump discontinuities.

MODEL PROBLEMS

1. What is the integral of a function, $g(x)$, over $[1, 8]$ if its integral over $[1, 5]$ is -7 and its integral from $[5, 8]$ is 9?

(A) -14

(B) 0

(C) 2

(D) 1

Solution

$\int_1^5 g(x) = -7$ $\int_5^8 g(x) = 9$	We restate the given information using mathematical notation.
$\int_1^8 g(x) = \int_1^5 g(x) + \int_5^8 g(x) = -7 + 9 = 2$	The upper bound of the first integral is the same as the lower bound of the second integral, so the third integral rule can be applied to find the answer. The correct answer is (C).

2. Consider the function $f(x) = \begin{cases} 4, & \text{for } x > 1 \\ x^2, & \text{for } x \le 1 \end{cases}$. What is $\displaystyle\int_{-2}^{10} f(x)\,dx$?

(A) 39

(B) 25

(C) −1

(D) 0

Graph the function and note that it is not continuous at $x = 1$.

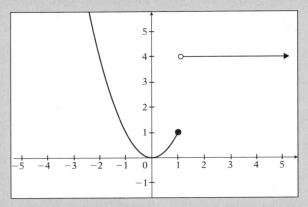

In this case, it is not division by 0 making the function discontinuous at this point; instead it is because LHL ≠ RHL. Let's just remove this discontinuity by rewriting the integral.

$$\int_{-2}^{10} f(x)\,dx = \int_{-2}^{1} f(x)\,dx + \int_{1}^{10} f(x)\,dx$$

Now that the function is continuous on each interval, you complete this problem.

3. What is $\displaystyle\int_{0}^{8} \frac{3x}{\sqrt[3]{64 - x^2}}\,dx$?

(A) 0

(B) 36

(C) 8

(D) 12

Solution

Begin this problem by noting that the integrand has a point of discontinuity at $x = 8$.

$\displaystyle\int_{0}^{8} \frac{3x}{\sqrt[3]{64 - x^2}}\,dx = \lim_{t \to 8^-} \int_{0}^{t} \frac{3x}{\sqrt[3]{64 - x^2}}\,dx$	Because $x = 8$ is the upper limit of integration, we can apply the limit definition of an integral.
For $\displaystyle\int \frac{3x}{\sqrt[3]{64 - x^2}}\,dx$, $u = 64 - x^2$, and $du = -2x\,dx$	The integrand is now continuous on $[0, t]$ for all $0 \le t < 8$ and we can use substitution to solve the integral.
After a lot of algebraic steps we find that $\displaystyle\int \frac{3x}{\sqrt[3]{64 - x^2}}\,dx = -\frac{9}{4}(64 - x^2)^{\frac{2}{3}} + c$. You try solving from this point.	

AP Calculus Exam-Type Questions

Multiple Choice Questions
No calculator permitted for these questions.

1. If $F(x) = \displaystyle\int_0^x \sin^2(2t)\,dt$, then $F'(x) =$

    (A) $-\cos^2(2x)$

    (B) $\cos^2(2x)$

    (C) $\sin^2(2x)$

    (D) $\frac{1}{2}\sin^2(2x)$

2. $\dfrac{d}{dx}\left(\displaystyle\int_2^5 (1 + t^{2/3})\,dt \right) =$

    (A) 0

    (B) $1 + 5^{2/3}$

    (C) $t + \frac{3}{5}t^{5/3}$

    (D) $5^{2/3} - 2^{2/3}$

3. $\dfrac{d}{dt}\left(\displaystyle\int_{6t}^1 (1 + \sqrt{x})^2\,dx \right) =$

    (A) $\sqrt{1 + 6t}$

    (B) $-\left(1 + \sqrt{6t}\right)^2$

    (C) $\left(1 + \sqrt{6t}\right)^2$

    (D) $-6\left(1 + \sqrt{6t}\right)^2$

For Questions 4 and 5, if $F(x) = \displaystyle\int_{-x}^x e^{-t^2}\,dt$, **then**

4. $F'(1) =$

    (A) 0

    (B) $2e^{-1}$

    (C) 2

    (D) $2e$

5. $F''(x) =$

    (A) 0

    (B) $-4xe^{-x^2}$

    (C) $-2xe^{-x^2}$

    (D) $4xe^{-x^2}$

For Questions 6–9, $f(x) = \displaystyle\int_0^x f'(t)\,dt$, **and the graph of** f' **is shown below.**

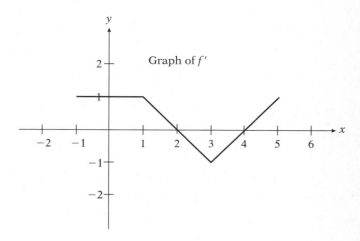

6. Which of the following are true?

    I. $f(-1) = -1$

    II. $f(1) < f(3)$

    III. $f'(1) < f'(3)$

    (A) I only

    (B) II only

    (C) III only

    (D) I and II

7. Which of the following are true about the graph of f?

    I. f is increasing on $(-1, 2)$ only

    II. f is increasing on $(-1, 2)$ and $(4, 5)$

    III. f is decreasing on $(1, 3)$

    (A) I only

    (B) II only

    (C) III only

    (D) I and III

8. Which of the following are true about the graph of f?

I. f is concave up on $(21, 1)$
II. f is concave up on $(1, 3)$
III. f is concave down on $(3, 5)$

(A) I only
(B) II only
(C) III only
(D) II and III

9. Which of the following are true about the graph of f?

I. f has a relative minimum at $x = 2$
II. f has a relative minimum at $x = 4$
III. f has a relative maximum at $x = 2$

(A) II only
(B) III only
(C) I and II
(D) II and III

10. If the integral $\int_1^5 x e^{x^2}\,dx$ is equal to some constant, c, then $\int_5^1 x e^{x^2}\,dx$ is

(A) 0
(B) $-c$
(C) 1
(D) c

11. The function $f(x) = \begin{cases} 4x, & \text{for } x > 1 \\ 3x^2, & \text{for } x \le 1 \end{cases}$. What is $\int_{-1}^4 f(x)\,dx$?

(A) 0
(B) 14
(C) 32
(D) -25

You will need a graphing calculator for Question #12.

12. $F(x) = \int \cos(x^2)\,dx$ and $F(2) = 10$. Find $F(3)$.

(A) 0.140
(B) 0.241
(C) 0.703
(D) 10.241

Free Response Questions
No calculator is allowed for these questions.

1. The graph of f, shown below, consists of a semicircle and two line segments on the interval $[-2, 6]$.

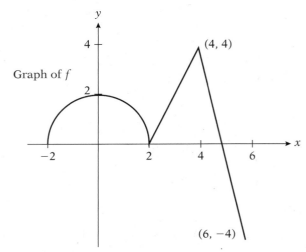

Graph of f

If $g(x) = \int_2^x f(t)\,dt$, use the graph of f to do the following:

(a) Find $g(-2)$, $g(0)$, $g(2)$, $g(4)$, and $g(6)$.
(b) Find the intervals where g is decreasing.
(c) Find the intervals where g is concave up.
(d) Find the absolute extrema of g on the interval $[-2, 6]$.
(e) Find the point(s) of inflection of g.
(f) Sketch g on the interval $[-2, 6]$.

2. The graph of $g(t)$ is shown on the interval

[0, 6] and $f(x) = \int_0^x g(t)\,dt$.

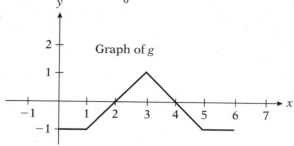

Graph of g

(a) Find the critical points of $f(x)$, and identify each as a relative maximum, a relative minimum, or neither.

(b) Find the absolute extrema of $f(x)$.

(c) If $f(0) = k$, is there a number c in the interval [0, 6] such that $f(c) = k$? Justify your conclusion.

(d) On what interval(s) is $f(x)$ concave up? On what interval(s) is $f(x)$ concave down?

(e) Sketch a graph of $f(x)$.

Lesson 5: Improper Integrals (BC Exam Only)

- Improper Integrals

In this lesson we take a brief break from proper integrals to discuss improper integrals. This topic is only found on the AP Calculus BC exam, so if you are sitting for the AB exam, you may skip this lesson.

Explain: Improper Integrals

There are two cases in which integrals are called **improper integrals:**

Case 1. One or both of the limits of the integral are ∞ or $-\infty$. The interval of integration is $[a, +\infty)$, $(-\infty, c]$, or $(-\infty, +\infty)$.

Case 2. The integrand is not continuous on the interval defined by the limits of the integration.

Improper integrals are evaluated by finding the antiderivative of the integrand and taking the limit(s) of the antiderivative expression. If the limit exists, the integral is said to converge to that number. If no limit exists, the integral is said to diverge.

In Case 1, if one or both of the limits of the integral are ∞ or $-\infty$, then we have either $\int_a^\infty f(x)\,dx$ or $\int_{-\infty}^c f(x)\,dx$, $\int_{-\infty}^\infty f(x)\,dx$.

$\int_a^\infty f(x)\,dx$ means $\lim\limits_{b\to\infty}\int_a^b f(x)\,dx$.

$\int_{-\infty}^c f(x)\,dx$ means $\lim\limits_{b\to-\infty}\int_b^c f(x)\,dx$.

$\int_{-\infty}^\infty f(x)\,dx$ means for some b, $-\infty < b < \infty$, $\lim\limits_{a\to-\infty}\int_a^b f(x)\,dx +$

$\lim\limits_{c\to\infty}\int_b^c f(x)\,dx$.

In Case 2, if the integrand is undefined at the left endpoint of $[a, b]$,

$\int_a^b f(x)\,dx = \lim\limits_{c\to a^+}\int_c^b f(x)\,dx$.

If the integrand is undefined at the right endpoint of $[a, b]$,

$\int_a^b f(x)\,dx = \lim\limits_{c\to b^-}\int_a^c f(x)\,dx$.

If the integrand is undefined at a point c in the interval $[a, b]$,

$\int_a^b f(x)\,dx = \lim\limits_{d\to c^-}\int_a^d f(x)\,dx + \lim\limits_{e\to c^+}\int_e^b f(x)\,dx$.

MODEL PROBLEMS

1. Find the value of $\displaystyle\int_0^\infty e^{-x}\,dx$, if it exists.

(A) 1

(B) 0

(C) −1

(D) 4

Solution

This is an example of Case 1. The interval of integration is $[0, +\infty)$.
By definition,

$$\int_0^\infty e^{-x}\,dx = \lim_{b\to\infty}\int_0^b e^{-x}\,dx.$$

The integral in the limit is

$$\int_0^b e^{-x}\,dx = \left[-e^{-x}\right]_0^b = -e^b - (-e^0) = -e^{-b} + 1.$$

Therefore,

$$\int_0^\infty e^{-x}\,dx = \lim_{b\to\infty}(-e^{-b} + 1) = 1.$$

The correct answer is (A).

2. Find the value of $\displaystyle\int_{-\infty}^{-1} \frac{1}{x^2}\,dx$.

(A) 0

(B) 1

(C) ∞

(D) $-\infty$

Solution

This is another example of Case 1. The interval of integration is $(-\infty, -1]$.

By definition, we know that $\displaystyle\int_{-\infty}^{-1} \frac{1}{x^2}\,dx = \lim_{b\to-\infty}\int_b^{-1} \frac{1}{x^2}\,dx$. Find the integral in the limit to finish solving.

3. Find the value of $\displaystyle\int_0^1 \frac{1}{\sqrt{x}}\,dx$, if it exists.

(A) $-\infty$

(B) 0

(C) 2

(D) 4

Solution

This is an example of Case 2. The integrand is not continuous at $x = 0$, which is the left endpoint of the interval $[0, 1]$. We know that $\displaystyle\int_0^1 \frac{1}{\sqrt{x}}\,dx = \lim_{b\to 0^+}\int_b^1 \frac{1}{\sqrt{x}}\,dx$ and that the integral in the limit is $\displaystyle\int_b^1 \frac{1}{\sqrt{x}}\,dx$. You finish solving from here.

AP Calculus Exam-Type Questions

Multiple Choice Questions
No calculator is allowed for these questions.

1. $\displaystyle\int_1^\infty \frac{2}{\sqrt[3]{x}}\,dx =$

   (A) ∞

   (B) 0

   (C) $\frac{2}{3}$

   (D) 1

2. $\displaystyle\int_0^1 \frac{dx}{\sqrt[3]{x-1}} =$

   (A) $-\infty$

   (B) $-\frac{3}{2}$

   (C) 0

   (D) 1

3. When r is a real number greater than
   $1, \displaystyle\int_1^r \frac{1}{x\ln x}\,dx =$

   (A) 1

   (B) $\ln r$

   (C) $-\infty$

   (D) ∞

4. When n is an integer greater than 1, $\displaystyle\int_0^1 \frac{1}{x^n}\,dx =$

   (A) 0

   (B) 1

   (C) $-\infty$

   (D) ∞

5. When n is an integer greater than 1, $\displaystyle\int_1^\infty \frac{1}{x^n}\,dx =$

   (A) 0

   (B) 1

   (C) $\frac{1}{n-1}$

   (D) $-\infty$

Free Response Questions

A graphing calculator is required for some questions.

Evaluate the following improper integrals, if they exist. If the integral does not exist, state so.

1. $\displaystyle\int_1^\infty \frac{1}{\sqrt{x}}\,dx$

2. $\displaystyle\int_0^{\frac{\pi}{2}} \tan x\,dx$

3. $\displaystyle\int_1^2 \frac{2}{x-1}\,dx$

4. $\displaystyle\int_{-1}^1 \frac{1}{x^2}\,dx$

5. For which range of values of p does each of the following integrals converge?

   (a) $\displaystyle\int_0^1 \frac{1}{x^p}\,dx$

   (b) $\displaystyle\int_1^\infty \frac{1}{x^p}\,dx$

   (c) $\displaystyle\int_0^1 \frac{1}{(\ln x)^p}\,dx$

   (d) $\displaystyle\int_1^\infty \frac{1}{(\ln x)^p}\,dx$

Lesson 6: Applications of the Integral: Accumulation and the Average Value of a Function

- Net Change
- Accumulation
- Average Value Function

Explain: Net Change

From the Fundamental Theorem of Calculus, we know that $\int_a^b f(x) = F(b) - F(a)$ where $f(x)$ has an antiderivative called $F(x)$. The function $f(x)$ represents the rate of change in $y = f(x)$ with respect to x and $F(b) - F(a)$ is the change in the y-variable as x moves from a to b. Thus we know that the integral of a rate of change is the net change in y. There are several places we can apply this principle.

MODEL PROBLEMS

1. Water flows out of a storage tank at a rate of $r(t) = 500 - 3t$ liters per minute where t is in minutes and $0 \le t \le 15$. Find, to the nearest liter, the amount of water that flows from the tank during the first 15 minutes.

   (A) 9,268 liters

   (B) 7,163 liters

   (C) 15,663 liters

   (D) 163 liters

   Solution

   To solve this problem, recognize that $r(t)$ is a function that represents a rate of change. Integrate that function from 0 to 15.

   $$\int_0^{15} (500 - 3t)\,dt \qquad \text{Set up the integration.}$$

   $$\left[500t - \frac{3t^2}{2} \right]_0^{15} = \qquad \begin{array}{l} \text{Integrate and evaluate.} \\ \text{The correct answer is (B).} \end{array}$$

   $$500(15) - \frac{3(225)}{2} = 7{,}163 \text{ liters}$$

2. A small rocket is launched directly upward with an initial velocity of 150 meters per second. The rocket's velocity as a function of elapsed time is given by $v(t) = 150 - 9.8t$, where t is in seconds and $t \ge 0$. Determine, to the nearest meter, the rocket's height above the launch site after 5 seconds.

   (A) 342 meters

   (B) 628 meters

   (C) 205 meters

   (D) 561 meters

Solution

This question is very similar to Model Problem #1. In this case, instead of the change representing the amount of water in a tank over time, it is the change in the position of the rocket over time. Integrate the given function over the indicated interval to solve.

3. A store you are shopping in on a rainy day has a leaky roof with a large bucket under the part of the roof that is leaking the most. During heavy rainfall, the height of the water inside the bucket increases at a rate of $r(t) = 2t^3 e^{-1.5t}$ feet per hour, where t is the time in hours since the rain began and $1 \leq t \leq 5$. At time $t = 1$ hour, the height of the water in the bucket is 0.80 feet. What is the height of the water in the bucket at time $t = 1.5$ hours?

(A) 1.03 feet

(B) 0.45 feet

(C) 0.30 feet

(D) 1.10 feet

Solution

If you are preparing for the AP Calculus AB exam, use your calculator to help you with the integration. If you are preparing for the AP Calculus BC exam, you will need to use integration by parts to solve. Consider also that you are given the height of the water in the bucket at $t = 1$. What does that mean for your integration interval? When you integrate over that interval, what does your answer represent in relation to the problem?

4. The marginal cost of manufacturing x yards of telecommunications cable is $C'(x) = 5 - 0.01x + 0.000004x^2$ (in dollars per yard). What is the increase in cost, to the nearest dollar, if the production level is raised from 2,000 to 3,000 yards?

(A) $6,621

(B) $8,298

(C) $5,333

(D) $4,254

Solution

Recall that marginal cost refers to the change in total cost that is incurred by manufacturing one more unit of an item, in this case, an additional yard of cable. Solve this problem in the same manner as Model Problems 1–3. Be sure to integrate over the correct interval.

Explain: Accumulation

When we calculate definite integrals, we get a single number that represents the area between the given function and the x-axis. In Lesson 3.4 we allowed either the lower or the upper limit of integration to vary as in $\int_a^x f(t) \, dt$, and we discussed how the accumulation function is simply a definite integral with a variable expression in one or more of its limits of integration. Remember that when we integrate these functions, the output will be a function, not a finite number. Here we briefly show some of the ways accumulation function questions have appeared on past AP Calculus exams.

MODEL PROBLEMS

FR 1. Liquid is pumped into storage tank at a constant rate of 5 gallons per minute. Unfortunately, some liquid is leaking out of the tank at the rate of $\sqrt{t + \frac{1}{2}}$ gallons per minute for $0 \le t \le 20$ minutes. At time $t = 0$, the tank contains 20 gallons of liquid.

(a) How many gallons of liquid leak out of the tank from time $t = 0$ to $t = 5$?

(b) How many gallons of liquid are in the tank at time $t = 5$ minutes?

(c) Write an expression, $A(t)$, for the total number of gallons of liquid in the tank at time t.

Solution

This problem combines net change and the accumulation function. We begin by integrating.

(a)	$\int_0^5 \sqrt{t + \frac{1}{2}} \, dt =$ $\left[\dfrac{2\left(t + \frac{1}{2}\right)^{\frac{3}{2}}}{3} \right]_0^5 = 8.36$ gallons	Determine how many gallons have leaked out of the tank by integrating the expression that represents the amount leaking out per minute.
(b)	$20 + 5 \cdot 5 - 8.36 = 36.64$ gallons	Determine how many gallons of liquid are in the tank at time $t = 5$. There were 20 gallons to begin with, 25 more pumped into the tank over the first five minutes, and then 8.36 gallons leaked out.
(c)	$A(t) = 20 + \int_0^t \left(5 - \sqrt{x + \frac{1}{2}} \right) dx$ $= 20 + 5t - \int_0^t \sqrt{x + \frac{1}{2}} \, dx$	Determine the accumulation function. This is the initial amount plus the integral of the rate of change.

FR 2. Grandmom's Manufacturing Company makes a variety of products, but its most popular is its heavy-duty climbing rope, which sells for $1.20 per foot. For climbing rope that is produced in fixed lengths, the cost of producing a portion of the climbing rope varies with its distance from the beginning of the rope. Grandmom's reports that the cost to produce a portion of a climbing rope that is x feet from the beginning of the rope is $0.15\sqrt{x + 1}$ per foot.

(a) Find Grandmom's profit on the sale of a 50-foot rope.

(b) Write an expression that represents Grandmom's profit on the sale of a climbing rope that is y feet in length.

Solution

(a)

$$1.20 \cdot 50 - \int_0^{50} 0.15\sqrt{x+1}\,dx$$

Recall that a company's profit is the amount for which it can sell a product minus the cost to produce the product. In this case, we know how much Grandmom's is selling the climbing rope for, as well as the amount it costs to produce, per foot. We've provided the set up to help you. Solve from this point.

(b) Here we are being asked for an accumulation function. Consider that the company will not make money if they do not produce a product. What does this mean for the initial value?

Explain: Average Value Function

If $f(x)$ is continuous on the interval $[a, b]$, then the **average value** of the function on the interval is

$$\frac{1}{b-a}\int_a^b f(x)\,dx.$$

This can also be expressed as

$$(\text{the average value of } f(x))(b - a) = \int_a^b f(x)\,dx.$$

If $f(x) \geq 0$ for the entire interval, the above expression can be represented as two areas that are equal. The right side of the equation represents the area under the curve, enclosed by the lines $x = a$, $x = b$, and the x-axis. The left side of the equation represents the area of a rectangle with $(b - a)$ as its base and the average value of the function as its height.

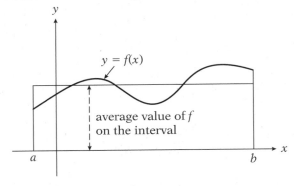

MODEL PROBLEMS

1. Find the average value of $f(x) = x^2$ on the interval $[0, 2]$.

(A) $\dfrac{4}{3}$

(B) 2

(C) 1

(D) $\dfrac{1}{2}$

Solution

$$\frac{1}{2}\int_0^2 x^2\,dx = \frac{4}{3}$$

Set up the calculation of the average value of $f(x) = x^2$ on the interval $[0, 2]$. The correct answer is (A).

2. Find the average value of $f(x) = \sin x$ on the interval $\left[0, \frac{\pi}{2}\right]$.

(A) π

(B) 1

(C) $\frac{2}{\pi}$

(D) 2π

Solution

To find this average value, we need to solve $\left(\dfrac{1}{\frac{\pi}{2} - 0}\right)\displaystyle\int_0^{\pi/2} \sin x\,dx$. You try solving from here.

3. Find the average value of $f(x) = e^{-x}$ on the interval $[0, 2]$.

(A) $2e^2$

(B) $\dfrac{e + 1}{2}$

(C) e

(D) $\dfrac{e^2 - 1}{2e^2}$

Solution

When you find the average value of this function, leave your answer in terms of e.

AP Calculus Exam-Type Questions

Multiple Choice Questions

A graphing calculator is required for some questions.

1. A monarch butterfly population has an initial population of 150 butterflies, and it increases at a rate of $b'(t)$ butterflies per week, where t denotes the elapsed time in weeks. What does the expression $150 + \displaystyle\int_0^5 b(t)\,dt$ represent?

(A) The number of butterflies in the population at any given time during the first 5 weeks.

(B) The total number of butterflies in the population at the end of 5 weeks.

(C) The overall change in the number of butterflies in the population over 5 weeks.

(D) The net change in the number of butterflies over 5 weeks.

2. If the growth rate of a child's height, in inches per year, is represented by $2 + \dfrac{1}{t^2}$, where t denotes the child's age in years, how many inches does the child gain between ages 4 and 8?

(A) $8\frac{1}{8}$ inches

(B) $5\frac{5}{8}$ inches

(C) $3\frac{1}{8}$ inches

(D) 6 inches

3. The marginal revenue function, $M'(x)$, is the derivative of the revenue function, $M(x)$. If x represents the number of units of product sold, what is $\int_{500}^{1000} M'(x)\, dx$?

(A) The total revenue collected on all product sales.

(B) The revenue the company made for selling 1,000 products.

(C) The amount of revenue collected by selling the 500th to 1,000th product.

(D) The profit earned by the company for selling 500 to 1000 products.

4. Find the average value of $f(x) = 2x - x^2$ on the interval $[0, 2]$.

(A) 0

(B) $\frac{1}{2}$

(C) 1

(D) $\frac{2}{3}$

5. Find the average value of $f(x) = x^2 - 2$ on the interval $[0, 2]$.

(A) $-\frac{4}{3}$

(B) $-\frac{2}{3}$

(C) 0

(D) $\frac{2}{3}$

6. Find the average value of $f(x) = \sqrt{x}$ on the interval $[1, 4]$.

(A) $\frac{1}{3}$

(B) $\frac{7}{9}$

(C) $\frac{14}{9}$

(D) $\frac{7}{2}$

7. Find the average value of $y = \sqrt[3]{x+3}$ on the interval $[-3, -2]$.

(A) 0.681

(B) 0.75

(C) 0.909

(D) 1.282

Free Response Questions

A graphing calculator is required for some questions.

1. At time $t = 0$, a bacteria population is 1,500. The bacteria's rate of growth is $500t^2$ bacteria per hour, where t denotes the elapsed time in hours.

(a) What is the bacteria's population after 4 hours? Round to the nearest whole number.

(b) Write a function that represents the number of bacteria in the population after any time k hours.

2. At a local gas station, an underground tank has a leak that has not yet been discovered. The gasoline is leaking from the tank at a rate of $r(t) = 10 - 5t$ gallons per day. How much gasoline has leaked out of the tank after 12 hours?

3. The average daily temperature (°F) in Atlanta, t months after July 1, is approximated by the function $T = 61 + 18\cos\frac{\pi t}{6}$. Find the average temperature between September 1 ($t = 2$) and December 1 ($t = 5$).

4. (a) Find the average value of $f(x) = \sqrt{x}$ on the interval $[0, 1]$.

(b) Find the average value of $f(x) = \sqrt[3]{x}$ on the interval $[0, 1]$.

(c) Find the average value of $f(x) = \sqrt[n]{x}$ on the interval $[0, 1]$.

(d) Find $\lim_{n \to \infty}$ (average value of) $f(x) = \sqrt[n]{x}$ on the interval $[0, 1]$.

5. Find the average value of $f(x) = \sqrt[3]{x}$ on the interval $[-a, a]$.

Lesson 7: Applications of the Integral: Motion and Volume

- Speed and Velocity
- Volume

Explain: Speed and Velocity

We reviewed in Lesson 2.7 that the position of an object at time t is denoted as $x(t)$ or $s(t)$ and is expressed in linear units like meters or feet. When we determine an object's **velocity**, we are calculating the rate of change of its position with respect to time, which is the time derivative of the position function. Recall also that velocity has both magnitude and direction and that acceleration is the derivative of the velocity function. Finally, we stated that the **speed** of an object tells us only how fast the object is moving and must have a positive value or be equal to 0. Speed is the absolute value of velocity. But what does any of this have to do with the definite integral?

Since velocity is the time derivative of position, and acceleration is the time derivative of velocity, we can conclude that velocity is the antiderivative of acceleration and position is the antiderivative of velocity! This means that we can use the Fundamental Theorem of Calculus to determine the displacement of an object over a given time interval. We demonstrate this concept in the first model problem below.

MODEL PROBLEMS

FR 1. Suppose that a particle is moving along a line with its velocity at time t given by $s'(t) = 3t^2 - 3$ for $t \geq 0$, where t is measured in seconds and s is measured in feet. Suppose the initial position of the particle is $s(0) = 5$. What is the particle's position at $t = 1$?

Solution

$\displaystyle\int_0^1 s'(t)dt$ $\displaystyle\int_0^1 \left(3t^2 - 3\right)dt$ $\left[t^3 - 3t\right]_0^1 = 1 - 3 = -2$	The particle's position at $t = 1$ is the change in position from $t = 0$ to $t = 1$, which is represented by the distance the particle moved in 1 second. We need to integrate $s'(t)$ over [0, 1]

During the first second of motion, the particle moves 2 feet to the left. Since it started at $s(0) = 5$, its position at $t = 1$ is $5 - 2 = 3$ feet.

2. A rubber band is shot with an initial velocity of 8 meters per second and accelerates at the rate of $a(t) = -2.4t$ meters per second squared for 2 seconds, after which it continues at constant velocity. What is the rubber band's velocity when 3 seconds are up?

(A) 3.2 m/s

(B) 1.5 m/s

(C) −2.8 m/s

(D) −3.2 m/s

3. A small go-kart traveling along a straight track has an initial velocity of 5 miles per hour. The driver accelerates at the rate of $a(t) = 1.6t$ mph per second for 8 seconds. How far goes the go-kart travel during those 8 seconds?

(A) 176.5 miles

(B) 51.2 miles

(C) 15.3 miles

(D) 0.05 miles

Solution

Consider how this problem is similar to both Model Problems #1 and #2. While you start this problem in the same way, there are a few more steps we must think about. Be sure to pay attention to the units throughout this problem.

Explain: Volume

Both the AP Calculus AB and BC courses include the application of integrals to finding the volumes of solids of revolution and solids with known cross-sections.

Solids of Revolution   A **solid of revolution** is formed by revolving an enclosed area around an **axis of revolution.** The axis of revolution may be vertical or horizontal. The first step in finding the volume of a solid of revolution is to sketch the area and to attempt to draw the solid. Though the drawing may not be perfect, it will assist you in visualizing the solid and identifying its radius or radii, which is necessary for finding the volume.

The figures on pages 250–251 are representative of solids of revolution that students will encounter on the AP Calculus examinations. The solids are formed by revolving the region A (enclosed by $y = x^2$, the x-axis, and $x = 2$) around the given axes of revolution.

The two main methods for finding the area of solids of revolution are the **disc method** and the **washer method.**

The Disc Method   To use the disc method, begin with the area of a disc (or circle), which is $A = \pi r^2$, where r is the radius of the circle. Write an expression for r, and write the formula for the area of the disc. The volume of the solid of revolution is the antiderivative of the area of the disc followed by dx if the axis of revolution is the x-axis or a line parallel to the x-axis, or followed by dy if the axis of revolution is the y-axis or a line parallel to the y-axis.

If the region enclosed by the graph of $f(x)$ and the x-axis on an interval $[a, b]$ is rotated around the x-axis, then slices in the region perpendicular to the x-axis are circles with radius $f(x)$. The area of each circle, or disc, is

$$\text{Area} = \pi(f(x))^2.$$

The thickness of the disc is a small dx, and the volume of the solid is given by the formula

$$\text{Volume} = \pi \int_a^b (f(x))^2 \, dx.$$

The Washer Method   To use the washer method, begin with the area of a washer, $A = \pi(R^2 - r^2)$, where R is the radius of the outer circle and r is the radius of the inner circle. Write expressions for R and r, and write the formula for the area of the washer. The volume of the solid of revolution is the antiderivative of the area of the washer.

If the region enclosed by the graphs of $f(x)$ and $g(x)$ on an interval $[a, b]$ where $f(x) \geq g(x)$ is rotated about the x-axis, then slices in the region perpendicular to the x-axis are washers with outer radius $R = f(x)$ and inner radius $r = g(x)$. The area of the washer is

$$A = \pi(R^2 - r^2) = \pi((f(x))^2 - (g(x))^2).$$

The thickness of the washer is a small dx, and the volume of the solid is given by the formula

$$V = \pi \int_a^b ((f(x))^2 - g((x))^2) dx.$$

If the region is rotated about a line other than the x-axis, draw a slice in the region perpendicular to the line of rotation. Extend the line segment drawn to the line of rotation. The length from the point on the line of rotation to the first point in the region is r and the length from the point on the line of rotation to the last point in the region is R.

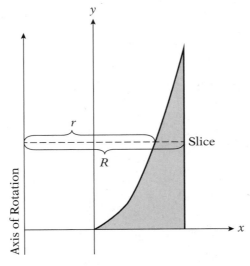

If $r = 0$, then the slice will become a disc when rotated; otherwise, the slice will become a washer when rotated.

The endpoints of the slice are the coordinates of the point or points on the graphs of $f(x)$ and $g(x)$. Use these coordinates to find expressions for r and R, the radius or radii of the disc or washer.

The designation dx or dy takes on greater importance here than in area problems. The thickness of the disc or washer is dx if it is measured in the x-direction (horizontally) or dy if it is measured in the y-direction (vertically). If an antiderivative is to be found with respect to x, then the integrand must be an expression in terms of x and the limits of the integral must be x-values. If the antiderivative is with respect to y, then the integrand must be in terms of y and the limits of the integral must be y-values.

	Horizontal Axis of Revolution	Vertical Axis of Revolution
Disc Method	$\pi \displaystyle\int_a^b r^2\,dx$	$\pi \displaystyle\int_a^b r^2\,dy$
Washer Method	$\pi \displaystyle\int_a^b (R^2 - r^2)\,dx$	$\pi \displaystyle\int_a^b (R^2 - r^2)\,dy$

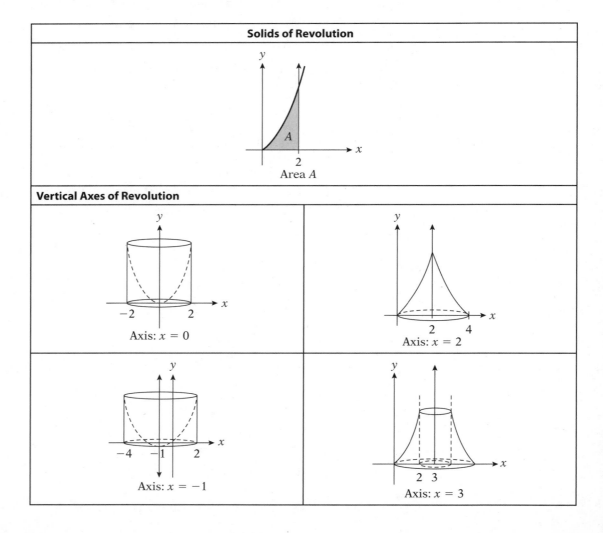

Solids of Revolution

Area A

Vertical Axes of Revolution

Axis: $x = 0$

Axis: $x = 2$

Axis: $x = -1$

Axis: $x = 3$

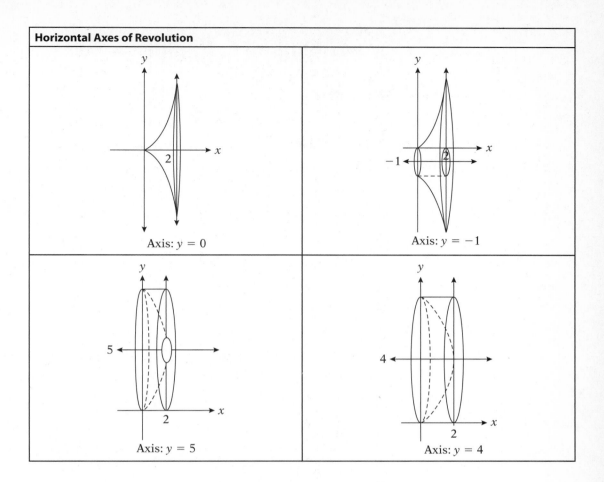

MODEL PROBLEMS

1. Find the volume of the solid generated when the region enclosed by the graph of $f(x) = x^2$ and the x-axis in the interval $[0, 2]$ is rotated about the x-axis.

(A) $\dfrac{32\pi}{5}$

(B) $\dfrac{22\pi}{5}$

(C) $\dfrac{5\pi}{3}$

(D) $\dfrac{2\pi}{5}$

Solution

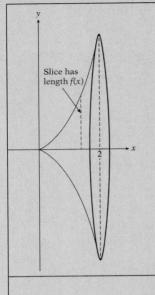	Begin by sketching the solid.
$A = \pi r^2 = \pi \left(x^2 \right)^2$	A slice in the region perpendicular to the *x*-axis has length $f(x)$ or x^2. When this slice is rotated about the *x*-axis, it will generate a disc with radius x^2. We find the formula for the area of the disc.
$V = \pi \displaystyle\int_0^2 \left(f(x) \right)^2 dx = \pi \displaystyle\int_0^2 x^4 \, dx$	Calculate the volume of the disc using the area formula.

Evaluate the integral either by hand or using a calculator. The volume is $\dfrac{32\pi}{5}$ and the correct answer is (A).

2. Using the region described in Model Problem #1, find the volume when the region is rotated about the *y*-axis.

(A) 12π

(B) 8π

(C) $\dfrac{5\pi}{3}$

(D) 6π

Solution

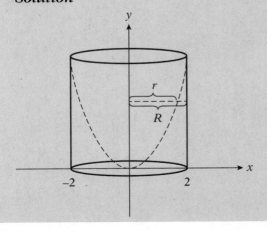

Again, we start by sketching the solid.

A slice drawn in the region perpendicular to the line of rotation will produce a washer with inner radius $r = x = \sqrt{y}$ and outer radius $R = 2$. The area of the washer is $A = \pi\left(2^2 - \left(\sqrt{y}\right)^2\right) = \pi(4 - y)$. You solve from this point. Keep in mind that the thickness is with respect to y, so the area must be expressed in terms of y, and the limits of integration must be y-values as well.

3. Rotate the region described in Model Problem #1 about the line $x = 2$. Find the volume of the solid generated.

(A) $\dfrac{2\pi}{5}$

(B) $\dfrac{4\pi}{5}$

(C) $\dfrac{8\pi}{3}$

(D) $\dfrac{2\pi}{3}$

Solution

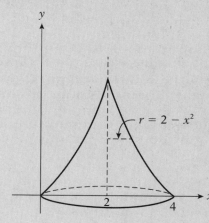

We provide the labeled sketch. A slice drawn perpendicular to the line $x = 2$ becomes a disc when rotated about that line. What does that mean for the radius of the disc?

4. Find the volume of the solid generated when the region enclosed by the graphs of $y = x^2$ and $y = \sqrt{x}$ is rotated about the x-axis.

(A) $\dfrac{3\pi}{10}$

(B) $\dfrac{4\pi}{5}$

(C) $\dfrac{8\pi}{3}$

(D) $\dfrac{2\pi}{3}$

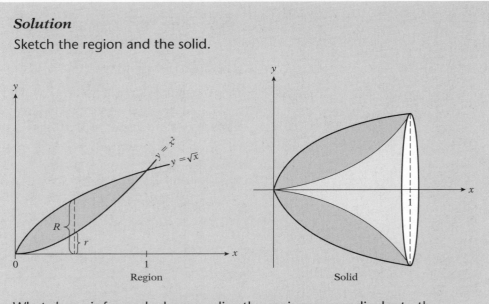

Solution

Sketch the region and the solid.

Region

Solid

What shape is formed when we slice the region perpendicular to the x-axis and then rotate it about the x-axis? What does that mean for the area of that shape and the volume of the solid?

Solids with Known Cross-Sections

Imagine taking an orange, cutting it in half, and placing one half cut-side down on a table. Next, imagine making paper-thin slices in one direction, perpendicular to the table. These slices are **cross sections.** Each cross section of the orange half is a semicircle, with each one having a different radius.

The sum of the areas of all these paper-thin semicircles form the volume of the orange.

Now imagine another solid, with cross-sectioned slices that are squares of different sizes. The sum of the areas of the paper-thin squares is the volume of the solid. In finding the volume of a solid with known cross sections, the base of the solid is given, as is the shape of the cross section. While this type of solid may be more difficult to visualize than the orange, finding its volume involves the same two-step process.

1. Find an expression for the area of the geometric shape of the cross section.
2. Take the antiderivative of the area expression.

Thus, the volume, V, of a solid with known cross sections is given by the formula

$$V = \int \text{Area}\,(dx \text{ or } dy).$$

Note: If the cross sections are perpendicular to the x-axis, the integral is with respect to dx. If the cross sections are perpendicular to the y-axis, the integral is with respect to dy.

MODEL PROBLEMS

1. A solid has a base that is a circle with equation $x^2 + y^2 = 1$. Cross sections perpendicular to the x-axis are semicircles with their diameters in the plane of the base. Find the volume of the solid.

(A) 8π cubic units

(C) $4\pi^3$ cubic units

(B) $\dfrac{2\pi}{3}$ cubic units

(D) $\dfrac{8\pi}{3}$ cubic units

Solution

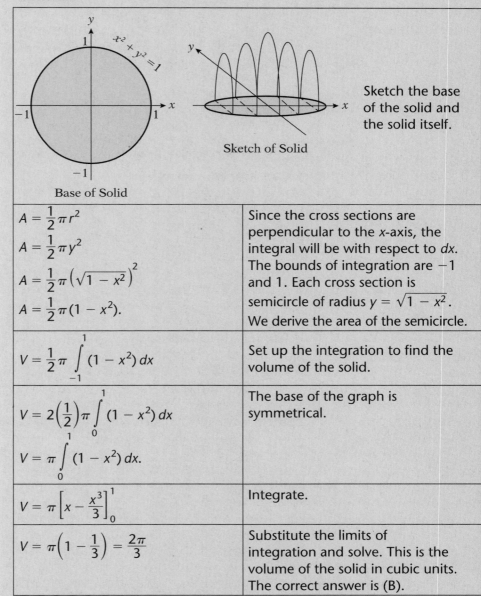

Base of Solid

Sketch of Solid

Sketch the base of the solid and the solid itself.

$A = \dfrac{1}{2}\pi r^2$ $A = \dfrac{1}{2}\pi y^2$ $A = \dfrac{1}{2}\pi\left(\sqrt{1-x^2}\right)^2$ $A = \dfrac{1}{2}\pi(1-x^2).$	Since the cross sections are perpendicular to the x-axis, the integral will be with respect to dx. The bounds of integration are -1 and 1. Each cross section is semicircle of radius $y = \sqrt{1-x^2}$. We derive the area of the semicircle.
$V = \dfrac{1}{2}\pi \displaystyle\int_{-1}^{1} (1-x^2)\,dx$	Set up the integration to find the volume of the solid.
$V = 2\left(\dfrac{1}{2}\right)\pi \displaystyle\int_{0}^{1} (1-x^2)\,dx$ $V = \pi \displaystyle\int_{0}^{1} (1-x^2)\,dx.$	The base of the graph is symmetrical.
$V = \pi\left[x - \dfrac{x^3}{3}\right]_{0}^{1}$	Integrate.
$V = \pi\left(1 - \dfrac{1}{3}\right) = \dfrac{2\pi}{3}$	Substitute the limits of integration and solve. This is the volume of the solid in cubic units. The correct answer is (B).

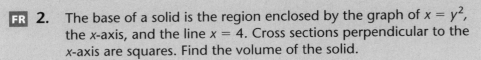

FR **2.** The base of a solid is the region enclosed by the graph of $x = y^2$, the x-axis, and the line $x = 4$. Cross sections perpendicular to the x-axis are squares. Find the volume of the solid.

Solution

Sketch the base of the solid and the solid itself.

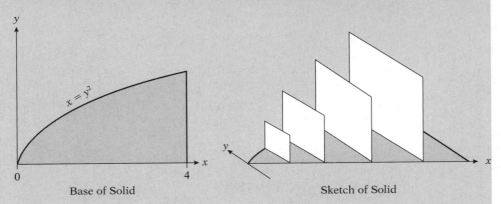

Base of Solid   Sketch of Solid

The cross sections are perpendicular to the x-axis, so the integral will be with respect to dx, and the integration bounds are 0 and 4. What is the length of the side of each square? Use that length to determine the area and then the volume of the solid.

3. The base of a solid is the region enclosed by the graphs of $y = \frac{1}{2}x^2$ and $y = 8$. Cross sections perpendicular to the y-axis are semicircles with diameter in the plane of the region. Find the volume of the solid.

(A) 18π cubic units

(B) 2π cubic units

(C) 32π cubic units

(D) π cubic units

Solution

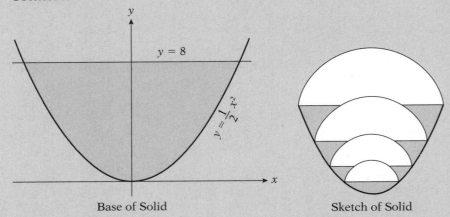

Base of Solid   Sketch of Solid

Sketch of the solid's base and the solid itself.

The cross sections are perpendicular to the y-axis. What does this mean for the integral? What variable will you integrate with respect to? How can you express the radius of the semicircles? How will you use that information to express the area of each semicircle?

AP Calculus Exam-Type Questions

Multiple Choice Questions
A graphing calculator is required for some questions.

1. The velocity of a certain object is given by $v(t) = \frac{t}{25}$. If the object is at position 0 when $t = 0$, what is the position of the object at $t = 16$?

   (A) 4.5 units

   (B) 0.32 units

   (C) 5.12 units

   (D) 0.98 units

2. A small car accelerates from rest at $2 + 3\sqrt{t}$ mph per second for 6 seconds, where t is in seconds, and continues at constant velocity after that. What is the car's velocity after 12 seconds?

   (A) 41.4 mph

   (B) 53.5 mph

   (C) 48.3 mph

   (D) 52.1 mph

3. The base of a solid is the region enclosed by $y = \sin x$ and the x-axis on the interval $[0, \pi]$. Cross sections perpendicular to the x-axis are semicircles with diameter in the plane of the base. Write an integral that represents the volume of the solid.

   (A) $\dfrac{\pi}{8} \displaystyle\int_0^{\pi} (\sin x)^2 \, dx$

   (B) $\dfrac{\pi}{8} \displaystyle\int_0^{1} (\sin x)^2 \, dx$

   (C) $\dfrac{\pi}{4} \displaystyle\int_0^{\pi} (\sin x)^2 \, dx$

   (D) $\dfrac{\pi}{8} \displaystyle\int_0^{\pi} \sin x \, dx$

4. The base of a solid is the region enclosed by $y = e^x$, the x-axis, the y-axis, and the line $x = \ln 3$. Cross sections perpendicular to the x-axis are squares. Write an integral that represents the volume of the solid.

   (A) $\displaystyle\int_0^{\ln 3} e^x \, dx$

   (B) $\displaystyle\int_0^{(\ln 3)^2} e^{2x} \, dx$

   (C) $\displaystyle\int_0^{\ln 3} e^{2x} \, dx$

   (D) $\pi \displaystyle\int_0^{\ln 3} e^{2x} \, dx$

5. The base of a solid is the region enclosed by the x-axis, $y = \tan x$, and the line $x = \frac{\pi}{4}$. Cross sections perpendicular to the x-axis are isosceles right triangles with one leg in the plane of the base. Write an integral that represents the volume of the solid.

   (A) $\dfrac{1}{2} \displaystyle\int_0^{\frac{\pi}{4}} \tan^2 x \, dx$

   (B) $\displaystyle\int_0^{\frac{\pi}{4}} \tan^2 x \, dx$

   (C) $\dfrac{\pi}{2} \displaystyle\int_0^{\frac{\pi}{4}} \tan^2 x \, dx$

   (D) $\dfrac{1}{2} \displaystyle\int_0^{1} \tan^2 x \, dx$

6. The base of a solid is the region enclosed by $y = e^x$ and the lines $y = 1$ and $x = \ln 3$. Cross sections perpendicular to the y-axis are squares. Write an integral that represents the volume of the solid.

(A) $\pi \displaystyle\int_1^3 (\ln 3 - \ln y)^2\, dy$

(B) $\displaystyle\int_1^3 (\ln 3 - \ln y)^2\, dy$

(C) $\displaystyle\int_0^{\ln 3} (\ln 3 - \ln y)^2\, dy$

(D) $\displaystyle\int_1^3 ((\ln 3)^2 - (\ln y)^2)\, dy$

7. Find the volume of the solid formed by rotating about the x-axis the region enclosed by the graph of $y = \sqrt{x} + 1$, the x-axis, the y-axis, and the line $x = 4$.

(A) 7.667 cubic units
(B) 9.333 cubic units
(C) 22.667 cubic units
(D) 37.699 cubic units

8. Find the volume of the solid formed by rotating the region bounded by the graph of $y = \sqrt{x} + 1$, the y-axis, and the line $y = 3$ about the y-axis.

(A) 6.40 cubic units
(B) 8.378 cubic units
(C) 20.106 cubic units
(D) 100.531 cubic units

9. Find the volume of the solid formed by rotating the region bounded by the graph of $y = \sqrt{x} + 1$, the y-axis, and the line $y = 3$ about the line $y = 5$.

(A) 13.333 cubic units
(B) 17.657 cubic units
(C) 41.888 cubic units
(D) 92.153 cubic units

10. The base of a solid is the region enclosed by the graph of $x^2 + 4y^2 = 4$. Cross sections of the solid perpendicular to the x-axis are squares. Find the volume of the solid.

(A) $\dfrac{8}{3}\pi$ cubic units

(B) $\dfrac{16}{3}$ cubic units

(C) $\dfrac{32}{3}$ cubic units

(D) $\dfrac{32}{3}\pi$ cubic units

11. Find the volume of the solid formed by rotating the graph of $x^2 + 4y^2 = 4$ about the x-axis.

(A) $\dfrac{8}{3}\pi$ cubic units

(B) $\dfrac{16}{3}$ cubic units

(C) $\dfrac{32}{3}$ cubic units

(D) $\dfrac{32}{3}\pi$ cubic units

12. Which of the following integrals represents the volume of the solid obtained by rotating the region bounded by the graph of $y = -\sqrt{x}$, the x-axis, and the line $x = 4$ about the x-axis?

(A) $\pi \displaystyle\int_0^4 y^2\, dy$

(B) $\pi \displaystyle\int_0^2 y^2\, dy$

(C) $\pi \displaystyle\int_0^4 (\sqrt{x})^2\, dx$

(D) $\pi \displaystyle\int_0^2 (-\sqrt{x})^2\, dx$

Free Response Questions

A graphing calculator is required for some questions.

1. The area enclosed by the graph of $x^2 + 4y^2 = 4$ is the base of a solid.

   (a) Find the ratio of the volume of the solid whose cross sections perpendicular to the x-axis are squares to the volume of the solid whose cross sections perpendicular to the x-axis are equilateral triangles.

   (b) Find the ratio of the volume of the solid whose cross sections perpendicular to the x-axis are squares to the volume of the solid whose cross sections perpendicular to the y-axis are squares.

2. Given the function $x^2 + 4y^2 = 4$,

   (a) find the ratio of the volumes of the solids generated by rotating the graph of the function about the x-axis and about the y-axis.

   (b) find the ratio of the volumes of the solids generated by rotating the graph of the function about the line $y = 2$ and about the line $x = 3$.

3. A cake is formed by rotating the region bounded by the graph of $y = \sqrt{25 - x^2}$, the y-axis, and the line $y = 3$ about the x-axis.

   (a) Find the volume of the cake.

   (b) If the cake weighs about 0.25 ounce/unit^3, about how much does the entire cake weigh?

4. A giant soda glass is formed by rotating the graph of
$$f(x) = \begin{cases} 0.03x^2 + 1.125, & 0 \le x < 5 \\ -0.2(x-5)^2 + 1.875, & 5 \le x < 6 \\ 0.1(x-6)^2 + 1.675, & 6 \le x \le 7 \end{cases}$$
   about the x-axis.

   (a) If the measurements are in inches, find the capacity of the glass in cubic inches.

   (b) If 16.387 cm^3 = 1 in.^{3}, and 1000 cm^3 = 1 liter, will the glass hold more than 0.5 liter of soda? Justify your conclusion.

5. R_1 is the region in the first quadrant bounded by the graph of $y = \frac{1}{2}x^2$, the y-axis, and the line $y = 2$. R_2 is the region in the first quadrant bounded by the graph of $y = \frac{1}{2}x^2$, the x-axis, and the line $x = 2$.

   (a) Find the ratio of the volumes of the solids generated when R_1 and R_2 are rotated about the x-axis.

   (b) Find the ratio of the volumes of the solids generated when R_1 and R_2 are rotated about the line $y = 2$.

Lesson 8: Integration with Parametric/Polar Functions (BC Exam Only)

- Displacement, Distance, and Position of a Particle
- The Length of a Planar Curve
- Areas Bounded by Polar Curves

This lesson discusses integration with parametric and polar functions. This topic is only found on the AP Calculus BC exam, so if you are sitting for the AB exam, you may skip this lesson.

Explain: Displacement, Distance, and Position of a Particle

Recall from Lesson 3.7 that velocity is the time derivative of position and acceleration is the time derivative of velocity. This means that position is the antiderivative of velocity and velocity is the antiderivative of acceleration.

Consider a particle moving along a straight line with a position function $s(t)$. The particle's velocity is then $v(t) = s'(t)$. The displacement of the particle over the time interval $T_1 \leq t \leq T_2$ is the net difference between the particle's starting position and ending position. Thus it follows from the Fundamental Theorem of Calculus that

$$\int_{T_1}^{T_2} v(t)dt = s(T_2) - s(T_1)$$

If we'd like to calculate the distance the particle has traveled during a time interval rather than its displacement, we need to consider both the intervals during which the particle moves to the right $(v(t) \geq 0)$ as well as the intervals during which the particle moves to the left $(v(t) \leq 0)$. In both cases, we integrate the particle's speed using

$$\int_{T_1}^{T_2} |v(t)|dt$$

MODEL PROBLEMS

FR 1. A particle moves along a line so that its velocity at time t is $v(t) = t^2 + 2t - 8$, measured in meters per second, where t is in seconds.

(a) Find the displacement of the particle during the time period $0 \leq t \leq 5$.

(b) What is the total distance the particle traveled during that time period?

Solution

(a) $\displaystyle\int_0^5 (t^2 + 2t - 8)\,dt =$ $\displaystyle\left[\frac{t^3}{3} + t^2 - 8t\right]_0^5 = \frac{80}{3}$	This is a simple integration of a polynomial over the given interval. At time $t = 5$, the particle is $\frac{80}{3} \approx 26.7$ meters to the right of its position at the start of the time period.
(b) $\displaystyle\int_0^2 [-v(t)]\,dt + \int_2^5 v(t)\,dt =$ $\displaystyle-\int_0^2 (t^2 + 2t - 8)\,dt + \int_2^5 (t^2 + 2t - 8)\,dt =$ $\displaystyle\left[-\frac{t^3}{3} - t^2 + 8t\right]_0^2 + \left[\frac{t^3}{3} + t^2 - 8t\right]_2^5 =$ $\displaystyle\frac{136}{3} \approx 45.3$ meters	Notice that we can factor $v(t) = t^2 + 2t - 8$ into $(t - 2)(t + 4)$, so we know that $v(t) \leq 0$ on the interval $[0, 2]$ and $v(t) \geq 0$ on $[2, 5]$. The particle has traveled approximately 45.3 meters.

2. At time $t \geq 0$, a particle moving in the xy-plane has velocity vector $v(t) = \langle 5e^{-t}, \sin(1 + t)\rangle$. What is the total distance the particle travels between $t = 0$ and $t = 2$?

(A) 1.861 meters

(B) 2.236 meters

(C) 1.695 meters

(D) 4.581 meters

Solution

For this question, we'll need to integrate the velocity vector. From previous knowledge, does the given vector express the initial or terminal point of the vector? How can we use that information to solve this problem? Over what interval do we integrate?

3. A moving particle has position $(x(t), y(t))$ at time t. The particle's position at time $t = 1$ is $(2, 6)$, and the velocity vector at any time $t > 0$ is given by $\left(1 - \frac{1}{t^2}, 2 + \frac{1}{t^2}\right)$. Find the position of the particle at time $t = 6$.

(A) $\left(\frac{25}{6}, \frac{65}{6}\right)$

(B) $\left(\frac{101}{6}, \frac{37}{6}\right)$

(C) $\left(\frac{65}{6}, \frac{25}{6}\right)$

(D) $\left(\frac{37}{6}, \frac{101}{6}\right)$

Explain: The Length of a Planar Curve

Arc Length   The process of finding the length of the arc of a curve is similar to the process described in Lesson 3.2 for finding the area under a curve. A function $y = f(x)$ is given on an interval $[a, b]$. The interval is partitioned into equal subintervals, each of length Δx. Each tiny piece of arc on the curve is approximated by the hypotenuse Δs of a right triangle with legs Δx and Δy.

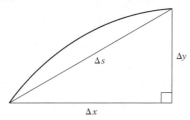

As the number of subintervals increases, the length of Δx approaches zero, and the length of the arc is closer to the hypotenuse of the triangle. The hypotenuse is expressed as

$$\Delta s = \sqrt{(\Delta x)^2 + (\Delta y)^2},$$

and the arc length is

$$\lim_{\Delta x \to 0} \sum \Delta s = \lim_{\Delta x \to 0} \sum \sqrt{(\Delta x)^2 + (\Delta y)^2}.$$

Thus, the formula for the arc length of a curve is

$$s = \int_a^b \sqrt{(dx)^2 + (dy)^2}.$$

Note: The formula in this form may be easier to remember, since the integrand is a form of the Pythagorean Theorem. In addition, by manipulating the integrand, formulas for arc length can be adjusted in the following ways:

If

y is a function of x, such as, $y = f(x)$,

Then

$$\sqrt{(dx)^2 + (dy)^2} = \sqrt{1 + \left(\frac{dy}{dx}\right)^2}\, dx,$$

and the length of the arc of the curve on $[a, b]$ is

$$s = \int_a^b \sqrt{1 + \left(\frac{dy}{dx}\right)^2}\, dx.$$

If

x is a function of y, such as, $x = f(y)$,

Then

$$\sqrt{(dx)^2 + (dy)^2} = \sqrt{1 + \left(\frac{dy}{dx}\right)^2}\, dy$$

and the length of the arc of the curve on $[c, d]$ is

$$s = \int_c^d \sqrt{1 + \left(\frac{dx}{dy}\right)^2}\, dy.$$

If

x and y are functions of a parameter t, that is, $x = x(t)$ and $y = y(t)$,

Then

$$\sqrt{(dx)^2 + (dy)^2} = \sqrt{\left(\frac{dx}{dt}\right)^2 + \left(\frac{dy}{dt}\right)^2}\, dt,$$

and the length of the arc on $[t_1, t_2]$ is

$$s = \int_{t_1}^{t_2} \sqrt{\left(\frac{dx}{dt}\right)^2 + \left(\frac{dy}{dt}\right)^2}\, dt.$$

Area of a Surface of Revolution   When the arc of a curve is rotated about a line, it forms a solid.

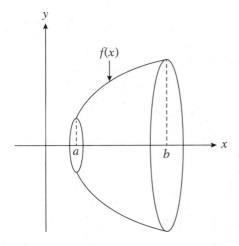

The area of the surface of revolution can be calculated by the formula

$$\text{S.A.} = \int 2\pi r\, ds,$$

where r is the distance between the curve and the line of rotation, and ds is given by one of the radical expressions.

If $y = f(x)$ on $[a, b]$ and the arc of the curve is rotated about the x-axis, then the surface area is given by

$$\text{S.A.} = \int_a^b 2\pi y \sqrt{1 + \left(\frac{dy}{dx}\right)^2}\, dx$$

If the same arc is rotated about the y-axis, then the surface area is

$$\text{S.A.} = \int_a^b 2\pi x = \sqrt{1 + \left(\frac{dy}{dx}\right)^2} \, dx.$$

MODEL PROBLEMS

1. Write an integral that represents the length of the arc of the graph of $y = x^2$ on $[0, 2]$.

   (A) $s = \int_0^2 2x \, dx$

   (B) $s = \int_0^2 \sqrt{1 + 4x^2} \, dx$

   (C) $s = \int_0^2 x^2 \, dx$

   (D) $s = \int_0^1 1 + 4x \, dx$

Solution

Since $y = x^2$, we know that $\frac{dy}{dx} = 2x$. We apply $s = \int_a^b \sqrt{1 + \left(\frac{dy}{dx}\right)^2} \, dx$ to find $s = \int_0^2 \sqrt{1 + 4x^2} \, dx$. The correct answer is (B).

2. Write an integral that represents the length of the arc of the graph of $x = \sqrt{y^2 + 1}$ on the interval for y from $[-1, 1]$.

   (A) $s = \int_{-1}^1 \sqrt{1 + \frac{y}{y+1}} \, dx$

   (C) $s = \int_{-1}^1 \sqrt{\frac{y^2}{y+1}} \, dx$

   (B) $s = \int_{-1}^2 \sqrt{1 + \frac{y^2}{y^2 + 1}} \, dy$

   (D) $s = \int_{-1}^1 \sqrt{1 + \frac{y^2}{y^2 + 1}} \, dy$

Solution

In this case, we know that $x = \sqrt{y^2 + 1}$, so $\frac{dy}{dx} = \frac{y}{(y^2 + 1)}$. You solve from here.

3. Write an integral in a single variable that represents the area of the surface when the arc of the graph of $y = x^2$ on $[0, 2]$ is rotated about the x-axis.

   (A) $\int_0^2 2\pi x^2 \sqrt{1 + 4x^2} \, dx$

   (B) $\int_0^2 2x^2 \sqrt{1 + 4x} \, dx$

   (C) $\int_1^2 2\pi y^2 \sqrt{1 + 4x^2} \, dx$

   (D) $\int_1^2 2y^2 \sqrt{1 + 4x^2} \, dx$

Explain: Areas Bounded by Polar Curves

In this section, we move from the rectangular coordinate system to the polar coordinate system. We begin by reviewing some basic facts. The **polar coordinate system** consists of points (r, θ), where r is the distance of the point from the pole (the origin of the rectangular coordinate system) and θ is the angle formed with the polar axis (the positive x-axis). An essential difference between the polar coordinate system and the rectangular coordinate system is that a point in the polar coordinate system does not have a unique representation; that is, a point can be represented in multiple ways with more than one set of coordinates. This is because r and θ may not be unique. It is important to remember this when working with polar equations. In some cases, it may make it difficult to identify all the points of intersection of polar graphs. The graphs may intersect at a point, but for different values of r or θ, or both.

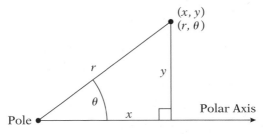

When r is positive, as in the figure above, the point is on the ray that is the terminal side of angle θ. When r is negative, the point is in the opposite direction from the ray that is the terminal side of θ. Therefore, as the following figure shows, the point $(-r, \theta)$ is the same as the point $(r, \theta + \pi)$.

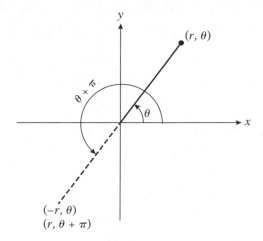

In some situations, it is very useful to locate points using polar coordinates. For example, some important curves have equations in the polar coordinate system that are much simpler than in the rectangular coordinate system. For this reason, it can be useful to convert rectangular coordinates (and vice versa).

Converting Polar Coordinates to Rectangular Coordinates

If a point has polar coordinates (r, θ), then the rectangular coordinates of the point are $(r \cos \theta, r \sin \theta)$. In other words, since $\cos \theta = \frac{x}{r}$ and $\sin \theta = \frac{y}{r}$,

$x = r \cos \theta$, and

$y = r \sin \theta$

Converting Rectangular Coordinates to Polar Coordinates

If a point has rectangular coordinates (x, y), then the polar coordinates of the point are (r, θ) where

$r^2 = x^2 + y^2$, or
$r = \sqrt{x^2 + y^2}$

and

$\theta = \arctan\left(\frac{y}{x}\right)$, or

$\theta = \tan^{-1}\left(\frac{y}{x}\right)$, or

$\tan \theta = \frac{y}{x}$

Note: Use the positive square root of $x^2 + y^2$ for r if $x > 0$, and the negative square root if $x \le 0$.

MODEL PROBLEM

FR **1.** (a) Find the polar equation for the curve represented by the rectangular coordinate equation $x\sqrt{x^2 + y^2} = 2y$.

(b) Find the rectangular coordinate equation for the curve represented by the polar equation $r = 3\cos 2\theta$.

Solution

(a)

$x\sqrt{x^2 + y^2} = (r\cos\theta)$, and $2y = 2r\sin\theta$. $(r\cos\theta)r = 2r\sin\theta$ $r = \dfrac{2r\sin\theta}{r\cos\theta}$ $r = 2\tan\theta$	Use the relationships given to convert both sides of the equation. Simplify.

The resulting polar equation is much simpler than the original rectangular coordinate equation.

(b)

$r = 3\cos^2\theta - 3\sin^2\theta$	Begin this part of the problem by applying the double angle formula.
$r^3 = 3(r\cos\theta)^2 - 3(r\sin\theta)^2$	Multiply through by r^2.
$r^3 = \left(\sqrt{x^2 + y^2}\right)^3$	Use the relationships given to convert both sides of the equation. Begin with the right-hand side.
$3(r\cos\theta)^2 - 3(r\sin\theta)^2 = 3(x)^2 - 3(y)^2$, or $3(r\cos\theta)^2 - 3(r\sin\theta)^2 = 3(x^2 - y^2)$	Now work the left-hand side.
$\left(x^2 + y^2\right)^3 = 9\left(x^2 - y^2\right)^2$	This is the rectangular coordinate equation. Again we see that the polar equation is much simpler than the rectangular coordinate equation.

Although the equations presented, which relate x, y, r, and θ, may be useful, the focus in Calculus BC is not on translating polar coordinates into rectangular coordinates (or vice versa). Rather, the focus is on graphing polar curves, investigating their properties, finding points of intersection, enclosed areas, and arc lengths.

Polar Curves A polar curve is represented by an equation of the form $r = f(\theta)$. The following are some curves and their equations that you should become familiar with and be able to sketch by hand. Note that curves that have a term with cosine are symmetric to the polar axis, while curves that have a term with sine are symmetric to the line perpendicular to the polar axis.

$r = a \cos \theta$

$r = a \sin \theta$

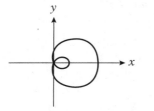

Note: These circles are completely drawn for $0 \le \theta \le \pi$.

Limaçon

$$r = a \pm b \cos \theta \quad \text{or} \quad r = a \pm b \sin \theta$$

If $a < b$, the limaçon has an inner loop.

If $a = b$, the limaçon is called a **cardioid.**

If $a > b$, the limaçon has a flattened end.

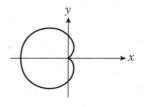
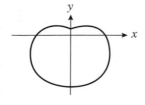

Petal Curves

$r = a \cos n\theta$ or $r = a \sin n\theta$

If n is a positive even integer, the curve has $2n$ petals.

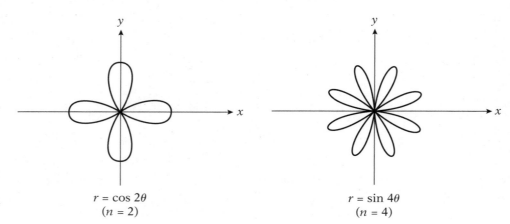

$r = \cos 2\theta$
$(n = 2)$

$r = \sin 4\theta$
$(n = 4)$

If n is a positive odd integer, the curve has n petals.

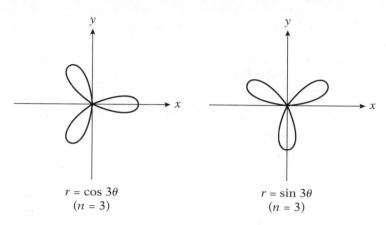

$r = \cos 3\theta$
$(n = 3)$

$r = \sin 3\theta$
$(n = 3)$

If n is not an integer, then the petals overlap.

Calculator Note

To graph a polar curve on the TI-83/84
Press MODE and scroll down and right to Pol. Press ENTER.
   Press Y= and enter the equation in r_1.
   Press GRAPH and adjust the window (if necessary) to see the entire graph.
Note: ZOOM 4 is a good window for most polar curves.
   Notice the values of θ in WINDOW. Some polar curves are traced from $\theta = 0$ to
   $\theta = \pi$. Other curves are traced from $\theta = 0$ to $\theta = 2\pi$.
   After graphing the curve, press TRACE to see coordinates. To change to polar
coordinates (r, θ), press 2nd ZOOM (FORMAT), scroll right to PolarGC, and press
ENTER.

To graph a polar curve on the TI-89
Press MODE. Go to Graph. Go to Polar. Press ENTER ENTER. Proceed as above.

To graph a polar curve on the TI-nspire
Create a new graph document. Press MENU, **Graph Type, Polar**. Note that
the symbol θ can be accessed by pressing CTRL and then the catalog button.

Here it is important to note that since each point in the plane has multiple representations in polar coordinates, solving for the points of intersection of two polar curves may require more than solving an equation.

MODEL PROBLEMS

FR 1. Find the points of intersection of $r = 2 \sin \theta$ and $r = 2 + 2 \cos \theta$.

Solution

$2 \sin \theta = 2 + 2 \cos \theta$	Start by simultaneously solving the equations.
$\sin^2 \theta = (1 + \cos \theta)^2$ $\sin^2 \theta = 1 + 2 \cos \theta + \cos^2 \theta$	Divide by 2 and then square both sides of the equation.
$1 - \cos^2 \theta = 1 + 2 \cos \theta + \cos^2 \theta$ $2 \cos^2 \theta + 2 \cos \theta = 0$	Now use the Pythagorean identity to replace $\sin^2 \theta$ with $1 - \cos^2 \theta$ and then simplify.
$2 \cos \theta (\cos \theta + 1) = 0$ $2 \cos \theta = 0$ or $\cos \theta + 1 = 0$ $\theta = \dfrac{\pi}{2}$ or $\theta = \pi$	Factor the equation.

The only solution for $2 \cos \theta = 0$ is $\theta = \dfrac{\pi}{2}$ since the domain for the circle $r = 2 \sin \theta$ is $0 \le \theta \le \pi$. Furthermore, the solution $\theta = \pi$ makes $r = 0$, and thus the point of intersection is at the pole. When $r = 0$ on both curves, for any value of θ, the pole is a point of intersection. Thus, the points of intersection are $\left(2, \dfrac{\pi}{2}\right)$ and the pole.

Looking at the graph, we see that these are the only two points of intersection.

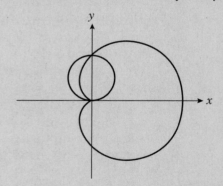

FR 2. Find the points of intersection of $r = \sin \theta$ and $r = 1 + 2 \sin \theta$.

Solution

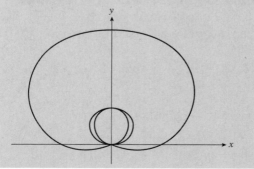

Consider the graph for these polar equations. There appear to be two points of intersection.

Solve the equation $\sin \theta = 1 + 2 \sin \theta$ to determine the coordinates of one of the points of intersection. Where does the other point lie? How do you know?

Area in Polar Coordinates

Now that we have briefly reviewed the polar coordinate system and finding the points of intersection of polar curves, we can move to calculating area in polar coordinates.

The formula for the area inside a polar curve is Area $= \int \frac{1}{2} r^2 \, d\theta$, where the limits of the integral are values of θ.

MODEL PROBLEMS

FR **1.** Write an integral that represents the area inside the circle $r = 2 \cos \theta$ from $\theta = 0$ to $\theta = \frac{\pi}{4}$. Find the value of the integral using a calculator.

Solution

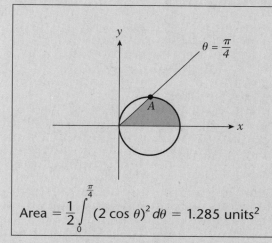

	Graph and shade the area you are trying to calculate.
Area $= \dfrac{1}{2} \displaystyle\int_{0}^{\frac{\pi}{4}} (2 \cos \theta)^2 \, d\theta = 1.285$ units^2	Now write and solve the integral.

FR **2.** Find the area common to the curves $r = 2 \cos \theta$ and $r = 2 + 2 \sin \theta$.

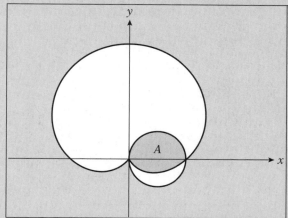

Again, start by graphing and shading the area you are trying to calculate.

Note there are two points of intersection, similar to the two points of intersection in Model Problem #2 on page 270. The equation you need to solve to find these points is $2 \cos \theta = 2 + 2 \sin \theta$. Once you have the points, consider that the area in common is the sum of the upper semicircle and part of the cardioid, so the area is the sum of two integrals.

Other Polar Curve Formulas The following two formulas for polar curves are used infrequently, but are given here for reference.

Slope of the Tangent Line to a Polar Curve

$$\frac{dy}{dx} = \frac{r\cos\theta + \frac{dr}{d\theta}\sin\theta}{-r\sin\theta + \frac{dr}{d\theta}\cos\theta}$$

Arc Length of a Polar Curve from $\theta = a$ to $\theta = b$

$$s = \int_a^b \sqrt{r^2 + \left(\frac{dr}{d\theta}\right)^2}\, d\theta$$

MODEL PROBLEMS

1. Find the perimeter of the polar curve $r = 2 - 2\cos\theta$.

(A) $\frac{\pi}{3}$

(B) 2π

(C) 16

(D) $\frac{3}{2}$

Solution

Since the graph of $r = 2 - 2\cos\theta$ is traced out once for values of θ between 0 and 2π, use the arc length formula with $a = 0$ and $b = 2\pi$.

$$s = \int_0^{2\pi} \sqrt{r^2 + (r')^2}\, d\theta = 16 \text{ units}$$

FR **2.** Find the perimeter of the inner loop of the graph of $r = 2 - 4\cos\theta$.

Solution

$2 - 4\cos\theta = 0$ $-4\cos\theta = -2$ $\cos\theta = \dfrac{1}{2}$	The first step is to find the values of θ that make $r = 0$. These are the values of θ where the curve intersects the pole. We use some algebra.
	Since $\cos\theta = \dfrac{1}{2}$, $\theta = \dfrac{\pi}{3}$ and $\theta = \dfrac{5\pi}{3}$. Graph and trace the curve on the calculator. We see that the bottom half of the inner loop runs from $\theta = 0$ and $\theta = \dfrac{\pi}{3}$.
What does this mean for the perimeter of the inner loop? What are the limits of integration in this case?	

FR 3. At what point(s) on the graph of $r = 2 - 4 \cos \theta$ is the tangent line

    (a) vertical?

    (b) horizontal?

Solution

The formula for $\frac{dy}{dx}$ on page 272 will give the slope of the tangent line to a polar curve.

(a) $-\sin \theta(2 - 4 \cos \theta) + 4 \sin \theta \cos \theta = 0$	To find the points at which the tangent line is vertical, set the denominator of $\frac{dy}{dx}$ equal to 0 and solve for θ.
How many solutions will this equation have? Make sure you express all your answers as coordinate points.	
(b) $2 \cos \theta - 4 \cos^2 \theta + 4 \sin^2 \theta = 0$	To find the points at which the tangent line is horizontal, set the numerator of $\frac{dy}{dx}$ equal to 0 and solve for θ.

To solve from here, consider using a Pythagorean identity and the quadratic formula. This part of the question will have four solutions.

AP Calculus Exam-Type Questions

Multiple Choice Questions

A graphing calculator is required for some of these questions.

1. A particle moves along a path described by $x = \cos^3 t$ and $y = \sin^3 t$. The distance that the particle travels along the path from $t = 0$ to $t = \frac{\pi}{2}$ is

    (A) 0.75 units

    (B) 1.75 units

    (C) 0 units

    (D) −0.50 units

2. A particle is moving along a curve in the xy-plane. Its position is given by $(x(t), y(t))$ where $\frac{dx}{dt} = \cos(t^2)$ and $\frac{dy}{dt} = \sin(t^3)$. At time $t = 0$, the object is at (4, 7). Where is the particle at time $t = 2$?

    (A) (−0.772, 0.548)

    (B) (4.46, 7.45)

    (C) (3.57, 7.65)

    (D) (5.68, −8.91)

3. Find the length of part of the parabola $y = \frac{1}{2}x^2$ on the interval $[-1, 1]$.

(A) 0.333 units

(B) 1.886 units

(C) 2.179 units

(D) 2.296 units

4. Find the length of the arc of the curve defined by the parametric equations $\begin{cases} x(t) = \sin t \\ y(t) = 1 - \cos t \end{cases}$ for values of t in the interval $\left[-\frac{\pi}{2}, \frac{\pi}{2}\right]$.

(A) $\frac{\pi}{2}$

(B) π

(C) $\pi + 1$

(D) $\pi - 1$

5. Find the area of the surface formed when the curve $y = e^{-x}$ on the interval $[0, 1]$ is rotated about the x-axis.

(A) 4.849 units²

(B) 0.772 units²

(C) 1.212 units²

(D) 1.544 units²

6. Find the area of the surface formed by rotating the graph of $f(x) = \sqrt[3]{x} - 1$ on the interval $[2, 3]$ about the y-axis.

(A) 8.111 units²

(B) 16.223 units²

(C) 4.056 units²

(D) 5.164 units²

7. The graph of $r = 4 \cos \theta$ is

(A) a circle with radius 4.

(B) a circle with radius 2.

(C) a four-petal rose.

(D) an eight-petal rose.

8. The graphs of $r = \cos \theta$ and $r = 2 \cos 2\theta$ intersect in how many points?

(A) 3

(B) 4

(C) 5

(D) 6

9. The graph of $r = 2 + 4 \sin \theta$ is symmetric to

(A) the polar axis.

(B) the line $\theta = \frac{\pi}{2}$.

(C) the line $\theta = \frac{\pi}{4}$.

(D) the line $\theta = \frac{\pi}{6}$.

10. The graph of the equation $r = \dfrac{2}{\cos \theta}$

(A) intersects the polar axis at one point.

(B) intersects the polar axis at two points.

(C) does not intersect the polar axis.

(D) intersects the line $\theta = \frac{\pi}{2}$ at one point.

Free Response Questions

A graphing calculator is required for some questions.

1. Find the length of the ellipse given by $x^2 + 4y^2 = 4$.

2. (a) Find the length of the graph given by $f(x) = \frac{1}{x}$ on the interval $[1, 2]$.

    (b) Find the volume of the solid generated by rotating $f(x) = \frac{1}{x}$ on the interval $[1, c]$ about the x-axis.

    (c) Find the limiting value of the volume of the solid found in part (b) as $c \to \infty$.

3. (a) Sketch a graph of the polar curves given below and find their points of intersection.
$r = 2(1 - \cos \theta)$
$r = 2 \cos \theta$

    (b) Find an expression for the slope of the tangent to the graph of $r = 2 \cos \theta$ in terms of θ.

    (c) Find the slope of the tangent to the graph of $r = 2 \cos \theta$ at each of the points of intersection in part (a).

4. Consider the polar curves $r = 1 - \sin \theta$ and $r = 2 \cos \theta$.

    (a) Identify each polar graph.

    (b) Find the points of intersection of the two graphs.

    (c) Sketch the graphs and shade the region common to both curves.

    (d) Find the area of the region common to both curves.

Lesson 9: Differential Equations

- Separable Differential Equations

Explain: Separable Differential Equations

A **differential equation** is an equation whose terms include the derivatives of a function with respect to an independent variable. A **separable differential equation** is a differential equation that can be separated so that one variable is on one side of the equation and the other variable is on the other side of the equation. If the variables are x and y, then separating the variables results in all the x and dx terms being on one side of the equation, and all the y and dy terms being on the other side of the equation. Separating the variables is the first step in solving a separable differential equation. The solution to a differential equation, as with any equation, is an expression that makes the equation true.

To solve a separable differential equation:

1. Separate the variables.

2. Find the antiderivative on each side of the equation.

3. Write the solution in the form y (or the dependent variable) = a function of x (or the independent variable).

MODEL PROBLEMS

FR 1. Show that $\frac{dy}{dx} = xy$ is a separable differential equation.

Solution

To show that this equation is a separable differential equation, we must show that we can collect all the terms with x in them on one side of the equation and all the terms with y in them on the other side of the equation.

$\frac{dy}{dx} = xy$ $\frac{dy}{y} = x\,dx$	Multiply both sides of the given equation by dx and then divide both sides by y. This is a separable differential equation.

FR 2. Separate the variables in the differential equation $\frac{dP}{dt} = kPt^2$

Solution

To solve this question, algebraically manipulate the equation. Note that the position of the k is irrelevant.

FR 3. Separate the variables in the differential equation $\frac{dy}{dx} = \frac{x}{y+1}$.

Solution

Solve this problem the same way we solved Model Problems #1 and #2.

FR **4.** Solve for y in the differential equation $\dfrac{dy}{dx} = xy$

Solution

$\displaystyle\int \frac{dy}{y} = \int x\, dx$	We already separated the variables in Model Problem #1, so we can start this problem by taking the antiderivative of each side.
$\ln\lvert y\rvert + c_1 = \dfrac{x^2}{2} + c_2$	We easily compute the antiderivative for each side of the equation where c_1 and c_2 are constants. Recall that the domain of the ln function is all positive real numbers so the absolute value sign ensures our value will be positive.
$\ln\lvert y\rvert + c_1 = \dfrac{x^2}{2} + c_2$ $\ln\lvert y\rvert = \dfrac{x^2}{2} + c_2 - c_1$ $\ln\lvert y\rvert = \dfrac{x^2}{2} + C$	We combine c_1 and c_2 into a single constant. Let $C = c_2 - c_1$.
$e^{\ln\lvert y\rvert} = e^{\frac{x^2}{2}+C}$ $\lvert y\rvert = e^{\frac{x^2}{2}+C}$	We solve for y. We can use the property that $e^{\ln\lvert y\rvert} = \lvert y\rvert$.
$e^{\frac{x^2}{2}+C} = e^{\frac{x^2}{2}} \cdot e^{C}$ $y = \pm e^{C} \cdot e^{\frac{x^2}{2}}$	Substitute.
$y = A e^{\frac{x^2}{2}}$	We denote $A = \pm e^{C}$. Note that this solution represents a family of curves where A is a constant.

5. Solve the differential equation $\dfrac{dP}{dt} = kPt^2$.

(A) $e^{\frac{t^3}{3}}$

(B) $A e^{\frac{kt^3}{3}}$

(C) $e^{\frac{kt^3}{3}}$

(D) $A e^{\frac{3}{kt^3}}$

Solution

Again, we already separated this differential equation in Model Problem #2. We can start by integrating both sides and then follow the guide in Model Problem #4 to solve.

6. (a) Find a general solution to the differential equation $\dfrac{dy}{dx} = \dfrac{x}{y+1}$.

(b) Find the solution for this equation that satisfies the initial condition $y(0) = 0$.

Solution

(a)

$\displaystyle\int (y+1)\,dy = \int x\,dx$ $\dfrac{y^2}{2} + y = \dfrac{x^2}{2} + c$	We separated the variables in Model Problem #3. Now we integrate both sides of the equation. This is the general solution.

(b)

$\dfrac{(0)^2}{2} + (0) = \dfrac{(0)^2}{2} + c$ $0 = c$	To find the solution that satisfies the given initial condition, substitute $x = 0$, $y = 0$ into the differential equation and solve for c.
$\dfrac{y^2}{2} + y = \dfrac{x^2}{2} + (0)$ $2 \cdot \left(\dfrac{y^2}{2} + y = \dfrac{x^2}{2} \right)$ $y^2 + 2y = x^2$	Substitute the value of c into the equation and then solve for y. We leave it to the student to finish the problem from this point.

As we have seen, solutions to differential equations are functions or families of functions. It is important to note that some solutions to differential equations may be subject to domain restrictions because the differential equation is only valid over a certain set of numbers. We also take this opportunity to formally state that the solution to the first order differential equation $\dfrac{dy}{dx} = f(x)$ is a function $F(x)$ such that $y = F(x)$ and $\dfrac{dy}{dx} = f(x)$. That is, any antiderivative $y = F(x)$ of $f(x)$ is a solution of the differential equation. Specifically, the antiderivative of $f(x)$ forms a family of functions that differ from each other by only a constant (as in Model Problem #4). Therefore, the general solution of the differential equation $\dfrac{dy}{dx} = f(x)$ is the family of functions $F(x)$ defined by $F(x) = C + \displaystyle\int_a^b f(t)\,dt$.

Furthermore, we can find a particular solution to the differential equation $\dfrac{dy}{dx} = f(x)$ by modifying the general solution slightly. When $F(a) = y_0$, our solution becomes $F(x) = y_0 + \displaystyle\int_a^b f(t)\,dt$.

AP Calculus Exam-Type Questions

Multiple Choice Questions
No calculator permitted for these questions.

1. The differential equation $\frac{dy}{dx} = xy + 2y$ in separable form is

    (A) $dy = (xy + 2y)\,dx$

    (B) $\frac{dy}{dx} - xy = 2y$

    (C) $dy = (x + 2)y\,dx$

    (D) $\frac{dy}{y} = (x + 2)\,dx$

2. A particle begins at $(0, 1)$ and moves up the y-axis so that at time t its velocity y' is double the position y. A solution to this differential equation could be

    (A) $y = 2e^{2t}$

    (B) $2y = e^{2t}$

    (C) $y = e^{2t} + 1$

    (D) $y = e^{2t}$

3. A possible solution to $\frac{dy}{dt} = y - 5$ is

    (A) $y = 5 + ce^{t}$

    (B) $y = ce^{t} - 5$

    (C) $y = 5e^{t}$

    (D) $y^2 - 5y = t + c$

4. The solution to the differential equation $\frac{dP}{dt} = -0.02P$ with $P(0) = 5$ is

    (A) $P = 5e^{-0.02t}$

    (B) $P = 5e^{-0.002t}$

    (C) $P = 5 + e^{-0.02t}$

    (D) $P = -0.02P^2 + c$

Free Response Questions

A graphing calculator is required for questions #2 and #3.

1. Solve the following differential equation using the separation of variables method.

    (a) $\frac{dy}{dx} = x^2 + x$

    (b) $\frac{dy}{dx} = \frac{y}{x^2}$

    (c) $\frac{dy}{dx} = y^3$ with the initial condition $y(0) = 1$

    (d) $\frac{dy}{dx} = xy + y$

2. A spherical snowball is melting so that the rate of change of the radius is 2 cm/hr.

    (a) Show that the rate of change of the volume is proportional to the surface area.

    (Volume $= \frac{4}{3}\pi r^3$, Surface Area $= 4\pi r^2$)

    (b) Find the constant of proportionality of the equation in part (a).

3. The slope of a curve is given by the formula $3x^2y^2$ at a point (x, y). Find the equation of the curve if the curve passes through the point $(1, -1)$.

Lesson 10: Exponential and Logistic Change

- Exponential Change
- Logistic Change (BC Exam Only)

Explain: Exponential Change

Many physical situations can be modeled as separable differential equations. Population growth can be modeled as follows. Suppose that the rate of change of a population P is proportional to the population at a time t.

This sentence translates into the differential equation $\frac{dP}{dt} = kP$.

Precalculus students may know the solution as $y = Ce^{kt}$. Calculus students can derive this formula. Separating the variables and taking the antiderivative of both sides of the equation $\frac{dP}{dt} = kP$, we get

$$\int \frac{dP}{P} = \int k \, dt$$

Solving for the antiderivative, $\ln|P| = kt + c$.

Using the techniques in the previous lessons, $P = Ce^{kt}$.

Other situations that can be modeled by similar differential equations and solutions are radioactive decay of an element and bacterial growth.

MODEL PROBLEMS

1. The rate of growth of a certain bacterium is proportional to the number present. In population B, there are 200 bacteria initially, and 500 bacteria five minutes later.

   (a) Write a differential equation that represents the rate of growth of the bacterial population B with respect to time t (in minutes).

   (b) Solve the differential equation for B using the given conditions.

   (c) Use the solution in part (b) to predict the value of B at $t = 10$.

   Solution

(a)	$\frac{dB}{dt} = kB$	We write the differential equation.
(b)	$B = Ce^{kt}$	Use the general equation to solve the differential equation from part (a).
	$200 = Ce^{k0}$ $200 = Ce^{0}$ $200 = C$	Solve for C. We know there are $B = 200$ bacteria at time $t = 0$.

$B = 200\,e^{kt}$ $500 = 200\,e^{k\cdot5}$ $k = \dfrac{1}{5}\ln\!\left(\dfrac{5}{2}\right) = 0.183$ $B = 200\,e^{0.183t}$	We substitute $C = 200$ into the differential equation and solve for k using the other given condition.
(c) $\quad B = 200\,e^{0.183(10)} = 1{,}250$ bacteria	Use the equation to predict the number of bacteria at time $t = 10$.

2. The half-life of a certain isotope is 890 years. If a sample of this isotope has a mass of 10 mg, find a formula for the mass that remains after t years.

(A) $5\,e^{\frac{-(\ln 2)t}{890}}$

(B) $10e^{\frac{0.5t}{890}}$

(C) $10\,e^{\frac{-(\ln 2)t}{890}}$

(D) $5\,e^{\frac{890\,t}{0.5}}$

Solution

In this instance, we are working with exponential decay rather than exponential growth, but we can use the same basic ideas. With exponential growth, the differential equation is generally $\dfrac{dP}{dt} = kP$ where k is a positive constant. For decay, we say that $\dfrac{dm}{dt} = km$ where k is a negative constant. Thus, radioactive substances decay at a rate that is proportional to the remaining mass and $m(t) = m_0e^{kt}$. Use the fact that at time $t = 0$, the mass is 10 mg and that at time $t = 890$, half of the original mass remains to find the formula.

3. Use your formula from Model Problem #2 to determine, to the nearest tenth of a milligram, the mass of the isotope sample remaining after 1,000 years.

(A)   9.9 mg

(B)   5.6 mg

(C)   3.9 mg

(D)   4.6 mg

Solution

Once you have the formula for decay, all you need to do to solve this problem is substitute in $t = 1{,}000$ and use your calculator to solve.

The next section of the lesson discusses models for logistic change. This topic is only found on the AP Calculus BC exam, so if you are sitting for the AB exam, you may skip this section of the lesson.

Explain: Logistic Change (BC Exam Only)

Lesson 3.9 and the previous section of this lesson described types of separable differential equations. With exponential change, we saw that the rate of change of the variable y at time t was proportional to the value of the variable y at time t. This model has a wide range of applications, the most common of which are population or bacterial growth or radioactive decay. It is possible, however, for y to represent the number of fish in an artificial pond or the number of people in a town who are infected with a contagious disease. In these cases, the growth is restricted; the value of the variable y has a limiting value a. The number of fish in the pond is limited due to the amounts of food and oxygen available. The number of people infected with the disease cannot exceed the population of the town. This type of restricted growth is called **logistic growth**. In the differential equation for logistic growth, the rate of change of the variable y is proportional not only to the value of y itself, but also to the difference between y and the carrying capacity a, such that $a > y$. Symbolically, the logistic growth model is

$$\frac{dy}{dt} = ky(a - y)$$

This differential equation is separable.

$\dfrac{dy}{y(a - y)} = k\,dt$	Separate the variables.
$\dfrac{1}{y(a - y)} = \dfrac{1}{a}\left(\dfrac{1}{y} + \dfrac{1}{a - y}\right)$ $\displaystyle\int \dfrac{1}{a}\left(\dfrac{1}{y} + \dfrac{1}{a - y}\right)dy = \int k\,dt$ $\dfrac{1}{a}\left(\ln|y| - \ln|a - y|\right) = kt + c$	Integrate by partial fractions (Lesson 3.1).
$y = \dfrac{a}{1 + Ae^{-akt}}$	Finally, we simply solve this equation for the variable y.
$y_0 = \dfrac{a}{1 + A}$ or $A = \dfrac{a}{y_0} - 1$	When $t = 0$, let $y = y_0$. Substitute those values into the equation.

The graph of the solution to a logistic growth model has a horizontal asymptote $y = a$.

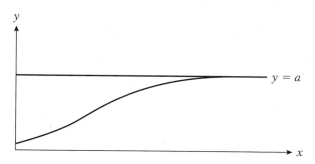

MODEL PROBLEMS

FR **1.** Show that the value of y at the point of inflection of

$$y = \frac{a}{1 + Ae^{-akt}} \text{ is } y = \frac{a}{2}.$$

Solution

$\frac{dy}{dt} = ky(a - y) = kay - ky^2$	Ultimately, to find a point of inflection, we need to calculate $\frac{d^2y}{dt^2}$. We start with $\frac{dy}{dt}$.
$\frac{d^2y}{dt^2} = ka\frac{dy}{dt} - ky\frac{dy}{dt} =$ $k\frac{dy}{dt}(a - 2y) = k^2y(a - y)(a - 2y)$	Now find $\frac{d^2y}{dt^2}$.
$k^2y(a - y)(a - 2y) = 0$ $y = 0, y = a, \text{ and } y = \frac{a}{2}$	Set $\frac{d^2y}{dt^2}$ equal to 0 and solve.

Since the range of y is between y_0 and a, the only value of y that is a possible point of inflection is $y = \frac{a}{2}$.

2. Which of the following differential equations are separable?

(a) $\frac{dy}{dt} + y = 5$ (e) $\frac{1}{y}\frac{dy}{dt} = 2t$

(b) $y\frac{dy}{dt} = 2t + 7$ (f) $\frac{dy}{dt} = 2t(10 - t)$

(c) $\frac{dy}{dt} = y^2 + t^2$ (g) $\frac{1}{y}\frac{dy}{dt} = 4(10 - y)$

(d) $\frac{dy}{dt} = 2y$

(A) (a), (b), and (c)

(B) (a), (b), (d), (e), and (g)

(C) (a), (b), (d), (e), (f), and (g)

(D) All are separable.

Solution

To determine if a given differential equation is separable, attempt to rewrite the equation so all the variables of one type are on a single side of the equation and all the variables of the other type are on the other side of the equation.

3. Which of the following equations are examples of the logistic growth model?

(a) $\dfrac{dy}{dt} + y = 5$

(b) $y\dfrac{dy}{dt} = 2t + 7$

(c) $\dfrac{dy}{dt} = y^2 + t^2$

(d) $\dfrac{dy}{dt} = 2y$

(e) $\dfrac{1}{y}\dfrac{dy}{dt} = 2t$

(f) $\dfrac{dy}{dt} = 2t(10 - t)$

(g) $\dfrac{1}{y}\dfrac{dy}{dt} = 4(10 - y)$

(A) (a), (b), and (g)

(B) (e) and (g)

(C) (g) only

(D) None of these are examples of the logistic growth model.

Solution

For a differential equation to be an example of logistic growth, it needs to be able to be expressed in the form $\dfrac{dy}{dt} = ky(a - y)$.

AP Calculus Exam-Type Questions

Multiple Choice Questions
No calculator permitted for these questions.

BC 1. Which of the following differential equations is an example of the logistic growth model?

(A) $\dfrac{dy}{dx} = 10x(5 - x)$

(B) $\dfrac{dy}{dx} = 10y(50 - y)$

(C) $\dfrac{dV}{dt} = 2V(5 - t)$

(D) $\dfrac{dR}{dt} = t(R - t)$

BC 2. Which of the following differential equations is separable, but NOT an example of the logistic growth model?

(A) $\dfrac{dy}{dx} = x + y$

(B) $\dfrac{dy}{dx} = 2y(10 - y)$

(C) $\dfrac{dy}{dx} = 21 - y$

(D) $\dfrac{dy}{dx} = x^2 + y^2$

BC 3. The solution to the equation $\dfrac{dy}{dx} = 2y^2$ with $y(1) = 2$ is

(A) $y = \sqrt{4 + e^{2x-2}}$

(B) $y = \sqrt{4 + e^{2x} - e^2}$

(C) $y = \sqrt[3]{\dfrac{3x + 13}{2}}$

(D) $y = \dfrac{2}{5 - 4x}$

BC 4. The solution to the equation $\dfrac{dy}{dt} = 2y(10 - y)$ with $y(0) = 1$ is

(A) $y = \dfrac{10}{1 - 9e^{-20t}}$

(B) $y = \dfrac{10}{1 + 9e^{20t}}$

(C) $y = \dfrac{10}{1 + 9e^{-20t}}$

(D) $y = \dfrac{20}{11 + 9e^{-20t}}$

Free Response Questions

A graphing calculator is required for some questions.

1. A radioactive element has a half-life of 1,000 years. (This means that the amount present initially will be halved after 1,000 years.)

   (a) If 100 grams of the element are present initially, how many grams remain after 5000 years?

   (b) If the rate of change of the number of grams present is proportional to the amount present, write and solve a differential equation that represents the amount y of the element remaining after t years

2. Solve the differential equation $\dfrac{dy}{dt} + y = 5$ when the initial condition is $y(0) = 1$.

3. Solve the differential equation $y\dfrac{dy}{dt} = 2t + 7$ when the initial condition is $y(1) = 4$.

4. Solve the differential equation $\dfrac{dy}{dt} = 2y$ when the initial condition is $y(0) = 10$.

5. Solve the differential equation $\left(\dfrac{1}{y}\right)\dfrac{dy}{dt} = 2t$ when the initial condition is $y(0) = 2$.

BC 6. Solve the differential equation $\dfrac{dy}{dt} = 2t(10 - t)$ when the initial condition is $y(3) = 0$.

BC 7. Solve the differential equation $\left(\dfrac{1}{y}\right)\dfrac{dy}{dt} = 4(10 - y)$ when the initial condition is $y(1) = 4$.

BC 8. In the logistic growth model $y = \dfrac{a}{1 + Ae^{akt}}$, the y-value of the inflection point of the graph is $y = \dfrac{a}{2}$. Find the value of t at the inflection point.

BC 9. (No calculator) Consider the differential equation $\dfrac{dy}{dt} = 2y(1 - t)$.

   (a) Sketch the graph of the solution to the differential equation on the slope field provided below with $y(0) = 5$.

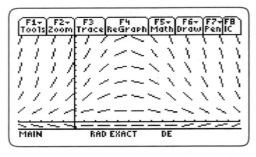

   (b) Solve the differential equation with $y(0) = 5$.

   (c) Find the coordinates of the points where the rate of change of y with respect to t is the greatest.

BC **10.** (Calculator required) Two dogs infected with a virus were admitted to a veterinary clinic, which holds a maximum of fifty dogs. The virus spread among the animals, and two days later ten dogs were infected.

(a) Assuming the logistic growth model for the spread of the virus $\frac{dy}{dt} = ky(M - y)$, find the values of M and k, and find y as a function of t.

(b) If spread of the virus is not halted, after how many days will 25 dogs be infected?

11. (Calculator required) The rate of growth of the fish population in an artificial pond is given by the differential equation $\frac{dy}{dt} = 0.003y(500 - y)$, where y is the number of fish in the pond after t days.

(a) What is the maximum number of fish that the fish pond can hold?

(b) Write the solution, y, to the differential equation if the pond is populated initially with 50 fish.

(c) What is the y-value at the point of inflection?

(d) Use a graphing calculator to draw a slope field of the differential equation, and draw a graph of the solution on the same set of axes.

(e) Find the number of fish in the pond after 1 day; 2 days; 3 days; 4 days; 5 days.

Lesson 11: Euler's Approximation Method (BC Exam Only)

- Euler's Approximation Method

This lesson discusses Euler's Approximation Method. This topic is only found on the AP Calculus BC exam, so if you are sitting for the AB exam, you may skip this lesson.

Explain: Euler's Approximation Method

In Lesson 2.9, we found graphical solutions to differential equations using slope fields. Euler's method is a simple but powerful tool, based on tangent line approximation, by which we can find numerical approximations to solutions of differential equations. Euler's method uses a point on the graph of a function and the differential equation for which the function is a solution to approximate values of a solution to the differential equation.

Given a differential equation with an initial value (x_0, y_0), we know that since $y = y_0$ when $x = x_0$, the solution y is known at only the initial point (x_0, y_0), while the derivative is known at all points (x, y).

To begin applying Euler's method, draw a line through (x_0, y_0) with slope equal to $\dfrac{dy}{dx}$. This is the line tangent to the graph of the function $f(x)$ at the point (x_0, y_0).

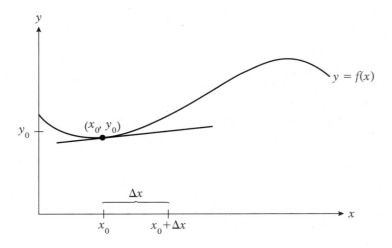

Use the tangent line to approximate the value of the function at (x_1, y_1), one small step Δx away from the initial value x_0. This is the process of linear approximation using the derivative of a function; that is, to approximate the value of the function at $x_1 = x_0 + \Delta x$, use the expression

$$f(x_0 + \Delta x) \approx f(x_0) + \frac{dy}{dx} \Delta x$$

Thus, $y_1 \approx y_0 + \dfrac{dy \Delta x}{dx}$. This gives us an approximate value for y one step away from the initial point (x_0, y_0).

To continue the process, take one more step Δx away from x_0 to $x_0 + 2\Delta x$. To approximate the value of the function at (x_2, y_2) when $x_2 = x_0 + 2\Delta x$, draw a line through (x_1, y_1) on the tangent line with x-coordinate $x_1 = x_0 + \Delta x$, using the slope formula $\frac{dy}{dx}$ at that point. This line is no longer tangent to the graph of the original function, but it does have the same slope as the tangent line at $x = x_i$. Use this line to approximate the value of the function at $x_2 = x_0 + 2\Delta x$.

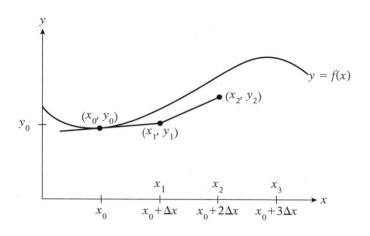

This process may be continued, but for each iteration the error in the approximation becomes greater. For small Δx, though, the approximation is quite close to the value of the function.

MODEL PROBLEMS

1. Given the differential equation $\frac{dy}{dx} = 2x$ with the initial point $(0, 1)$, use Euler's method with a step size of 0.1 to approximate the value of y at $x = 0.3$.

(A) 1.06

(B) 1

(C) 0

(D) 1.02

Solution

Since $\frac{dy}{dx} = 2x$, the slope of the tangent line at $(0, 1)$ is zero. The equation of the tangent line at $(0, 1)$ is then $y = 1$. Taking a step $\Delta x = 0.1$ away from $x = 0$, the new value $x_1 = x_0 + \Delta x = 0.1$.

The new value y_1 is found by using the equation of the tangent line, $y = 1$. Thus, $y_1 = 1$ (which is the same as y_0). The point (x_1, y_1) is $(0.1, 1)$.

Now take another step Δx to $x_2 = 0.2$. To find the approximate value of y_2 at $x_2 = 0.2$, draw a line from $(0.1, 1)$ with slope equal to $\frac{dy}{dx}$; that is, the slope is $2(0.1) = 0.2$. The approximate value of y_2 at $x_2 = 0.2$ is calculated by taking the y-value at $(0.1, 1)$ and adding the change in y, Δy, where $\Delta y = \frac{dy}{dx} \Delta x = 2x_0 \Delta x$. Thus, $\Delta y = 2(0.1)(0.1) = 0.02$, the value of y_2 is 1.02, and the point (x_2, y_2) is $(0.2, 1.02)$.

Before iterating a third time, it will be useful to organize the data into a table:

Old Point (x, y)	Equation of Tangent Line at (x, y) $\left(\text{Slope} = \frac{dy}{dx} \right)$	New Point (x, y)
$(0, 1)$	$y - 1 = 2(0)(x - 0)$ $y = 1$	$(0.1, 1)$
$(0.1, 1)$	$y - 1 = 2(0.1)(x - 0.1)$ $y = 0.2x + 0.98$	$(0.2, 1.02)$
$(0.2, 1.02)$	$y - 1.02 = 2(0.2)(x - 0.2)$ $y = 0.4x + 0.94$	$(0.3, 1.06)$

Thus $f(0.3) \approx 1.06$.

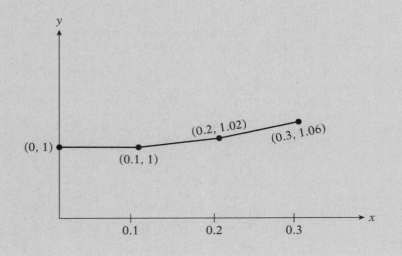

2. Given the differential equation $\frac{dy}{dx} = x^2$ with the initial condition $y(0) = 1$, use Euler's method with a step size of 0.1 to approximate the value of y at $x = 0.2$.

(A) 1

(B) 1.001

(C) 0.998

(D) 1.002

Solution

Set up a chart similar to what was shown above to organize your work.

Old Point (x, y)	Equation of the tangent line at (x, y) $\left(\text{Slope} = \frac{dy}{dx}\right)$	New Point (x, y)
(0, 1)		

AP Calculus Exam-Type Questions

Multiple Choice Questions
No calculator allowed for these questions.

1. $\frac{dy}{dx} = \frac{x}{1 + x^2}$ and $y(0) = 0$. Using Euler's method with step $\Delta x = 0.2$, $y(0.2)$ is approximately

   (A) 0
   (B) 0.0196
   (C) 0.192
   (D) 0.2

2. $\frac{dy}{dx} = x + y$ and $y(0) = 1$. Using Euler's method with step $\Delta x = 0.5$, approximate the value of $y(0.5)$.

   (A) 0
   (B) 1
   (C) 1.5
   (D) 1.797

3. $x^2 \frac{dy}{dx} = y - 1$ and $y(1) = 2$. Use Euler's method with step $\Delta x = 0.1$ to approximate $y(1.2)$.

   (A) 2.091
   (B) 2.1
   (C) 2.181
   (D) 2.191

4. $(x^2 + 1) \frac{dy}{dx} = y - 1$ and $y(0) = 3$. What is the approximate value of $y(0.1)$ using Euler's method with step $\Delta x = 0.1$?

   (A) −0.891
   (B) 3
   (C) 3.2
   (D) 3.21

Free Response Questions
A graphing calculator is required for some questions.

1. $\frac{dy}{dx} = \frac{1}{x}$ and $y(1) = 0$.

   (a) Use Euler's method with step $\Delta x = 0.2$ to complete the table.

x	y (approximate)
1	0 (actual value)
1.2	
1.4	

   (b) Find the equation of the lines tangent to the graph of $y(x)$ at each of the points in the table above using slope $= \frac{dy}{dx}$.

   (c) Graph a segment of the first tangent line on the interval $[1, 1.2)$, the second tangent line on the interval $[1.2, 1.4)$, and the third tangent line on the interval $[1.4, 1.6)$.

2. Given the differential equation $\frac{dy}{dx} = x + 2$ with the initial point $(0, 1)$, use Euler's method with a step size of 0.1 to approximate the value of $f(0.2)$.

3. Given the differential equation $\frac{dy}{dx} = 3x$ with the initial condition $f(1) = 1$, use Euler's method with a step size of 0.1 to approximate the value of $f(1.2)$.

CALCULUS AB/BC

SECTION I, Part A

Time – 60 minutes
Number of problems – 30

A graphing calculator is not permitted for these problems.

1. $\int (\sqrt{x} + 5)^2 \, dx =$

   (A) $\frac{x^2}{2} + 25x + \frac{20}{3}x^{\frac{2}{3}} + c$

   (B) $\frac{(\sqrt{x} + 5)^3}{3} + c$

   (C) $(\sqrt{x} + 5) + c$

   (D) $1 + \frac{5}{\sqrt{x}} + c$

2. If $\int_1^5 f(x) \, dx = 3$ and $\int_1^{10} f(x) \, dx = -7$, then $\int_5^{10} f(x) \, dx =$

   (A) -10
   (B) -4
   (C) -2
   (D) 4

3. $\int_{-1}^{1} \left(e^x - 1 \right) dx =$

   (A) -2
   (B) 0
   (C) $\frac{e^2 - 2e - 1}{e}$
   (D) $\frac{e^2 - 2e + 1}{e}$

4. Find the area enclosed by the graphs of $y = \sqrt{x}$ and $y = x^3$.

   (A) $\frac{1}{4}$

   (B) $\frac{1}{3}$

   (C) $\frac{5}{12}$

   (D) $\frac{2}{3}$

5. Find the average value of $f(x) = \sqrt{x}$ on the interval $[1, 4]$.

   (A) $\frac{1}{3}$

   (B) $\frac{7}{9}$

   (C) $\frac{14}{9}$

   (D) $\frac{7}{2}$

6. The base of a solid is the region enclosed by the graph of $x^2 + 4y^2 = 4$. Cross sections of the solid perpendicular to the x-axis are squares. Find the volume of the solid.

   (A) $\frac{8}{3}$

   (B) $\frac{8}{3}\pi$

   (C) $\frac{16}{3}$

   (D) $\frac{32}{3}\pi$

7. Which of the following integrals represents the volume of the solid obtained by rotating the region bounded by the graph of $y = -\sqrt{x}$, the x-axis, and the line $x = 4$ about the x-axis?

   (A) $\pi \int_0^4 y^2 \, dy$

   (B) $\pi \int_0^2 y^2 \, dy$

   (C) $\pi \int_0^4 (\sqrt{x})^2 \, dx$

   (D) $\pi \int_0^2 (-\sqrt{x})^2 \, dx$

8. $\int \dfrac{x^4 - 3x^2 + 2}{x^2 - 2} =$

(A) $\dfrac{1}{3}x^3 - x + c$

(B) $3x^3 - x^2 + x + c$

(C) $\dfrac{1}{3}x^3 - 6x^2 + x + c$

(D) $\dfrac{1}{3}x^3 - 6x + c$

9. If $F(x) = \displaystyle\int_0^x \sin^2(2t)\, dt$, then $F'(x) =$

(A) $-\cos^2(2x)$

(B) $\cos^2(2x)$

(C) $\sin^2(2x)$

(D) $\dfrac{1}{2}\sin^2(2x)$

10. $\dfrac{d}{dx}\left(\displaystyle\int_2^5 (1 + t^{\frac{2}{3}})\, dt \right) =$

(A) 0

(B) $1 + 5^{\frac{2}{3}}$

(C) $t + \dfrac{3}{5}t^{\frac{2}{3}}$

(D) $5^{2/3} - 2^{\frac{2}{3}}$

11. If $F(x) = \displaystyle\int_{-x}^x e^{-t^2}\, dt$, then $F'(1) =$

(A) 0

(B) $2e^{-1}$

(C) 2

(D) $2e$

12. Which of the following is true for the lower sum of $f(x) = \dfrac{1}{x}$ on the interval $[1, 2]$ for any number of subintervals?

(A) lower sum $> \ln 2$

(B) lower sum $\geq \dfrac{1}{2}$

(C) lower sum $= \ln 2$

(D) lower sum $= \dfrac{1}{2}$

13. Find the area between the x-axis and the graph of $y = 3 - |x|$ on the interval $[0, 6]$.

(A) 0

(B) $\dfrac{9}{2}$

(C) 9

(D) 18

14. Which of the following integrals can be used to find the area of the region enclosed by the graphs of $x = y^2$ and $x = y + 2$?

(A) $\displaystyle\int_0^1 (\sqrt{x} - (-\sqrt{x}))dx$

(B) $\displaystyle\int_{-1}^2 (y + 2 - y^2)dy$

(C) $\displaystyle\int_1^4 (\sqrt{x} - (x + 2))dx$

(D) $\displaystyle\int_1^4 (y - 2 - y^2)dy$

15. Find $\displaystyle\int \dfrac{e^x}{e^x + 4}\, dx$.

(A) $\dfrac{1}{e^x(e^x + 4)} + c$

(B) $e^x \ln(e^x + 4) + c$

(C) $\dfrac{(e^x + 4)^{-2}}{-2} + c$

(D) $\ln(e^x + 4) + c$

16. Find the area under the curve $y = \sec^2 x$ on the interval $\left[0, \dfrac{\pi}{3}\right]$.

(A) $\dfrac{1}{2}$

(B) $\sqrt{3}$

(C) $\dfrac{\sqrt{3}}{3}$

(D) $\sqrt{3} - 1$

17. Find the area of the region enclosed by $y = \sin x$ and $y = \cos x$ on the interval $[0, 2\pi]$.

    (A) $\sqrt{2}$

    (B) $4\sqrt{2}$

    (C) $\dfrac{\sqrt{2}}{2}$

    (D) 1

18. $\displaystyle\int \dfrac{4}{\sqrt{x}}\,dx =$

    (A) $8\sqrt{x} + c$

    (B) $2\sqrt{x} + c$

    (C) $\dfrac{6}{\sqrt{x}} + c$

    (D) $-2x\sqrt{x} + c$

19. $\displaystyle\int \dfrac{x}{x+4}\,dx =$

    (A) -4

    (B) 1

    (C) $x - 4\ln|x + 4| + c$

    (D) $\dfrac{x^2}{x^2 + 8} + c$

20. If $\displaystyle\int_{0}^{a} \sin x\,dx = b$, then $\displaystyle\int_{-a}^{a} \sin x\,dx =$

    (A) b

    (B) $2b$

    (C) 0

    (D) $b + 1$

21. $\displaystyle\int_{-a}^{a} \dfrac{x}{x^2 + 1}\,dx =$

    (A) 0

    (B) $2\displaystyle\int_{0}^{a} \dfrac{x}{x^2 + 1}\,dx$

    (C) $-\dfrac{1}{\left(a^2 + 1\right)^2}$

    (D) $\dfrac{1}{a}$

22. $\displaystyle\int x^2 e^{x^3}\,dx =$

    (A) $e^{x^3} + c$

    (B) $2x e^{x^3} + c$

    (C) $\dfrac{x^3}{3} e^{x^3} + c$

    (D) $\dfrac{1}{3} e^{x^3} + c$

23. $\displaystyle\int \dfrac{\left(\ln(x+1)\right)}{x+1}\,dx =$

    (A) $\dfrac{\left(\ln(x+1)\right)^2}{2} + c$

    (B) $\ln(x+1) + c$

    (C) $\dfrac{1}{x+1} + c$

    (D) $\dfrac{1}{(x+1)^2} + c$

24. $\displaystyle\int e^{\ln x^2}\,dx =$

    (A) $2x + c$

    (B) $x^2 + c$

    (C) $\dfrac{x^3}{3} + c$

    (D) $e^{\ln x^2} + c$

25. $\displaystyle\int \dfrac{\sin\sqrt{x}}{\sqrt{x}}\,dx =$

    (A) $-\cos\sqrt{x} + c$

    (B) $-2\cos\sqrt{x} + c$

    (C) $-\dfrac{1}{2}\cos\sqrt{x} + c$

    (D) $\dfrac{1}{2}\cos\sqrt{x} + c$

26. $\displaystyle\int \tan^2 x\, \sec^2 x\,dx =$

    (A) $\dfrac{\tan^3 x}{3} + c$

    (B) $\dfrac{\tan^3 x\, \sec^3 x}{9} + c$

    (C) $\dfrac{\sec^3 x}{3} + c$

    (D) $4\tan x\, \sec x + c$

27. $\int x \ln x \, dx =$

(A) $2x^2 \ln x - 4x + c$

(B) $\dfrac{1}{x^2} \ln x - \dfrac{x^2}{4} + c$

(C) $\dfrac{x^2}{2} \ln x - \dfrac{x^2}{4} + c$

(D) $\dfrac{1}{x^2} \ln x - 4x^2 + c$

28. Which of the following is the correct set up for evaluating $\displaystyle\int_0^1 \dfrac{1}{\sqrt{x}} \, dx$? Justify your answer.

(A) We must use $\displaystyle\lim_{b \to 0} \int_b^1 \left(x^{\frac{1}{2}}\right) dx$ since the integrand is discontinuous at $x = 0$.

(B) We must use $\displaystyle\lim_{b \to 0^+} \int_0^b \dfrac{1}{\sqrt{x}} \, dx$ because the integrand is continuous on $[0, 1]$.

(C) We must use $\displaystyle\lim_{b \to 0^+} \int_b^a \left(x^{-\frac{1}{2}}\right) dx$ because the integrand is continuous at every point in its domain.

(D) We must use $\displaystyle\lim_{b \to 0^+} \int_b^1 \dfrac{1}{\sqrt{x}} \, dx$ because the integrand is not continuous at $x = 0$.

29. Find the area bounded by $y = \ln x$ and the x-axis on the interval $[b, 1]$ for $0 < b < 1$.

(A) $1 + b \ln b + b$

(B) $-b \ln b$

(C) $1 + b \ln b - b$

(D) $b \ln b - b - 1$

30. $\dfrac{d}{dt}\left(\displaystyle\int_1^{2t^2} (1 + \sin x) \, dx \right) =$

(A) $1 + \sin(2t^2)$

(B) $4t\left(1 + \cos(2t^2)\right)$

(C) $1 + \cos(2t^2)$

(D) $4t\left(1 + \sin(2t^2)\right)$

CALCULUS AB/BC

SECTION I, Part B
Time – 45 minutes
Number of problems – 15

A graphing calculator is required for these problems.

1. Which of the following expressions is the Trapezoidal Rule approximation for $y = x^2$ on the interval [0, 2] with 10 equal subintervals?

   (A) $\frac{1}{20}\left[(0.2)^2 + 2(0.4)^2 + \cdots + 2(1.8)^2 + 2^2\right]$

   (B) $\frac{1}{10}\left[2(0.2)^2 + 2(0.4)^2 + \cdots + 2(1.8)^2 + 2^2\right]$

   (C) $\frac{1}{5}\left[2(0.2)^2 + 2(0.4)^2 + \cdots + 2(1.8)^2 + 2^2\right]$

   (D) $\frac{1}{20}\left[2(0.2)^2 + 2(0.4)^2 + \cdots + 2(1.8)^2 + 2^2\right]$

2. Which of the following is true about the trapezoidal approximation for the graph of $f(x) = e^{-x}$ on the interval [−1, 1] with n equal subintervals?

   (A) Using $n = 5$ gives a closer approximation to the area under the curve than $n = 10$.

   (B) The trapezoidal approximation on the interval [−1, 0] is equal to the trapezoidal approximation on the interval [0, 1].

   (C) The trapezoidal approximation is greater than the area under the curve.

   (D) The trapezoidal approximation is greater than the upper sum.

3. Find the volume of the solid formed by rotating the region bounded by the graph of $y = \sqrt{x} + 1$, the y-axis, and the line $y = 3$ about the line $y = 5$.

   (A) 13.333

   (B) 17.657

   (C) 41.888

   (D) 92.153

4. Find the volume of the solid formed by rotating the graph of $x^2 + 4y^2 = 4$ about the x-axis.

   (A) $\frac{8}{3}$

   (B) $\frac{8}{3}\pi$

   (C) $\frac{16}{3}$

   (D) $\frac{32}{3}$

5. The lower sum of $f(x) = \sqrt{x}$ on the interval [0, 1] with four equal subintervals is

   (A) 0.25

   (B) 0.518

   (C) 0.667

   (D) 0.768

6. Find the volume of the solid generated by rotating $y = e^{-x}$ on the interval $[b < 0, 0]$ about the x-axis.

(A) $\frac{\pi}{4}(e^{-2b} + 1)$

(B) $\frac{\pi}{2}(e^{-2b} - 1)$

(C) $\frac{\pi}{4}(e^{2b} - 1)$

(D) $\frac{\pi}{2}\left(e^{-\frac{1}{2}b} + 1\right)$

7. Find the average value of $f(x) = x^2 - 2$ on the interval $[0, 2]$.

(A) $-\frac{4}{3}$

(B) $-\frac{2}{3}$

(C) 0

(D) $\frac{2}{3}$

For Questions 8–11, $f(x) = \int\limits_{0}^{x} f'(t)\, dt$ **and the graph of** f' **is shown.**

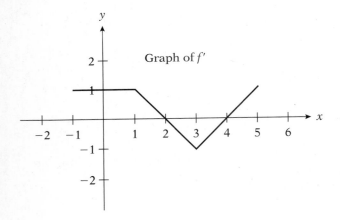

8. Which of the following are true?

I. $f(-1) = -1$

II. $f(1) < f(3)$

III. $f'(1) < f'(3)$

(A) I only

(B) II only

(C) III only

(D) I and II

9. Which of the following are true about the graph of f?

I. f is increasing on $(-1, 2)$ only

II. f is increasing on $(-1, 2)$ or $(4, 5)$

III. f is increasing on $(1, 3)$

(A) I only

(B) II only

(C) III only

(D) None

10. Which of the following are true about the graph of f?

I. f is concave up on $(-1, 1)$

II. f is concave up on $(1, 3)$

III. f is concave down on $(3, 5)$

(A) I only

(B) II only

(C) III only

(D) None

11. Which of the following are true about the graph of f?

I. f has a relative minimum at $x = 2$

II. f has a relative minimum at $x = 4$

III. f has a relative maximum at $x = 2$

(A) I only

(B) II only

(C) III only

(D) II and III

12. The graph of any solution to the differential equation $\dfrac{dy}{dx} = \dfrac{1}{1 + x^2}$

(A) is monotonically increasing.

(B) is always concave up.

(C) is symmetric to the y-axis.

(D) is symmetric to the origin.

13. A particle begins at (0, 1) and moves up the y-axis so that at time t its velocity, y', is double the position y. A solution to this differential equation could be

(A) $y = 2e^{2t}$

(B) $2y = e^{2t}$

(C) $y = e^{2t} + 1$

(D) $y = e^{2t}$

14. The solution to the differential equation $\frac{dP}{dt} = -0.02P$ with $P(0) = 5$ is

(A) $P = 5e^{-0.02t}$

(B) $P = 5e^{-0.002t}$

(C) $P = 5 + e^{-0.02t}$

(D) $P = -0.02P^2 + c$

15. $\frac{dy}{dx} = x + 2xy$ and $y(0) = 1$. Find y as a function of x.

(A) $y = 3e^{x^2} - 2$

(B) $y = 3^{x^2} + 1$

(C) $y = \frac{3}{2}e^{x^2} - \frac{1}{2}$

(D) $y = 3\ln(x^2 + 1) + 1$

Main Idea 3: Integrals and the Fundamental Theorem of Calculus
Summary Assessment

CALCULUS AB/BC

SECTION II, Part A

Time – 30 minutes
Number of problems – 2

A graphing calculator is required for these problems.

1. For each of the following regions (a)–(e), write one or more integral expressions that represent the area of the region. Then compute the area of the region.

   (a) $y = \cos x$ on the interval $\left[-\frac{\pi}{2}, \frac{\pi}{2}\right]$

   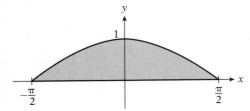

   (b) $y = e^x - 1$ on the interval $[0, 1]$

   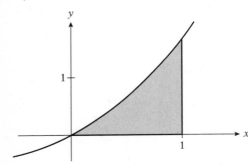

   (c) The region in the first quadrant enclosed by the graphs of $y = 4 - x^2$, $y = 4x - x^2$, and $x = 0$.

   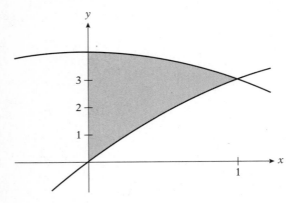

   (d) The region enclosed by $y = x^4 - 1$ and $y = -x + 1$.

   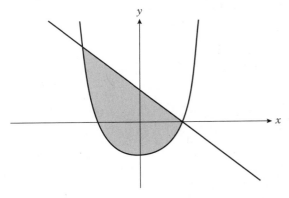

   (e) The region above the x-axis enclosed by $y = x^3 + 1$ and $y = -x + 3$.

   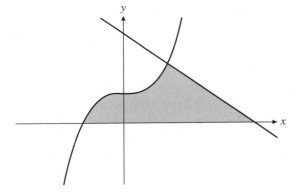

2. Sketch the graph of $y = \sqrt{1 - x^3}$ on the interval $[0, 1]$ and use five subintervals to approximate the area under the curve using

   (a) left-hand sums.

   (b) right-hand sums.

   (c) midpoint sums.

   (d) the trapezoidal approximation.

CALCULUS AB/BC

SECTION II, Part B

Time – 60 minutes
Number of problems – 4

A graphing calculator is not permitted for these problems.

1. The graph of f is a semicircle and two line segments. Find the area between the graph of f on the interval $[-8, 8]$ and the x-axis.

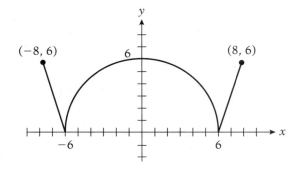

2. Given the differential equation $x^2 \dfrac{dy}{dx} - y^2 = 1$, with initial condition $y(1) = 0$:

   (a) Write the equation of the line tangent to the graph of the solution of the differential equation at $x = 1$.

   (b) Is the graph of the solution to the differential equation concave up or concave down at $x = 1$? Explain your answer.

   (c) Find the solution to the differential equation.

3. The graph of $g(t)$ is shown on the interval $[0, 6]$ and $f(x) = \displaystyle\int_0^x g(t)\, dt$.

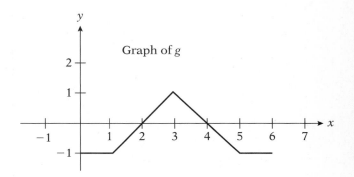

   (a) Find the critical points of $f(x)$, and identify each as a relative maximum, a relative minimum, or neither. Justify your conclusion.

   (b) Find the absolute extrema of $f(x)$. Justify your conclusion.

   (c) If $f(0) = k$, is there a number c in the interval $[0, 6]$ such that $f(c) = k$? Justify your conclusion.

   (d) On what interval(s) is $f(x)$ concave up? On what interval(s) is $f(x)$ concave down?

   (e) Sketch a graph of $f(x)$.

4. Match the differential equations from (a) – (f) with the slope fields I – VI.

Differential Equation		Slope field
(a) $\dfrac{dy}{dx} = x + xy^2$	I.	
(b) $\dfrac{dy}{dx} = -\dfrac{x}{y}$	II.	
(c) $\dfrac{dy}{dx} = -y + 1$	III.	
(d) $\dfrac{dy}{dx} = \dfrac{y^2}{x}$	IV.	
(e) $\dfrac{dy}{dx} = x + y$	V.	
(f) $\dfrac{dy}{dx} = x + xy$	VI.	

CORRELATION CHART

Use the given charts to mark the questions you missed. Then go back and review the suggested lesson(s) to improve your understanding of the concepts.

Section I, Part A (No Calculator Allowed)

Missed?	Question Number	Review the information in...
	1	Lesson 1
	2	Lesson 3
	3	Lesson 3
	4	Lesson 2, Lesson 3
	5	Lesson 6
	6	Lesson 7
	7	Lesson 7
	8	Lesson 1
	9	Lesson 3
	10	Lesson 3
	11	Lesson 3
	12	Lesson 2
	13	Lesson 2, Lesson 3
	14	Lesson 2
	15	Lesson 1
	16	Lesson 2, Lesson 3
	17	Lesson 2, Lesson 3
	18	Lesson 1
	19	Lesson 1
	20	Lesson 4
	21	Lesson 4
	22	Lesson 1 (BC Exam Only)
	23	Lesson 1
	24	Lesson 1
	25	Lesson 1
	26	Lesson 1 (BC Exam Only)
	27	Lesson 1 (BC Exam Only)
	28	Lesson 5 (BC Exam Only)
	29	Lesson 1, Lesson 2, Lesson 3
	30	Lesson 3

Section I, Part B (Calculator Required)

Missed?	Question Number	Review the information in...
	1	Lesson 2
	2	Lesson 2
	3	Lesson 7
	4	Lesson 7
	5	Lesson 2
	6	Lesson 7
	7	Lesson 1
	8	Lesson 3, Lesson 6
	9	Lesson 3, Lesson 6
	10	Lesson 3, Lesson 6
	11	Lesson 3, Lesson 6
	12	Lesson 9
	13	Lesson 8 (BC Exam Only)
	14	Lesson 9
	15	Lesson 9

Section II, Part A (Calculator Required)

Missed?	Question Number	Review the information in...
	1(a)	Lesson 1, Lesson 2
	1(b)	
	1(c)	
	1(d)	
	1(e)	
	2	Lesson 2

Section II, Part B (No Calculator Allowed)

Missed?	Question Number	Review the information in...
	1	Lesson 3, Lesson 4
	2(a)	Lesson 9
	2(b)	
	2(c)	
	3(a)	Lesson 3, Lesson 4
	3(b)	
	3(c)	
	3(d)	
	3(e)	
	4	Lesson 9

MAIN IDEA 4
Series

Lesson 1: Sequence and Series: Definitions, Sums, and Convergence

- Definitions and Sigma Notation
- Types of Series and Convergence

This Main Idea discusses topics unique to the AP Calculus BC exam. If you are sitting for the AB exam, you may skip this Main Idea.

We open this unit with a discussion of sequence and series; it is important to thoroughly understand sequences in order to work with series. Here we would like to note that although many students do not find series to be useful outside of a textbook or the AP exam, it does play a very important role in the study of ordinary differential equations. There are many applications of this topic that are beyond the scope of a typical AP Calculus course or review book. Carefully study these concepts as you will see them again as you move through higher math courses in college.

Explain: Definitions and Sigma Notation

A **sequence** is simply an ordered list of numbers. A few sequences are listed below.

$$1, \frac{1}{2}, \frac{1}{3}, \frac{1}{4}, \frac{1}{5}, \ldots \qquad 1, 2, 4, 8, 16, 32, 64, \ldots$$

$$1, 1, 2, 3, 5, 8, 13, 21, \ldots \qquad 1, \frac{1}{4}, \frac{1}{9}, \frac{1}{16}, \frac{1}{25}, \frac{1}{36}, \ldots$$

In a sequence, the first term is denoted a_1, the second is a_2, and the nth term is a_n.

The sum of a few or all of the terms in a sequence is called a **series**. We can sum any of the terms in a sequence. We concisely express sums with many terms using sigma notation, in which the Greek letter sigma stands for summation.

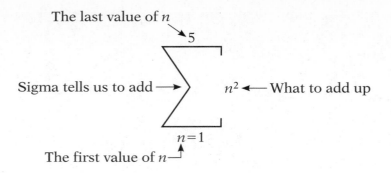

The last value of n

Sigma tells us to add →

n^2 ← What to add up

$n=1$

The first value of n →

The symbol $\sum\limits_{n=1}^{5} n^2$ denotes that n starts as 1 and takes on the values of consecutive integers ending with 5. The expression n^2 tells us to take the sum of the squares, $1^2 + 2^2 + 3^2 + 4^2 + 5^2$, which equals 55.

There is no unique way of expressing a sum in sigma notation. For example, we can **re-index** the sum as $\sum\limits_{n=0}^{4} (n+1)^2$ or $\sum\limits_{n=2}^{6} (n-1)^2$.

There are three basic rules for working with sigma notation. If c is any constant then:

1. $\sum\limits_{k=m}^{n} ca_k = c \sum\limits_{k=m}^{n} a_k$

2. $\sum\limits_{k=m}^{n} (a_k + b_k) = \sum\limits_{k=m}^{n} a_k + \sum\limits_{k=m}^{n} b_k$

3. $\sum\limits_{k=m}^{n} (a_k - b_k) = \sum\limits_{k=m}^{n} a_k - \sum\limits_{k=m}^{n} b_k$

MODEL PROBLEMS

1. Evaluate $\sum\limits_{k=2}^{4} (2k+1)$.

(A) 14

(B) 21

(C) 24

(D) 18

Solution

$(2 \cdot 2 + 1) + (2 \cdot 3 + 1) + (2 \cdot 4 + 1)$	Starting with $k = 2$, find the value of the terms through $k = 4$.
$5 + 7 + 9 = 21$	Simplify and sum. The correct answer is (B).

FR **2.** Write the sum $\frac{1}{2} + \frac{1}{3} + \frac{1}{4} + \ldots + \frac{1}{10}$ in sigma notation.

Solution

The first value of n is clearly 2 and the last value is 10, so we just need to find the expression we are summing. Examining the sum, we see that the denominator of each successive term is one more than the previous. The sigma notation is $\sum\limits_{n=2}^{10} \frac{1}{n}$.

FR **3.** Write the sum $\frac{1}{2} + \frac{1}{4} + \frac{1}{8} + \frac{1}{16} + \ldots + \frac{1}{128}$ in sigma notation.

Solution

Examine the denominators of the fractions. Are they increasing in a familiar pattern? Use that pattern to write the summation.

4. Find $\sum_{i=1}^{n}(i^2 + 1)$.

(A) $1 + (1^2 + 2^2 + 3^2 + \ldots + n^2 + 1)$

(B) $1 + (1^2 + 2^2 + 3^2 + \ldots + n^2)$

(C) $1 - n + (1^2 + 2^2 + 3^2 + \ldots + n^2)$

(D) $n + (1^2 + 2^2 + 3^2 + \ldots + n^2)$

Solution

Starting with $i = 1$, begin to evaluate the terms in this series. Is there a pattern you can generalize? Consider factoring out a common term.

5. Find $\sum_{k=2}^{5}\frac{1}{10}(k^3 - k^2)$.

(A) 17

(B) 167

(C) 278

(D) 45

Solution

Consider rewriting this sum using rules 1 and 3 from page 304. You will then need to solve $\frac{1}{10}\sum_{k=2}^{5}k^3 - \frac{1}{10}\sum_{k=2}^{5}k^2$.

Explain: Types of Series and Convergence

There are several types of series you need to understand in order to be successful on the AP Calculus BC exam, including geometric series, *p*-series, telescoping series, and harmonic series. It is important to remember; however, that when studying a series of numbers, the major goal is to determine whether the series has a limit. Does the sum of the terms approach a finite value? If the series has a limit, it is said to **converge** to that value. If the series does not have a limit, it is said to **diverge**.

Consider a square with a side length of 1 unit. Draw a line through the center of the square and shade one side. That represents $\frac{1}{2}$. Next, divide the unshaded portion in half and shade half of that. The shaded portion now represents $\frac{1}{2} + \frac{1}{4}$. If we repeat the procedure, the shaded portion will represent $\frac{1}{2} + \frac{1}{4} + \frac{1}{8}$.

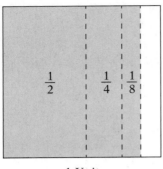

1 Unit

We see that we can go on indefinitely and that the following series results:

$$\frac{1}{2} + \frac{1}{4} + \frac{1}{8} + \ldots + \frac{1}{2^n} + \ldots = 1.$$

This is an example of an infinite series. Notice that although the number of terms in the series is infinite, the series does have a finite sum. If we look at the partial sums of the series, we see that they appear to converge to 1.

$$S_1 = \frac{1}{2} = 0.50$$

$$S_2 = \frac{1}{2} + \frac{1}{4} = 0.75$$

$$S_3 = \frac{1}{2} + \frac{1}{4} + \frac{1}{8} = 0.875$$

$$S_4 = \frac{1}{2} + \frac{1}{4} + \frac{1}{8} + \frac{1}{16} = 0.9375$$

Geometric Series In a geometric sequence, the first term is denoted a_1 and succeeding terms are each multiplied by a constant r. The geometric series formed by adding successive terms of a geometric sequence has a limit when $|r| < 1$. The sum of the terms of a convergent geometric series is given by the formula $S = \frac{a_1}{1 - r}$. What makes a geometric series special is that we know not only whether the series converges, but also the value to which it converges.

The *p*-Series The *p*-series, like the geometric series, is easy to test for convergence.

The *p*-series $\sum\limits_{n=1}^{\infty} \frac{1}{n^p} = \frac{1}{1^p} + \frac{1}{2^p} + \frac{1}{3^p} + \ldots$ converges for $p > 1$.

The *p*-series diverges for $p \leq 1$.

In the case of a *p*-series, we can determine if the series converges, but we cannot always determine the value to which it converges.

Telescoping Series   A third series whose convergence is easily tested is the telescoping series. One example of a telescoping series is

$$\sum_{n=1}^{\infty}\left(\frac{1}{n} - \frac{1}{n+1}\right) = \left(1 - \frac{1}{2}\right) + \left(\frac{1}{2} - \frac{1}{3}\right) + \left(\frac{1}{3} - \frac{1}{4}\right) + \dots.$$

Notice that the terms of this series cancel in pairs: $-\frac{1}{2}$ and $\frac{1}{2}$, $-\frac{1}{3}$ and $\frac{1}{3}$, etc. This causes the sum to collapse like a telescope.

The sequence of even-numbered partial sums, S_n, for the telescoping series listed above is:

$$S_2 = \frac{2}{3}$$

$$S_4 = \frac{4}{5}$$

$$S_6 = \frac{6}{7}$$

Thus, $S_n = \frac{n}{n+1}$, and the sum of the series S is $\lim_{n\to\infty} S_n = \lim_{n\to\infty} \frac{n}{n+1} = 1$.

Thus, $S_{2n} = \frac{n}{n+1}$, and the sum of the series S is $\lim_{n\to\infty} S_{2n} = \lim_{n\to\infty} \frac{n}{n+1} = 1$.

Harmonic Series   The harmonic series is a special case of the p-series where $p = 1$. It has the form

$$\sum_{n=1}^{\infty}\frac{1}{n} = 1 + \frac{1}{2} + \frac{1}{3} + \frac{1}{4} + \frac{1}{5} + \dots.$$

We can observe partial sums to determine whether the harmonic series converges or diverges:

$$S_1 = 1$$

$$S_2 = 1 + \frac{1}{2}$$

$$S_4 = 1 + \frac{1}{2} + \left(\frac{1}{3} + \frac{1}{4}\right)$$

Notice that in S_4, $\left(\frac{1}{3} + \frac{1}{4}\right) > 2\left(\frac{1}{4}\right)$, or $\frac{1}{2}$.

$$S_8 = 1 + \frac{1}{2} + \left(\frac{1}{3} + \frac{1}{4}\right) + \left(\frac{1}{5} + \frac{1}{6} + \frac{1}{7} + \frac{1}{8}\right)$$

Again, notice that in S_8, $\left(\frac{1}{5} + \frac{1}{6} + \frac{1}{7} + \frac{1}{8}\right) > 4\left(\frac{1}{8}\right)$, or $\frac{1}{2}$.

By increasing n, it is possible to make the partial sum of the harmonic series arbitrarily large. As $n \to \infty$, the partial sum $\to \infty$, or $\lim_{x\to\infty} S_n = \infty$. Since the sequence of partial sums diverges, the harmonic series diverges, and $\sum_{n=1}^{\infty}\frac{1}{n} = \infty$. The harmonic series is an important example of a series that diverges, yet has terms that approach zero.

MODEL PROBLEMS

1. Find the sum of the series formed by adding successive terms of the sequence $1, \frac{1}{2}, \frac{1}{4}, \frac{1}{8}, \ldots$.

(A) 2

(B) $\frac{1}{2}$

(C) 0

(D) 1

Solution

Begin by determining the type of series represented. Notice that each successive term of the series can be found by multiplying the preceeding term by $\frac{1}{2}$, so this is a geometric series with $r = \frac{1}{2}$. The sum of the terms in this series is $S = \dfrac{1}{1 - \frac{1}{2}} = 2$. The correct answer is (A).

2. Find the sum of the series $3 + 1 + \frac{1}{3} + \frac{1}{9} + \ldots$

(A) 4.5

(B) 1

(C) 0

(D) 3.5

Solution

Again, start by determing the type of series presented. Is there a constant ratio from one term to the next? If so, it is a geometric series and you need to determine the value of r.

3. Find the value of $\sum_{n=0}^{\infty} (0.5^n - 0.2^n)$.

(A) 0.50

(B) 0

(C) 0.75

(D) 1

Solution

Consider rewriting this series using rule 3 from page 304. If you do, you need to find the value of $\sum_{n=0}^{\infty} 0.5^n - \sum_{n=0}^{\infty} 0.2^n$. Look at each sum separately to find the constant ratio and the first term of the sum. Then use the formula $S = \dfrac{a_1}{1 - r}$ as many times as needed to complete the calculation.

FR **4.** Test the convergence of $\sum_{n=1}^{\infty} \frac{1}{n^2}$.

Solution

This is a p-series where $p = 2$. Since $p > 1$, this series converges.

5. Does the series $\sum_{n=1}^{\infty} \left(\frac{1}{n^3} - 0.9^n \right)$ converge?

Solution

We use rule 3 from page 304 to split the series into two parts:

$$\sum_{n=1}^{\infty} \frac{1}{n^3} - \sum_{n=1}^{\infty} 0.9^n.$$

Now we can evaluate each part separately; one part is a *p*-series and the other is a geometric series. If each part of the series converges, the entire series converges. If one part of the series diverges, the entire series diverges.

6. Determine whether the series $\sum_{n=1}^{\infty} \left(\frac{3}{n} - \frac{3}{n+2} \right)$ converges and, if possible, find its sum.

(A) The series diverges and there is no sum.

(B) The series converges and the sum is 4.5.

(C) The series diverges but the sum is 2.5.

(D) The series converges but there is no sum.

Solution

Rewrite the series as $3\sum_{n=1}^{\infty} \left(\frac{1}{n} - \frac{1}{n+2} \right)$ and find the first few terms. We see they are $3\left[\left(1 - \frac{1}{3} \right) + \left(\frac{1}{2} - \frac{1}{4} \right) + \left(\frac{1}{3} - \frac{1}{5} \right) + \left(\frac{1}{4} - \frac{1}{6} \right) \dots \right]$. Are there like terms with opposite signs? What type of series is this? How can we find the sum?

7. Determine if the series $\sum_{n=1}^{\infty} \frac{2}{8n}$ is convergent.

Solution

Try rewriting the series to reveal its structure. Remember that if the rewritten series is convergent, the original series is also convergent.

8. Determine if the series $\sum_{n=1}^{\infty} \frac{2n+1}{n^3}$ is convergent.

Solution

We rewrite the given series using the basic rules for working sigma notation on page 304. Then $\sum_{n=1}^{\infty} \frac{2n+1}{n^3} = \sum_{n=1}^{\infty} \frac{2}{n^2} + \frac{1}{n^3}$. You try solving from this point.

9. Determine the sum $\sum_{n=2}^{\infty} \left(\frac{4}{n-1} - \frac{4}{n} \right)$.

(A) ∞

(B) 2

(C) 4

(D) 1

Solution

You need to rewrite this sum using the rules on page 304 and then find the first few terms. The type of series and solution will become apparent.

10. Determine if the series $\sum\limits_{n=1}^{\infty} \dfrac{3^{n-2}}{4^{2n-1}}$ is convergent.

Solution

$$\sum_{n=1}^{\infty} \frac{3^{n-2}}{4^{2n-1}} = \sum_{n=1}^{\infty} \frac{3^n \cdot 3^{-2}}{4^{2n} \cdot 4^{-1}} = \sum_{n=1}^{\infty} \frac{4 \cdot 3^n}{9 \cdot 4^{2n}}$$

$$= \sum_{n=1}^{\infty} \frac{4 \cdot 3^n}{9 \cdot \left(4^2\right)^n}$$

We need to use the laws of indices (you learned these in Algebra 1) to rewrite the fraction. You continue solving from this point.

AP Calculus Exam-Type Questions

Multiple Choice Questions
No calculator permitted for these questions.

1. Written in sigma notation, $\dfrac{2}{2} + \dfrac{3}{2} + \dfrac{4}{2} + \dfrac{5}{2} + \dots$ is

 (A) $\sum\limits_{n=0}^{4} \dfrac{n+2}{2}$

 (B) $\sum\limits_{n=0}^{4} \dfrac{2n}{2}$

 (C) $\sum\limits_{n=1}^{\infty} \dfrac{n+2}{2}$

 (D) $\sum\limits_{n=1}^{\infty} \dfrac{n+1}{2}$

2. $1 + \dfrac{1}{2} + \dfrac{1}{6} + \dfrac{1}{24} + \dfrac{1}{120} =$

 (A) $\sum\limits_{n=0}^{5} \dfrac{1}{2^n}$

 (B) $\sum\limits_{n=0}^{5} \dfrac{1}{2n}$

 (C) $\sum\limits_{n=1}^{5} \dfrac{1}{n!}$

 (D) $\sum\limits_{n=1}^{\infty} \dfrac{1}{n!}$

3. The sum $\sum\limits_{n=1}^{\infty} \dfrac{n+1}{n}$ represents which of the following expressions?

 (A) $2 + \dfrac{3}{2} + \dfrac{4}{3} + \dfrac{5}{4} + \cdots$

 (B) $\dfrac{3}{2} + \dfrac{4}{3} + \dfrac{5}{4} + \cdots$

 (C) $2 + 1 + \dfrac{1}{2} + \dfrac{1}{4} + \cdots$

 (D) $\dfrac{3}{2} - \dfrac{4}{3} + \dfrac{5}{4} - \cdots$

4. Find the value of r (if it exists) in the series

$$3 - \dfrac{9}{2} + \dfrac{27}{4} - \cdots$$

 (A) $-\dfrac{3}{2}$

 (B) $-\dfrac{2}{3}$

 (C) $\dfrac{3}{2}$

 (D) No r exists

5. Find the sum of the series $\left(1 - \dfrac{1}{3}\right) +$

$$\left(\dfrac{1}{3} - \dfrac{1}{5}\right) + \left(\dfrac{1}{5} - \dfrac{1}{7}\right) + \cdots$$

 (A) $\dfrac{2}{3}$

 (B) 1

 (C) $\dfrac{4}{5}$

 (D) Does not exist

6. What type of series is represented by $\sum\limits_{n=1}^{\infty} \dfrac{4}{20n}$?

 (A) Geometric series

 (B) Harmonic series

 (C) Telescoping series

 (D) p-series

7. Write $1 + 3 + 5 + 7 + 9$ using sigma notation.

(A) $\displaystyle\sum_{n=1}^{5} 2n + 1$

(B) $\displaystyle\sum_{n=1}^{\infty} 2n - 1$

(C) $\displaystyle\sum_{n=0}^{4} 2n + 1$

(D) $\displaystyle\sum_{n=0}^{5} 2n - 1$

Questions 8–16: Test each of the following series for convergence.

8. $\displaystyle\sum_{n=1}^{\infty} \frac{n+3}{9n}$

(A) Converges to $\frac{1}{9}$

(B) Converges to $\frac{1}{3}$

(C) Converges to 0

(D) Diverges

9. $\displaystyle\sum_{n=1}^{3} \frac{1}{n}$

(A) Converges to $\frac{1}{3}$

(B) Converges to $\frac{11}{6}$

(C) Converges to $\frac{5}{6}$

(D) Diverges

10. $\displaystyle\sum_{n=1}^{\infty} \frac{n+3}{n}$

(A) Converges to 3

(B) Converges to 1

(C) Converges to 4

(D) Diverges

11. $\displaystyle\sum_{n=0}^{\infty} \frac{4^n}{6^n}$

(A) Converges to 3

(B) Converges to $\frac{3}{2}$

(C) Converges to $\frac{2}{3}$

(D) Diverges

12. $\displaystyle\sum_{n=0}^{\infty} \frac{2}{8^n}$

(A) Converges to $\frac{7}{8}$

(B) Converges to $\frac{8}{7}$

(C) Converges to $\frac{16}{7}$

(D) Diverges

13. $\displaystyle\sum_{n=3}^{\infty} \left(\frac{10}{n-2} - \frac{10}{n-1} \right)$

(A) Converges to 10

(B) Converges to 5

(C) Converges to -5

(D) Diverges

14. $\displaystyle\sum_{n=0}^{\infty} \frac{n^8 + 3n^7}{n^7}$

(A) 3

(B) 4

(C) 0

(D) Diverges

15. $\displaystyle\sum_{n=0}^{\infty} \frac{2^{n+1}}{3^{n-3}}$

(A) Converges to 3

(B) Converges to 162

(C) Converges to 54

(D) Diverges

16. $\displaystyle\sum_{n=0}^{\infty} \frac{2^{3n-5}}{8^n}$

(A) Converges to $\frac{1}{4}$

(B) Converges to 1

(C) Converges to 0

(D) Diverges

Free Response Questions

A graphing calculator is required for some questions.

1. Evaluate the following sums:

   (a) $\displaystyle\sum_{n=1}^{5} (n^2 + 1)$

   (b) $\displaystyle\sum_{n=1}^{5} n(n + 1)$

   (c) $\displaystyle\sum_{n=2}^{6} n(n - 1)$

   (d) $\displaystyle\sum_{n=0}^{4} (n^2 + 3n + 2)$

2. (a) Write each sum in sigma notation.

   (b) Evaluate each sum.

   i. $\left(1 - \dfrac{1}{2}\right) + \left(1 - \dfrac{1}{3}\right) + \left(1 - \dfrac{1}{4}\right)$
   $+ \cdots + \left(1 - \dfrac{1}{10}\right)$

   ii. $\left(1 - \dfrac{1}{2}\right) + \left(\dfrac{1}{2} - \dfrac{1}{3}\right) + \left(\dfrac{1}{3} - \dfrac{1}{4}\right)$
   $+ \cdots + \left(\dfrac{1}{9} - \dfrac{1}{10}\right)$

   iii. $\left(1 - \dfrac{1}{3}\right) + \left(\dfrac{1}{3} - \dfrac{1}{5}\right) + \left(\dfrac{1}{5} - \dfrac{1}{7}\right)$
   $+ \cdots + \left(\dfrac{1}{9} - \dfrac{1}{11}\right)$

   iv. $\left(1 - \dfrac{1}{3}\right) + \left(1 - \dfrac{1}{5}\right) + \left(1 - \dfrac{1}{7}\right)$
   $+ \cdots + \left(1 - \dfrac{1}{11}\right)$

3. Find the sum $\displaystyle\sum_{n=1}^{\infty} \dfrac{5^{n-1}}{4^{n+1}}$, if it converges. If it does not converge, state so.

4. Test if the following sequence converges.

   $$\sum_{n=0}^{\infty} \dfrac{3^{n+1}}{4^n}$$

5. Find the sum $\displaystyle\sum_{n=0}^{\infty} \dfrac{2^n}{3^{2n-1}}$, if it converges.

6. Test if the following sequence converges.

   $$\sum_{n=1}^{\infty} n^2$$

7. Test if the following sequence converges.

   $$\sum_{n=0}^{\infty} \left(\dfrac{3^n}{4^n}\right)$$

8. Determine the sum $\displaystyle\sum_{n=1}^{\infty} \left(\dfrac{6}{n} - \dfrac{6}{n + 1}\right)$, if it converges.

Lesson 2: More on Tests of Convergence

- Other Tests of Convergence
- Alternating Series and Error Formula
- Absolute and Conditional Convergence

Explain: Other Tests of Convergence

So far, we have discussed the most common types of series, geometric, p-series, telescoping, and harmonic series, and the conditions for their convergence. We began with these series as they are easily tested for convergence. Series other than these exist and can also be tested for convergence. The convergence tests for a series of positive terms are:

> The Ratio Test
>
> The Limit Comparison Test
>
> The Direct Comparison Test
>
> The Integral Test

Additionally, the Alternating Series Test applies specifically to a series in which the terms alternate in sign. Aside from the special case of alternating series, there is no best or right test for convergence of a series. Generally, the convergence tests can be applied effectively in the order in which they appear on the list. After some practice, however, the best method is the one that is the easiest to do.

Before testing for convergence of a series $\sum_{n=1}^{\infty} a_n$, always use the **divergence test**.

Divergence Test

If

$$\lim_{n \to \infty} a_n \neq 0,$$

Then

$$\sum_{n=1}^{\infty} a_n \text{ diverges.}$$

Keep in mind that the divergence test is inconclusive if $\lim_{n \to \infty} a_n = 0$. Even if a limit is 0, you may not have convergence. Be careful not to use the converse of the statement.

The Ratio Test Given a series such that $\sum_{n=1}^{\infty} a_n$, we can use the ratio test to determine whether it converges. To do so, we find $\lim_{n \to \infty} \left| \dfrac{a_{n+1}}{a_n} \right|$. If the limit is less than 1, the series converges, but if the limit is greater than 1, the series diverges. When $\lim_{n \to \infty} \left| \dfrac{a_{n+1}}{a_n} \right| = 1$, the test is inconclusive.

MODEL PROBLEMS

FR **1.** Does the series $\sum\limits_{n=1}^{\infty} \dfrac{n}{n+1}$ converge or diverge?

Solution

$\lim\limits_{n\to\infty} \dfrac{n}{n+1} = 1$	We begin this problem using the divergence test.
Since the limit of a_n is not 0, this series diverges.	

FR **TT** **2.** Does the series $\sum\limits_{n=1}^{\infty} \dfrac{n^3}{n!}$ converge or diverge?

Solution

$\lim\limits_{n\to\infty} \dfrac{n^3}{n!} = 0$	Reasoning our way through the limit, the value of the numerator will grow less quickly than the value of the denominator, so the limit is 0 (see Main Idea 1, Lesson 5). Since divergence test results in 0, the test is inconclusive.
$\lim\limits_{n\to\infty}\left\|\dfrac{\dfrac{(n+1)^3}{(n+1)!}}{\dfrac{n^3}{n!}}\right\|$ $= \lim\limits_{n\to\infty}\left(\dfrac{(n+1)^3\, n!}{(n+1)!\, n^3}\right)$ $= \lim\limits_{n\to\infty}\left(\dfrac{(n+1)^2}{n^3}\right) = 0$	We move to the ratio test to confirm our reasoning and determine whether the series converges or diverges.
Because the limit of the series by the ratio test is 0 and $0 < 1$, the series converges.	

FR **3.** Does the series $\sum\limits_{n=1}^{\infty} \dfrac{2^n}{n^2}$ converge or diverge?

Solution

Use the divergence test. If the results are inconclusive, move to the ratio test.

FR **4.** Use the ratio test to determine if $\sum\limits_{n=1}^{n} \dfrac{n+1}{4^n}$ is convergent or divergent.

Solution

To use the ratio test, find $\lim\limits_{n\to\infty}\left|\dfrac{a_{n+1}}{a_n}\right|$ and compare your results to 1. If the limit is less than 1, the series converges, but if the limit is greater than 1, the series diverges.

FR **5.** Test for the convergence of $\sum_{n=1}^{\infty} \dfrac{kn^2}{n!}$, where k is a constant.

Solution

Again, you need to evaluate $\lim_{n\to\infty}\left|\dfrac{a_{n+1}}{a_n}\right|$. In this case, $a_n = \dfrac{kn^2}{n!}$ and

$a_{n+1} = \dfrac{k(n+1)^2}{(n+1)!} = \dfrac{k(n+1)^2}{(n+1)n!} = \dfrac{k(n+1)}{n!}$. You finish solving the problem from this point.

Limit Comparison Test and Direct Comparison Test

In both the limit comparison test and the direct comparison test, a series whose convergence is being tested, say $\sum_{n=1}^{\infty} a_n$, is compared with a series whose convergence is known, say $\sum_{n=1}^{\infty} b_n$. The limit comparison test is easier to use since it involves taking the limit of the ratio of the terms of the two series, while the direct comparison test involves establishing an inequality between the terms of the two series. Note that for the direct comparison test, the inequality listed below does not need to be true for all n. It is enough that the inequality is eventually true.

The Limit Comparison Test

If $\sum a_n$ and $\sum b_n$ are series of positive terms, and $\lim_{n\to\infty}\dfrac{a_n}{b_n}$ is a positive finite number,

Then the series $\sum_{n=1}^{\infty} a_n$ and $\sum_{n=1}^{\infty} b_n$ either both converge or both diverge.

The Direct Comparison Test

If $0 \le a_n \le b_n$ and the series $\sum_{n=1}^{\infty} a_n$ diverges,

Then $\sum_{n=1}^{\infty} b_n$ diverges.

If $0 \le a_n \le b_n$ and the series $\sum_{n=1}^{\infty} b_n$ converges,

Then $\sum_{n=1}^{\infty} a_n$ converges.

MODEL PROBLEMS

FR **1.** Test $\sum_{n=2}^{\infty} \dfrac{1}{n^2 - 1}$ for convergence.

Solution

$\lim_{n\to\infty} \dfrac{\frac{1}{n^2-1}}{\frac{1}{n^2}} = \lim_{n\to\infty} \dfrac{n^2}{n^2-1} = 1$	We will use the limit comparison test to compare the given series to $\sum_{n=1}^{\infty} \dfrac{1}{n^2}$.

Since the limit is a positive finite number and the series $\sum_{n=1}^{\infty} \dfrac{1}{n^2}$ converges (this is a p-series where $p = 2$), the given series also converges.

2. Test $\displaystyle\sum_{n=1}^{\infty} \frac{1}{n+1}$ for convergence.

Solution

To solve this question use the limit comparison test to compare the given series to $\displaystyle\sum_{n=1}^{\infty} \frac{1}{n}$. See page 306 to recall important information about *p*-series.

FR **3.** Test the series $\displaystyle\sum_{n=1}^{\infty} \frac{1}{3^n}$ using the direct comparison test with the series $\displaystyle\sum_{n=1}^{\infty} \frac{1}{n^2}$.

Solution

In the direct comparison test, we need to establish one of two inequalities. For this problem, we think that $\displaystyle\sum_{n=1}^{\infty} \frac{1}{3^n}$ converges, since $\displaystyle\sum_{n=1}^{\infty} \frac{1}{n^2}$ does converge (this is a *p*-series with $p = 2$), so we need to show that $\frac{1}{3^n} \leq \frac{1}{n^2}$.

We can use our graphing calculators to do this, either by graphing the two functions 3^n and n^2 (substituting x for n) or by making a table of values for positive integers.

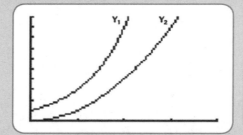 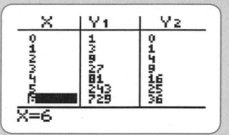

We see that the graphs do not intersect for positive values of x and that 3^x is always greater than x^2, which verifies the inequality. The series converges.

FR **4.** Test the series $\displaystyle\sum_{n=1}^{\infty} \frac{1}{2^n}$ using the direct comparison test with the series $\displaystyle\sum_{n=1}^{\infty} \frac{1}{n^2}$.

Solution

We know that $\displaystyle\sum_{n=1}^{\infty} \frac{1}{n^2}$ does converge (*p*-series with $p = 2$), so you need to show that $\frac{1}{2^n} \leq \frac{1}{n^2}$ or that $2^n \geq n^2$. Remember that the inequality does not have to be true for all positive integers, n. It is sufficient that the inequality be true for all n that are greater than some positive integer.

FR **5.** Use the limit comparison test to determine if $\displaystyle\sum_{n=1}^{\infty} \frac{n}{(n+1)!}$ converges or diverges.

Solution

Compare $\displaystyle\sum_{n=1}^{\infty} \frac{n}{(n+1)!}$ with the related series $\displaystyle\sum_{n=1}^{\infty} \frac{n}{n!}$ and test to see if the $\displaystyle\lim_{n\to\infty} \frac{a_n}{b_n}$ is finite where $a_n = \frac{n}{(n+1)!}$ and $b_n = \frac{n}{n!}$. If so, then determine if both series converge or diverge.

FR **6.** Using direct comparison, determine if $\sum_{n=1}^{\infty} \dfrac{n^2 + 1}{8n^5 - 4}$ is convergent.

Solution

Let $\sum_{n=1}^{\infty} \dfrac{n^2 + 1}{8n^5 + 4}$ be such that $a_n = \dfrac{n^2 + 1}{8n^5 + 4}$ and let us have another

series $\sum_{n=1}^{\infty} \dfrac{n^2 + 1}{8n^5}$ where $b_n = \dfrac{n^2 + 1}{8n^5}$. Now compare a_n and b_n. Note that

both fractions have the same numerator, so focus on the denominator.

You also know that $8n^5 \leq 8n^5 + 4$, so $\dfrac{n^2 + 1}{8n^5} \geq \dfrac{n^2 + 1}{8n^5 + 4}$. You solve this
problem from here.

The Integral Test   The terms of the a series $\sum_{n=1}^{\infty} a_n$ can be thought of as outputs of a function

$f(x)$ whose domain is the positive integers and where $f(n) = a_n$ for all

positive intergers, n. The existence of the sum of the series $\sum_{n=1}^{\infty} a_n$ is related

to $\int_{1}^{\infty} f(x)\,dx$ as follows:

If $\int_{1}^{\infty} f(x)\,dx$ converges,

Then $\sum_{n=1}^{\infty} a_n$ converges.

If $\int_{1}^{\infty} f(x)\,dx$ diverges,

Then $\sum_{n=1}^{\infty} a_n$ diverges.

For both of these to be true, the function f needs to be decreasing,
continuous, and non-negative.

MODEL PROBLEMS

FR **1.** Determine, using the integral test, if $\sum_{n=1}^{\infty} \dfrac{2n}{n^2 + 4}$ converges.

Solution

Let $f(x) = \dfrac{2x}{x^2 + 4}$. Then the equivalent integral is $\int_{1}^{\infty} \dfrac{2x}{x^2 + 4}\,dx$, which
we solve using improper integrals (see Main Idea, Lesson 5).

$\displaystyle\int_{1}^{\infty} \dfrac{2x}{x^2 + 4}\,dx = \lim_{t\to\infty} \int_{1}^{t} \dfrac{2x}{x^2 + 4}\,dx$	Let $u = x^2 + 4$; $du = 2x\,dx$.
$\displaystyle\lim_{t\to\infty} \int_{1}^{t} \dfrac{2x}{x^2 + 4}\,dx = \lim_{t\to\infty} \int_{5}^{t^2+4} \dfrac{du}{u} = \lim_{t\to\infty} [\ln u]_{5}^{t^2+4}$	When $x = 1$, $u = 5$ and when $x = t$, $u = t^2 + 4$. We substitute these values.
$\displaystyle\lim_{t\to\infty} \left[\ln(t^2 + 4) - \ln 5\right] = \lim_{t\to\infty}\left[\ln\left(\dfrac{t^2 + 4}{5}\right)\right] = \infty$	We finish solving and find that the integral does not converge. From this we know that the series $\displaystyle\sum_{n=1}^{\infty} \dfrac{2n}{n^2 + 4}$ does not converge.

Explain: Alternating Series and Error Formula

Another type of series is an **alternating series**, which is often of the form $a_1 - a_2 + a_3 - a_4 + a_5 - \ldots = \sum_{n=1}^{\infty}(-1)^{n+1} a_n$. As with other series, our main interest here is to determine if the series converges.

Alternating Series Test

If

　　1. $\lim_{n \to \infty} a_n = 0$, and

　　2. $a_{n+1} \leq a_n$,

Then

$$\sum_{n=1}^{\infty}(-1)^{n+1} a_n \text{ converges.}$$

We can also calculate the error associated with computing a partial sum of an alternating series.

If

an alternating series $\sum_{n=1}^{\infty}(-1)^{n+1} a_n$ converges,

Then

its sum can be approximated by the sum of the first n terms of the series, and the error in the approximation is less than the $(n+1)^{\text{st}}$ term.

MODEL PROBLEMS

FR **1.** Does the alternating series $\sum_{n=1}^{\infty}(-1)^{n+1}\frac{1}{n}$ converge or diverge?

Solution

$\lim_{n \to \infty} \frac{1}{n} = 0$	There are two conditions the alternating series must fulfill to converge. We start by checking the limit. It is equal to 0, so we move to the second condition.

| $\dfrac{1}{n+1} \leq \dfrac{1}{n}$ | We check to make sure $a_{n+1} \leq a_n$. This condition is satisfied so the given series converges. |

FR **2.** Determine if $\displaystyle\sum_{n=1}^{\infty}(-1)^{n+1}\dfrac{1}{2n}$ diverges or converges.

Solution

This is an alternating series, so both test conditions must be met in order for the series to converge. The limit of $\dfrac{1}{2n}$ is $\displaystyle\lim_{n\to\infty}a_n = \lim_{n\to\infty}\dfrac{1}{2n} = \dfrac{1}{2}\lim_{n\to\infty}\dfrac{1}{n}$. Does $\dfrac{1}{n}$ look familiar? What is the value of this limit? Finish this problem from here.

FR **3.** (a) Use the first four terms to approximate the series $\displaystyle\sum_{n=1}^{\infty}(-1)^{n+1}\dfrac{1}{n^2}$.

(b) Determine the error associated with this approximation.

Solution

| (a) | $\displaystyle\sum_{n=1}^{4}(-1)^{n+1}\dfrac{1}{n^2} = 1 - \dfrac{1}{2^2} + \dfrac{1}{3^2} - \dfrac{1}{4^2}$ $\displaystyle\sum_{n=1}^{4}(-1)^{n+1}\dfrac{1}{n^2} = 1 - \dfrac{1}{4} + \dfrac{1}{9} - \dfrac{1}{16} = \dfrac{115}{144}$ | We approximate the series using $n = 1, 2, 3,$ and 4. |
| (b) | $\left|\dfrac{1}{5^2}\right| = \dfrac{1}{25} = 0.04$ | The error is less than the value of the $(n + 1)^{th}$ term. We calculate the value of the fifth term. The error in the approximation is less than 0.04. |

4. If the first five terms of the series $\displaystyle\sum_{n=1}^{\infty}(-1)^{n+1}\dfrac{1}{n}$ are used to approximate the sum, what is the error estimate on this approximation?

(A) $-\dfrac{1}{5}$

(B) 0.25

(C) $\dfrac{1}{6}$

(D) -0.50

Solution

We showed that the given alternating series converges in Model Problem #1. Use the error formula to estimate the error.

Explain: Absolute and Conditional Convergence

If an alternating series $a_1 - a_2 + a_3 - a_4 + \cdots = \sum\limits_{n=1}^{\infty}(-1)^{n+1}a_n$ converges and the series of positive terms $\sum\limits_{n=1}^{\infty}a_n$ converges, then the alternating series $\sum\limits_{n=1}^{\infty}(-1)^{n+1}a_n$ is said to be **absolutely convergent**.

If an alternating series $a_1 - a_2 + a_3 - a_4 + \cdots = \sum\limits_{n=1}^{\infty}(-1)^{n+1}a_n$ converges and the series of positive terms $\sum\limits_{n=1}^{\infty}a_n$ diverges, then the alternating series $\sum\limits_{n=1}^{\infty}(-1)^{n+1}a_n$ is said to be **conditionally convergent**.

To expedite the process of deciding if an alternating series is absolutely or conditionally convergent, first test the series of positive terms. If the series of positive terms converges, then the alternating series must converge as well, and the alternating series is absolutely convergent.

On the other hand, if the series of positive terms diverges, then use the alternating series test to test the convergence of the alternating series. If the alternating series converges, then the alternating series is conditionally convergent. Otherwise, the alternating series diverges.

MODEL PROBLEM

FR 1. Is the series $\sum\limits_{n=1}^{\infty}(-1)^{n+1}\dfrac{3}{4n^3}$ absolutely or conditionally convergent?

Solution

$\sum\limits_{n=1}^{\infty}a_n = \sum\limits_{n=1}^{\infty}\dfrac{3}{4n^3} = \dfrac{3}{4}\sum\limits_{n=1}^{\infty}\dfrac{1}{n^3}$	We first determine if the sum of the positive terms of the sequence is convergent. We know that $\sum\limits_{n=1}^{\infty}\dfrac{1}{n^3}$ is a p-series with $p = 3$ so the series is convergent. Since the series of positive terms converges, the series is absolutely convergent.

FR 2. Is the series $\sum\limits_{n=1}^{\infty}(-1)^{n+1}\dfrac{1}{n}$ absolutely or conditionally convergent?

Solution

First test the series of positive terms for convergence. The p-series $\sum\limits_{n=1}^{\infty}\dfrac{1}{n}$ has $p = 1$, so this series diverges. Now use the alternating series test to see if the alternating series converges or diverges.

FR 3. Is the series $\sum\limits_{n=1}^{\infty}(-1)^{n+1}\dfrac{1}{n\cdot\sqrt{n}}$ absolutely convergent?

Solution

Use the procedure explained in Model Problems #1 and #2 to work through this question.

AP Calculus Exam-Type Questions

Multiple Choice Questions
No calculator permitted for these questions.

1. How many terms of the series $\sum_{n=1}^{\infty}(-1)^{n+1}\frac{1}{n^4}$ are needed to approximate the sum of the series with error <0.001?

   (A) 3

   (B) 4

   (C) 5

   (D) 6

2. If the series $\sum_{n=1}^{\infty}\frac{1}{n^{1.01}}$ converges, which of the following series also converges by the direct comparison test?

   (A) $\sum_{n=1}^{\infty}\frac{1}{n}$

   (B) $\sum_{n=1}^{\infty}\frac{1}{\sqrt{n}}$

   (C) $\sum_{n=1}^{\infty}(-1)^{n+1}\frac{1}{n^{1.01}}$

   (D) $\sum_{n=1}^{\infty}\frac{1}{n^{0.9}}$

3. Which of the following series is absolutely convergent?

   (A) $\sum_{n=1}^{\infty}\frac{(-1)^{n+1}}{n^{0.99}}$

   (B) $\sum_{n=1}^{\infty}\frac{(-1)^{n+1}}{n^2}$

   (C) $\sum_{n=1}^{\infty}\frac{(-1)^{n+1}}{n}$

   (D) $\sum_{n=1}^{\infty}(-1)^{n+1}3^n$

4. If $\sum_{n=1}^{\infty}\frac{1}{n}$ diverges, which of the following series also diverges?

   (A) $\sum_{n=1}^{\infty}\frac{1}{n^2}$

   (B) $\sum_{n=1}^{\infty}\frac{(-1)^{n+1}}{n}$

   (C) $\sum_{n=1}^{\infty}\frac{0.5}{n}$

   (D) $\sum_{n=1}^{\infty}\frac{10^6}{n^2}$

5. A student states: "If the series $\sum_{n=1}^{\infty}a_n$ converges, then $\sum_{n=1}^{\infty}|a_n|$ converges." Which of the following series makes this statement false?

   (A) $\sum_{n=1}^{\infty}\frac{(-1)^{n+1}}{n^3}$

   (B) $\sum_{n=1}^{\infty}\frac{(-1)^{n+1}}{n}$

   (C) $\sum_{n=1}^{\infty}\frac{\cos n\pi}{n^2}$

   (D) $\sum_{n=1}^{\infty}\frac{(-1)^{n+1}}{n^{1.5}}$

6. A student uses the ratio test to determine the convergence of the series $\sum_{n=1}^{\infty}a_n$. Which value of the limit will ensure that the series converges?

   (A) 1

   (B) 2

   (C) $\frac{\pi}{2}$

   (D) $\frac{1}{2}$

7. Which of the following statements is true about the series $\sum_{n=1}^{\infty}\frac{7}{n+1}$?

   (A) It is conditionally convergent.

   (B) It is convergent by the comparison test.

   (C) It is divergent.

   (D) It is absolutely convergent

8. Identify the series that is absolutely convergent.

   (A) $\sum_{n=1}^{\infty}(-1)^{n+1}\sin(n\pi)$

   (B) $\sum_{n=1}^{\infty}(-1)^{n+1}\frac{3n-2}{n}$

   (C) $\sum_{n=1}^{\infty}(-1)^{n+1}\frac{6+2n}{n^3}$

   (D) $\sum_{n=1}^{\infty}(-1)^{n+1}\frac{n}{n^{0.98}}$

Questions 9–12: Use the series

$$\sum_{n=1}^{\infty}(-1)^{n+1}\frac{4n}{e^{2n}}.$$

9. Identify the series type.

   (A) p-series

   (B) Alternating series

   (C) Harmonic series

   (D) Geometric series

10. Evaluate $\lim_{n\to\infty}\frac{4n}{e^{2n}}$.

    (A) 4

    (B) 0

    (C) ∞

    (D) e

11. Compare a_{n+1} and a_n.

    (A) $a_{n+1}=a_n$

    (B) $a_{n+1}\geq a_n$

    (C) $a_{n+1}\leq a_n$

    (D) Not enough information

12. Based on the above information, what can we say about the series above?

    (A) It is divergent.

    (B) It is absolutely convergent.

    (C) It is conditionally convergent.

    (D) It is convergent.

13. Find the error when the alternating series $\sum_{n=0}^{\infty}(-0.25)^n$ is approximated by the first four terms of the series.

    (A) 0.00098

    (B) 0.1992

    (C) 0.2002

    (D) 0.3906

Free Response Questions

A graphing calculator is required for some questions.

1. Consider the series $\sum_{n=1}^{\infty}\frac{(-1)^{n+1}}{n^p}$.

   (a) Determine the values of p for which the series converges.

   (b) Find the maximum value of the error if k terms are used to approximate the sum of the series.

2. Do the following series converge absolutely, coverge conditionally, or diverge?

   (a) $\sum_{n=2}^{\infty}(-1)^n\frac{1}{\ln n}$

   (b) $\sum_{n=0}^{\infty}(-1)^n\left(\frac{x}{2}\right)^n$, when $x=1?\,x=2?\;x=3?$

   (c) $\sum_{n=2}^{\infty}(-1)^n\left(\frac{n+1}{n^3}\right)$

3. (a) Find $\sum_{n=1}^{10}\frac{(-1)^{n+1}}{n^n}$.

   (b) What is the maximum value of the error if $\sum_{n=1}^{\infty}\frac{(-1)^{n+1}}{n}$ is approximated by the answer to part (a)?

   (c) If the sum of the first 20 terms was used instead in part (a), would the error in part (b) be increased or decreased? Explain your answer.

4. (a) Find the sum of the series $\sum_{n=1}^{\infty}\frac{1}{n^2}$ correct to three decimal places and state the number of terms needed to arrive at this answer.

   Use the sum and seq commands found in CATALOG.

   (b) Find the sum of the series $\sum_{n=1}^{\infty}\frac{1}{n!}$ correct to three decimal places and state the number of terms needed to arrive at this answer.

   (c) Describe in a sentence or two your conclusions about the convergence of each of the two series in parts (a) and (b).

Lesson 3: Taylor Polynomials

- Introduction and Taylor Coefficients
- The Taylor Polynomial Formula
- Lagrange Error Bounds
- Alternating Series Error Bound
- Taylor Series

Explain: Introduction and Taylor Coefficients

The algebra of polynomials—adding, subtracting, multiplying, and dividing—is straightforward. Finding derivatives of polynomial functions consists of repeated application of a few simple rules. If only all functions were polynomials! This is the wish that is answered by Taylor polynomials. Any function that has derivatives of a certain order can be approximated by a polynomial of that order. This includes logarithmic, exponential, trigonometric, and many other functions. There is also a formula that gives an upper bound on the error in using a Taylor polynomial of a certain degree to approximate a function.

The tangent line to the graph of a function $f(x)$ at a point $(a, f(a))$ is the first-degree Taylor polynomial for the function at that point. As we have seen, the tangent line provides a linear approximation of the function at values close to the given point. The slope of the tangent line is $f'(a)$. Thus, the equation of the tangent line in point-slope form is

$$y - f(a) = f'(a)(x - a) \text{ or}$$
$$y = f(a) + f'(a)(x - a),$$

which is a first-degree polynomial.

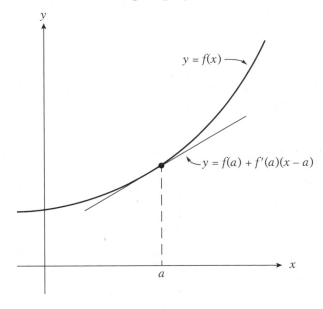

We know that zooming in at a point on the graph of a function gives a picture of the graph that looks like the tangent line. By local linearity, we also know that the tangent line approximates f near values of x close to a. As the tangent line moves farther away from the point of tangency $(a, f(a))$, the linear approximation becomes less accurate. Extend this idea to the Taylor polynomials: as the degree of a Taylor polynomial increases, the interval where the polynomial is a good approximation of the function also increases. If the degree of the Taylor polynomial increases without bound, the polynomial becomes a **Taylor series.**

MODEL PROBLEMS

1. The function $f(x) = x^4 - 2x^2$ has three zeros. Find the slope of the first-degree Taylor polynomial for $f(x)$ at the largest zero.

(A) $\sqrt{2}$

(B) 2

(C) $2\sqrt{2}$

(D) $4\sqrt{2}$

Solution

We begin by finding the zeros of the function. We can quickly determine that they are $x = 0$, $\pm\sqrt{2}$, the largest of which is $\sqrt{2}$. We find the slope of the first-degree Taylor polynomial at $x = \sqrt{2}$.

$f'(x) = 4x^3 - 4x$	Find the derivative of the given function.
$f'(\sqrt{2}) = 4(\sqrt{2})^3 - 4(\sqrt{2})$ $f'(\sqrt{2}) = 8\sqrt{2} - 4\sqrt{2} = 4\sqrt{2}$	The slope of the polynomial is represented by $f'(a)$. We calculate this value. The correct answer is option (D).

2. The linear approximation function for $f(x) = \sqrt{x - 1}$ at $x = 2$ is

(A) $x - 2y = 0$

(B) $y - 2 = \frac{1}{2}(x - 1)$

(C) $y - 1 = \frac{2}{3}(x - 2)$

(D) $x - 2y = 1$

Solution

$f'(x) = \dfrac{1}{2\sqrt{x - 1}}$	For this problem we need to determine the equation of the line at the given value. We start by finding the derivative of the given function.

$y = f(a) + f'(a)(x - a)$ $y = \sqrt{2 - 1} + \dfrac{1}{2\sqrt{2 - 1}}(x - 2)$ $y = 1 + \dfrac{1}{2}(x - 2)$ $y = \dfrac{x}{2}$ $x - 2y = 0$	We use the formula given on page 323 where $a = 2$ and completely simplify. The correct answer is (A).

At times it is difficult to determine the value of a function, such as in the neighborhood of a removable discontinuity. Using the Taylor formula, however, we can approximate any function to a polynomial and then use the approximation to evaluate the value of a function around only that point.

In general, the Taylor polynomial to approximate the value of $f(x)$ at $x = a$ is

$$f(x) \approx f(a) + f'(a)(x - a) + \frac{f''(a)}{2!}(x - a)^2 + \frac{f'''(a)}{3!}(x - a)^3 + \ldots + \frac{f^n(a)}{n!}(x - a)^n.$$

Using sigma notation, we can write this as

$$f(x) \approx \sum_{k=0}^{n} \frac{f^k(a)}{k!}(x - a)^k$$

The values $\dfrac{f^k(a)}{k!}$, sometimes denoted a_k, are called **Taylor polynomial coefficients**.

Using this new notation for coefficients, we have

$$f(x) \approx \sum_{k=0}^{n} a_k (x - a)^k \text{ where } a_k = \frac{f^k(a)}{k!}.$$

Before moving forward with the Model Problems, we want to clarify our use of the approximation symbol ($\approx$). We are not approximating the entire function. Only the function near the specific, given point.

MODEL PROBLEMS

1. Find the coefficient of the third term of a Taylor polynomial for $f(x) = \cos(2x)$ at $x = 0$.

(A) 4

(B) −4

(C) 0

(D) −2

Solution

$\dfrac{f''(a)}{2!}$	We look to the Taylor polynomial to find the coefficient formula for the third term.
$f(x) = \cos(2x)$ $f'(x) = -2\sin(2x)$ $f''(x) = -4\cos(2x)$	We need to find the second derivative of the given function, $f(x)$.

$f''(0) = -4\cos(0) = -4$	Now evaluate the second derivative at $x = 0$.
$\dfrac{f''(a)}{2!} = -\dfrac{4}{2} = -2$	Determine the coefficient. The correct option is (D).

2. Determine the fourth Taylor polynomial coefficient for $f(x) = \sin(2x)$ at $x = \dfrac{\pi}{4}$.

(A) -8

(B) 0

(C) -4

(D) 8

Solution

The fourth Taylor polynomial coefficient is given by $\dfrac{f'''(a)}{3!}$. The second derivative of the given function is $f''(x) = -4\sin(2x)$. You finish solving from this point.

3. Determine the second Taylor polynomial coefficient for $f(x) = e^{-3x+2}$ at $x = 0$.

(A) $-3\,e^2$

(B) -3

(C) e^2

(D) 1

Solution

The second Taylor polynomial coefficient is given by $\dfrac{f'(a)}{1!}$. Find the derivative of the given function and evaluate it at the necessary point.

Explain: The Taylor Polynomial Formula

We now proceed to approximating functions of degree n using Taylor polynomial

$$f(x) \approx f(a) + f'(a)(x - a) + \frac{f''(a)}{2!}(x - a)^2 + \frac{f'''(a)}{3!}(x - a)^3 + \ldots + \frac{f^n(a)}{n!}(x - a)^n = \sum_{k=0}^{n} \frac{f^k(a)}{k!}(x - a)^k$$

The first few terms of the formula may look familiar to you as we have already used them to approximate linear functions. It is important to note that the degree of the polynomial is equal to the highest power on $(x - a)$, which is also equal to the number of times a function is differentiated.

MODEL PROBLEMS

FR **1.** (a) Find a third-degree Taylor polynomial centered at $x = 1$ for $f(x) = \sqrt{x}$ and use the polynomial to approximate $\sqrt{1.2}$.

(b) Use your graphing calculator to graph $f(x)$ and the Taylor polynomial on the same set of axes. Sketch what you see.

Solution

The given function is not a polynomial since polynomials have positive integer exponents. We are going to use a polynomial to approximate the given function near $x = 1$.

(a)

$f(1) = \sqrt{1}$ $\qquad$ $f(1) = 1$ $\qquad$ $a_0 = 1$ $f'(x) = \dfrac{1}{2\sqrt{x}}$ $\qquad$ $f'(1) = \dfrac{1}{2}$ $\qquad$ $a_1 = \dfrac{1}{2}$ $f''(x) = -\dfrac{1}{4}x^{-3/2}$ $\quad$ $f''(1) = -\dfrac{1}{4}$ $\quad$ $a_2 = -\dfrac{1}{8}$ $f'''(x) = \dfrac{3}{8}x^{-5/2}$ $\quad$ $f'''(1) = \dfrac{3}{8}$ $\quad$ $a_3 = \dfrac{1}{16}$	We calculate the Taylor coefficients.
$P_3 = 1 + \dfrac{1}{2}(x - 1) - \dfrac{1}{8}(x - 1)^2 + \dfrac{1}{16}(x - 1)^3$	Write the Taylor polynomial based on the calculated coefficients.

(b)

$\sqrt{1.2} = 1 + \dfrac{1}{2}(1.2 - 1) - \dfrac{1}{8}(1.2 - 1)^2$ $+ \dfrac{1}{16}(1.2 - 1)^3 = 1.0955$ $\sqrt{1.2} = 1.0955$	Approximate the value of $\sqrt{1.2}$.
	Graph the function and its polynomial approximation.

While the Taylor polynomial can be derived for any function $f(x)$ by using the formula (provided that the derivatives are of a certain order), the AP Calculus exam emphasizes knowing and applying the Taylor polynomials for commonly used functions like those given in the table:

Function	Taylor Polynomial	Sigma Notation	Center
e^x	$1 + x + \dfrac{x^2}{2!} + \dfrac{x^3}{3!} + \dfrac{x^4}{4!} + \cdots + \dfrac{x^n}{n!}$	$\displaystyle\sum_{k=0}^{n} \dfrac{x^k}{k!}$	0
$\ln x$	$(x - 1) - \dfrac{(x - 1)^2}{2} + \dfrac{(x - 1)^3}{3} - \dfrac{(x - 1)^4}{4} + \cdots + \dfrac{(-1)^{n+1}(x - 1)^n}{n}$	$\displaystyle\sum_{k=1}^{n} \dfrac{(-1)^{k+1}(x - 1)^k}{k}$	1
$\sin x$	$x - \dfrac{x^3}{3!} + \dfrac{x^5}{5!} - \dfrac{x^7}{7!} + \cdots + \dfrac{(-1)^n x^{2n+1}}{(2k + 1)!}$	$\displaystyle\sum_{k=1}^{n} \dfrac{(-1)^k x^{2k+1}}{(2k + 1)!}$	0
$\cos x$	$1 - \dfrac{x^2}{2!} + \dfrac{x^4}{4!} - \dfrac{x^6}{6!} + \cdots + \dfrac{(-1)^n x^{2n}}{(2n)!}$	$\displaystyle\sum_{k=0}^{n} \dfrac{(-1)^k x^{2k}}{(2k)!}$	0
$\dfrac{1}{1 - x}$	$1 + x + x^2 + x^3 + \cdots + x^n$	$\displaystyle\sum_{k=0}^{n} x^k$	0

MODEL PROBLEMS

1. Find a third-degree Taylor's polynomial for $f(x) = 2e^{3x}$ at $x = 1$.

(A) $f(x) \approx \left(9x^3 - 18x^2 + 51x - 4\right)e^3$

(B) $f(x) \approx \left(9x^3 + 18x^2 + 51x - 4\right)e^3$

(C) $f(x) \approx \left(9x^3 - 18x^2 + 15x - 4\right)e^3$

(D) $f(x) \approx \left(9x^3 + 36x^2 + 51x - 4\right)e^3$

Solution

$f'(x) = 6e^{3x}$	$f'(1) = 6e^3$	$a_1 = 6e^3$	We calculate the Taylor coefficients.
$f''(x) = 18e^{3x}$	$f''(1) = 18e^3$	$a_2 = 9e^3$	
$f'''(x) = 54e^{3x}$	$f'''(1) = 54e^3$	$a_3 = 9e^3$	
$f(x) \approx 2e^3 + 6e^3(x-1) + 9e^3(x-1)^2 + 9e^3(x-1)^3$			Write the polynomial. This is not one of the answer options, so we continue manipulating.
$(x-1)^2 = x^2 - 2x + 1$ $(x-1)^3 = x^3 - 3x^2 + 3x - 1$			Apply binomial expansion.
$f(x) \approx 2e^3 + 6e^3(x-1) + 9e^3(x^2 - 2x + 1) +$ $\qquad 9e^3(x^3 - 3x^2 + 3x - 1)$ $f(x) \approx 9e^3 x^3 - 18e^3 x^2 + 15e^3 x - 4e^3$ $f(x) \approx \left(9x^3 - 18x^2 + 15x - 4\right)e^3$			Substitute and simplify. The correct answer is (C).

FR 2. (a) Find the first-, third-, and fifth-degree Taylor polynomials for the function $f(x) = \sin(x)$ at $x = 0$.

(b) Use a graphing calculator to graph $f(x)$ with each of the polynomials from part (a). Sketch what you see.

(c) Which polynomial is the best approximation of $f(x) = \sin(x)$ at $x = 0$? Justify your answer.

Solution

(a)	$f(x) = \sin(x)$ $\qquad$ $f(0) = 0$ $f'(x) = \cos(x)$ $\qquad$ $f'(0) = 1$ $P_1 = x$	We find the derivative of the given function and use it to write a first-degree Taylor polynomial. You continue part (a) from here.
(b)		We graph $f(x)$ and P_1 on the same set of axes. You graph $f(x)$ with each of P_3, and P_5.
(c)	Examine your graphs of $f(x)$ with P_1, P_3, and P_5. Which of the polynomials best matches $f(x)$ around $x = 0$?	

Explain: Lagrange Error Bounds

Taylor polynomials are approximations of a given function. As they are not exact duplicates of the original function, there is a margin of error in any Taylor polynomial. The error in an approximation is the difference between the approximated value and the actual value; however, there are times in which we are only interested in determining the largest error one can attain. The largest error is called the **error bound**. We can measure the error bound in a Taylor polynomial using the **Lagrange error bound**.

The Lagrange error bound in approximating a polynomial of degree n using Taylor's formula is

$$R_n = \frac{f^{(n+1)}(z)}{(n+1)!}(x-a)^{n+1}$$ where z is a number between x and a.

MODEL PROBLEMS

FR 1. Find the Lagrange error bound at $x = 0.1$ when we approximate $f(x) = \dfrac{1}{2-3x}$ using a quadratic Taylor polynomial around $x = 0$.

Solution

In quadratic approximation $n = 2$, so the Lagrange error bound (centered at $x = 0$) is $R_2 = \dfrac{f'''(0)}{(3)!}(x-0)^3$. Begin by differentiating the given function.

$f(x) = \dfrac{1}{2-3x} = (2-3x)^{-1}$ $f'(x) = 3(2-3x)^{-2}$ $f''(x) = 18(2-3x)^{-3}$ $f'''(x) = 162(2-3x)^{-4}$	Differentiation.
$f'''(0) = 162(2-0)^{-4} = \dfrac{162}{2^4} = \dfrac{162}{16} = 10.125$	Evaluate $f'''(x)$ at 0.
$R_2 = \dfrac{f'''(0)}{(3)!}(x-0)^3 = \dfrac{10.125}{6}(0.1-0)^3 = 0.0016875$	Calculate the error bound.

FR 2. Given that $f(x) = \dfrac{1}{x^2+1}$, find the Lagrange error bound in evaluating $f(1.2)$ if we use a linear approximation on $f(x)$ around $x = 1$.

(A) 0.002

(B) 0.5

(C) 0.04

(D) 0.01

Solution

When using a linear approximation $n = 1$, and the Lagrange error bound is $R_1 = \dfrac{f''(z)}{(2)!}(x-a)^2$. Find the needed derivative(s) of the function, evaluate the correct deriviate at $x = 1$, and then use the Lagrange error bound formula.

FR 3. How many terms are needed to approximate $e^{-1.5}$ using a Taylor polynomial centered at $x = 0$ so that the error bound is less than 0.001?

Solution

In this case, the function is $f(x) = e^x$ and we want to know the value of n such that $R_n = \dfrac{f^{(n+1)}(z)}{(n+1)!}(x-a)^{n+1} = 0.001$. All values less than that will have an error of less than 0.001. To approximate $e^{-1.5}$, we consider a Taylor polynomial evaluated around $x = 0$. But we know that

$f^{(n+1)}(x) = f(x) = e^x$ for all values of x and that $f^{(n+1)}(z) = e^0 = 1$.

Thus, $R_n = \dfrac{f^{(n+1)}(z)}{(n+1)!}(x-a)^{n+1} = 0.001$ reduces to

$R_n = \dfrac{1}{(n+1)!}(-1.5)^{n+1} = 0.001$. From here, use a calculator to determine the value of n that makes the error bound less than 0.001.

Explain: Alternating Series Error Bound

If a Taylor polynomial has alternating positive and negative signs, then the polynomial's error can be approximated using the alternating series error bound. For these polynomials, the error bound is the absolute value of the $(n + 1)^{\text{st}}$ term.

MODEL PROBLEMS

FR 1. (a) Find a fourth-degree Taylor polynomial for $f(x) = \dfrac{1}{1 + 4x}$ around $x = 0$.

(b) Determine the error bound for $f(0.3)$.

Solution

(a)

$f(x) = (1 + 4x)^{-1}$	$f(0) = 1$	We find the values needed for the Taylor polynomial.
$f'(x) = -4(1 + 4x)^{-2}$	$f'(0) = -4,$	
$f''(x) = 32(1 + 4x)^{-3}$	$f''(0) = 32$	
$f'''(x) = -384(1 + 4x)^{-4}$	$f'''(0) = -384$	
$f^{(4)}(x) = 6144(1 + 4x)^{-5}$	$f^{(4)}(0) = 6144$	
$f(x) \approx 1 - 4x + 16x^2 - 64x^3 + 256x^4$		Create the Taylor polynomial. This is an alternating polynomial.

(b)

$R_4 = \left| \dfrac{f^5(a)}{5!}(x-a)^5 \right|$	We use the alternating series error bound to determine the error bound for $f(0.3)$. This is the formula for the error bound.
$f^{(5)}(x) = -122880(1+4x)^{-6}$	Find the fifth derivative.
$f^{(5)}(0) = -122880$	Evaluate at $x = 0$.
$\left\| \dfrac{-122880}{5!}(x-0)^5 \right\| = \left\| \dfrac{-122880}{120}(0.3-0)^5 \right\|$ $= 2.488$	Calculate the error bound.

2. Determine the error bound for evaluating $f(0.55)$ around $x = 0.5$ given that $f(x) = \dfrac{1}{1+2x}$ is approximated by a third-degree polynomial.

Solution

Since this is a third-degree polynomial, if it alternates, then its error can be approximated by the absolute value of the fourth term. Calculate the fourth derivative; as a check the second derivative is $f''(x) = 8(1+2x)^{-3}$. Then use the alternating series error bound formula.

3. Determine the maximum error in approximating $f(1.5)$ by its first-degree Taylor polynomial centered at $x = 1$.

(A) 0.0625

(B) 0.125

(C) 0.25

(D) 0.03125

Solution

How many times should we differentiate $f(x)$ to determine the error bound? At which value should that term be evaluated? How do we use that information to calculate the error bound if the terms in the polynomial alternate?

Explain: Taylor Series

We have learned that an nth degree Taylor polynomial is the expression

$$f(x) \approx f(a) + f'(a)(x-a) + \frac{f''(a)}{2!}(x-a)^2 + \frac{f'''(a)}{3!}(x-a)^3 + \ldots + \frac{f^n(a)}{n!}(x-a)^n,$$

or in sigma notation, it is $f(x) \approx \displaystyle\sum_{k=0}^{n} \frac{f^k(a)}{k!}(x-a)^k$. There are times that we may be interested in representing a function by an infinite series rather than stopping at a specific term. That approximation is $\displaystyle\sum_{k=0}^{\infty} \frac{f^k(a)}{k!}(x-a)^k$ and it is called a **Taylor series.** If we compare the Taylor series and an nth degree Taylor polynomial, we notice that

$$\sum_{k=0}^{n} \frac{f^{(k)}(a)}{k!}(x-a)^k \leq \sum_{k=0}^{\infty} \frac{f^{(k)}(a)}{k!}(x-a)^k$$

So we can say that an nth degree Taylor polynomial is a partial sum of a Taylor series.

MODEL PROBLEMS

FR **1.** Given that $f(x) = e^{2x}$,
(a) find the fifth-degree Taylor polynomial around $x = 0$.
(b) find the Taylor series for the function.
(c) find the difference between the two expressions in (b) and (a).

Solution

(a)
$f(x) = e^{2x}$	$f(0) = 1$	Determine the fifth derivative and evaluate.
$f'(x) = 2e^{2x}$	$f'(0) = 2$	
$f''(x) = 4e^{2x}$	$f''(0) = 4$	
$f'''(x) = 8e^{2x}$	$f'''(0) = 8$	
$f^{(4)}(x) = 16e^{2x}$	$f^{(4)}(0) = 16$	
$f^{(5)}(x) = 32e^{2x}$	$f^{(5)}(0) = 32$	
$f(x) \approx 1 + 2x + \dfrac{4}{2}(x)^2 + \dfrac{8}{6}(x)^3 + \dfrac{16}{24}(x)^4 + \dfrac{32}{120}x^5$ $f(x) \approx \displaystyle\sum_{n=0}^{5} \dfrac{(2x)^n}{n!}$		Write the Taylor polynomial in both expanded and sigma notation.

(b)
$f(x) \approx 1 + \dfrac{2}{1!}x + \dfrac{4}{2!}(x)^2 + \dfrac{8}{3!}(x)^3 + \dfrac{16}{4!}(x)^4$ $+ \dfrac{32}{5!}x^5 + \ldots = \displaystyle\sum_{n=0}^{\infty} \dfrac{(2x)^n}{n!}$	Examine your Taylor polynomial to write the Taylor series using sigma notation.

(c)
$\displaystyle\sum_{n=0}^{\infty} \dfrac{(2x)^n}{n!} - \sum_{n=0}^{5} \dfrac{(2x)^n}{n!} = \sum_{n=6}^{\infty} \dfrac{(2x)^n}{n!}$	We can clearly see that the fifth-degree polynomial is a partial sum of the Taylor series. We calculate the difference.

2. What is the Taylor series for $f(x) = \cos(2x)$ at $x = 0$?

(A) $\displaystyle\sum_{k=0}^{\infty} (-1)^{k+1} \dfrac{(2x)^{2k}}{(2k)!}$

(B) $\displaystyle\sum_{k=0}^{\infty} (-1)^{k} \dfrac{(2x)^{2k+1}}{(2k)!}$

(C) $\displaystyle\sum_{k=0}^{\infty} (-1)^{k} \dfrac{(2x)^{2k}}{(2k)!}$

(D) $\displaystyle\sum_{k=0}^{\infty} (-1)^{k+1} \dfrac{(2x)^{2k+2}}{(2k)!}$

Solution

We know that a Taylor polynomial of nth degree is the partial sum of that Taylor series. We use this information to determine the series and start by finding some derivatives of $f(x) = \cos(2x)$.

$f(x) = \cos(2x)$	$f(0) = 1$
$f'(x) = -2\sin(2x)$	$f'(0) = 0$
$f''(x) = -4\cos(2x)$	$f''(0) = -4$
$f'''(x) = 8\sin(2x)$	$f'''(0) = 0$
$f^4(x) = 16\cos(2x)$	$f^4(0) = 16$
$f^5(x) = -32\sin(2x)$	$f^5(0) = 0$
$f^6(x) = -64\cos(2x)$	$f^6(0) = -64$
$f^7(x) = 128\sin(2x)$	$f^7(0) = 0$

Examining the Taylor polynomial, we see that $f(x) \approx 1 - \frac{4}{2!}x^2 + \frac{16}{4!}x^4 - \frac{64}{6!}x^6$.
The positive values in the numerators create a geometric series where the first term is 1, the common ratio is $4x^2 = (2x)^2$ and the signs alternate after one term. Use this information to write the Taylor polynomial in sigma notation and determine the Taylor series.

AP Calculus Exam-Type Questions

Multiple Choice Questions

A graphing calculator is required for some questions.

1. Using linear approximation of $f(x) = 2x^4 - 2x + 7$ around $x = 1$, estimate $f(1.2)$.

   (A) 8.2

   (B) 8.4

   (C) 7.2

   (D) 8.7

2. Using the alternating series error bound, find the error approximating $f(x) = \frac{1}{1 + 5x}$ at $x = 0.3$ with its second degree Taylor polynomial centered at $x = 0.2$.

   (A) 0.0625

   (B) 0.007813

   (C) 0.04688

   (D) 0.0500

3. Find the fifth-degree Taylor polynomial for $f(x) = \cos(4x)$ at $x = 0$.

   (A) $f(x) = -4x + \frac{32}{3}x^3 - \frac{128}{15}x^5$

   (B) $f(x) = 1 - 8x^2 + \frac{32}{3}x^4$

   (C) $f(x) = 1 - 16x^2 + 256x^4$

   (D) $f(x) = 1 + 8x^2 + \frac{32}{3}x^4$

4. Find the Lagrange error bound when $f(1.2)$ is approximated around $x = 1$ using a quadratic approximation of $f(x) = \frac{2}{3 - x}$.

   (A) 0.006

   (B) 0.001

   (C) 0.125

   (D) 0.075

5. Find the linear approximation of

$g(x) = \dfrac{2}{3 + 4x^2}$ at $x = 1$.

(A) $y - \dfrac{2}{7} = \dfrac{16}{49}(x - 1)$

(B) $y - \dfrac{2}{7} = \dfrac{16}{49}(1 - x)$

(C) $y = \dfrac{16}{49}(x - 1) - \dfrac{2}{7}$

(D) $y = \dfrac{16}{49}(1 - x) - \dfrac{2}{7}$

6. Find the slope of the tangent to the curve
$y = e^{-x} + 3$ at $x = 0$.

(A) -1

(B) 4

(C) $3 + e$

(D) $3 - e$

7. Determine the coefficient of the third term of
a Taylor polynomial for the function
$f(x) = \dfrac{1}{8 - x}$ at $x = 6$.

(A) 0.125

(B) 0.1667

(C) 0.0104

(D) 0.0625

8. Using the formula for the error E, what
is the maximum value of the error in
approximating 1.2 with a Taylor polynomial
of degree three centered at $x = 1$?

(A) 0.000345

(B) 0.0004

(C) 0.00666

(D) 0.1813

9. Find the third-degree Taylor polynomial for
$f(x) = \sqrt{x - 1}$ at $x = 2$.

(A) $f(x) \approx 1 - \dfrac{1}{2}(x - 2) - \dfrac{1}{8}(x - 2)^2 + \dfrac{1}{16}(x - 2)^3$

(B) $f(x) \approx 1 + \dfrac{1}{2}(x - 2) - \dfrac{1}{8}(x - 2)^2 + \dfrac{1}{16}(x - 2)^3$

(C) $f(x) \approx 1 + \dfrac{1}{2}(x - 2) - \dfrac{1}{4}(x - 2)^2 + \dfrac{3}{8}(x - 2)^3$

(D) $f(x) \approx 1 - \dfrac{1}{2}(x - 2) + \dfrac{1}{4}(x - 2)^2 - \dfrac{3}{8}(x - 2)^3$

Questions 10–13: Use the function
$g(x) = 2 \cos\left(2x - \dfrac{\pi}{2}\right)$.

10. What is $g^5(x)$?

(A) $g^{(5)}(x) = 64\cos\left(2x - \dfrac{\pi}{2}\right)$

(B) $g^{(5)}(x) = -64\cos\left(2x - \dfrac{\pi}{2}\right)$

(C) $g^{(5)}(x) = -64\sin\left(2x - \dfrac{\pi}{2}\right)$

(D) $g^{(5)}(x) = 64\sin\left(2x - \dfrac{\pi}{2}\right)$

11. Evaluate $g'''(0)$.

(A) 0

(B) 16

(C) -1

(D) -16

12. Determine the fifth-degree Taylor polynomial
at $x = 0$.

(A) $g(x) \approx 4x - \dfrac{8}{3}x^3 + \dfrac{8}{15}x^5$

(B) $g(x) \approx 2 - 4x^2 + \dfrac{4}{3}x^4$

(C) $g(x) \approx 4x - 16x^3 + 64x^5$

(D) $g(x) \approx 2 - 8x^2 - 32x^4$

13. Estimate $g(1)$.

(A) 52

(B) -0.6667

(C) 1.867

(D) 0.8

14. Use the error formula to estimate the error
if $\sin^2(0.2)$ is approximated with a Taylor
polynomial of degree four centered at $x = 0$
for $\sin^2 x$.

(A) 0

(B) 0.01333

(C) 0.00002133

(D) 0.06667

15. Find an equation of the line tangent to $y = \sqrt{2x + 9}$ at $x = 0$.

(A) $y - 3 = 3x$

(B) $\frac{1}{9}x = y - 3$

(C) $3y - 9 - x = 0$

(D) $y = \frac{1}{3}x - 3$

6. Find the quadratic approximation of $f(x) = \sqrt{8x + 1}$ around $x = 0$.

7. A Taylor polynomial of degree n approximates the value of cos (0.5) with error < 0.001. Find the smallest value of n.

Free Response Questions

A graphing calculator is required for some questions.

1. Find a quadratic approximating polynomial for $f(x) = \dfrac{1}{2 + x}$ around $x = 0$.

2. (a) Find all roots of $h(x) = 9x^3 - 16x$.

(b) Identify the smallest root of $h(x)$.

(c) Find the second-degree Taylor polynomial for $h(x)$ around the smallest root.

3. (a) For the function $f(x) = e^{3x}$, find the equation of the tangent line at $x = 0$.

(b) Use the equation of the tangent line to estimate $f(0.8)$.

4. (a) Derive a second-degree Taylor polynomial for $f(x) = \sqrt[3]{x}$, centered at $x = 1$.

(b) Use the Taylor polynomial in part (a) to approximate $\sqrt[3]{2}$.

(c) Find the error in the approximation in part (b).

5. (a) Use division to find a Taylor polynomial of degree n for $f(x) = \dfrac{1 + 2x}{1 + x}$.

(b) Write the Taylor polynomial in part (a) in sigma notation.

Lesson 4: Maclaurin Series

- Maclaurin Series Defined
- Maclaurin Series for $\dfrac{1}{1-x}$

Explain: Maclaurin Series Defined

A Maclaurin series is a Taylor polynomial series that is centered at $x = 0$. There are functions whose Maclaurin series is fundamental

in expressing their exact form, including e^x, $\sin(x)$, $\cos(x)$, and $\dfrac{1}{1-x}$. Let us consider the Maclaurin series for $f(x) = e^x$.

For $f(x) = e^x$, we know that $f'(x) = f''(x) = f'''(x) = \ldots f^{(n)}(x) = e^x$. We can evaluate all these functions at $x = 0$ to find that $f'(0) = f''(0) = f'''(0) = \ldots f^{(n)}(0) = e^0 = 1$.

Thus, the series is $f(x) = 1 + \dfrac{x}{1!} + \dfrac{x^2}{2!} + \dfrac{x^3}{3!} + \dfrac{x^4}{4!} + \ldots + \dfrac{x^n}{n!} + \ldots = \displaystyle\sum_{n=0}^{\infty} \dfrac{x^n}{n!} = e^x$.

The fundamental Maclaurin series are

$$e^x = 1 + \frac{x}{1!} + \frac{x^2}{2!} + \frac{x^3}{3!} + \frac{x^4}{4!} + \ldots + \frac{x^n}{n!} + \ldots = \sum_{n=0}^{\infty} \frac{x^n}{n!}$$

$$\sin x = x - \frac{x^3}{3!} + \frac{x^5}{5!} - \frac{x^7}{7!} + \ldots + \frac{(-1)^n x^{2n+1}}{(2n+1)!} + \ldots = \sum_{n=0}^{\infty} \frac{(-1)^n x^{2n+1}}{(2n+1)!}$$

$$\cos x = 1 - \frac{x^2}{2!} + \frac{x^4}{4!} - \frac{x^6}{6!} + \ldots + \frac{(-1)^n x^{2n}}{(2n)!} + \ldots = \sum_{n=0}^{\infty} \frac{(-1)^n x^{2n}}{(2n)!}$$

Using these fundamental Maclaurin series, we can determine the series of other functions, as well as the exact values of other series.

MODEL PROBLEMS

1. Which of the following is the fifth-degree Taylor polynomial for $\sin\frac{1}{2}x$?

(A) $\dfrac{x}{2} - \dfrac{x^3}{2(3)} + \dfrac{x^5}{2(5)}$

(B) $\dfrac{x}{2} - \dfrac{x^3}{2(3!)} + \dfrac{x^5}{2(5!)}$

(C) $\dfrac{x}{2} + \dfrac{x^3}{2^3(3!)} + \dfrac{x^5}{2^5(5!)}$

(D) $\dfrac{x}{2} - \dfrac{x^3}{2^3(3!)} + \dfrac{x^5}{2^5(5!)}$

Solution

We know the series for $\sin x$ is $x - \dfrac{x^3}{3!} + \dfrac{x^5}{5!} - \dfrac{x^7}{7!} + \ldots + \dfrac{(-1)^n x^{2n+1}}{(2n+1)!} + \ldots$

$= \displaystyle\sum_{n=1}^{\infty} \dfrac{(-1)^n x^{2n+1}}{(2n+1)!}$. The fifth-degree polynomial would then be

$\sin x = x - \dfrac{x^3}{3!} + \dfrac{x^5}{5!}$. To find the series for $\sin\frac{1}{2}x$, we substitute $\frac{1}{2}x$ for x in the series to find $\sin\frac{1}{2}x = \frac{1}{2}x - \dfrac{\left(\frac{1}{2}x\right)^3}{3!} + \dfrac{\left(\frac{1}{2}x\right)^5}{5!} = \dfrac{x}{2} - \dfrac{x^3}{2^3 \cdot 3!} + \dfrac{x^5}{2^5 \cdot 5!}$, which is answer option (D).

2. Which of the following is the third-degree Maclaurin polynomial for $f(x) = \ln(1-x)$?

(A) $-x - \dfrac{x^2}{2} - \dfrac{x^3}{3}$

(B) $-x - \dfrac{x^2}{2!} - \dfrac{x^3}{3!}$

(C) $(1-x) - \dfrac{(1-x)^2}{2} + \dfrac{(1-x)^3}{3}$

(D) $-x + \dfrac{x^2}{2!} - \dfrac{x^3}{3!}$

Solution

A Maclaurin polynomial is simply a Taylor polynomial that is centered at $x = 0$. We follow the solution process outlined in Lesson 4.3 to determine the answer. Begin by differentiating the given function three times and then evaluating where needed to determine the coefficients.

FR **3.** Find the exact value of each given series.

(a) $1 - \dfrac{\pi^2}{2!} + \dfrac{\pi^4}{4!} - \dfrac{\pi^6}{6!} + \ldots$

(b) $\dfrac{3\pi}{2} - \dfrac{27\pi^3}{8(3!)} + \dfrac{243\pi^5}{32(5!)} - \dfrac{2187\pi^7}{128(7!)} + \ldots$

Solution

The key to solving problems such as these is to rewrite the given series into something more familiar. For part (a), we see that

$1 - \dfrac{(\pi)^2}{2!} + \dfrac{(\pi)^4}{4!} - \dfrac{(\pi)^6}{6!} + \ldots$ is simply the cosine series where $x = \pi$.

We can substitute to find that $1 - \dfrac{(\pi)^2}{2!} + \dfrac{(\pi)^4}{4!} - \dfrac{(\pi)^6}{6!} + \ldots = \cos\pi = -1$.

Therefore $1 - \dfrac{(\pi)^2}{2!} + \dfrac{(\pi)^4}{4!} - \dfrac{(\pi)^6}{6!} + \ldots = -1$. You try the same idea with part (b).

4. Find the fourth-degree Taylor polynomial centered at $x = 0$ for $f(x) = 1 - \cos x$.

(A) $1 - \dfrac{x^2}{2!} + \dfrac{x^4}{4!}$

(B) $1 + \dfrac{x^2}{2!} + \dfrac{x^4}{4!}$

(C) $-\dfrac{x^2}{2!} + \dfrac{x^4}{4!}$

(D) $\dfrac{x^2}{2!} - \dfrac{x^4}{4!}$

Solution

The series for $\cos x$ is $1 - \frac{x^2}{2!} + \frac{x^4}{4!} - \frac{x^6}{6!} + \dots + \frac{(-1)^n x^{2n}}{(2n)!} + \dots = \sum_{n=1}^{\infty} \frac{(-1)^n x^{2n}}{(2n)!}$. Use this information to derive the required fourth-degree Taylor polynomial.

FR 5. (a) Write the Taylor polynomial of degree four for $f(x) = e^x$.

(b) Use the Taylor polynomial in part (a) to write an expression for $f(\ln x)$.

(c) Using TABLE in the calculator, make a table of five values of x and $f(\ln x)$.

(d) Write a sentence drawing a conclusion based on the values of x and $f(\ln x)$ in the table.

Solution

(a) $e^x = 1 + \frac{x}{1!} + \frac{x^2}{2!} + \frac{x^3}{3!} + \frac{x^4}{4!}$	Use the series on page 336 to write the polynomial.
(b) $f(\ln x) = 1 + \frac{\ln x}{1!} + \frac{(\ln x)^2}{2!} + \frac{(\ln x)^3}{3!} + \frac{(\ln x)^4}{4!}$	We substitute $\ln x$ for x in the series.
(c) Compare 5 values for x and $f(\ln x)$. Write down your values so you can support your answer to (d).	
(d) How do your values of x compare to the values of $f(\ln x)$? Why is this notable?	

FR 6. Find the Maclaurin series for $e^{0.2x}$.

Solution

Use the general series on page 336 to determine this series.

Explain: Maclaurin Series for $\frac{1}{1-x}$

We now derive the Maclaurin series of the function $f(x) = \frac{1}{1-x}$.

For $f(x) = \frac{1}{1-x} = (1-x)^{-1}$, we know that $f'(x) = (1-x)^{-2}$, $f''(x) = 2(1-x)^{-3}$, and $f'''(x) = 6(1-x)^{-4}$. Evaluating these derivatives at $x = 0$, we have $f(0) = f'(0) = 1$, $f''(0) = 2$, and $f'''(0) = 6$. Substituting into the Taylor series expression, we get $f(x) = 1 + x + \frac{2x^2}{2!} + \frac{6x^3}{3!} = 1 + x + x^2 + x^3 + \dots x^n + \dots = \sum_{n=0}^{\infty} x^n$. It is clear that this is a geometric series with a first term 1 and a common ratio of x.

Like other Maclaurin series, we can use this series to generate other similar series or determine the exact value of other series.

MODEL PROBLEMS

FR **1.** Find the Maclaurin polynomial of degree four for $\dfrac{1}{1-3x}$ and write it in sigma notation.

Solution

$\begin{aligned}&1 + (3x) + (3x)^2 + (3x)^3 + (3x)^4 =\\&1 + 3x + 9x^2 + 27x^3 + 81x^4\end{aligned}$	Substitute $3x$ for x in the Maclaurin polynomial of degree four for $\dfrac{1}{1-x}$.
$\displaystyle\sum_{n=0}^{4}(3x)^n$	Express in sigma notation.

FR **2.** Find the Maclaurin polynomial of degree eight for $\dfrac{1}{1+x^2}$ and write the polynomial in sigma notation.

Solution

Substitute $-x^2$ for x in the Maclaurin polynomial of degree four for $\dfrac{1}{1-x}$ and simplify. Then write the polynomial in sigma notation.

FR **3.** Find the Maclaurin polynomial of degree four for $\dfrac{1}{2-x}$ and write the polynomial in sigma notation.

Solution

We begin by rewriting $\dfrac{1}{2-x}$ as $\dfrac{1}{2\left(1-\frac{x}{2}\right)} = \dfrac{1}{2}\cdot\dfrac{1}{1-\frac{x}{2}}$. Now we can

substitute $\dfrac{x}{2}$ for x in the Maclaurin series for $\dfrac{1}{1-x}$. We will need to

multiply our final polynomial by $\dfrac{1}{2}$.

FR **4.** Find a Maclaurin polynomial of degree eight for $\dfrac{x^2}{1-x^2}$ in the following ways:

(a) Use the Maclaurin polynomial for $f(x) = \dfrac{1}{1-x}$.

(b) Show that $\dfrac{x^2}{1-x^2} = \dfrac{1}{1-x^2} - 1$ using the polynomial for $\dfrac{x^2}{1-x^2}$.

(c) Show that $\dfrac{1}{1-x^2} = \dfrac{1}{2}\left(\dfrac{1}{1+x} + \dfrac{1}{1-x}\right)$ using the polynomials $\dfrac{1}{1-x}$ and $\dfrac{1}{1+x}$.

Solution

(a)	$\begin{aligned}\displaystyle\sum_{n=0}^{8}x^n &= 1 + x + x^2 + x^3 + x^4 +\\&\quad x^5 + x^6 + x^7 + x^8\end{aligned}$	We quickly write the eighth-degree polynomial using the given Maclaurin polynomial.
	For $\dfrac{x^2}{1-x^2}$ to take the form $\dfrac{1}{1-x}$ we write $x^2 \cdot \dfrac{1}{1-x^2}$ and substitute x^2 for x. Finish by simplifying.	
(b)	The expansion of $\dfrac{1}{1-x^2}$ is $\displaystyle\sum_{n=0}^{8}x^{2n} = 1 + x^2 + x^4 + x^6 + x^8 + x^{10} + x^{12} + x^{14} + x^{16}$. Use this and your final answer to part (a) to show that the equivalency is true.	

(c) We know that $\dfrac{1}{1-x} = \sum\limits_{n=0}^{\infty} x^n = 1 + x + x^2 + x^3 + x^4 + x^5 + x^6 + x^7 + x^8 + \ldots$ and $\dfrac{1}{1+x} = \sum\limits_{n=0}^{\infty} (-x)^n = 1 - x + x^2 - x^3 + x^4 - x^5 + x^6 - x^7 + x^8 + \ldots$. We can use this information and derivations from part (b) to prove $\dfrac{1}{1-x^2} = \dfrac{1}{2}\left(\dfrac{1}{1+x} + \dfrac{1}{1-x}\right)$ is true.

AP Calculus Exam-Type Questions

Multiple Choice Questions
A graphing calculator is required for some questions.

1. Write the Maclaurin series for $\dfrac{1}{1-3x}$.

   (A) $1 + 3x + 9x^2 + 27x^3 + \ldots$

   (B) $1 - 3x + 3x^2 - 3x^3 + \ldots$

   (C) $1 + 3x + 3x^2 + 3x^3 + \ldots$

   (D) $1 - 3x + 9x^2 - 27x^3 + \ldots$

2. Determine the exact value of the series
   $1 - 3 + 9 - 27 + 81 + \ldots$ using the series for $\dfrac{1}{1-x}$.

   (A) $\dfrac{1}{4}$

   (B) $\dfrac{1}{3}$

   (C) $-\dfrac{1}{2}$

   (D) $\dfrac{1}{2}$

3. Find the third-degree polynomial for
   $f(x) = \dfrac{1}{3+7x}$ that is centered at $x = 0$.

   (A) $1 - \dfrac{7}{3}x + \dfrac{49}{9}x^2 - \dfrac{343}{27}x^3$

   (B) $\dfrac{1}{3} + \dfrac{7}{9}x + \dfrac{49}{27}x^2 + \dfrac{343}{81}x^3$

   (C) $\dfrac{1}{3} - \dfrac{7}{9}x + \dfrac{49}{27}x^2 - \dfrac{343}{81}x^3$

   (D) $1 + \dfrac{7}{3}x + \dfrac{49}{9}x^2 + \dfrac{343}{27}x^3$

4. Find the function whose series is
   $-x + \dfrac{x^3}{3!} - \dfrac{x^5}{5!} + \dfrac{x^7}{7!} + \ldots$.

   (A) $\cos(-x)$

   (B) e^{-x}

   (C) $\sin(-x)$

   (D) $\cos(x)$

5. Find the exact expression of the series
   $\dfrac{1}{3} - \dfrac{4x^2}{3} + \dfrac{16x^4}{3} - \dfrac{64x^6}{3} + \dfrac{256x^8}{3} - \ldots$
   using the series for $\dfrac{1}{1-x}$.

   (A) $\dfrac{1}{3 - 4x^2}$

   (B) $\dfrac{1}{12x^2 + 3}$

   (C) $\dfrac{1}{1 + 12x^2}$

   (D) $\dfrac{1}{3 - 12x^2}$

6. Find the series of the function $\dfrac{1}{x + 6x^2}$ and express it in sigma notation.

   (A) $\sum\limits_{n=0}^{\infty} -6^n x^{n-1}$

   (B) $\sum\limits_{n=0}^{\infty} 6^n x^n$

   (C) $\sum\limits_{n=0}^{\infty} (-6)^n x^{n+1}$

   (D) $\sum\limits_{n=0}^{\infty} (-6)^n x^{n-1}$

7. Find third-degree Maclaurin series for $y = \cos\left(\frac{1}{4}x\right)$.

(A) $1 - \frac{x^2}{16 \cdot 2!} + \frac{x^4}{256 \cdot 4!} - \frac{x^6}{4096 \cdot 6!} + \cdots$

(B) $1 + \frac{x}{4 \cdot 1!} + \frac{x^2}{16 \cdot 2!} + \frac{x^3}{64 \cdot 3!} + \cdots$

(C) $1 - \frac{16x^2}{2!} + \frac{256x^4}{4!} - \frac{4096x^6}{6!} + \cdots$

(D) $1 + 4x + \frac{16x^2}{2!} + \frac{64x^3}{3!} + \cdots$

8. Using the series for $\cos x$, find the series for $\cos\left(x^2\right)$.

(A) $1 - \frac{x^4}{2!} + \frac{x^6}{4!} - \frac{x^8}{6!} + \cdots$

(B) $1 + x^3 + \frac{x^4}{2!} + \frac{x^6}{3!} + \frac{x^8}{4!} + \cdots$

(C) $1 + x^3 + \frac{x^4}{2!} + \frac{x^5}{3!} + \frac{x^6}{4!} + \cdots$

(D) $1 - \frac{x^4}{2!} + \frac{x^8}{4!} - \frac{x^{12}}{6!} + \cdots$

9. Find the approximate value of the function whose series is $1 + \frac{2}{3 \cdot 1!} + \frac{4}{9 \cdot 2!}$ $+ \frac{8}{27 \cdot 3!} + \cdots$

(A) 0.9999

(B) 1.948

(C) 0.01164

(D) 0.5134

10. Find the third-degree Maclaurin series for $y = \sin\left(\frac{1}{3}x\right)$.

(A) $1 - \frac{9x^2}{2!} + \frac{81x^4}{4!} - \frac{729x^6}{6!} + \cdots$

(B) $1 - \frac{x^2}{9 \cdot 2!} + \frac{x^4}{81 \cdot 4!} - \frac{x^6}{729 \cdot 6!} + \cdots$

(C) $3x - \frac{27x^3}{3!} + \frac{243x^5}{5!} - \frac{2187x^7}{7!} + \cdots$

(D) $\frac{x}{3} - \frac{x^3}{27 \cdot 3!} + \frac{x^5}{243 \cdot 5!} - \frac{x^7}{2187 \cdot 7!} + \cdots$

11. Find the series of the function e^{-4x}.

(A) $1 - \frac{4x}{1!} + \frac{16x^2}{2!} - \frac{64x^3}{3!} + \frac{256x^4}{4!} + \cdots$

(B) $1 - \frac{16x^2}{2!} + \frac{256x^4}{4!} - \frac{4096x^6}{6!} + \cdots$

(C) $1 - \frac{4x}{1!} - \frac{16x^2}{2!} - \frac{64x^3}{3!} - \frac{256x^4}{4!} - \cdots$

(D) $1 - \frac{x}{4} + \frac{x^2}{16 \cdot 2!} - \frac{x^3}{64 \cdot 3!} + \frac{x^4}{256 \cdot 4!} - \cdots$

12. Given the Maclaurin series for $\frac{1}{1 - x^2} = 1 + \frac{9}{25} + \frac{81}{625} + \frac{729}{15625} + \cdots$, find the exact value of the series.

(A) $\frac{25}{16}$

(B) $\frac{25}{9}$

(C) $\frac{34}{25}$

(D) $\frac{25}{34}$

13. Find the exact expression of the series $1 - \frac{2}{x} + \frac{4}{x^2} - \frac{8}{x^3} + \frac{16}{x^4} - \cdots$ using the series for $\frac{1}{1 - x}$.

(A) $\frac{x}{x - 2}$

(B) $\frac{x}{2 - x}$

(C) $\frac{x}{x + 2}$

(D) $\frac{2}{2 + x}$

14. Determine the Maclaurin series for $\frac{x^2}{1 - x^5}$ using the series for $\frac{1}{1 - x}$.

(A) $\sum_{n=0}^{\infty} x^{5n-2}$

(B) $\sum_{n=0}^{\infty} x^{25n}$

(C) $\sum_{n=0}^{\infty} x^{\frac{5}{2}n}$

(D) $\sum_{n=0}^{\infty} x^{5n+2}$

15. Determine the series of the function e^{x^2}.

(A) $1 + x^3 + \dfrac{x^4}{2!} + \dfrac{x^5}{3!} + \dfrac{x^6}{4!} + \ldots$

(B) $1 + x^2 + \dfrac{x^4}{2!} + \dfrac{x^6}{3!} + \dfrac{x^8}{4!} + \ldots$

(C) $x^2 - \dfrac{x^4}{2!} + \dfrac{x^8}{4!} - \dfrac{x^{12}}{6!} + \ldots$

(D) $x^2 + x^3 + x^4 + x^5 + x^6 + \ldots$

16. Find fourth-degree Maclaurin series for $y = e^{2x}$.

(A) $\displaystyle\sum_{n=0}^{\infty} \dfrac{2^n x^n}{n!}$

(B) $\displaystyle\sum_{n=0}^{\infty} \dfrac{2x^n}{n!}$

(C) $\displaystyle\sum_{n=1}^{\infty} \dfrac{2^n x^n}{n!}$

(D) $\displaystyle\sum_{n=1}^{\infty} \dfrac{2x^n}{n!}$

17. Find the exact value of the series $2 + 10 + 50 + 250 + 1250 + \ldots$ using the series for $\dfrac{1}{1-x}$.

(A) $\dfrac{2}{5}$

(B) $-\dfrac{1}{3}$

(C) $-\dfrac{1}{2}$

(D) $\dfrac{1}{3}$

Free Response Questions

A graphing calculator is required for some questions.

1. (a) Write the fourth-degree Taylor polynomial for $f(x) = \dfrac{1}{1-x}$ centered at $x = 0$.

(b) Use the Taylor polynomial in part (a) to write a fourth-degree Taylor polynomial for $g(x) = \dfrac{1}{5-x}$. State the center.

(c) Use the Taylor polynomial in part (a) to write a fourth-degree Taylor polynomial for $h(x) = \dfrac{1}{5-x^2}$. State the center.

2. (a) Find the Maclaurin series for $f(x) = \dfrac{1}{9-x^2}$ using the series for $\dfrac{1}{1-x}$.

(b) Determine the sigma notation for the series above.

3. Using the series for $\dfrac{1}{1-x}$, write the sigma notation of the series $\dfrac{2x}{4-x^2}$.

4. (a) Using the series for $g(x) = \cos x$, find the series for $8\cos 2x$.

(b) Write the sigma notation for the above series.

5. (a) Using the series for $\dfrac{1}{1-x}$, find the Maclaurin series for $\dfrac{1}{1-2x^2}$.

(b) Write the exact value of the series $1 + 8 + 64 + 512 + \ldots$

Lesson 5: Power Series

- Power Series Introduction
- Other Methods of Determining a Power Series
- Radius of Convergence and Types of Power Series Convergence
- Radius of Convergence and the Taylor Series
- Radius of Convergence for Term-by-Term Differentiation and Integration

Explain: Power Series Introduction

In Lesson 4.3, we discussed the Taylor polynomial of a function $f(x)$ given by

$$f(x) = f(a) + f'(a)(x - a) + \frac{f''(a)}{2!}(x - a)^2 + \frac{f'''(a)}{3!}(x - a)^3 + \ldots = \sum_{n=0}^{\infty} \frac{f^{(m)}(x)}{m!}(x - a)^m$$

where $\frac{f^{(m)}(x)}{m!}$ are the coefficients of the Taylor series. For the power series,

$\frac{f^{(m)}(c)}{m!} = a_n$, where m is one of the values on n. Thus,

---

A power series centered at c is a series of the form

$$a_0 + a_1(x - c) + a_2(x - c)^2 + a_3(x - c)^3 + \cdots = \sum_{n=0}^{\infty} a_n(x - c)^n,$$

where a_n are constants.

MODEL PROBLEMS

FR 1. What is the power series of $f(x) = \dfrac{3}{4 + 10x}$ centered at $x = 0.1$?

(A) $\displaystyle\sum_{n=0}^{\infty} \frac{3^{n+1}}{5}(x - 0.1)^n$

(B) $\displaystyle\sum_{n=1}^{\infty} \frac{3^{n+1}}{5}(x - 0.1)^n$

(C) $\displaystyle\sum_{n=1}^{\infty} \frac{3^n}{5}(x - 0.1)^n$

(D) $\displaystyle\sum_{n=0}^{\infty} \frac{3^n}{5}(x - 0.1)^n$

Solution

$f'(x) = -30(4 + 10x)^{-2}$ $f''(x) = 600(4 + 10x)^{-3}$ $f'''(x) = -18000(4 + 10x)^{-4}$ $f^4(x) = 720000(4 + 10x)^{-5}$	We determine the first four derivatives of the given function to try to find the pattern.

$f(0.1) = \dfrac{3}{5}$	$a_0 = \dfrac{3}{5} \cdot \dfrac{1}{0!} = \dfrac{3}{5}$	
$f'(x) = -\dfrac{6}{5}$	$a_1 = -\dfrac{6}{5} \cdot \dfrac{1}{1!} = -\dfrac{6}{5}$	Evaluate the derivatives at $c = 1$ and calculate the coefficients, a_n.
$f''(x) = \dfrac{24}{5}$	$a_2 = \dfrac{24}{5} \cdot \dfrac{1}{2!} = \dfrac{12}{5}$	
$f'''(x) = -\dfrac{144}{5}$	$a_3 = -\dfrac{144}{5} \cdot \dfrac{1}{3!} = -\dfrac{24}{5}$	
$f^4(x) = \dfrac{1152}{5}$	$a_4 = \dfrac{1152}{5} \cdot \dfrac{1}{4!} = \dfrac{48}{5}$	

$\dfrac{3}{5} - \dfrac{6}{5}(x - 0.1) + \dfrac{12}{5}(x - 0.1)^2 - \dfrac{24}{5}(x - 0.1)^3$ $+ \dfrac{48}{5}(x - 0.1)^4 + \dots$	Use the formula for power series.
$\dfrac{3}{5} - \dfrac{6}{5}(x - 0.1) + \dfrac{12}{5}(x - 0.1)^2 - \dfrac{24}{5}(x - 0.1)^3$ $+ \dfrac{48}{5}(x - 0.1)^4 + \dots + \dfrac{3^{n+1}}{5}(x - 0.1)^n + \dots$	Introduce the nth term for $n = 1, 2, 3, \dots$.
$= \displaystyle\sum_{n=0}^{\infty} \dfrac{3^{n+1}}{5}(x - 0.1)^n$	Generalize. The correct answer is (A).

FR **2.** Find the power series of $f(x) = \cos\left(\dfrac{1}{4}x\right)$ at $x = 2\pi$.

Solution

$f'(x) = -\dfrac{1}{4}\sin\left(\dfrac{1}{4}x\right)$	$f''(x) = -\dfrac{1}{16}\cos\left(\dfrac{1}{4}x\right)$	
$f'''(x) = \dfrac{1}{64}\sin\left(\dfrac{1}{4}x\right)$	$f^4(x) = \dfrac{1}{256}\cos\left(\dfrac{1}{4}x\right)$	We must calculate some derivatives of the given function to try to determine the pattern.
$f^5(x) = -\dfrac{1}{1024}\sin\left(\dfrac{1}{4}x\right)$	$f^6(x) = -\dfrac{1}{4096}\cos\left(\dfrac{1}{4}x\right)$	
$f^7(x) = \dfrac{1}{16384}\sin\left(\dfrac{1}{4}x\right)$		

$f(2\pi) = \cos\left(\frac{\pi}{2}\right) = 0$	$f'(2\pi) = -\frac{1}{4}\sin\left(\frac{\pi}{2}\right) = -\frac{1}{4}$	Evaluate the function and each of its derivatives at the given value.
$f''(2\pi) = -\frac{1}{16}\cos\left(\frac{\pi}{2}\right) = 0$	$f'''(2\pi) = \frac{1}{64}\sin\left(\frac{\pi}{2}\right) = \frac{1}{64}$	
$f^4(2\pi) = \frac{1}{256}$ $\cos\left(\frac{\pi}{2}\right) = 0$	$f^5(2\pi) = -\frac{1}{1024}$ $\sin\left(\frac{\pi}{2}\right) = -\frac{1}{1024}$	
$f^6(2\pi) = -\frac{1}{4096}$ $\cos\left(\frac{\pi}{2}\right) = 0$	$f^7(2\pi) = \frac{1}{16384}$ $\sin\left(\frac{\pi}{2}\right) = \frac{1}{16384}$	
$a_0 = -\frac{1}{4} \cdot 1 = -\frac{1}{4}$	$a_1 = \frac{1}{64} \cdot \frac{1}{3!} = \frac{1}{64} \cdot \frac{1}{3!}$	Now calculate the coefficients of the series.
$a_2 = -\frac{1}{1024} \cdot \frac{1}{5!}$	$a_3 = \frac{1}{16384} \cdot \frac{1}{7!}$	

Notice that the terms in the series alternate signs and that the numbers that have the factorial symbol are all odd. Examine the work presented so far to see if you can spot any other patterns that will help you write the general term of the power series.

Explain: Other Methods of Determining a Power Series

There are a number of methods of determining the power series of a function. In the last section, we simply used the Taylor series to determine the power series. This is not always possible. Sometimes we must use substitution, properties of the geometric series, or operations such as term-by-term integration or term-by term differentiation.

Substitution We use the series of known functions like cosine, sine, e^x, or $\ln x$. We repeat these known basic series here.

$$\cos x = 1 - \frac{x^2}{2!} + \frac{x^4}{4!} - \frac{x^6}{6!} + \dots + \frac{(-1)^n x^{2n}}{(2n)!} + \dots = \sum_{n=0}^{\infty} \frac{(-1)^n x^{2n}}{(2n)!}$$

$$\sin x = x - \frac{x^3}{3!} + \frac{x^5}{5!} - \frac{x^7}{7!} + \dots + \frac{(-1)^n x^{2n+1}}{(2n+1)!} + \dots = \sum_{n=0}^{\infty} \frac{(-1)^n x^{2n+1}}{(2n+1)!}$$

$$e^x = 1 + \frac{x}{1!} + \frac{x^2}{2!} + \frac{x^3}{3!} + \frac{x^4}{4!} + \dots + \frac{x^n}{n!} + \dots = \sum_{n=0}^{\infty} \frac{x^n}{n!}$$

$$\ln x = (x-1) - \frac{(x-1)^2}{2} + \frac{(x-1)^3}{3} - \frac{(x-1)^4}{4} + \dots + \frac{(-1)^{n+1}(x-1)^n}{n} + \dots$$

MODEL PROBLEMS

1. Find the series of the function $f(x) = 4e^{2x}$ at $x = 0$.

(A) $\displaystyle\sum_{n=0}^{\infty} \frac{(2x)^n}{n!}$

(B) $\displaystyle\sum_{n=0}^{\infty} \frac{2^{n+2}x^n}{n!}$

(C) $\displaystyle\sum_{n=0}^{\infty} \frac{2^{n-2}x^n}{n!}$

(D) $\displaystyle\sum_{n=0}^{\infty} \frac{2^3 x^n}{n!}$

Solution

$e^x = 1 + \dfrac{x}{1!} + \dfrac{x^2}{2!} + \dfrac{x^3}{3!} + \dfrac{x^4}{4!} + \ldots + \dfrac{x^n}{n!} + \ldots = \displaystyle\sum_{n=0}^{\infty} \dfrac{x^n}{n!}$	We will use the series for e^x.
$e^{2x} = 1 + 2x + \dfrac{(2x)^2}{2!} + \dfrac{(2x)^3}{3!} + \dfrac{(2x)^4}{4!} + \ldots +$ $\dfrac{(2x)^n}{n!} + \ldots = \displaystyle\sum_{n=0}^{\infty} \dfrac{(2x)^n}{n!}$	Substitute $2x$.
$4e^{2x} = 4\displaystyle\sum_{n=0}^{\infty} \dfrac{(2x)^n}{n!} = \displaystyle\sum_{n=0}^{\infty} \dfrac{4(2x)^n}{n!} = \displaystyle\sum_{n=0}^{\infty} \dfrac{2^2 2^n x^n}{n!} = \displaystyle\sum_{n=0}^{\infty} \dfrac{2^{n+2}x^n}{n!}$	Determine the series for $f(x) = 4e^{2x}$. The correct answer is (B).

FR **2.** Find the series of $f(x) = \cos(3x)$ at $x = 2$.

Solution

The value $x = 2$ implies $x - 2 = 0$. Therefore, the factor $x - 2$ must be in our expansion.

$f(x) = \cos 3x = \cos\big(3(x - 2 + 2)\big) = \cos\big(3(x - 2) + 6\big)$ $\cos\big(3(x - 2) + 6\big) = \cos\big(3(x - 2)\big)\cos 6 - \sin\big(3(x - 2)\big)\sin 6$	We modify $f(x) = \cos(3x)$, to include the said factor.
$\cos\big(3(x - 2) + 6\big) = 0.9602\cos\big(3(x - 2)\big) + 0.2794\sin\big(3(x - 2)\big)\sin 6$	Calculate the cosine and sine of 6 (in radians).
$0.9602\displaystyle\sum_{n=0}^{\infty} \frac{(-1)^n\big(3(x-2)\big)^{2n}}{(2n)!} + 0.2794\displaystyle\sum_{n=0}^{\infty} \frac{(-1)^n\big(3(x-2)\big)^{2n+1}}{(2n+1)!}$	Generalize.
$\displaystyle\sum_{n=0}^{\infty} \frac{(-1)^n 0.9602\big(3(x-2)\big)^{2n}}{(2n)!} + \displaystyle\sum_{n=0}^{\infty} \frac{(-1)^n 0.2794\big(3(x-2)\big)\big(3(x-2)\big)^{2n}}{(2n+1)(2n)!}$	
$\displaystyle\sum_{n=0}^{\infty} \frac{(-1)^n 0.9602\big(3(x-2)\big)^{2n}}{(2n)!} + \frac{(-1)^n 0.2794\big(3(x-2)\big)\big(3(x-2)\big)^{2n}}{(2n+1)(2n)!}$	Simplify.

$$\sum_{n=0}^{\infty} \frac{(-1)^n 0.9602(2n+1)\big(3(x-2)\big)^{2n} + (-1)^n 0.2794\big(3(x-2)\big)\big(3(x-2)\big)^{2n}}{(2n+1)(2n)!}$$

$$\sum_{n=0}^{\infty} \frac{(-1)^n(1.9204n + 0.8382x - 0.7144)\big(3(x-2)\big)^{2n}}{(2n+1)!}$$

3. Find the series for $f(x) = e^x$ evaluated at $x = 3$.

(A) $\displaystyle\sum_{n=0}^{\infty} \frac{e^3 (x-3)^n}{n!}$

(B) $\displaystyle\sum_{n=0}^{\infty} \frac{(x-3)^n}{n!}$

(C) $\displaystyle\sum_{n=0}^{\infty} \frac{e^{x-3} (x)^n}{n!}$

(D) $\displaystyle\sum_{n=0}^{\infty} \frac{e^3 (x+3)^n}{n!}$

Solution

This problem is similar to Model Problem #1. Use the series for e^x and modify it for $x - 3$.

FR **4.** Find the series for $f(x) = 8e^{2x}$ evaluated at $x = 2$.

Solution

Again, use the series for e^x and modify it as needed.

Geometric Properties We apply this method to functions that are similar to, or can be expressed in, the form $\dfrac{1}{1-x}$ so that we can use the series

$$\frac{1}{1-x} = 1 + x + x^2 + x^3 + \ldots = \sum_{n=0}^{\infty} x^n.$$

We can also use the alternating geometric series,

$$\frac{1}{1+x} = 1 - x + x^2 - x^3 + \ldots = \sum_{n=0}^{\infty} (-1)^{n+1} x^n.$$

MODEL PROBLEMS

1. Find the Taylor series for the function $f(x) = \dfrac{1}{2-x}$ centered at $x = 4$.

(A) $\displaystyle\sum_{n=0}^{\infty} (-1)^{n+1} \frac{(x-4)^n}{2^n}$

(B) $\displaystyle\sum_{n=0}^{\infty} (-1)^{n+1} \frac{(x-4)^n}{2^{n+1}}$

(C) $\displaystyle\sum_{n=0}^{\infty} (-1)^{n+2} \frac{(x-4)^n}{2^{n+1}}$

(D) $\displaystyle\sum_{n=0}^{\infty} (-1)^n \frac{(x-4)^n}{2^n}$

Solution

$f(x) = \dfrac{1}{2-x} = \dfrac{1}{2-x+4-4} = \dfrac{1}{2-(x-4)-4}$ $= \dfrac{1}{-2-(x-4)}$	Our expansion must have the factor $x-4$, so we modify the function.
$f(x) = \dfrac{1}{-2\left(1+\dfrac{(x-4)}{2}\right)} = -\dfrac{1}{2}\cdot\dfrac{1}{1+\dfrac{(x-4)}{2}}$	We must have $1+a$ or $1-a$ where a has the factor $x-4$.
$\dfrac{1}{1+x} = \sum_{n=0}^{\infty}(-1)^{n+1}x^n$ $f(x) = -\dfrac{1}{2}\cdot\dfrac{1}{1+\dfrac{x-4}{2}} = -\dfrac{1}{2}\sum_{n=0}^{\infty}(-1)^{n+1}\left(\dfrac{x-4}{2}\right)^n$ $f(x) = \sum_{n=0}^{\infty}\dfrac{(-1)}{2}(-1)^{n+1}\dfrac{(x-4)^n}{2^n}$	We use the alternating series summation.
$f(x) = \sum_{n=0}^{\infty}(-1)^{n+2}\dfrac{(x-4)^n}{2^{n+1}}$	Simplify. Answer choice (C) is correct.

2. Find the series for $f(x) = \dfrac{4}{1+x}$, centered at $x=1$.

(A) $\displaystyle\sum_{n=0}^{\infty}(-1)^{n+1}\dfrac{(x-1)^n}{2^n}$

(B) $\displaystyle\sum_{n=0}^{\infty}(-1)^{n+1}\dfrac{(x-1)^n}{2^{2n}}$

(C) $\displaystyle\sum_{n=0}^{\infty}(-1)^{n+1}\dfrac{(x-1)^n}{2^{n+1}}$

(D) $\displaystyle\sum_{n=0}^{\infty}(-1)^{n+1}\dfrac{(x-1)^n}{2^{n-1}}$

Solution

$f(x) = \dfrac{4}{1+x} = \dfrac{4}{1+(x-1)+1} = \dfrac{4}{2+(x-1)}$	We modify the function so that it has a factor of $x-1$.
$\dfrac{4}{2+(x-1)} = \dfrac{4}{2\left(1+\dfrac{(x-1)}{2}\right)} = \dfrac{2}{1+\dfrac{(x-1)}{2}}$ $= 2\cdot\dfrac{1}{1+\dfrac{(x-1)}{2}}$	We must have $1+a$ or $1-a$ where a has the factor $x-1$.
Continue solving from here. You know that $\dfrac{1}{1+x} = \sum_{n=0}^{\infty}(-1)^{n+1}x^n$. Use this general pattern to finish the question.	

3. The power series for $f(x) = \dfrac{3}{3-x}$ centered at $x = 0$ is

(A) $\displaystyle\sum_{n=0}^{\infty} \left(\dfrac{x}{3}\right)^n$

(B) $3\displaystyle\sum_{n=0}^{\infty} \left(\dfrac{x}{3}\right)^n$

(C) $\dfrac{1}{3}\displaystyle\sum_{n=0}^{\infty} \left(\dfrac{x}{3}\right)^n$

(D) $\displaystyle\sum_{n=1}^{\infty} \left(\dfrac{x}{3}\right)^n$

Solution

$f(x) = \dfrac{3}{3-x} = \dfrac{3}{3\left(1 - \frac{x}{3}\right)} = \dfrac{1}{\left(1 - \frac{x}{3}\right)}$	We modify the function $f(x) = \dfrac{3}{3-x}$ so that the denominator is of the form $1 - a$ or $1 + a$ where a should be the product of x and a constant. You solve from this point.

FR **4.** Find the power series for $g(x) = \dfrac{8}{x}$ centered at $x = -4$.

Solution

We modify the function to have the term $x + 4$ since $x = -4$ implies $x + 4 = 0$. From this point, restate the denominator in the correct form and then completely simplify the series.

Term-by-Term Differentiation

Before we take a look at some problems where we must use term-by-term differentiation to determine the power series, we highlight how to differentiate a general power series,

$$f(x) = \sum_{n=0}^{\infty} a_n (x - c)^n.$$

Since a_n is a constant with respect to x, we differentiate $(x - c)^n$ using the power rule. The derivative is $n(x - c)^{n-1}$. Thus, we have

$$f'(x) = \sum_{n=1}^{\infty} na_n (x - c)^{n-1}.$$

The summation is from $n = 0$, but we move this ahead to 1 because the first term (the constant) of the original series is lost due to integration. This process is called **index shift**. If the index has to be moved backwards to a number t units less, we add t to the values of n. If it has to be moved forward by t units, we subtract t to the values of n. For example,

$$\sum_{n=3}^{\infty} a_n (x - c)^{n-3} = \sum_{n=0}^{\infty} a_{n+3} (x - c)^n \qquad \text{Moved backwards by 3 units}$$

$$\sum_{n=3}^{\infty} a_n (x - c)^{n-3} = \sum_{n=7}^{\infty} a_{n-4} (x - c)^{n-4} \qquad \text{Moved forward by 4 units}$$

MODEL PROBLEMS

FR 1. Find the power series of $g(x) = \dfrac{2}{(1-2x)^2}$ using term-by-term differentiation.

Solution

$\dfrac{d}{dx}\left(\dfrac{1}{1-2x}\right) = \dfrac{2}{(1-2x)^2}$ and $\dfrac{1}{1-2x} = \sum\limits_{n=0}^{\infty}(2x)^n$ $g(x) = \dfrac{2}{(1-2x)^2} = \dfrac{d}{dx}\left(\dfrac{1}{1-2x}\right) = \dfrac{d}{dx}\left(\sum\limits_{n=0}^{\infty}(2x)^n\right)$ $= \sum\limits_{n=1}^{\infty}2n(2x)^{n-1}$	Determine the expansion of the series $\dfrac{1}{1-2x}$.
$\dfrac{2}{(1-2x)^2} = \sum\limits_{n=0}^{\infty}2(n+1)(2x)^{(n+1)-1} = \sum\limits_{n=0}^{\infty}(2n+2)(2x)^n$	Shift the index.
$g(x) = \dfrac{2}{(1-2x)^2} = \sum\limits_{n=0}^{\infty}(2n+2)(2x)^n$	State the answer.

FR 2. Find the power series of $g(x) = \dfrac{6x}{\left(1-x^2\right)^2}$ using term-by-term differentiation.

Solution

$\dfrac{d}{dx}\left(\dfrac{3}{1-x^2}\right) = \dfrac{6x}{\left(1-x^2\right)^2}$ and $3\cdot\dfrac{1}{1-x^2} = 3\sum\limits_{n=0}^{\infty}\left(x^2\right)^n = \sum\limits_{n=0}^{\infty}3x^{2n}$	Determine the expansion of the series.
$\dfrac{d}{dx}\left(\dfrac{3}{1-x^2}\right) = \dfrac{d}{dx}\sum\limits_{n=0}^{\infty}3x^{2n} = \dfrac{6x}{\left(1-x^2\right)^2}$	From this point, shift the index and simplify the answer. Use the process in Model Problem #1, above, to help you.

Term-by-Term Integration

Like differentiation, we can use integration to determine a power series, $\displaystyle\int\sum_{n=0}^{\infty}a_n(x-c)^n = k + \sum_{n=0}^{\infty}a_n\dfrac{(x-c)^{n+1}}{n+1}$, where k is the constant of integration.

MODEL PROBLEMS

1. Find the power series for $\ln(1-3x)$ using term-by-term integration.

(A) $\displaystyle\sum_{n=0}^{\infty}\dfrac{-3^{n+1}}{n+1}x^{n+1}$

(B) $1 - \displaystyle\sum_{n=0}^{\infty}\dfrac{3^{n+1}}{n+1}x^{n+1}$

(C) $1 + \displaystyle\sum_{n=0}^{\infty}\dfrac{3^{n+1}}{n+1}x^{n+1}$

(D) $\displaystyle\sum_{n=0}^{\infty}\dfrac{3^{n+1}}{n+1}x^{n+1}$

Solution

$\dfrac{3}{1-3x} = 3 \cdot \dfrac{1}{1-3x}$ $3 \cdot \dfrac{1}{1-3x} = 3\sum_{n=0}^{\infty}(3x)^n = \sum_{n=0}^{\infty}3(3x)^n$ $= \sum_{n=0}^{\infty}3 \cdot 3^n x^n = \sum_{n=0}^{\infty}3^{n+1}x^n$	We know that $\ln(1-3x) =$ $\displaystyle\int \dfrac{-3}{1-3x}dx = -\int\dfrac{3}{1-3x}dx$, so we need to determine the series for $\dfrac{3}{1-3x}$ first.
$\ln(1-3x) = -\displaystyle\int\dfrac{3}{1-3x}dx = -3 \cdot \dfrac{1}{1-3x} = -\int\sum_{n=0}^{\infty}3^{n+1}x^n = -\sum_{n=0}^{\infty}\dfrac{3^{n+1}}{n+1}x^{n+1}+k$ $\ln(1-3x) = k - \displaystyle\sum_{n=0}^{\infty}\dfrac{3^{n+1}}{n+1}x^{n+1}$	
$\ln(1-3(0)) = k - \displaystyle\sum_{n=0}^{\infty}\dfrac{3^{n+1}}{n+1}(0)^{n+1}$ $\ln(1-3x) = \displaystyle\sum_{n=0}^{\infty}\dfrac{-3^{n+1}}{n+1}x^{n+1}$	Above, k is the constant of integration. To determine the value of k, we take $x = 0$ and find $\ln 1 = k$ and since $\ln 1 = 0$, we have $k = 0$ and the correct answer is (A).

FR **2.** Find the power series for $\tan^{-1}\left(\dfrac{x}{2}\right)$.

Solution

We know that $\tan^{-1}\left(\dfrac{x}{2}\right) = \displaystyle\int \dfrac{1}{2} \cdot \dfrac{1}{1+\left(\frac{x}{2}\right)^2}\,dx$ and $\dfrac{1}{1+x} = \displaystyle\sum_{n=0}^{\infty}(-1)^{n+1}x^n$ becomes

$\dfrac{1}{2} \cdot \dfrac{1}{1+\left(\frac{x}{2}\right)^2} = \dfrac{1}{2}\displaystyle\sum_{n=0}^{\infty}(-1)^{n+1}\left(\left(\dfrac{x}{2}\right)^2\right)^n = \dfrac{1}{2}\displaystyle\sum_{n=0}^{\infty}(-1)^{n+1}\left(\dfrac{x}{2}\right)^{2n}$. Simplifying

further, we get $\dfrac{1}{2}\displaystyle\sum_{n=0}^{\infty}(-1)^{n+1}\left(\dfrac{x}{2}\right)^{2n} = \dfrac{1}{2}\displaystyle\sum_{n=0}^{\infty}(-1)^{n+1}\dfrac{x^{2^n}}{2^{2n}} = \displaystyle\sum_{n=0}^{\infty}(-1)^{n+1}\dfrac{x^{2^n}}{2^{2n+1}}$.

You try solving from here.

3. Find the power series for $\ln(4-x)$.

(A) $\displaystyle\sum_{n=0}^{\infty}\dfrac{x^{n+1}}{(n+1)4^n}$

(B) $\displaystyle\sum_{n=0}^{\infty}\dfrac{x^{n-1}}{(n-1)4^{n+1}}$

(C) $\displaystyle\sum_{n=0}^{\infty}\dfrac{x^{n+1}}{(n+1)4^{n-1}}$

(D) $\displaystyle\sum_{n=0}^{\infty}\dfrac{x^{n+1}}{(n+1)4^{n+1}}$

Solution

We know that $\ln(4-x) = \displaystyle\int\dfrac{1}{4-x}dx$ and the series expansion is

$\dfrac{1}{4-x} = \dfrac{1}{4\left(1-\frac{x}{4}\right)} = \dfrac{1}{4} \cdot \dfrac{1}{1-\frac{x}{4}}$. Then, since $\dfrac{1}{1-x} = \displaystyle\sum_{n=0}^{\infty}x^n$,

we have $\dfrac{1}{4-x} = \dfrac{1}{4} \cdot \dfrac{1}{1-\frac{x}{4}} = \dfrac{1}{4}\displaystyle\sum_{n=0}^{\infty}\left(\dfrac{x}{4}\right)^n = \displaystyle\sum_{n=0}^{\infty}\dfrac{1}{4}\left(\dfrac{x}{4}\right)^n = \displaystyle\sum_{n=0}^{\infty}\dfrac{x^n}{4 \cdot 4^n} = \displaystyle\sum_{n=0}^{\infty}\dfrac{x^n}{4^{n+1}}$.

You solve from this point.

Explain: Radius of Convergence and Types of Power Series Convergence

A power series may converge or diverge for a given value of x. The number, R, which represents R-units around a point within which the series converges is called the **radius of convergence**. For any point outside this area, the series diverges. We can usually determine the value of R using ratio test (see page 313).

Suppose that c is the center of convergence. Then for a given power series there are only three cases for convergence.

Case I	The series converges for only a single value. By convention, the radius of convergence in this case is $R = 0$.
Case II	The series converges for all the values of x. By definition, the radius of convergence here is $R = \infty$.
Case III	There is some positive number R such that the series will converge when $|x - c| < R$ and will diverge when $|x - c| > R$. We can rewrite these inequalities as $x - c < R < x + c$.

In the event where $x = c \pm R$, the series can either diverge or converge.

MODEL PROBLEMS

FR **1.** Determine if $\displaystyle\sum_{n=0}^{\infty} \frac{(x-2)^n}{n!}$ converges.

Solution

$a_n = \dfrac{(x-2)^n}{n!}$; $a_{n+1} = \dfrac{(x-2)^{n+1}}{(n+1)!}$	We find the values of a_n and $a_{n+1} + 1$ so that we may use the ratio test.
$\displaystyle\lim_{n\to\infty}\left\|\frac{a_{n+1}}{a_n}\right\| = \lim_{n\to\infty}\left\|\frac{(x-2)^{n+1}}{(n+1)!}\cdot\frac{n!}{(x-2)^n}\right\|$ $= \displaystyle\lim_{n\to\infty}\left\|\frac{(x-2)^{n+1}}{(n+1)n!}\cdot\frac{n!}{(x-2)^n}\right\|$ $\displaystyle\lim_{n\to\infty}\left\|\frac{(x-2)}{(n+1)}\right\| = (x-2)\lim_{n\to\infty}\left\|\frac{1}{(n+1)}\right\| = (x-2)\cdot 0 < 1$	Calculate the limit.
Thus, we have R equal to infinity and the radius of convergence is ∞. This summation converges for all values of x.	

2. Determine the radius of convergence for $\displaystyle\sum_{n=0}^{\infty}\frac{x^n}{2}$.

(A) 2

(B) ∞

(C) $\dfrac{1}{2}$

(D) 1

Solution

$a_n = \dfrac{x^n}{2}; a_{n+1} = \dfrac{x^{n+1}}{2}$	Find the values of a_n and $a_n + 1$.
$\lim\limits_{n\to\infty}\left\|\dfrac{a_{n+1}}{a_n}\right\| = \lim\limits_{n\to\infty}\left\|\dfrac{x^{n+1}}{2} \cdot \dfrac{2}{x^n}\right\| = \lim\limits_{n\to\infty}\|x\| = \|x\|$	Calculate the limit. What does this value mean for the radius of convergence?

FR 3. What is the radius of convergence of $\sum\limits_{n=0}^{\infty}(8x)^n$?

Solution

Follow the steps outlined in Model Problems #1 and #2.

FR 4. Find the values of x for which the series $\sum\limits_{n=0}^{\infty}(3x)^n$ converges. State the radius of convergence.

Solution

Use the ratio test to find the limit.

$$\lim\limits_{n\to\infty}\left\|\dfrac{(3x)^{n+1}}{(3x)^n}\right\| = \lim\limits_{n\to\infty}\|3x\| = \|3x\|$$

The series converges if $\|3x\| < 1$. Therefore, the interval of convergence is $\|x\| < \dfrac{1}{3}$, or $-\dfrac{1}{3} < x < \dfrac{1}{3}$, and the radius of convergence is $R = \dfrac{1}{3}$.

To check the endpoints, substitute $x = -\dfrac{1}{3}$ and $x = \dfrac{1}{3}$ into the series.

Both $\sum\limits_{n=0}^{\infty}(-1)^n$ and $\sum\limits_{n=0}^{\infty}(1)^n$ diverge. Therefore, the interval of convergence of $\sum\limits_{n=0}^{\infty}(3x)^n$ is $-\dfrac{1}{3} < x < \dfrac{1}{3}$.

FR 5. Find the interval of convergence for the series $\sum\limits_{n=1}^{\infty}\dfrac{(x-1)^n}{n}$.

Solution Use the ratio test to find the limit.

$$\lim\limits_{n\to\infty}\left\|\dfrac{\dfrac{(x-1)^{n+1}}{n+1}}{\dfrac{(x-1)^n}{n}}\right\| = \lim\limits_{n\to\infty}\left\|\dfrac{n}{n+1}(x-1)\right\| = \|x-1\|$$

The interval of convergence is $\|x-1\| < 1$ or $0 < x < 2$.

To check the endpoints, substitute $x = 0$ and $x = 2$ into the series.

At $x = 0$, the series becomes $\sum\limits_{n=1}^{\infty}\dfrac{(-1)^n}{n}$. This alternating series converges by the alternating series test.

At $x = 2$, the series becomes $\sum\limits_{n=1}^{\infty}\dfrac{1}{n}$. This is a p-series with $p = 1$. Since $p \leq 1$, this series diverges.

Thus, the interval of convergence for the series $\sum\limits_{n=1}^{\infty}\dfrac{(x-1)^n}{n}$ includes 0 but excludes 2. The interval of convergence is $0 \leq x < 2$.

FR **6.** Test the series $\sum_{n=0}^{\infty} \dfrac{(x-3)^n}{3^n}$ for convergence.

Solution

For this problem, you could use the ratio test to find the limit, then check the endpoints to see if the series converges or diverges. You could also look to see if it is a geometric series.

Explain: Radius of Convergence and the Taylor Series

Suppose that the ratio test results in a positive radius of convergence for a given power series. Then we know that power series is a Taylor series of the function to which it converges over the open interval.

MODEL PROBLEM

FR **1.** Determine if $\sum_{n=0}^{\infty} \dfrac{(x-1)^n}{n!}$ is a Taylor series.

Solution

Let $a_n = \dfrac{(x-1)^n}{n!}$ and $a_{n+1} = \dfrac{(x-1)^{n+1}}{(n+1)!}$, then the ratio is

$\dfrac{a_{n+1}}{a_n} = \dfrac{(x-1)^{n+1}}{(n+1)!} \cdot \dfrac{n!}{(x-1)^n} = \dfrac{x-1}{n+1}$. We must have $\dfrac{x-1}{n+1} > 0$ or $x > 1$

for the ratio to be a Taylor series. Thus, the series is a Taylor series for $x > 1$.

FR **2.** Determine if $\sum_{n=0}^{\infty} (-1)^{n+1} \dfrac{(x-1)^{2n}}{2n!}$ is a Taylor series.

Solution

Find the expressions for a_n and a_{n+1} and then use the ratio test to determine convergence.

Explain: Radius of Convergence for Term-by-Term Differentiation and Integration

The derivative and the antiderivative of a power series are again power series. The intervals of convergence of the derivative and the antiderivative of a power series have the same center and radius as the interval of convergence of the original power series, but the endpoints may differ. The interval of convergence of the derivative of a power series may lose endpoints, while the antiderivative of a power series may gain endpoints.

The derivative of $\sum_{n=0}^{\infty} a_n (x-c)^n$ is $\sum_{n=1}^{\infty} n a_n (x-c)^{n-1}$.

The antiderivative of $\sum_{n=0}^{\infty} a_n (x-c)^n$ is $k + \sum_{n=0}^{\infty} a_n \dfrac{(x-c)^{n+1}}{n+1}$, where k is a constant.

354 Main Idea 4: Series

In other words, the derivative and the antiderivative of a power series are obtained by integrating and differentiating, respectively, each individual term in the original series.

MODEL PROBLEMS

FR 1. (a) Write the series for e^x centered at $x = 0$, and find its interval of convergence.

(b) Find the series for the derivative of e^x, and the series for the antiderivative of e^x, and state the interval of convergence for each.

Solution

(a)

$$\lim_{n \to \infty} \left| \frac{\frac{x^{n+1}}{(n+1)}}{\frac{x^n}{n}} \right| = \lim_{n \to \infty} \left| \frac{x}{n+1} \right| = 0$$	The series for e^x is $\sum_{n=0}^{\infty} \frac{x^n}{n!}$. We use the ratio test to determine the interval of convergence. Since the limit is less than 1 for all values of x, the interval of convergence is all real numbers.

(b)

$$\sum_{n=0}^{\infty} \frac{x^n}{n!} = 1 + x + \frac{x^2}{2!} + \frac{x^3}{3!} + \ldots =$$ $$\sum_{n=1}^{\infty} \frac{x^{n-1}}{(n-1)!} = 1 + x + \frac{x^2}{2!} + \frac{x^3}{3!} \ldots$$	We find the derivative for e^x. It is e^x.
$$\sum_{n=1}^{\infty} \frac{x^n}{n!} = 1 + x + \frac{x^2}{2!} + \frac{x^3}{3!} + \ldots \text{ is}$$ $$k + x + \frac{x^2}{2!} + \frac{x^3}{3!} + \ldots = k + \sum_{n=0}^{\infty} \frac{x^{n+1}}{(n+1)!}$$	We find the antiderivative of e^x. It is e^x.
When $x = 0$, $k = 1$ and the series for the antiderivative is identical to the derivative, which is identical to e^x. All three have the same interval of convergence, $-\infty < x < \infty$.	

FR 2. (a) Write the power series for ln x centered at $x = 1$, and find its interval of convergence.

(b) Find the power series for the derivative of ln x and for the antiderivative of ln x. State the interval of convergence for each power series.

Solution

(a)

$$(x - 1) - \frac{(x-1)^2}{2} + \frac{(x-1)^3}{3} -$$ $$\ldots = \sum_{n=1}^{\infty} \frac{(x-1)^n}{n}$$	Determine the power series for ln x, centered at $x = 1$. Determine the interval of convergence using the ratio test. Be sure to test the endpoints.

(b)

$$\sum_{n=1}^{\infty} (-1)^{n+1} (x-1)^{n-1}$$	Find the power series for the derivative of ln x at $x = 1$. What does this mean for the interval of convergence?
Now find the power series for the antiderivative for ln x and determine the interval of convergence.	

AP Calculus Exam-Type Questions

Multiple Choice Questions
No calculator permitted for these questions.

1. Write the power series for $\frac{1}{x}$ centered at $x = 2$.

(A) $\displaystyle\sum_{n=0}^{\infty} -\frac{(x+2)^n}{2^{n+1}}$

(B) $\displaystyle\sum_{n=0}^{\infty} \frac{(-1)^{n+1}(x-2)^n}{2^{n+1}}$

(C) $\displaystyle\sum_{n=0}^{\infty} \frac{(x-2)^n}{2^{n+1}}$

(D) $\displaystyle\sum_{n=0}^{\infty} \frac{(-1)^{n+1}(x+2)^n}{2^{n+1}}$

2. Find the power series for e^{2x} at $x = 1$.

(A) $\displaystyle\sum_{n=0}^{\infty} \frac{2^n(x-1)^n}{n!e^2}$

(B) $\displaystyle\sum_{n=0}^{\infty} \frac{2(x+1)^n e^2}{n!}$

(C) $\displaystyle\sum_{n=0}^{\infty} \frac{2(x-1)^n}{n!e^2}$

(D) $\displaystyle\sum_{n=0}^{\infty} \frac{2^n(x-1)^n e^2}{n!}$

3. Determine the radius of convergence of the series $\displaystyle\sum_{n=0}^{\infty} \frac{(x+2)^{n+1}}{2^n}$.

(A) 4

(B) $\frac{1}{2}$

(C) 2

(D) 1

4. Find the power series for e^{-x} at $x = -1$.

(A) $\displaystyle\sum_{n=0}^{\infty} -\frac{(-1)^n(x+1)^n e}{n!}$

(B) $\displaystyle\sum_{n=0}^{\infty} -\frac{(x-1)^n}{n!e}$

(C) $\displaystyle\sum_{n=0}^{\infty} -\frac{(-1)^n(x+1)^n}{n!e}$

(D) $\displaystyle\sum_{n=0}^{\infty} -\frac{(x-1)^n e}{n!}$

5. Determine the radius of convergence for the series $\displaystyle\sum_{n=0}^{\infty} \frac{(x-1)^n}{4^n}$.

(A) 4

(B) 1

(C) $\frac{1}{4}$

(D) $\frac{1}{2}$

6. Find the power series of $f(x) = \tan^{-1}(x)$ centered at $x = 0$.

(A) $\displaystyle\sum_{n=0}^{\infty} \frac{(-1)^{n+1}x^{n+1}}{n+1}$

(B) $\displaystyle\sum_{n=0}^{\infty} (-1)^{n+1}x^{2n}$

(C) $\displaystyle\sum_{n=0}^{\infty} \frac{(-1)^{n+1}x^{2n+1}}{2n+1}$

(D) $\displaystyle\sum_{n=0}^{\infty} (-1)^{n+1}x^n$

7. Find the radius of convergence of $\displaystyle\sum_{n=0}^{\infty}\frac{8(x+1)^{n+1}}{2^n}$.

(A) 4

(B) $\dfrac{1}{8}$

(C) $\dfrac{1}{4}$

(D) 8

8. Find the power series of $f(x) = \dfrac{1}{2+x}$ centered at $x = -1$.

(A) $\displaystyle\sum_{n=0}^{\infty}(x+1)^n$

(B) $\displaystyle\sum_{n=0}^{\infty}(-1)^{n+1}(x+1)^n$

(C) $\displaystyle\sum_{n=0}^{\infty}\frac{(x-1)^n}{3^{n+1}}$

(D) $\displaystyle\sum_{n=0}^{\infty}\frac{(-1)^{n+1}(x-1)^n}{3^{n+1}}$

9. The power series $\displaystyle\sum_{n=1}^{\infty}\frac{(-1)^{n+1}(3x-1)^n}{n}$ is equivalent to $f(x) =$

(A) e^{3x-1}

(B) $\ln(3x-1)$

(C) $\ln(3x)$

(D) $\ln(3x) - 1$

10. The interval of convergence of the series $\displaystyle\sum_{n=0}^{\infty}\frac{3^n(x-2)^n}{n!}$ is

(A) $(-\infty, \infty)$

(B) $[2, \infty)$

(C) $(-\infty, 2]$

(D) $\left(\dfrac{5}{3}, \dfrac{7}{3}\right)$

11. For which of the following values of x does the series $\displaystyle\sum_{n=0}^{\infty}\left(\frac{5x}{3}\right)^n$ converge?

(A) $|x| \le \dfrac{3}{5}$

(B) $|x| < \dfrac{3}{5}$

(C) $|x| \le \dfrac{5}{3}$

(D) $|x| \le 1$

12. The number e can be represented by which of the following power series?

(A) $\displaystyle\sum_{n=0}^{\infty}\frac{(-1)^n}{n!}$

(B) $\displaystyle\sum_{n=1}^{\infty}\frac{(-1)^n}{n!}$

(C) $\displaystyle\sum_{n=0}^{\infty}\frac{1}{n!}$

(D) $\displaystyle\sum_{n=1}^{\infty}\frac{1}{n!}$

13. Find the interval of convergence of $\displaystyle\sum_{n=0}^{\infty}\frac{(x+4)^n}{n!}$

(A) Converges for the interval $|x+4| < 1$.

(B) Converges only for the point $x = 4$.

(C) Converges for all the values of x.

(D) Converges for the interval $|x+4| < \dfrac{1}{4}$.

14. The series $\displaystyle\sum_{n=0}^{\infty}\frac{(2x-1)^n}{n!}$ converges for which of the following values of x?

(A) all real numbers

(B) $0 < x < 1$

(C) $0 < x \le 1$

(D) No values of x

Free Response Questions

A graphing calculator is required for some questions.

1. Find the interval of convergence of $\displaystyle\sum_{n=0}^{\infty} \frac{(x-3)^{2n}}{2^{2n+1}}$.

2. Test the following series for convergence. If the series converges, give the interval of convergence:

   (a) $\displaystyle\sum_{n=0}^{\infty} \frac{(x-4)^{2n}}{4^{2n}}$

   (b) $\displaystyle\sum_{n=0}^{\infty} \frac{(x-4)^{2n}}{4^{2n+1}}$

   (c) $\displaystyle\sum_{n=0}^{\infty} \frac{(x+4)^{2n}}{4^{2n}}$

3. Find the power series for $\dfrac{1}{(1-x)^2}$ using the power series for $\dfrac{1}{1-x}$, and state its interval of convergence.

4. Find the power series for $\dfrac{1}{(1-x)^3}$ using the power series for $\dfrac{1}{1-x}$, and state its interval of convergence.

5. (a) Find a function $f(x)$ that represents the sum of the series $\displaystyle\sum_{n=0}^{\infty} \left(\frac{x}{3}\right)^n$, and state the domain of $f(x)$.

   (b) Find a function $g(x)$ where $g'(x) = f(x)$.

   (c) Write the power series for $g(x)$, and state the values of x for which the power series converges to $g(x)$.

   (d) Approximate $g(1)$ to three decimal places.

6. Rewrite $\frac{1}{x}$ as $\dfrac{1}{1+(x-1)}$ to

   (a) Write a Taylor series for $\frac{1}{x}$ centered at $x = 1$.

   (b) Find the interval of convergence for the series in part (a).

   (c) Find the Taylor series centered at $x = 1$ for the derivative of $\frac{1}{x}$, and find the interval of convergence.

   (d) Find the Taylor series centered at $x = 1$ for $\displaystyle\int \frac{1}{x}\,dx$, and find the interval of convergence.

7. (a) Write a power series for $f(x) = e^{2x} - 1$ and state its interval of convergence.

   (b) Find the power series for $f'(x)$ by differentiating the power series found in part (a).

   (c) Use the power series for $f(x)$ to find the power series for $f'(x)$ by a method other than taking the derivative.

   (d) Write an expression for $f'(0.5)$ in sigma notation.

CALCULUS BC

SECTION I, Part A

Time – 60 minutes
Number of problems – 30

A graphing calculator is not permitted for these problems.

1. The interval of convergence of the series $\sum_{n=1}^{\infty} \frac{(x-1)^n}{n}$ is

   (A) $0 \le x < 2$

   (B) $0 < x < 2$

   (C) $0 < x \le 2$

   (D) $0 \le x \le 2$

2. The series $\sum_{n=0}^{\infty} \frac{(2x-1)^n}{n!}$ converges for which of the following values of x?

   (A) All real numbers

   (B) $0 < x < 1$

   (C) $0 < x \le 1$

   (D) $0 \le x \le 1$

3. For which of the following values of x does the series $\sum_{n=0}^{\infty} \left(\frac{5x}{3}\right)^n$ converge?

   (A) All real numbers

   (B) $|x| \le \frac{3}{5}$

   (C) $|x| < \frac{3}{5}$

   (D) $|x| \le \frac{5}{3}$

4. The power series for $f(x) = \frac{3}{3-x}$ centered at $x = 0$ is

   (A) $\sum_{n=0}^{\infty} \left(\frac{x}{3}\right)^n$

   (B) $3\sum_{n=0}^{\infty} \left(\frac{x}{3}\right)^n$

   (C) $9\sum_{n=0}^{\infty} \left(\frac{x}{3}\right)^n$

   (D) $\frac{1}{3}\sum_{n=0}^{\infty} \left(\frac{x}{3}\right)^n$

5. The number e can be represented by which of the following power series?

   (A) $\sum_{n=0}^{\infty} \frac{(-1)^n}{n!}$

   (B) $\sum_{n=1}^{\infty} \frac{(-1)^n}{n!}$

   (C) $\sum_{n=0}^{\infty} \frac{1}{n!}$

   (D) $\sum_{n=1}^{\infty} \frac{1}{n!}$

6. The power series $\sum_{n=1}^{\infty} \frac{(-1)^{n+1}(3x-1)^n}{n}$ is equivalent to $f(x) =$

   (A) e^{3x-1}

   (B) $\ln(3x-1)$

   (C) $\ln(3x)$

   (D) $\ln(3x) - 1$

7. For values of x in the interval $-5 < x < 5$, the sum of the series $\sum_{n=1}^{\infty} \left(\frac{x}{5}\right)^n$ is equal to

   (A) $\frac{x}{5-x}$

   (B) $\frac{5}{5-x}$

   (C) $\frac{1}{5-x}$

   (D) $\frac{5}{x-5}$

8. On the interval $(-3, 3)$, the sum of the series $\sum_{n=1}^{\infty} n\left(\frac{x}{3}\right)^{n-1}$ can be represented by

   (A) $f(x) = \frac{9}{(3-x)^2}$

   (B) $f(x) = \frac{3}{(3-x)^2}$

   (C) $f(x) = -\frac{3}{(3-x)^2}$

   (D) $f(x) = \frac{x}{3-x}$

9. Find the error estimate in approximating $\sum\limits_{n=1}^{\infty} (-1)^n \frac{1}{n}$ with the first ten terms of the series.

(A) $\frac{1}{9}$

(B) $\frac{1}{10}$

(C) $\frac{1}{11}$

(D) $\frac{1}{12}$

10. What type of series is $\sum\limits_{n=0}^{\infty} \left(\frac{2}{5}\right)^n$?

(A) p-series

(B) geometric series

(C) alternating series

(D) telescoping series

11. What type of series is $\sum\limits_{n=2}^{\infty} \left(\frac{1}{n-1} - \frac{1}{n}\right)$?

(A) p-series

(B) geometric series

(C) alternating series

(D) telescoping series

12. What type of series is $\sum\limits_{n=1}^{\infty} \frac{(-1)^{n-1} n!}{n^n}$?

(A) p-series

(B) geometric series

(C) alternating series

(D) telescoping series

13. $\sum\limits_{n=1}^{\infty} \left(-\frac{1}{5}\right)^n$

(A) converges to $-\frac{1}{6}$.

(B) converges to $-\frac{1}{5}$.

(C) converges to $-\frac{1}{4}$.

(D) converges to 0.

14. The series $1 - \frac{1}{2} + \frac{1}{3} - \frac{1}{4} + \cdots$

(A) converges to $\frac{2}{3}$.

(B) converges to ln 2.

(C) converges to e.

(D) diverges.

15. Find the sum $\sum\limits_{n=1}^{\infty} n \left(\frac{1}{4}\right)^{n-1}$.

(A) $\frac{9}{16}$

(B) $\frac{16}{25}$

(C) $\frac{4}{3}$

(D) $\frac{16}{9}$

16. The series $\sum\limits_{n=0}^{\infty} \frac{(-1)^n \pi^{2n+1}}{(2n+1)!}$ has a sum of

(A) -1

(B) 0

(C) 1

(D) π

17. $\sum\limits_{n=1}^{\infty} \frac{(-1)^n \left(\frac{\pi}{3}\right)^{2n}}{(2n)!} =$

(A) $-\frac{1}{2}$

(B) $\frac{1}{2}$

(C) $\frac{3}{3-\pi}$

(D) $\frac{3}{3+\pi}$

18. The series $\sum\limits_{n=0}^{\infty} \left(\frac{2^n}{3^n} - 1\right)$

(A) converges to $\frac{2}{3}$.

(B) converges to 2.

(C) converges to 0.

(D) diverges.

19. Determine the sum of the series $\frac{1}{2} - \frac{1}{6} + \frac{1}{24} - \cdots$

(A) 1

(B) 2

(C) $\frac{1}{e}$

(D) e

20. The error in estimating e^{-2} using five terms of the Taylor series for e^{-x} is not greater than

(A) $\frac{2^4}{4!}$

(B) $\frac{2^5}{5!}$

(C) $\frac{2^6}{6!}$

(D) $\frac{2^5}{5!}$

21. The interval of convergence of the series $\sum\limits_{n=0}^{\infty}\dfrac{3^n(x-2)^n}{n!}$ is

(A) $(-\infty, \infty)$
(B) $[2, \infty)$
(C) $[-\infty, 2)$
(D) $\left(\dfrac{5}{3}, \dfrac{7}{3}\right)$

22. Find the values of x for which the series $\sum\limits_{n=0}^{\infty}\dfrac{5^n}{2^n}(x+1)^n$ converges.

(A) Nwo values of x
(B) $-\dfrac{7}{5} < x < -\dfrac{3}{5}$
(C) $-\dfrac{5}{2} < x < \dfrac{5}{2}$
(D) $x = 0$ only

23. The series represented by $\sum\limits_{n=0}^{\infty}\left(\dfrac{1}{5}\right)^n$ is

(A) a p-series.
(B) a geometric series.
(C) a telescoping series.
(D) a power series.

24. $\sum\limits_{n=1}^{\infty}\dfrac{2^n}{n}$ can be described as a series that is

(A) geometric and convergent.
(B) alternating.
(C) a power series.
(D) divergent.

25. The fourth-degree Taylor polynomial for $\dfrac{1}{1-x}$ centered at $x = -1$ is

(A) $\sum\limits_{n=0}^{4} x^n$

(B) $\sum\limits_{n=0}^{4} (x+1)^n$

(C) $\sum\limits_{n=0}^{4} \dfrac{(x+1)^n}{2^{n+1}}$

(D) $\sum\limits_{n=0}^{4} \dfrac{(x+1)^n}{2^n}$

26. What is the sum of the series $\sum\limits_{n=0}^{\infty}\dfrac{\left(\frac{\pi}{6}\right)^{2n}}{n!}$, if it exists?

(A) $\dfrac{6}{6-\pi}$

(B) $\dfrac{1}{2}$

(C) $\dfrac{\sqrt{3}}{2}$

(C) $e^{\pi^2/36}$

27. $\dfrac{d}{dx}\left(\sum\limits_{n=1}^{\infty}\dfrac{x^{2n}}{n!}\right) =$

(A) $-2x\sin(x^2)$
(B) $\cos(x^2)$
(C) e^{x^2}
(D) $2xe^{x^2}$

28. The series $\sum\limits_{n=0}^{\infty}\left(\dfrac{2^n - n^2}{3^n}\right)$

(A) converges to 0.
(B) converges to $\dfrac{32}{81}$.
(C) converges to $\dfrac{7}{243}$.
(D) converges but the sum can only be approximated.

29. How many terms of the series $\sum\limits_{n=1}^{\infty}(-1)^{n+1}\dfrac{1}{n^4}$ are needed to approximate the sum of the series with error <0.001?

(A) 3
(B) 4
(C) 5
(D) 6

30. Find the value of r (if it exists) in the series $3 - \dfrac{9}{2} + \dfrac{27}{4} - \cdots$.

(A) $-\dfrac{3}{2}$

(B) $-\dfrac{2}{3}$

(C) $\dfrac{2}{3}$

(D) $\dfrac{3}{2}$

Main Idea 4: Series (BC Exam Only)
Summary Assessment

CALCULUS BC

SECTION I, Part B
Time – 45 minutes
Number of problems – 15

A graphing calculator is required for these problems.

1. Use the power series for e^x to find the exact value of $\sum_{n=0}^{\infty} \frac{(0.5)^n}{n!}$.

   (A) 1
   (B) $\sqrt{2}$
   (C) $\sqrt{e}$
   (D) e

2. Use the power series for $\sin x$ to find the exact value of $\sum_{n=0}^{\infty} (-1)^n \frac{\left(\frac{\pi}{2}\right)^{2n+1}}{(2n+1)!}$.

   (A) 0
   (B) 1
   (C) $\frac{\pi}{2}$
   (D) π

3. For the series $\sum_{n=1}^{\infty} \frac{1}{4^n n^4}$, which test is most appropriate to show its convergence or divergence?

   (A) ratio test
   (B) limit comparison test
   (C) direct comparison test
   (D) integral test

4. For the series $\sum_{n=1}^{\infty} \frac{n}{\sqrt{n^2 + 1}}$, which test is most appropriate to show its convergence or divergence?

   (A) ratio test
   (B) limit comparison test
   (C) direct comparison test
   (D) integral test

5. For the series $\sum_{n=0}^{\infty} \frac{2^n}{n!}$, which test is most appropriate to show its convergence or divergence?

   (A) ratio test
   (B) limit comparison test
   (C) direct comparison test
   (D) integral test

6. For what values of x does $\sum_{n=0}^{\infty} (2x)^{2n}$ converge?

   (A) For no values of x
   (B) $|x| < \frac{1}{2}$
   (C) $|x| \leq \frac{1}{2}$
   (D) $|x| < 2$

7. Find the interval of convergence for $\sum_{n=1}^{\infty} \frac{(2x)^n}{n^2}$.

   (A) $\left(-\frac{1}{2}, \frac{1}{2}\right)$
   (B) $\left[-\frac{1}{2}, \frac{1}{2}\right)$
   (C) $\left(-\frac{1}{2}, \frac{1}{2}\right]$
   (D) $\left[-\frac{1}{2}, \frac{1}{2}\right]$

8. Find the interval of convergence for $\sum_{n=0}^{\infty} \frac{(x-5)^{n+1}}{n+1}$.

   (A) $(4, 6)$
   (B) $[4, 6)$
   (C) $(4, 6]$
   (D) $[4, 6]$

9. Find the interval of convergence for $\sum\limits_{n=1}^{\infty}(-1)^{n+1}\dfrac{(2x-3)^{n}}{n^{3/2}}$.

(A) $(1, 2)$

(B) $[1, 2)$

(C) $(1, 2]$

(D) Not given

10. Find the sum of the series
$$\left(1-\frac{1}{3}\right)+\left(\frac{1}{3}-\frac{1}{5}\right)+\left(\frac{1}{5}-\frac{1}{7}\right)+\cdots.$$

(A) $\dfrac{2}{3}$

(B) $\dfrac{4}{5}$

(C) $\dfrac{6}{7}$

(D) 1

11. Which of the following series is absolutely convergent?

(A) $\sum\limits_{n=1}^{\infty}\dfrac{(-1)^{n+1}}{n^{0.99}}$

(B) $\sum\limits_{n=1}^{\infty}\dfrac{(-1)^{n+1}}{n^{2}}$

(C) $\sum\limits_{n=1}^{\infty}\dfrac{(-1)^{n+1}}{n}$

(D) $\sum\limits_{n=1}^{\infty}(-1)^{n+1}3^{n}$

12. Of the following, which series is conditionally convergent?

(A) $\sum\limits_{n=1}^{\infty}\dfrac{(-1)^{n+1}}{n^{2}}$

(B) $\sum\limits_{n=1}^{\infty}\dfrac{(-1)^{n+1}}{\sqrt{n}}$

(C) $\sum\limits_{n=1}^{\infty}\dfrac{(-1)^{n+1}}{n^{3}}$

(D) $\sum\limits_{n=1}^{\infty}\dfrac{(-1)^{n+1}}{n!}$

13. $\sum\limits_{n=0}^{\infty}\left(\dfrac{2}{5}\right)^{n}=$

(A) $\dfrac{2}{5}$

(B) $\dfrac{2}{3}$

(C) 1

(D) $\dfrac{5}{3}$

14. What does the series $\dfrac{\pi}{2}\sum\limits_{n=0}^{\infty}\cos(n\pi)\dfrac{\left(\frac{\pi}{2}\right)^{2n}}{(2n+1)!}$ converge to?

(A) -1

(B) 0

(C) 1

(D) $\dfrac{2}{2-\pi}$

15. For what value(s) of p does $\sum\limits_{n=2}^{\infty}\dfrac{(-1)^{n}}{(\ln n)^{p}}$ converge?

(A) $p \neq 0$

(B) $p < 0$

(C) $p > 0$

(D) $p \geq 1$

CALCULUS BC

SECTION II, Part A

Time – 30 minutes
Number of problems – 2

> A graphing calculator is required for these problems.

1. Consider the series $\dfrac{x^3}{2!} - \dfrac{x^5}{4!} + \dfrac{x^7}{6!} - \cdots$.

   (a) Find a function, $f(x)$, to which the series converges.

   (b) If $F'(x) = f(x)$, find a power series representation for $F(x)$.

2. If $f(x)$ is a function with $f(1) = 1$, $f'(1) = 2$, $f''(1) = 3$, and $f'''(1) = -2$,

   (a) Write a third-degree Taylor polynomial, $P_3(x)$, for $f(x)$ centered at $x = 1$.

   (b) Use the polynomial in part (a) to approximate $f(0.9)$.

   (c) Explain why $P_3(0.9) \neq f(0.9)$.

CALCULUS BC

SECTION II, Part B

Time – 60 minutes
Number of problems – 4

A graphing calculator is not permitted for these problems.

1. (a) Find a function $f(x)$ that represents the sum of the series $\sum_{n=0}^{\infty}\left(\frac{x}{3}\right)^n$, and state the domain of $f(x)$.

   (b) Find a function $g(x)$ where $g'(x) = f(x)$.

   (c) Write the power series for $g(x)$, and state the values of x for which the power series converges to $g(x)$.

2. Given a function $f(x)$ with $f(2) = \frac{1}{2}$,
   $f'(2) = -\frac{1}{4}, f''(2) = \frac{1}{4}, f'''(2) = -\frac{3}{8}$,

   (a) Write a Taylor polynomial of degree 3 for $f(x)$ centered at $x = 2$.

   (b) Write a Taylor polynomial of degree 2 for $f'(x)$ centered at $x = 2$.

   (c) Write a Taylor polynomial of degree 4 for $\int f(x)\,dx$ centered at $x = 2$.

3. Rewrite $\frac{1}{x}$ as $\frac{1}{1 + (x - 1)}$ to

   (a) write a Taylor series for $\frac{1}{x}$ centered at $x = 1$.

   (b) find the interval of convergence for the series in part (a).

   (c) find the Taylor series centered at $x = 1$ for the derivative of $\frac{1}{x}$, and find the interval of convergence.

   (d) find the Taylor series centered at $x = 1$ for $\int \frac{1}{x}\,dx$, and find the interval of convergence.

4. Use the series $1 - x + x^2 - x^3 + x^4 - \cdots$
   $= \frac{1}{1 + x}$ for $|x| < 1$ to find the exact value of each of the following series:

   (a) $1 - \frac{1}{2} + \frac{1}{4} - \frac{1}{8} + \cdots$

   (b) $\sum_{n=0}^{\infty}(-1)^n\left(\frac{1}{3}\right)^n$

   (c) $\sum_{n=1}^{\infty}(-1)^{n+1}(0.7)^n$

Main Idea 4: Summary Assessment

CORRELATION CHART

Use the given charts to mark the questions you missed. Then go back and review the suggested lesson(s) to improve your understanding of the concepts.

Section I, Part A (No Calculator Allowed)

Missed?	Question Number	Review the information in...
	1	Lesson 1, Lesson 2
	2	Lesson 1, Lesson 2
	3	Lesson 1, Lesson 2
	4	Lesson 5
	5	Lesson 5
	6	Lesson 5
	7	Lesson 1
	8	Lesson 1
	9	Lesson 3
	10	Lesson 3
	11	Lesson 1
	12	Lesson 1
	13	Lesson 1, Lesson 2
	14	Lesson 1
	15	Lesson 2
	16	Lesson 2
	17	Lesson 2
	18	Lesson 1
	19	Lesson 1
	20	Lesson 3
	21	Lesson 1, Lesson 2, Lesson 5
	22	Lesson 1, Lesson 2, Lesson 5
	23	Lesson 1
	24	Lesson 1, Lesson 2
	25	Lesson 3
	26	Lesson 1, Lesson 2, Lesson 5
	27	Lesson 1, Lesson 2, Lesson 5
	28	Lesson 1
	29	Lesson 3
	30	Lesson 1

Section I, Part B (Calculator Required)

Missed?	Question Number	Review the information in...
	1	Lesson 5
	2	Lesson 5
	3	Lesson 2
	4	Lesson 2
	5	Lesson 2
	6	Lesson 1
	7	Lesson 1, Lesson 2
	8	Lesson 1, Lesson 2
	9	Lesson 1, Lesson 2
	10	Lesson 1
	11	Lesson 2
	12	Lesson 2
	13	Lesson 1, Lesson 2
	14	Lesson 1
	15	Lesson 1, Lesson 2

Section II, Part A (Calculator Required)

Missed?	Question Number	Review the information in...
	1(a)	Lesson 2, Lesson 5
	1(b)	
	2(a)	Lesson 3, Lesson 4
	2(b)	
	2(c)	

Section II, Part B (No Calculator Allowed)

Missed?	Question Number	Review the information in...
	1(a)	Lesson 5
	1(b)	
	1(c)	
	2(a)	Lesson 3, Lesson 4
	2(b)	
	2(c)	
	3(a)	Lesson 3, Lesson 4
	3(b)	
	3(c)	
	3(d)	
	4(a)	Lesson 1, Lesson 2, Lesson 5
	4(b)	
	4(c)	

AB Model Examination 1

CALCULUS AB

SECTION I, Part A
Time – 60 minutes
Number of problems – 30

> A graphing calculator is not permitted for these problems.

1. If $xy - y = 2x + 4$, $\dfrac{dy}{dx}$ is

   (A) $\dfrac{y-2}{x-1}$

   (B) $\dfrac{2-y}{x-1}$

   (C) $\dfrac{y-6}{x-1}$

   (D) $\dfrac{2}{x-1}$

2. Let $f(x)$ be an odd function and $g(x)$ be and even function. Which of the following statements are true?

   I. $\displaystyle\int_{-2}^{2} f(x)\,dx = 0$

   II. $\displaystyle\int_{-2}^{2} g(x)\,dx = 0$

   III. $\displaystyle\int_{-2}^{2} f(x)g(x)\,dx = 0$

   (A) II
   (B) III
   (C) I and II
   (D) I and III

3. $\displaystyle\lim_{x\to 0} \dfrac{\sin 3x}{5x} =$

   (A) $\dfrac{3}{5}$

   (B) $\dfrac{5}{3}$

   (C) 3

   (D) 5

4. For which of the following x-values on the graph of $y = 2x - x^2$ is $\dfrac{dy}{dx}$ the largest?

   (A) –2.7
   (B) –2.2
   (C) 1
   (D) 2.7

5. If $y = e^{2x} + \tan 2x$, then $y'(\pi) =$

   (A) $2e^{2\pi}$
   (B) $e^{2\pi} + 1$
   (C) $2e^{2\pi} + 2$
   (D) $2e^{\pi} - 2$

6. Write the equation of the line tangent to $y = e^{x+1}$ at $x = 0$.

   (A) $y = ex + e$
   (B) $y = x + 1$
   (C) $y = x + e$
   (D) $y = ex + 1$

7. If the acceleration of a particle is given by $a(t) = 2e^t$ and when $t = 1$ the velocity is 2, then $v(0)$ is

   (A) 0
   (B) $2 - 2e$
   (C) $2 - \dfrac{1}{2}e$
   (D) $4 - 2e$

8. If $3xy + 2y^2 = 5$, find $\dfrac{dy}{dx}$ at $(1, 1)$.

   (A) $-\dfrac{3}{7}$
   (B) 0
   (C) $\dfrac{3}{7}$
   (D) 7

9. The graph of $y = \dfrac{\ln(1-x)}{x+1}$ has vertical asymptote(s) at

(A) $x = 1$

(B) $x = 0$

(C) $x = \pm 1$

(D) $x = -1$

10. $\dfrac{d}{dt}\displaystyle\int_t^{t^2} \dfrac{1}{x}\,dx =$

(A) $\dfrac{1}{t^2}$

(B) $\ln(t)$

(C) $\ln(t^2)$

(D) $\dfrac{1}{t}$

11. $\displaystyle\lim_{h\to 0} \dfrac{\cos\left(\dfrac{\pi}{4}+h\right) - \cos\left(\dfrac{\pi}{4}\right)}{h} =$

(A) $-\dfrac{\sqrt{3}}{2}$

(B) $-\dfrac{\sqrt{2}}{2}$

(C) 0

(D) $\dfrac{\sqrt{2}}{2}$

12. $\displaystyle\int (3x^2 - \cos x)\,dx =$

(A) $6x + \sin(x) + c$

(B) $x^3 + \sin(x) + c$

(C) $x^3 - \sin(x) + c$

(D) $6x - \sin(x) + c$

13. Find the area under the curve $y = x^2 + 1$ on the interval $[1, 2]$.

(A) $\dfrac{7}{3}$

(B) 3

(C) $\dfrac{10}{3}$

(D) 4

14. $\displaystyle\int_{-1}^{2} \dfrac{x}{x^2+1}\,dx =$

(A) $\ln\dfrac{2}{5}$

(B) 0

(C) $\dfrac{1}{2}\ln\dfrac{5}{2}$

(D) $\dfrac{1}{2}\ln 3$

15. $\displaystyle\int_0^1 e^{3x+2}\,dx =$

(A) $\dfrac{1}{3}e^5$

(B) $\dfrac{1}{3}(e^5 - e^2)$

(C) $\dfrac{1}{3}(e^5 - 1)$

(D) $e^5 - 1$

16. If $y = \sin^2 5x$, $\dfrac{dy}{dx} =$

(A) $5 \sin 10x$

(B) $5 \cos 5x$

(C) $5 \sin 5x$

(D) $10 \sin 10x$

17. For what values of x is $f(x) = 2x^3 - x^2 + 2x$ concave up?

(A) $x < \dfrac{1}{6}$

(B) $x < 0$

(C) $x > 0$

(D) $x > \dfrac{1}{6}$

Questions 18 and 19 refer to the graph of the velocity, $v(t)$, of an object at time t shown below.

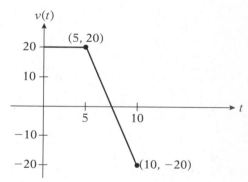

18. If $x(t)$ is the position of the object at time t, and $a(t)$ is the acceleration of the object at time t, which of the following is true?

(A) $v(5) > v(2)$

(B) $x(5) > x(2)$

(C) $a(6) > a(2)$

(D) $x(10) < x(5)$

19. $\displaystyle\int_{0}^{10} v(t)\,dt =$

(A) 0

(B) 50

(C) 75

(D) 100

20. If $f(1) = 2$ and $f'(1) = 5$, use the equation of the line tangent to the graph of f at $x = 1$ to approximate $f(1.2)$.

(A) 1

(B) 1.2

(C) 3

(D) 5.4

21. The equation of the line tangent to $y = \tan^2(3x)$ at $x = \dfrac{\pi}{4}$ is

(A) $y = -12x + 3\pi - 1$

(B) $y = -12x + 3\pi + 1$

(C) $y = -6x + \dfrac{3\pi}{2} + 1$

(D) $y = -12x + 3\pi + 3$

22. The graph of $f'(x)$ is shown below.

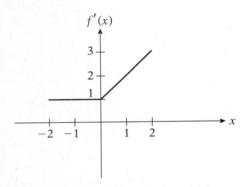

Which of the following could be the graph of f?

(A)

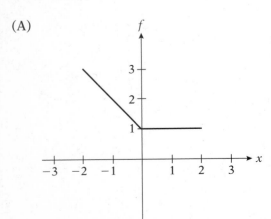

(B)

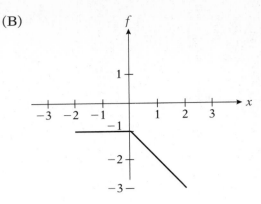

(C)

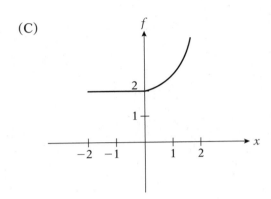

(D)

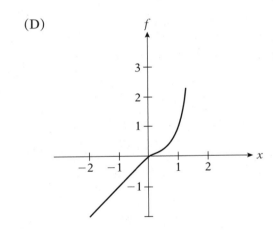

23. At what value of x is the line tangent to the graph of $y = x^2 + 3x + 5$ perpendicular to the line $x - 2y = 5$?

(A) $-\dfrac{5}{2}$

(B) -2

(C) $-\dfrac{1}{2}$

(D) $\dfrac{1}{2}$

24. The function $f(x)$, graphed here, is called a sawtooth wave. Which of the following statements about this function is true?

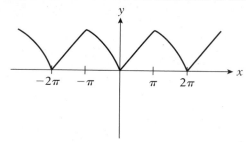

(A) $f(x)$ is continuous everywhere.
(B) $f(x)$ is differentiable everywhere.
(C) $f(x)$ is continuous everywhere but $x = n\pi$.
(D) $f(x)$ is an even function.

25. Find the derivative of $y = x^2 e^{x^2}$.

(A) $2x e^{x^2}(x^2 + 1)$
(B) $2x e^{x^2}$
(C) $2x^3 e^{x^2}$
(D) $4x^2 e^{x^2}$

26. $\displaystyle\int_{0}^{\frac{\pi}{2}} e^{2-\cos x} \sin x \; dx =$

(A) $e^2 - e$
(B) 1
(C) 0
(D) e^2

27. The average value of $f(x) = -\dfrac{1}{x^2}$ on $\left[\dfrac{1}{2}, 1\right]$ is

(A) -2
(B) -1
(C) $-\dfrac{1}{2}$
(D) 2

28. $f(x) = \left|x^2 - 3x\right|$. Find $f'(1)$.

(A) -3
(B) -1
(C) 1
(D) 3

29. $\displaystyle\lim_{x \to \infty} \frac{3 - \cos x}{x + 4} =$

(A) 0
(B) $\dfrac{1}{2}$
(C) $\dfrac{3}{4}$
(D) Does not exist

30. $\displaystyle\lim_{x \to 0} \tan \frac{1}{x}$

(A) 0
(B) 1
(C) ∞
(D) Does not exist

CALCULUS AB

SECTION I, Part B

Time – 45 minutes
Number of problems – 15

A graphing calculator is required for these problems.

1. Which of the following statements is true about the figure?

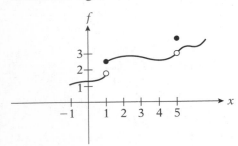

   (A) $\lim\limits_{x \to 5} f(x)$ exists

   (B) $\lim\limits_{x \to 1} f(x)$ exists

   (C) $\lim\limits_{x \to 5} f(x) = f(5)$

   (D) $\lim\limits_{x \to 1} f(x) = f(1)$

2. How many points of inflection are there for the function $y = x + \cos 2x$ on the interval $[0, \pi]$?

   (A) 0

   (B) 1

   (C) 2

   (D) 3

3. The graph of the function $f(x)$ is shown below.

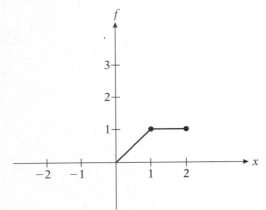

If $F'(x) = f(x)$, and $F(0) = -3$, then $F(2) =$

   (A) -4.5

   (B) -1.5

   (C) 1.5

   (D) 3

4. If $\lim\limits_{h \to 0} \dfrac{f(3 + h) - f(3)}{h} = 0$, then which of the following must be true?

   I. f has a derivative at $x = 3$.
   II. f is continuous at $x = 3$.
   III. f has a critical value at $x = 3$.

   (A) I only

   (B) I and II

   (C) I and III

   (D) I, II, and III

5. Consider the function $y(x) = x^3 - x^2 - 1$. For what value(s) of x is the slope of the tangent equal to 5?

   (A) -1 only

   (B) $\dfrac{5}{3}$ only

   (C) -1 and $\dfrac{5}{3}$

   (D) $\dfrac{1}{3}$ only

6. A pebble thrown into a pond creates circular ripples such that the rate of change of the circumference is 12π cm/s. How fast is the area of the ripple changing when the radius is 3 cm?

   (A) 6π cm²/s

   (B) 2π cm²/s

   (C) 12π cm²/s

   (D) 36π cm²/s

7. If $y = x^2 + 1$, what is the smallest positive value of x such that $\sin y$ is a relative maximum?

(A) 0.756

(B) 0.841

(C) 1

(D) 1.463

8. Find the area in the first quadrant bounded by $y = 2 \cos x$, $y = 3 \tan x$, and the y-axis.

(A) 0.347

(B) 0.374

(C) 0.432

(D) 0.568

9. In the following figure, the equations $y = x^2$ and $x = 4$ bound the region R and form the base of a solid. The cross sections are semicircles perpendicular to the base whose diameters are in the plane of the region R.

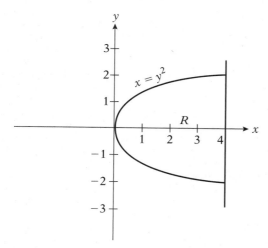

Which of the following represents the volume of the solid?

(A) π

(B) 4π

(C) 8π

(D) $\dfrac{32}{3}\pi$

10. $f'(x) = x^3 (x - 2)^4 (x - 3)^2 \cdot f(x)$ has a relative maximum at $x =$

(A) 2

(B) 2 and 3

(C) 0 and 3

(D) There is no relative maximum.

11. $a(t) = \dfrac{5t^2 + 1}{5t}$ and $v(1) = 1$. Find $v(2)$.

(A) 1.139

(B) 2.10

(C) 2.139

(D) 2.639

12. Use the table shown to approximate the area under the curve of $y = f(x)$ using trapezoids.

x	y
0	1
1	2
3	4
4	1

(A) 5.5

(B) 8

(C) 10

(D) 11

13. In the figure shown, which of the following is true?

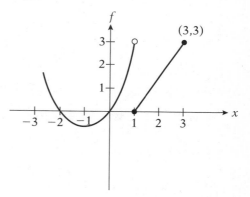

(A) $\lim\limits_{x \to 1} f(x) = 3$

(B) $f'(1) = 1$

(C) $f(1) = 3$

(D) The average rate of change of $f(x)$ on $[1, 3]$ equals $f'(2)$.

14. The region enclosed by the graphs of $y = \sqrt{x}$, $y = 2$, and the y-axis is rotated about the line $y = 4$. Write an integral that represents the volume of the solid generated.

(A) $2\pi \displaystyle\int_0^2 \sqrt{x}\, dx$

(B) $\pi \displaystyle\int_0^2 (4 - \sqrt{x})\, dx$

(C) $\pi \displaystyle\int_0^4 \left((4 - \sqrt{x})^2 - 4\right) dx$

(D) $\pi \displaystyle\int_0^2 \left((4 - \sqrt{x})^2 - 4\right) dx$

15. Find the value of c guaranteed by the Mean Value Theorem for $f(x) = \dfrac{2}{x-1}$ on the interval $[3, 5]$.

(A) $1 + 2\sqrt{2}$

(B) $2\sqrt{2}$

(C) $1 + \sqrt{2}$

(D) $1 - 2\sqrt{2}$

AB Model Examination 1

CALCULUS AB

SECTION II, Part A
Time – 30 minutes
Number of problems – 2

A graphing calculator is required for these problems.

1. A rocket is launched with an initial velocity of zero, and with acceleration in feet per second per second defined by

$$a(t) = \begin{cases} 20e^{-t/2}, & \text{for } 0 \le t \le 10 \text{ seconds} \\ -16, & \text{for } t > 10 \text{ seconds} \end{cases}.$$

(a) At what time does the rocket begin to descend?

(b) What is the rocket's maximum height?

(c) What is the velocity when the rocket impacts the earth?

2. A leaky cylindrical oilcan has a diameter of 4 inches and a height of 6 inches. The can is full of oil and is leaking at the rate of 2 in.^{3}/hr. The oil leaks into an empty conical cup with vertex down and with a diameter of 8 inches and a height of 8 inches.

(a) At what rate is the depth of the oil in the conical cup rising when the oil in the cup is 3 inches deep?

(b) When the oilcan is empty, what is the depth of the oil in the conical cup?

CALCULUS AB

SECTION II, Part B

Time – 60 minutes
Number of problems – 4

> **A graphing calculator is not permitted for these problems.**

1. Region R is bounded by the graph of $y = x^{2/3}$, the x-axis, and the line $x = 8$.

    (a) For what value of k, $0 < k < 8$, does the line $x = k$ divide region R into two parts equal in area?

    (b) Region R is rotated about the x-axis. Find the value of p if the lines $x = p$ and $x = q$ $(p < q)$ divide the solid into three parts that have the same volume.

2. Consider the graph of $f(x)$, shown below, which consists of four straight line segments.

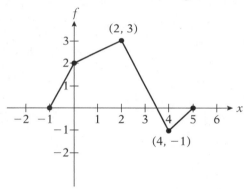

If $h(x) = \displaystyle\int_1^x f(t)\, dt$,

    (a) Find $h(2)$ and $h(-1)$.

    (b) On what interval(s) is $h(x)$ decreasing?

    (c) What are the critical values of h? Justify your answer.

    (d) What are the points of inflection of h? Justify your answer.

    (e) Find the absolute maximum and the absolute minimum of h. Justify your answer.

3. (a) Draw a slope field for the differential equation $\dfrac{dy}{dx} = x(y - 1)$ for integer values in $0 \le x \le 2$ and $0 \le y \le 3$.

    (b) On the slope field drawn in part (a), sketch a solution to the differential equation with initial condition $y(0) = 2$.

    (c) Solve the differential equation with initial condition $y(0) = -1$.

4. Consider the graph of the derivative of f.

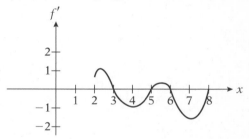

    (a) At what value(s) of x does f have a relative maximum? Justify your answer.

    (b) On what intervals is f concave up?

    (c) At what value(s) of x does f have a point of inflection? Justify your answer.

    (c) Is $f(3) > f(2)$? Justify your answer.

AB Model Examination 2

CALCULUS AB

SECTION I, Part A
Time – 60 minutes
Number of problems – 30

> **A graphing calculator is not permitted for these problems.**

1. $f(x) = 2x^3 - 6x^2 + 6x - 1$ has a point of inflection located at

   (A) $(0, -1)$

   (B) $(1, 1)$

   (C) $(2, 3)$

   (D) $(1, 0)$

2. Find the average value of $f(x)$ on the interval $[-1, 4]$ in the figure shown.

   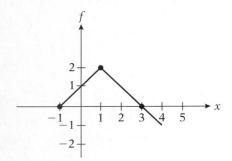

   (A) $-\dfrac{1}{5}$

   (B) $\dfrac{7}{10}$

   (C) $\dfrac{9}{10}$

   (D) $\dfrac{7}{2}$

3. $\displaystyle\int_{\frac{\pi}{2}}^{\pi} \sin x \cos x \, dx =$

   (A) -1

   (B) $-\dfrac{1}{2}$

   (C) 0

   (D) $\dfrac{1}{2}$

4. A function $f(x)$ is continuous on the closed interval $[a, b]$. Which of the following must be true?

   (A) $f(x)$ has a maximum on $[a, b]$.

   (B) $f(x)$ has a point of inflection on $[a, b]$.

   (C) $f'(c) = \dfrac{f(b) - f(a)}{b - a}$ for at least one c in the interval $[a, b]$.

   (D) $f'(c) = 0$ for at least one c in the interval $[a, b]$.

5. Find the slope of the line tangent to the graph of $3xy - 2x + 3y^2 = 5$ at the point $(2, 1)$.

   (A) $-\dfrac{1}{3}$

   (B) $-\dfrac{1}{12}$

   (C) $\dfrac{1}{12}$

   (D) 1

6. If $f(x) = \big(g(x)\big)^5$, $g(2) = -1$, and $f'(2) = 5$, find $g'(2)$.

   (A) -5

   (B) 0

   (C) $\dfrac{1}{5}$

   (D) 1

7. $\dfrac{d}{dx}\left(\dfrac{x+1}{x+2}\right) =$

(A) 1

(B) $\dfrac{1}{x+2}$

(C) $\dfrac{1}{(x+2)^2}$

(D) $-\dfrac{1}{(x+2)^2}$

8. What is the instantaneous rate of change of $f(x) = \ln(\tan^2 x)$ at $x = \dfrac{\pi}{4}$?

(A) 0

(B) 1

(C) $\dfrac{\sqrt{3}}{2}$

(D) 4

9. Consider the function

$$f(x) = \begin{cases} 2x^2 - x^3, & x < 2 \\ e^{2x-4}, & x \geq 2 \end{cases}.$$

Find $\lim\limits_{x \to 2} f(x)$.

(A) 0

(B) 1

(C) 2

(D) Does not exist

10. If $f(x) = e^{\sin^2 x}$, then $f'(x) =$

(A) $e^{\sin^2 x}$

(B) $2 \sin x e^{\sin^2 x}$

(C) $2 \sin x \cos x e^{\sin^2 x}$

(D) $e^{2\cos x}$

11. $\displaystyle\int_0^{\frac{\pi}{3}} \sec x \tan x \, dx =$

(A) 0

(B) 1

(C) $\sqrt{2} - 1$

(D) $\sqrt{3} - 1$

12. The position function for a particle's motion on a line is $x(t) = t^3 - t^2 - t + 1, t \geq 0$. At what value(s) of t is the particle at rest?

(A) $t = 0$

(B) $t = 1$

(C) $t = -1$ and $t = 1$

(D) $t = \dfrac{1}{3}$

13. At which value(s) of x on $[-3, 3]$ is $f(x)$ discontinuous?

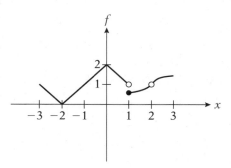

(A) $x = -2$

(B) $x = -2$ and $x = 1$

(C) $x = 1$

(D) $x = 1$ and $x = 2$

14. $\displaystyle\int_0^1 \dfrac{x^2 - 1}{x^2 + 1} \, dx =$

(A) -1

(B) $1 - \dfrac{\pi}{2}$

(C) $1 - \dfrac{\pi}{3}$

(D) $1 - \dfrac{\pi}{4}$

15. $\dfrac{d}{dx}\left(\displaystyle\int_2^{2x} \sqrt[3]{1 + t} \, dt\right) =$

(A) $\sqrt[3]{1 + 2x} - \sqrt[3]{3}$

(B) $2\sqrt[3]{1 + 2x} - \sqrt[3]{3}$

(C) $2\sqrt[3]{1 + 2x}$

(D) $\sqrt[3]{1 + 4x^2}$

16. Consider the graph of *f* shown.

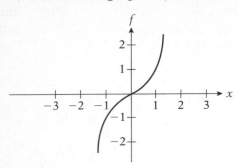

Which of the following is the graph of *f'*?

(A)

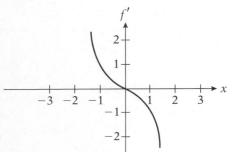

(B)

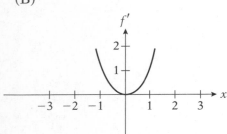

(C)

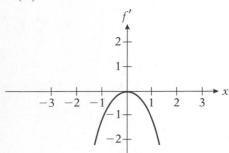

(D)

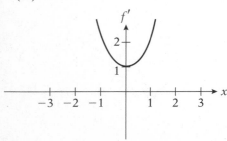

17. Find the equation of the line tangent to $y = \tan^2 x$ at $x = \frac{\pi}{3}$.

(A) $y - 3 = 8\sqrt{3}\left(x - \frac{\pi}{3}\right)$

(B) $y - 3 = 4\sqrt{3}\left(x - \frac{\pi}{3}\right)$

(C) $y - 1 = 4\left(x - \frac{\pi}{3}\right)$

(D) $y - 1 = 4\sqrt{3}\left(x - \frac{\pi}{3}\right)$

18. If $f'(x) = 2x(x + 1)(x + 2)^2$, then $f(x)$ has

(A) a relative maximum at $x = -1$ and a relative minimum at $x = 0$.

(B) relative maxima at $x = -1$ and $x = -2$, and a relative minimum at $x = 0$.

(C) a relative maximum at $x = -2$ and a relative minimum at $x = 0$.

(D) only a relative minimum at $x = 0$.

19. The area under the graph of $y = \frac{1}{x}$ from $x = 1$ to $x = a$ (where $a > 1$) is equal to the area under the curve from $x = p$ (where $p < 1$) to $x = 1$. Express p in terms of a.

(A) $p = \frac{1}{a}$

(B) $p = -a$

(C) $p = \frac{1}{a^2}$

(D) $p = \frac{1}{\ln a}$

20. $\frac{dy}{dt} = ky$ and $y(1) = 1$. Find $y(t)$ in terms of k and t.

(A) $y = kt^2$

(B) $y = k\sqrt{t}$

(C) $y = e^{-kt}$

(D) $y = e^{k(t-1)}$

21. Consider the function $f(x) = x^4 + 2x^2 + 1$. On what interval is $f(x)$ increasing?

(A) $(-\infty, \infty)$

(B) $(-\infty, 0)$

(C) $(0, \infty)$

(D) $(1, \infty)$

22. $a(t) = 6t - 12$ for $0 \le t \le 4$. If $v(0) = 18$, find the maximum velocity on the interval $[0, 4]$.

(A) 2

(B) 4

(C) 6

(D) 18

23. If $f(x) = \frac{1}{2}(2x + 5)^3$, then $f'(x) =$

(A) $\frac{3}{2}(2x + 5)^2$.

(B) $3(2x + 5)^2$.

(C) $3(2x + 5)$.

(D) $\frac{3}{2}(2x + 5)$.

24. The area enclosed by the curves $y = x^2 - 4$ and $y = 2x - 4$ can be represented by the integral

(A) $\displaystyle\int_{-4}^{0} (x^2 - 2x)\,dx.$

(B) $\displaystyle\int_{0}^{2} (2x - x^2)\,dx.$

(C) $\displaystyle\int_{-4}^{0} (2x - x^2)\,dx.$

(D) $\displaystyle\int_{0}^{2} (x^2 - 2x)\,dx.$

25. $\displaystyle\lim_{x \to -\infty} \frac{2x}{\sqrt{x^2 + 1}} =$

(A) -2

(B) -1

(C) 1

(D) 2

26. $g(x)$ is a differentiable function on the closed interval $[a, b]$. Which of the following must be true?

(A) For every x in $[a, b]$, $g(x)$ is between $g(a)$ and $g(b)$.

(B) For every k between $g(a)$ and $g(b)$, there is a value c in $[a, b]$ such that $g(c) = k$.

(C) There is at least one x in $[a, b]$ such that $g'(x) = 0$.

(D) $\displaystyle\lim_{x \to \infty} g(x)$ does not exist.

27. The region enclosed by the graphs of $y = x^{2/3}$, $y = 4$, and the y-axis is rotated about the line $y = 4$. The volume of the solid generated can be represented by the integral

(A) $2\pi \displaystyle\int_{0}^{8} (4 - x^{2/3})^2\,dx.$

(B) $\pi \displaystyle\int_{0}^{8} (4 - x^{2/3})^2\,dx.$

(C) $2\pi \displaystyle\int_{0}^{4} (4 - x^{2/3})^2\,dx.$

(D) $\pi \displaystyle\int_{0}^{4} (16 - x^{4/3})\,dx.$

28. On what interval(s) is the graph of $f(x) = \dfrac{x}{x^2 + 1}$ concave down?

(A) $\left(0, \sqrt{3}\right)$

(B) $\left(-\sqrt{3}, 0\right)$

(C) $(0, \infty) \cup \left(-\sqrt{3}, 0\right)$

(D) $(-\infty, -\sqrt{3}) \cup \left(0, \sqrt{3}\right)$

29. $\displaystyle\lim_{x \to \infty} \frac{\sin x}{x} =$

(A) 0

(B) 1

(C) -1

(D) Does not exist

30. $\displaystyle\lim_{x \to 1} \cos\frac{x + 1}{x - 1} =$

(A) 0

(B) 1

(C) -1

(D) Does not exist

CALCULUS AB

SECTION I, Part B

Time – 45 minutes
Number of problems – 15

A graphing calculator is required for these problems.

1. Find $\dfrac{dy}{dx}$ when $y = 0$ if $x \cos y - \sin x - 2 = 0$.

(A) 0

(B) 0.637

(C) 2.554

(D) undefined

2. If $v(t) = \ln(t^2 + t + 1)$, then $a(1) =$

(A) $\dfrac{1}{3}$.

(B) $\dfrac{2}{3}$.

(C) 1.

(D) $\dfrac{4}{3}$.

3. $y = \sec^2(2x + \pi)$. Find $y'\left(\dfrac{\pi}{2}\right)$.

(A) 0

(B) 2

(C) 4

(D) 8

4. $y = \dfrac{e^{2x-1}}{x}$ has

  I. a relative minimum at $x = \dfrac{1}{2}$.

  II. a horizontal asymptote $y = 0$.

  III. a vertical asymptote $x = 0$.

(A) I and II

(B) I and III

(C) II and III

(D) I, II, and III

5. If $\displaystyle\int_0^a \sin(x)\,dx = b$, then $\displaystyle\int_{-a}^a \sin(x)\,dx =$

(A) b.

(B) $2b$.

(C) 0.

(D) $b + 1$.

6. $\dfrac{d}{dx}\left(\displaystyle\lim_{h \to 0} \dfrac{\ln(x + h) - \ln x}{h}\right) =$

(A) $-\dfrac{1}{x^2}$

(B) $\dfrac{1}{x}$

(C) -1

(D) 0

7. Assuming that the graph of $g(x)$, shown below, behaves likes that of e^{-x} except at $x = 0$, identify the false statement among the following:

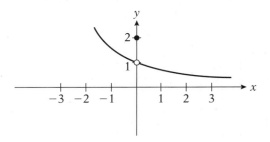

(A) $\displaystyle\lim_{x \to 0} g(x) = 1$.

(B) $\displaystyle\lim_{x \to \infty} g(x) = 0$.

(C) $g'(x) < 0$ for $x \neq 0$.

(D) $g'(0) = 2$.

8. For what value(s) of x are the lines tangent to $f(x) = \frac{1}{3}x^3 + 5$ and $g(x) = 4 + 2x - \frac{x^2}{2}$ parallel?

   (A) $x = -2$ and $x = 1$
   (B) $x = -2$ only
   (C) $x = 1$ only
   (D) $x = -3.475$ only

9. The equation of the line tangent to $y = \dfrac{x^2}{x^2 + 1}$ at $x = 1$ is

   (A) $y = -2x$.
   (B) $y = -2x - 1$.
   (C) $y = -2x + 2.5$.
   (D) $y = \frac{1}{2}x$.

10. A box with a square base is needed to package 100 cm^3 of powdered milk. Find the dimensions of the box that will use the minimum amount of material.

    (A) length = 3.89 cm, width = 4.12 cm
    (B) length = width = 4.64 cm
    (C) length = 5.02 cm, width = 5.05 cm
    (D) length = width = 6.55 cm

11. The derivative of $y(x) = \arcsin\left(\frac{x}{2}\right)$ on $-1 < x < 1$ is

    (A) $y = \dfrac{1}{2\sqrt{1 - \frac{x^2}{4}}}$

    (B) $y = \dfrac{1}{2\sqrt{1 - \sin(x)}}$

    (C) $y = \dfrac{1}{2\cos\left(\arcsin\left(\frac{x}{2}\right)\right)}$

    (D) $y = \dfrac{\arccos\left(\frac{x}{2}\right)}{2}$

12. In the graph shown, at which point is $\dfrac{dy}{dx} > 0$ and $\dfrac{d^2y}{dx^2} < 0$?

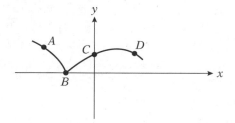

    (A) A
    (B) B
    (C) C
    (D) D

13. If $f(x) = \begin{cases} x^2 + 2, & x < 1 \\ 2x + 1, & x \geq 1 \end{cases}$, which of the following is true about $f(x)$?

    (A) The function is not continuous and not differentiable at $x = 1$.
    (B) The function is continuous, but not differentiable at $x = 1$.
    (C) The function is differentiable, but not continuous at $x = 1$.
    (D) The function is both continuous and differentiable at $x = 1$.

14. If $f(x) = 3x^2 - 4$, then $\lim\limits_{x \to a} \dfrac{f'(x) - f'(a)}{x - a} =$

    (A) $3a^2 - 4$
    (B) $6a$
    (C) 6
    (D) 0

15. Find the area of the region enclosed by the semicircle $y = \sqrt{16 - x^2}$ and the line $y = 2$.

    (A) 3.653 units^2
    (B) 4.913 units^2
    (C) 7.306 units^2
    (D) 9.827 units^2

CALCULUS AB

SECTION II, Part A
Time – 30 minutes
Number of problems – 2

> A graphing calculator is required for these problems.

1. The velocity, $v(t)$, of an object is a differentiable function of t. The table shows values of the velocity for integral values of t on the interval $[0, 4]$:

t	$v(t)$
0	5
1	8
2	15
3	10
4	5

   (a) Show that the acceleration equals zero at least once in the interval $[0, 4]$. Justify your answer.

   (b) Find the average rate of change of the velocity on the interval $[1, 4]$.

   (c) If $x(t) = \int v(t)\,dt$ and $x(0) = 2$, use the Trapezoidal Rule with four equal subintervals on $[0, 4]$ to estimate $x(4)$.

2. Consider the function $y = \dfrac{kx}{x - k}$.

   (a) Show that y is symmetric with respect to the line $y = x$.

   (b) Write the equations of the horizontal and vertical asymptotes of y.

   (c) Find the points(s) of intersection of y with the line $x + y = -2k$, and find the slope of the tangent line (to the first equation) at the point(s) of intersection.

CALCULUS AB
SECTION II, Part B
Time – 60 minutes
Number of problems – 4

> **A graphing calculator is not permitted for these problems.**

1. Food is being poured into Fluffy the cat's bowl at the constant rate of 1 gram per day. Simultaneously, Fluffy is consuming the food at the rate of $\ln(t + 1)$ grams per day. At time $t = 0$, there are two grams of food in the bowl.

   (a) Find an expression for $B(t)$, the amount of food in the bowl at time t.

   (b) After four days, Joe, a dog who eats cat food, chases Fluffy away. How much food is in the bowl for Joe?

   (c) At what point is the bowl at its fullest?

   (d) At what point is the bowl empty?

2. Consider the function $f(x) = \dfrac{\sin(2x)}{x}$.

   (a) Find the domain of f.

   (b) State the interval(s) where f is increasing on $0 \leq x \leq 2\pi$. Justify your answer.

   (c) State the interval(s) where f is concave down on $0 \leq x \leq 2\pi$. Justify your answer.

   (d) Find $\lim\limits_{x \to 0} f(x)$.

3. A spherical object with initial velocity 20 cm/s is rolled down a smooth surface. The velocity of the object is described by the differential equation $\dfrac{dv}{dt} = -2v + 8$.

   (a) Find the velocity v of the object as a function of time t.

   (b) Find $\lim\limits_{t \to \infty} v(t)$, the limiting velocity of the object.

4. A line tangent to $y = x^2 + 1$ at $x = a$, $a > 0$, intersects the x-axis at point P.

   (a) Write an expression for the area of the triangle formed by the tangent line, the x-axis, and the line $x = a$.

   (b) For what value of a is the area of the triangle a minimum? Justify your answer.

CALCULUS BC

SECTION I, Part A
Time – 60 minutes
Number of problems – 30

A graphing calculator is not permitted for these problems.

1. If $f(x) = 2\sin^2 5x$, $f'(x) =$

   (A) $10\sin(10x)$.
   (B) $20\sin(5x)$.
   (C) $10\sin(5x)$.
   (D) $4\cos(5x)$.

2. Find the x-intercept of the line tangent to $y = \ln(\ln(x))$ at $x = e$.

   (A) $x = -1$
   (B) $x = 0$
   (C) $x = 1$
   (D) $x = e$

3. $a(t) = 2e^t$ and $v(1) = 2$. Find $v(t)$.

   (A) $2(e^t - e + 1)$
   (B) $2(e^{t-1} + 1)$
   (C) $2t + 1$
   (D) $2e^t + e$

4. $\displaystyle\lim_{x \to -\infty} \frac{\ln(1-x)}{x^2 + 1} =$

   (A) $-\infty$
   (B) -1
   (C) 0
   (D) 1

5. $y = \dfrac{e^{2x-1}}{x}$ has

   I. a relative minimum at $x = \frac{1}{2}$.
   II. a horizontal asymptote $y = 0$.
   III. a vertical asymptote $x = 0$.

   (A) I and II
   (B) I and III
   (C) II and III
   (D) I, II and III

6. For $f(x) = \begin{cases} x^2 + 2, & x < 1 \\ 2x + 1, & x \geq 1 \end{cases}$, which of the following is true?

   (A) $f(x)$ is not continuous at $x = 1$.
   (B) $f(x)$ is continuous but not differentiable at $x = 1$.
   (C) $f(x)$ is differentiable but not continuous at $x = 1$.
   (D) $f(x)$ is continuous and differentiable at $x = 1$.

7. $\displaystyle\int_1^e x \ln x \, dx =$

   (A) $\dfrac{e^2 + 1}{4}$
   (B) $2e^2 - 1$
   (C) $\dfrac{e^2 - e - 1}{2}$
   (D) $2e^2 + 1$

8. $f(x) = \cos x$. Which of the following are true?

   I. $\displaystyle\int_{-a}^{a} \cos x \, dx = 2\int_0^a \cos x \, dx$

   II. $\displaystyle\int_a^c \cos x \, dx + \int_c^b \cos x \, dx = \int_a^b \cos x \, dx$

   III. $\displaystyle\int_{-a}^{a} \cos x \, dx = 0$

   (A) I only
   (B) II only
   (C) I and II
   (D) II and III

9. $\dfrac{d}{dt}\left(\displaystyle\int_0^{2t} \dfrac{1 - \cos x}{x}\,dx\right) =$

(A) $\dfrac{1 - \cos 2t}{t}$

(B) $\dfrac{1 - \cos 2t}{2t}$

(C) $\sin 2t$

(D) $2 \sin 2t$

10. Find the area under the curve of $\dfrac{14x + 16}{x^2 + x - 20}$ on the interval $[5, 10]$.

(A) $4 \ln\left(\dfrac{2}{3}\right) + 3 \ln(5)$

(B) $-40 \ln(5) + 54 \ln\left(\dfrac{3}{2}\right)$

(C) $8 \ln(6) + 6 \ln\left(\dfrac{3}{2}\right)$

(D) $9 \ln\left(\dfrac{4}{32}\right)$

11. Write an integral that represents the length of one arch of $y = \sin\ x$.

(A) $\displaystyle\int_0^{\frac{\pi}{2}} \sqrt{1 + \cos^2 x}\ dx$

(B) $\displaystyle\int_0^{\pi} \sqrt{1 + \cos^2 x}\ dx$

(C) $\displaystyle\int_0^{\frac{\pi}{2}} (1 + \cos x)\ dx$

(D) $\displaystyle\int_0^{\frac{\pi}{2}} \sin^2 x\ dx$

12. For what values of a and c is the function

$f(x) = \begin{cases} x + c, & x > 2 \\ ax^2, & x \leq 2 \end{cases}$ differentiable at $x = 2$?

(A) $a = \dfrac{1}{2}, c = 0$

(B) $a = \dfrac{1}{4}, c = -1$

(C) $a = 1, c = 6$

(D) $a = 0, c = -2$

13. The slope field below depicts a certain differential equation. Which of the following choices could be a solution to that equation?

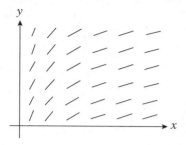

(A) $y = \ln(x)$

(B) $y = e^{-x}$

(C) $y = \sin(x)$

(D) $y = e^x$

14. The motion of a particle is given by the parametric equations $x = t^2 + t$ and $y = 3t - 2$. The speed of the particle at $t = 2$ is

(A) $2\sqrt{2}$.

(B) $\sqrt{26}$.

(C) $\sqrt{34}$.

(D) 6.

15. $h(x) = \dfrac{f(x)}{(g(x))^2}$. If $f'(x) = g(x), g'(x) = \dfrac{1}{f(x)}$, and $g(x) > 0$ for all real x, then $h'(x) =$

(A) $\dfrac{2}{(g(x))^3} - \dfrac{1}{g(x)}$.

(B) $\dfrac{1}{g(x)} - \dfrac{2}{(g(x))^3}$.

(C) $(g(x))^2 - 2$.

(D) $\dfrac{1}{g(x)} - \dfrac{2f(x)}{(g(x))^3}$.

16. Which of the following series converge?

I. $\displaystyle\sum_1^{\infty} \dfrac{k}{n^2}$, where k is a constant

II. $\displaystyle\sum_1^{\infty} \dfrac{(-1)^n}{\sqrt{n}}$

III. $\displaystyle\sum_1^{\infty} (0.4)^{n-1}$

(A) I only

(B) III only

(C) I and III

(D) I, II, and III

17. The maximum value of $f(x) = \dfrac{\sqrt{x}-3}{x}$ occurs at $x =$

(A) -6.

(B) $\dfrac{\sqrt{3}}{3}$.

(C) 3.

(D) 6.

18. $y' = 2y + 5$. Find y'' in terms of y.

(A) 0

(B) 2

(C) $4y + 5$

(D) $4y + 10$

19. For what value of c does $y = cx + \dfrac{3}{x}$ have a relative minimum at $x = 2$?

(A) $-\dfrac{2}{3}\ln 2$

(B) 0

(C) $\dfrac{3}{8}$

(D) $\dfrac{3}{4}$

20. $f(x) = 3(x-2)^2 + 6(x-2) + 1$. Find the equation of the line tangent to $f(x)$ at $x = 2$.

(A) $6x - y = 11$

(B) $y = 0$

(C) $6x - y = 12$

(D) $6x - y = 13$

21. Which formula could be used to calculate the average rate of change of $f(x)$ on the closed interval $[0, 4]$?

(A) $\dfrac{f(4) - f(0)}{2}$

(B) $\dfrac{f(0) + f(4)}{2}$

(C) $\dfrac{f(4) - f(0)}{4}$

(D) $\dfrac{f(0) + f(4)}{4}$

22. $f(x) = \dfrac{x}{x-3}$. If $f^{-1}(x)$ is the inverse of $f(x)$, find the derivative of f^{-1} at $x = -2$.

(A) -3

(B) $-\dfrac{1}{3}$

(C) $\dfrac{1}{3}$

(D) 1

23. An ellipse with equation $x^2 + 9y^2 = 9$ is the base of a solid in which each cross section perpendicular to the x-axis is a square. Find the volume of the solid.

(A) 4 units^3

(B) 8 units^3

(C) 16 units^3

(D) 32 units^3

24. $f(x) = 3x^3 - 4$. Find $\displaystyle\lim_{x \to 2} \dfrac{f(x) - f(2)}{x - 2}$.

(A) 18

(B) 24

(C) 32

(D) 36

25. The graph of $f(x)$ is shown.

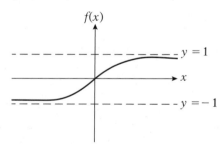

If $g(x) = f\left(\dfrac{1}{x}\right)$, find the value of $\displaystyle\lim_{x \to 0^+} g(x)$.

(A) -1

(B) 0

(C) 1

(D) ∞

26. If $y = \ln(\cos^2 x)$, then $y' =$

(A) $-2\tan x$.

(B) $\sec^2 x$.

(C) $2\sec x$.

(D) $2\tan x$.

27. Write the equation of the line perpendicular to the tangent of the curve represented by the equation $y = e^{x+1}$ at $x = 0$.

(A) $y = -\frac{1}{e}x$

(B) $y = -\frac{1}{e}x + e$

(C) $y = ex + e$

(D) $y = \frac{1}{e}x + e$

28. $\displaystyle\int_1^\infty xe^{-x^2}dx$ is

(A) $\frac{1}{2}$

(B) 1

(C) $\frac{1}{2e}$

(D) 2

29. Find the area bounded by the graph of $y = \dfrac{x}{x^2 - 1}$ and the x-axis on the interval $\left[-\frac{1}{2}, \frac{1}{2}\right]$.

(A) $\ln\left(\dfrac{3}{4}\right)$

(B) 0

(C) $\dfrac{1}{2}\ln\left(\dfrac{4}{3}\right)$

(D) $\ln\left(\dfrac{4}{3}\right)$

30. $F(x)$ is the antiderivative of $f(x)$, $F(5) = 7$, and $\displaystyle\int_2^5 f(x)\, dx = 9$. Find $F(2)$.

(A) -7

(B) -2

(C) 2

(D) 16

CALCULUS BC

SECTION I, Part B

Time – 30 minutes
Number of problems – 15

A graphing calculator is required for these problems.

1. The region in the first quadrant bounded by $y = \sqrt[3]{x}$ and the line $x = 8$ forms the base of a solid. Cross sections of the solid perpendicular to the x-axis are squares. For what value of k does the line $x = k$ divide the solid into two solids of equal volume?

   (A) 4
   (B) 4.138
   (C) 5.278
   (D) $\dfrac{16}{3}$

2. Find the slope of the tangent to the graph of $x \ln y + e^x = y$ at the point $(0, 1)$.

   (A) -1
   (B) 0
   (C) 1
   (D) 2

3. The graph of $f(x)$ is shown.

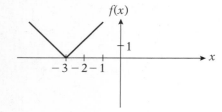

   Which of the following could be the graph of $f'(x)$?

   (A)

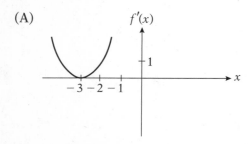

(B)

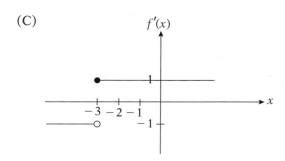

(C)

(D)

4. Let $f(x) = \sqrt{x^2 - x}$. Find $f'(1)$.

   (A) $-\dfrac{1}{2}$
   (B) 0
   (C) 1
   (D) Does not exist

5. Which of the following is NOT true about the function $f(x)$ shown?

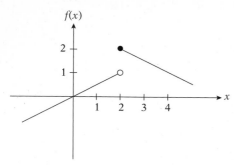

(A) $f(2) = 2$

(B) $\lim\limits_{x \to 2^-} f(x) = 1$

(C) $\lim\limits_{x \to 2} f(x) = 1$

(D) $f'(0) = \dfrac{1}{2}$

6. The fourth-degree Taylor polynomial for $y = e^{x/4}$, centered at $x = 0$, is

(A) $\displaystyle\sum_{n=0}^{4} \left(\dfrac{x}{4}\right)^n$.

(B) $\displaystyle\sum_{n=1}^{4} \dfrac{x^n}{n(4^n)}$.

(C) $\displaystyle\sum_{n=1}^{4} \dfrac{x^n}{(4^n)n!}$.

(D) $\displaystyle\sum_{n=0}^{4} \dfrac{x^n}{n!(4^n)}$.

7. $f'(x) = 0.25(x + 1)^3(2x + 5)(x - 3)^2$. The graph of $f(x)$ has

(A) no critical points.

(B) one relative minimum and one relative maximum.

(C) two relative minima and one relative maximum.

(D) two relative minima and two relative maxima.

8. Consider the function $y = \dfrac{x}{x^2 + 1}$. At what value of x is $\dfrac{dy}{dx}$ the largest?

(A) $-\sqrt{3}$

(B) -1

(C) 0

(D) 1

9. The acceleration s, in ft/s², of an object is given by the equation $a = -v$, where v is the velocity of the object in ft/s. If the initial velocity is 1 ft/s, then the position function could be

(A) Ce^{-t}.

(B) Ce^t.

(C) $e^t + c$.

(D) $e^{-t} + c$.

10. Find the area of the region inside the limaçon $r = 2 - \cos\theta$, but outside the circle $r = \cos\theta$.

(A) $\dfrac{9}{2}\pi$

(B) $\dfrac{3}{4}\pi$

(C) $\dfrac{15}{4}\pi$

(D) $\dfrac{17}{4}\pi$

11. The series $\displaystyle\sum_{n=1}^{\infty} \dfrac{1}{(12n + 1)(15n + 2)}$

(A) converges by the comparison test.

(B) diverges by the p-series test.

(C) converges by the ratio test.

(D) diverges by the ratio test.

12. For $t \geq 0$, a particle moves along a line with position $s(t) = 2t^3 - 9t + 1$. What is the acceleration when the particle is at rest?

(A) -9

(B) -6.348

(C) 0

(D) 14.697

13. A taxi driver is going from LaGuardia Airport to Kennedy Airport at an average speed of v miles per hour. The distance is thirty miles and gas costs \$1.33 per gallon. The taxi consumes gas at a rate of $f(v) = 2 + \dfrac{v^2}{600}$ gallons per hour where $10 \leq v \leq 55$. What average speed will minimize the total cost of fuel?

(A) 10.0 mph

(B) 25.823 mph

(C) 40.00 mph

(D) 34.641 mph

14. The series $\sum\limits_{n=0}^{\infty} \left(\dfrac{4}{k}\right)^n$ converges to 5. Find the value of k.

(A) 1

(B) 2

(C) 4.5

(D) 5

15. Which of the following is the smallest order Taylor polynomial, centered at $x = 1$, that will approximate on the domain $-1 \leq x \leq 3$ with Lagrange error bound less than 0.27?

(A) 3

(B) 5

(C) 7

(D) 9

CALCULUS BC

SECTION II, Part A
Time – 30 minutes
Number of problems – 2

A graphing calculator is required for these problems.

1. $\frac{dy}{dt} = 0.03y(100 - y)$. If $y(0)=10$,

   (a) for what values of y is y increasing?

   (b) for what value of y is y increasing the fastest?

   (c) use Euler's method, the initial value, and a step $\Delta t = 0.1$ to approximate $y(0.2)$.

2. The motion of a particle is described by the parametric equations $x = \frac{t}{5} + 1$ and $y = 2t - e^{t/2} + 1$, for $0 \le t \le 5$.

   (a) Find the coordinates of the absolute maximum and minimum. Justify your answer.

   (b) Find the x-intercept of the line tangent to the graph at $t = 2$.

   (c) Find the length of the graph from $t = 0$ to $t = 5$.

CALCULUS BC

SECTION II, Part B
Time – 60 minutes
Number of problems – 4

> A graphing calculator is not permitted for these problems.

1. Let R be the region bounded by $y = \sin x$ and $y = \cos x$ on the interval $\left[\frac{\pi}{4}, \frac{5\pi}{4}\right]$.

   (a) Find the area of region R.

   (b) Write, but do not evaluate, an integral expression for the volume of the solid obtained when R is rotated about the line $y = -1$.

   (c) A solid is formed with region R as the base and such that each cross section perpendicular to the x-axis is a square. Find the volume of the solid.

2. Consider the function $y wx) = \sqrt[3]{x^3 - 1}$.

   (a) Find the coordinates of the points on the graph where the tangent line is vertical or horizontal.

   (b) Find $\lim\limits_{x \to \infty} \frac{\sqrt[3]{x^3 - 1}}{x}$ and $\lim\limits_{x \to -\infty} \frac{\sqrt[3]{x^3 - 1}}{x}$. Interpret the end behavior of the graph of $y = \sqrt[3]{x^3 - 1}$ using the values of these limits.

   (c) Use the information in parts (a) and (b) to sketch the graph of y.

3. (a) Write the first four terms of the Maclaurin series for $f(x) = \dfrac{1}{1 + 2x}$, and express the series in sigma notation. State the interval of convergence for the series.

   (b) Use the series in part (a) to write the first four terms of the Maclaurin series for $\dfrac{1}{(1 + 2x)^2}$, and express the series in sigma notation. State the interval of convergence for the series.

   (c) Use the series in part (a) to write the Maclaurin series for $\ln(1 + 2x)$, and express the series in sigma notation. State the interval of convergence for the series.

4. The graph of the function $f(x)$ on the interval $[-2, 2]$ consists of two line segments and a semicircle, as shown below.

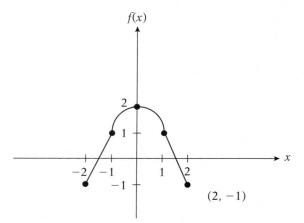

   If $g(x) = \displaystyle\int_0^x f(t)\, dt$,

   (a) find $g(0)$ and $g(2)$.

   (b) find the values of x where the relative maxima and minima of g occur. Justify your answer.

   (c) find the point(s) of inflection of g. Justify your answer.

   (d) sketch a graph of $g(x)$ on the interval $[-2, 2]$.

CALCULUS BC
SECTION I, Part A
Time – 60 minutes
Number of problems – 30

A graphing calculator is not permitted for these problems.

1. The sum $\frac{2}{5} + \frac{3}{5^2} + \frac{4}{5^3} + \ldots + \frac{n}{5^{n-1}} + \ldots$ approaches what value?

   (A) $\frac{1}{16}$

   (B) $\frac{1}{15}$

   (C) $\frac{1}{2}$

   (D) $\frac{9}{16}$

2. Write the equation of the line tangent to the graph of $y = \frac{x+3}{x}$ at $x = 1$.

   (A) $3x + y = 7$

   (B) $-3x + y = 1$

   (C) $3x + y = 13$

   (D) $x - 3y + 11 = 0$

3. For what value of c does $y = cx + \frac{3}{x^2}$ have a relative minimum at $x = 2$?

   (A) $-\frac{3}{4}$

   (B) $-\frac{3}{8}$

   (C) 0

   (D) $\frac{3}{4}$

4. $f(x) = \frac{5x}{x-5}$. Find the average rate of change of $f'(x)$ on the closed interval $[0, 4]$.

   (A) -12.6

   (B) $-\frac{13}{2}$

   (C) -6

   (D) -5

5. In the graph below, $g = f'$ and $f(x) = 2$.

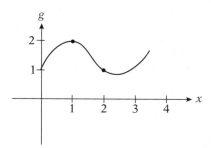

   Which of the following are true?
   - I. $g(1) > g(2)$
   - II. $f(1) < f(2)$
   - III. $f''(3) > 0$

   (A) I only

   (B) I and II

   (C) I and III

   (D) I, II, and III

6. $\int_{0}^{\infty} \frac{\ln(x)}{x} dx =$

   (A) 0

   (B) $\frac{1}{2}$

   (C) 1

   (D) diverges

7. For what values of a and c is the function
$$f(x) = \begin{cases} ax^2, & x \leq 2 \\ x + c, & x > 2 \end{cases}$$ differentiable for all real values of x?

   (A) $a = \frac{1}{2}, c = 0$

   (B) $a = \frac{1}{4}, c = -1$

   (C) $a = 1, c = 6$

   (D) $a = 0, c = -2$

8. $\lim\limits_{x\to\infty}\dfrac{\ln(\ln(x))}{\ln(x)} =$

(A) diverges

(B) 0

(C) $\dfrac{1}{2}$

(D) 1

9. $\lim\limits_{x\to\infty} x^5 e^{-x/5} =$

(A) $-\infty$

(B) 0

(C) 1

(D) ∞

10. $\dfrac{dx}{dt} = 5x^2$ and $x = 5$ when $t = 0$. Find the value of x when $t = 1$.

(A) $-\dfrac{5}{24}$

(B) $\dfrac{5}{24}$

(C) $\dfrac{e}{5}$

(D) $\dfrac{5}{4}$

11. A particle travels on a number line with velocity $v(t) = t \cos t$. Find the distance traveled from $t = 0$ to $t = \dfrac{\pi}{2}$.

(A) $\dfrac{\pi}{2}$

(B) $\dfrac{\pi}{2} - 1$

(C) $\dfrac{\pi}{2} + 1$

(D) 1

12. Given $\dfrac{dy}{dx} = x^2 y + x^2 + y + 1$, and $y(0) = 0$, then $y =$

(A) $e^{(x^2/2)+1} - 1$.

(B) $\dfrac{x^3}{3} + x$.

(C) $e^{(x^3/3)+x} - 1$.

(D) $e^{(x^3/3)+x+1}$.

13. $f(x) = \ln\left|x^2 - 2x\right|$. $f'(x) =$

(A) $\dfrac{2x - 2}{x^2 - 2x}$

(B) $\left|\dfrac{2x - 2}{x^2 - 2x}\right|$

(C) $\dfrac{\left|2x - 2\right|}{x^2 - 2x}$

(D) $\dfrac{2x - 2}{\left|x^2 - 2x\right|}$

14. Find the interval of convergence of the series $\sum\limits_{n=1}^{\infty} \left(\dfrac{x}{n}\right)^n$, where x is a real number.

(A) $[0, \infty)$

(B) $[-1, 1]$

(C) $[0, 1]$

(D) $(-\infty, \infty)$

15. What function is approximated by the following series?

$$(x - 2) - \dfrac{(x - 2)^2}{2} + \dfrac{(x - 2)^3}{3} - \cdots$$

(A) e^{x-2}

(B) $\ln(x - 2)$

(C) $\ln(x - 1)$

(D) $\sin(x - 2)$

16. $\dfrac{dy}{dx} = 5e^{-y}$ and $y(0) = 0$. Find the value of $\dfrac{d^2 y}{dx^2}$ at $x = 0$.

(A) -25

(B) -5

(C) 0

(D) 5

17. A company has 1,000 widgets and will be able to sell them all if the price is a dollar. The company will sell one less widget for each 10-cent increase in the price it charges. What price will maximize revenues, where revenue is the selling price times the quantity sold?

(A) $14.50

(B) $22.30

(C) $25.30

(D) $50.50

18. $\int x^2 \sqrt{x+1} \, dx =$

(A) $\frac{2}{7}(x+1)^{7/2} - \frac{4}{5}(x+1)^{5/2} + \frac{2}{3}(x+1)^{3/2} + c$

(B) $\frac{2}{7}(x+1)^{7/2} - \frac{2}{5}(x+1)^{5/2} + \frac{4}{3}(x+1)^{3/2} + c$

(C) $\frac{10}{7}(x+1)^{7/2} - 2x^{1/2} + c$

(D) $(x+1)^{3/2}\left(\frac{4}{5}x^2 - x + 1\right) + c$

19. If f is continuous for all real numbers, find

$$\lim_{h \to 0^+} \frac{\displaystyle\int_0^{h^2} f(t)\,dt}{h}.$$

(A) $f(h^2) - f(0)$

(B) $2h \, f(h^2)$

(C) $2h \, f(h^2) - f(0)$

(D) 0

20. Which of the following statements are true about $\displaystyle\sum_{n=3}^{\infty} \frac{1}{\sqrt[3]{n(n-1)(n-2)}}$?

   I. Converges by the p-series test
   II. Diverges by comparison test
   III. Grows less quickly than

   $$1 + \frac{1}{2} + \frac{1}{3} + \frac{1}{4} + \dots$$

(A) I only

(B) II only

(C) III only

(D) I and III

21. Which of the following is the series representation for $\dfrac{1}{1+5x}$?

(A) $\displaystyle\sum_{n=0}^{\infty} (-1)^n (5x)^n$

(B) $\displaystyle\sum_{n=0}^{\infty} (-1)^{n+1} (5x)^n$

(C) $\displaystyle\sum_{n=0}^{\infty} (-1)^n \frac{(5x)^n}{n!}$

(D) $\displaystyle\sum_{n=0}^{\infty} \frac{(5x)^n}{n}$

22. If the motion of a particle on a number line is described by $a(t) = 2t + 2$ and $v(1) = 4$ for $t \geq 0$, find the distance traveled by the particle in the first three seconds.

(A) 8 units

(B) 15 units

(C) 21 units

(D) 24 units

23. Find the equation of the line tangent to $y = (\arctan x)^2$ at $x = 1$.

(A) $y = \frac{\pi}{4}x + \frac{\pi^2}{16}$

(B) $y = \frac{\pi}{4}x - \frac{\pi^2}{16}$

(C) $y = \frac{\pi}{4}x + \frac{\pi(\pi - 4)}{16}$

(D) $y = \frac{\pi}{4}x$

24. Find the area of the inner loop of the polar curve $r = 1 + 2\cos\theta$.

(A) $2\pi - 3\sqrt{3}$

(B) 3π

(C) $\pi + \frac{3\sqrt{3}}{2}$

(D) $\pi - \frac{3\sqrt{3}}{2}$

25. $g(x) = \displaystyle\int_e^x \ln(1+t)\,dt$. Find the derivative of $(g'(x))^2$ at $x = e - 1$.

(A) 0

(B) $\frac{2}{e}$

(C) 1

(D) 2

26. Find the derivative of $\ln|x^2 - 2x|$.

(A) $\dfrac{1}{|x^2 - 2x|}$

(B) $\dfrac{2x - 2}{|x^2 - 2x|}$

(C) $\left|\dfrac{2x - 2}{x^2 - 2x}\right|$

(D) $\dfrac{2x - 2}{x^2 - 2x}$

27. Let $f(x) = xe^{x^2}$. If g is the inverse of f, then $g'(e) =$

   (A) 0.

   (B) $\frac{1}{4e}$.

   (C) $\frac{1}{3e}$.

   (D) $\frac{1}{e}$.

28. The voltage in a particular electrical circuit is $v(t) = 2\sin(3\pi t)$. The current through the circuit is $i(t) = \dfrac{dv}{dt}$. If the power consumed by the circuit is $p(t) = i(t)v(t)$, find the average power consumed for $0 < t < \pi$.

   (A) 0

   (B) $\frac{1}{\pi}(1 - \cos(6\pi^2))$

   (C) $-\frac{2}{\pi}(\cos(6\pi^2))$

   (D) $\frac{4}{\pi}(\sin^2(3\pi^2))$

29. F is the antiderivative of $f(x) = -2x^2 + 4x$. If $F(0) = 5$, then $F(1) =$

   (A) $\frac{4}{3}$.

   (B) $\frac{7}{3}$.

   (C) $\frac{11}{3}$.

   (D) $\frac{19}{3}$.

30. Find the linear approximation to $e^{\frac{x}{2}}$ at $x = 0$, and use it to approximate $\sqrt{e}$.

   (A) 0.75

   (B) 1.25

   (C) 1.5

   (D) 2

CALCULUS BC

SECTION I, Part B

Time – 45 minutes

Number of problems – 15

A graphing calculator is required for these problems.

1. Find the remainder when $\frac{1}{\sqrt{e}}$ is approximated by a third-degree Maclaurin polynomial.

   (A) 0.0024

   (B) 0.0208

   (C) 0.2916

   (D) 0.5833

2. Find the area in the first quadrant bounded by the graphs of $y = \frac{1}{x} - 1$, $y = 2x$, and the x-axis.

   (A) 0.443 units².

   (B) 0.5 units².

   (C) 0.886 units².

   (D) 1 units².

3. Find the length of the curve described by the parametric equations $x(t) = 2\sin(t)$ and $y(t) = 2\ln(\sin t)$ on $0.1 \leq t \leq 1.0$.

   (A) 2.042 units²

   (B) 3.243 units²

   (C) 4.491 units²

   (D) 4.587 units²

4. Find the value of
$$\lim_{x \to \infty} \frac{1}{n}\left(\sqrt{1 - \frac{1}{n^2}} + \sqrt{1 - \frac{4}{n^2}} + \sqrt{1 - \frac{9}{n^2}} \right.$$
$$\left. + \ldots + \sqrt{1 - \left(\frac{n-1}{n}\right)^2} \right).$$

   (A) π

   (B) $\frac{\pi}{4}$

   (C) $\frac{\pi}{2}$

   (D) 2

5. $\int_0^1 \frac{1}{\sqrt{1-x^2}}\, dx =$

   (A) $-\frac{\pi}{2}$

   (B) $\frac{1}{2}$

   (C) 1

   (D) $\frac{\pi}{2}$

6. The area of $r = 2 + \cos(\theta)$ on $0 \leq \theta \leq \pi$ is

   (A) 2π units².

   (B) $\frac{9\pi}{4}$ units².

   (C) π units².

   (D) $\frac{5\pi}{4}$ units².

7. $f(x) = 4x - x^3$ on the interval $[0, 2]$. Find the point of intersection of the lines tangent to the graph of f at the endpoints of the interval.

   (A) (1.333, 5.333)

   (B) (1, 3)

   (C) (1, 4)

   (D) (0.75, 3.578)

8. Use the Trapezoidal Rule with five equal sub-intervals to approximate $\int_0^1 \ln(x^2 + 1)\, dx$.

   (A) 0.264

   (B) 0.267

   (C) 0.337

   (D) 0.385

9. $y' = xy + 2y$ and $y(0) = 1$. What is the result when you use Euler's method with $\Delta x = 0.1$ to approximate $y(0.3)$?

   (A) 1.452
   (B) 1.771
   (C) 1.906
   (D) 2.338

10. If $h(x) = \sqrt{\sin(f(x))}$, $f(0) = \frac{\pi}{3}$, and $f'(0) = e$, approximate $h'(0)$.

   (A) -0.84321
   (B) -0.3102
   (C) 0.6409
   (D) 0.73024

11. Water leaks from a storage tank at a rate $R(t) = 2te^{-0.5t}$, in thousands of gallons per day, $t \geq 0$. How many gallons have leaked at the end of the first week, to the nearest gallon?

   (A) 3,456 gallons
   (B) 6,191 gallons
   (C) 6,407 gallons
   (D) 6,913 gallons

12. If $y = 2x(x-2)^2 - p$, for how many integer values of p does y have three distinct zeros?

   (A) 0
   (B) 1
   (C) 2
   (D) 3

13. $g(x) = \displaystyle\int_0^x (\ln(1+t))^2 \, dt$. Find $g'(e-1)$.

   (A) 1
   (B) $\dfrac{2}{e}$
   (C) $\dfrac{2\ln(1+e)}{e}$
   (D) $\dfrac{2\ln(1+e)}{e+1}$

14. Which of the following series are conditionally convergent?

   I. $\displaystyle\sum_0^\infty \frac{(-1)^n}{n!}$

   II. $\displaystyle\sum_0^\infty \frac{(-1)^{n+1}n^2}{n^2+n}$

   III. $\displaystyle\sum_0^\infty \frac{(-1)^{n+1}3^n}{5^n}$

   (A) None
   (B) I only
   (C) I and II
   (D) II and III

15. The hyperbolic sine function is defined as $\sinh x = \dfrac{e^x - e^{-x}}{2}$. A third-order Taylor polynomial approximation is $\sinh x \approx x + \dfrac{x^3}{3!}$. If this is used to approximate $\sinh x$ for $|x| \leq 2$, what is the LaGrange error bound?

   (A) 0.484
   (B) 0.363
   (C) 0.272
   (D) 0.266

CALCULUS BC

SECTION II, Part A
Time – 30 minutes
Number of problems – 2

A graphing calculator is required for these problems.

1. Given $y = \ln(x - 1)$ on the closed interval $[2, e + 1]$,

   (a) find the average value of y on the interval.

   (b) find the value of k so that the line $x = k$ divides the area under the curve into two regions of equal area.

   (c) write an integral for the volume of the solid generated when the area under the curve is rotated about the line $y = 1$.

2. Consider the function $f(x) = x^2 + 2$.

   (a) Write the equation of the line tangent to $f(x)$ at point $P(a, f(a))$, where $0 < a < 4$.

   (b) Write an expression for $A(x)$ in terms of a, where $A(x)$ is the area of the triangle formed by the tangent line in part (a), the x-axis, and the line joining P and $(4, 0)$.

   (c) Find the value of a that makes $A(x)$ a minimum. Justify your answer.

CALCULUS BC
SECTION II, Part B
Time – 60 minutes
Number of problems – 4

> **A graphing calculator is not permitted for these problems.**

1. $f(x)$ has derivatives of all orders for all real numbers. Suppose that

   $f(1) = 1$ and $f^{(n)}(1) = \frac{n}{2^n}$ for $n \geq 1$.

   (a) Write a 3rd-degree Taylor polynomial for $f(x)$ centered at $c = 1$ and use it to approximate $f(1.2)$.

   (b) Write a 4th-degree Taylor polynomial for $F(x) = \int_1^x f(t)\,dt$ centered at $c = 1$.
   Determine the exact value of $F(2)$, or explain why it cannot be determined.

   (c) Suppose $g(x) = (x - 1)\,f(x)$. Use part (a) to find a 2nd-degree Taylor polynomial for $g'(x)$. Then use it to approximate $g'(2)$.

2. Consider the differential equation $\frac{dy}{dt} = 5y - 5$.

   (a) Draw a slope field for the given differential equation for $-3 < t < 3$.

   (b) Solve the differential equation given that $y(0) = 5$.

   (c) Find the equation of the horizontal asymptote of the graph of the solution in part (b).

3. A water balloon is filled at a rate of 20 cubic inches per second. Assume that the balloon is a perfect sphere. Volume of sphere $= \frac{4}{3}\pi r^3$.

   (a) Write an equation for the change in volume as a function of the change in radius.

   (b) How fast is the radius of the balloon increasing when the radius is 10 inches?

   (c) Suppose the balloon later develops a tiny hole from which water escapes at the rate of $e^{-V/3}$ cubic in./s. Find an expression for $\frac{dV}{dt}$ under this condition.

   (d) How fast is the radius of the leaky balloon changing when the radius is 10 inches?

4. Consider the function $y = \frac{e^{2-2x^2}}{x}$.

   (a) Find y' and determine whether y' is even, odd, or neither.

   (b) On what interval(s) is y decreasing?

   (c) Find the coordinates of the point of inflection.

   (d) On what interval(s) is y concave up?

   (e) Find the range of y.

CORRELATION CHART

Use the given charts to mark the questions you missed. Then go back and review the suggested lesson(s) to improve your understanding of the concepts.

Section I, Part A (No Calculator Allowed)

Missed?	Question Number	Review the information in Lesson (Main Idea #. Lesson #)...
	1	2.3
	2	3.3
	3	1.2
	4	2.4
	5	2.3
	6	2.5
	7	2.7
	8	2.3
	9	1.3
	10	3.3
	11	1.2
	12	3.1
	13	3.3
	14	3.3
	15	3.3
	16	2.3
	17	2.6
	18	3.7
	19	3.7
	20	2.5
	21	2.5
	22	2.4
	23	2.5
	24	2.5
	25	2.2
	26	3.3
	27	3.6
	28	2.2
	29	1.2
	30	1.3

Section I, Part B (Calculator Required)

Missed?	Question Number	Review the information in Lesson (Main Idea #. Lesson #)...
	1	1.3
	2	2.6
	3	3.2
	4	1.4, 2.4, 2.5
	5	2.1
	6	2.7
	7	2.4
	8	3.3
	9	3.7
	10	2.4
	11	3.7
	12	3.2
	13	1.3, 2.1
	14	3.7
	15	2.10

Section II, Part A (Calculator Required)

Missed?	Question Number	Review the information in Lesson (Main Idea #. Lesson #)...
	1(a)	2.7
	1(b)	
	1(c)	
	2(a)	2.7
	2(b)	

Section II, Part B (No Calculator Allowed)

Missed?	Question Number	Review the information in Lesson (Main Idea #. Lesson #)...
	1(a)	3.7
	1(b)	
	2(a)	2.4, 2.6, 3.3
	2(b)	
	2(c)	
	2(d)	
	2(e)	
	3(a)	2.9, 3.9
	3(b)	
	3(c)	
	4(a)	2.4, 2.6
	4(b)	
	4(c)	
	4(d)	

CORRELATION CHART

Use the given charts to mark the questions you missed. Then go back and review the suggested lesson(s) to improve your understanding of the concepts.

Section I, Part A (No Calculator Allowed)

Missed?	Question Number	Review the information in Lesson (Main Idea #. Lesson #)...
	1	2.6
	2	3.6
	3	3.3
	4	2.4, 2.6, 2.10
	5	2.5
	6	2.1, 2.3
	7	2.2
	8	2.1
	9	1.3
	10	2.2, 2.3
	11	3.1, 3.3
	12	2.7
	13	1.4, 2.5
	14	3.3
	15	3.3
	16	2.1, 2.4, 2.6
	17	2.5
	18	2.4
	19	3.2, 3.3
	20	3.9
	21	2.4
	22	2.7
	23	2.2, 2.3
	24	3.2, 3.3
	25	1.2
	26	2.10
	27	3.7
	28	2.6
	29	1.3
	30	1.3

Section I, Part B (Calculator Required)

Missed?	Question Number	Review the information in Lesson (Main Idea #. Lesson #)...
	1	2.3
	2	2.6
	3	2.2, 2.3
	4	1.1, 2.4
	5	3.3, 3.4
	6	2.1, 2.2
	7	1.3, 1.4, 2.2
	8	2.5
	9	2.5
	10	2.7
	11	2.2, 2.3
	12	2.2, 2.4, 2.6
	13	1.4, 2.5
	14	2.1, 2.2
	15	3.2, 3.3

Section II, Part A (Calculator Required)

Missed?	Question Number	Review the information in Lesson (Main Idea #. Lesson #)...
	1(a)	3.6, 3.7
	1(b)	
	1(c)	
	2(a)	1.1, 2.5
	2(b)	
	2(c)	

Section II, Part B (No Calculator Allowed)

Missed?	Question Number	Review the information in Lesson (Main Idea #. Lesson #)...
	1(a)	3.1, 3.6
	1(b)	
	1(c)	
	1(d)	
	2(a)	1.3, 2.4, 2.6
	2(b)	
	2(c)	
	2(d)	
	3(a)	1.2, 3.9
	3(b)	
	4(a)	2.4, 2.7
	4(b)	

CORRELATION CHART

Use the given charts to mark the questions you missed. Then go back and review the suggested lesson(s) to improve your understanding of the concepts.

Section I, Part A (No Calculator Allowed)

Missed?	Question Number	Review the information in Lesson (Main Idea #. Lesson #)...
	1	2.2, 2.3
	2	2.5
	3	3.1, 3.3
	4	2.2
	5	2.4
	6	1.4, 2.5
	7	3.3
	8	3.4
	9	3.3
	10	3.2, 3.3
	11	3.8
	12	2.5
	13	2.9
	14	2.8
	15	2.2, 2.3
	16	4.1, 4.2, 4.5
	17	2.4
	18	2.6
	19	2.4
	20	2.5
	21	2.1
	22	2.3
	23	3.7
	24	2.2
	25	1.2
	26	2.2, 2.3
	27	2.5
	28	3.5
	29	3.2, 3.3
	30	3.2, 3.3

Section I, Part B (Calculator Required)

Missed?	Question Number	Review the information in Lesson (Main Idea #. Lesson #)...
	1	3.7
	2	2.5
	3	2.4, 2.6
	4	2.2, 2.3
	5	1.3, 1.4
	6	4.3
	7	2.4
	8	2.2, 2.4
	9	2.7
	10	3.8
	11	4.2
	12	2.7
	13	2.7
	14	4.1, 4.2
	15	4.3

Section II, Part A (Calculator Required)

Missed?	Question Number	Review the information in Lesson (Main Idea #. Lesson #)...
	1(a)	3.11
	1(b)	
	1(c)	
	2(a)	2.8, 3.8
	2(b)	
	2(c)	

Section II, Part B (No Calculator Allowed)

Missed?	Question Number	Review the information in Lesson (Main Idea #. Lesson #)...
	1(a)	3.2, 3.3, 3.7
	1(b)	
	1(c)	
	2(a)	1.1, 1.2
	2(b)	
	2(c)	
	3(a)	4.4
	3(b)	
	3(c)	
	4(a)	2.4, 2.6, 3.3
	4(b)	
	4(c)	
	4(d)	

CORRELATION CHART

Use the given charts to mark the questions you missed. Then go back and review the suggested lesson(s) to improve your understanding of the concepts.

Section I, Part A (No Calculator Allowed)

Missed?	Question Number	Review the information in Lesson (Main Idea #. Lesson #)...
	1	4.1
	2	2.5
	3	2.4
	4	2.1
	5	2.4
	6	3.5
	7	2.5
	8	1.5
	9	1.5
	10	2.2, 2.3
	11	3.8
	12	3.9
	13	2.2, 2.3
	14	4.1
	15	4.2, 4.4
	16	2.6
	17	2.7
	18	3.1
	19	3.2, 3.3
	20	4.2
	21	4.3
	22	3.8
	23	2.5
	24	3.8
	25	3.3, 3.4
	26	2.2, 2.3
	27	2.3
	28	3.6
	29	3.2, 3.3
	30	2.5

Section I, Part B (Calculator Required)

Missed?	Question Number	Review the information in Lesson (Main Idea #. Lesson #)...
	1	4.4
	2	3.2, 3.3
	3	3.8
	4	4.1
	5	3.3
	6	3.8
	7	2.5
	8	3.2
	9	3.11
	10	3.2, 3.3
	11	3.6
	12	2.1, 2.5
	13	3.3
	14	4.2
	15	4.4

Section II, Part A (Calculator Required)

Missed?	Question Number	Review the information in Lesson (Main Idea #. Lesson #)...
	1(a)	3.1, 3.7
	1(b)	
	1(c)	
	2(a)	2.5, 3.3
	2(b)	
	2(c)	

Section II, Part B (No Calculator Allowed)

Missed?	Question Number	Review the information in Lesson (Main Idea #. Lesson #)...
	1(a)	4.4
	1(b)	
	1(c)	
	2(a)	2.9, 3.9
	2(b)	
	2(c)	
	3(a)	2.7, 3.6
	3(b)	
	3(c)	
	3(d)	
	4(a)	2.2, 2.3, 2.4, 2.6
	4(b)	
	4(c)	
	4(d)	
	4(e)	

Index